Muslim Pilgrimage in the Modern World

ISLAMIC CIVILIZATION AND MUSLIM NETWORKS

Carl W. Ernst and Bruce B. Lawrence, editors

Highlighting themes with historical as well as contemporary significance, Islamic Civilization and Muslim Networks features works that explore Islamic societies and Muslim peoples from a fresh perspective, drawing on new interpretive frameworks or theoretical strategies in a variety of disciplines. Special emphasis is given to systems of exchange that have promoted the creation and development of Islamic identities—cultural, religious, or geopolitical. The series spans all periods and regions of Islamic civilization.

A complete list of titles published in this series appears at the end of the book.

Muslim Pilgrimage in the Modern World

EDITED BY
Babak Rahimi and Peyman Eshaghi

The University of North Carolina Press CHAPEL HILL

This book is published with appreciation for Florence and James Peacock and their generous support of the University of North Carolina Press.

© 2019 The University of North Carolina Press
All rights reserved
Set in Merope Basic by Westchester Publishing Services
Manufactured in the United States of America

The University of North Carolina Press has been a member of the Green Press Initiative since 2003.

Library of Congress Cataloging-in-Publication Data
Names: Rahimi, Babak, editor. | Eshaghi, Peyman, editor.
Title: Muslim pilgrimage in the modern world / edited by Babak Rahimi and Peyman Eshaghi.
Description: University of North Carolina Press : Chapel Hill, [2019] | Series: Islamic civilization and Muslim networks | Includes bibliographical references and index.
Identifiers: LCCN 2018049445 | ISBN 9781469651453 (cloth : alk. paper) | ISBN 9781469651460 (pbk : alk. paper) | ISBN 9781469651477 (ebook)
Subjects: LCSH: Muslim pilgrims and pilgrimages—History—21st century.
Classification: LCC BP187 .M87 2019 | DDC 297.3/5—dc23
LC record available at https://lccn.loc.gov/2018049445

Cover illustration: *Pilgrimage to a Ritual* © Reza Masoudi Nejad.
The congregation of Bohras from all over the world for the service session on Ashura day, Bhendi Bazaar area, Mumbai, India, December 2010.

Contents

Acknowledgments and Note on Transliteration ix

Introduction 1
BABAK RAHIMI AND PEYMAN ESHAGHI

PART I | *Rethinking Muslim Pilgrimage: History, Politics, and Transnationalism*

1. Sacrifice and Pilgrimage 49
   Body Politics and the Origins of Muslim Pilgrimage
   BRANNON WHEELER

2. The Hajj and Politics in China 68
   ROBERT R. BIANCHI

3. Pilgrimage and Transnational Religious Imagination in the Muslim Communities of Brazil 89
   PAULO G. PINTO

4. Red, White, and Blue 112
   American Muslims on Hajj and the Politics of Pilgrimage
   SOPHIA ROSE ARJANA AND ROSE ASLAN

PART II | *Embodiment, Memory, and Materiality*

5. Pilgrimages of the Dream 133
   On Wings of State in Sehwan Sharif, Pakistan
   OMAR KASMANI

6. Shrines and Pilgrimage in Southern Kazakhstan 149
   AZIM MALIKOV

7. Economies of Piety at the Syrian Shrine of Sayyida Zaynab 172
   EDITH SZANTO

8   Grave Visiting (*Ziyara*) in Indonesia   183
     JULIAN MILLIE AND LEWIS MAYO

PART III | *Communication, (New) Media, and Space*

9   Jamkaran   207
     *Embodiment and Messianic Experience in the
     Making of Digital Pilgrimage*
     BABAK RAHIMI

10   On Mediation and Magnetism:
     Or, Why Destroy Saint Shrines?   223
     EMILIO SPADOLA

11   Pilgrimage to a Ritual   240
     The Fluid Sacred Geography of the Bohras' Muharram
     REZA MASOUDI NEJAD

Glossary   259

Contributor Biographies   265

Index   269

Figures, Graphs, Map, and Tables

FIGURES

4.1 Religious souvenirs, Mecca 122

5.1 A view of Akram's dwelling in Lal-bagh 140

9.1 A young pilgrim after dropping his letter down the well, Jamkaran, June 25, 2016 219

11.1 Dr. Sayyidna Mohammed Burhanuddin (1915–2014), the spiritual leader of the Dawoodi Bohra, after one of his Muharram sermons, December 2010, Mumbai 241

11.2 A Bohras' *sabil* in Bohra Muhalla, Mumbai, December 2009 245

11.3 The Bohras packed the Bendi Bazaar area during the Muharram service session, December 2010, Mumbai 247

11.4 An emotional time for the Bohras at Rowzat al-Tahirah, when their spiritual leader visits his fathers' shrine after giving his Muharram sermon 250

11.5 Dongri area, looking toward Bohra Muhalla (to the east), April 2010, Mumbai 253

GRAPHS

2.1 Hajj rates and female participation in Lanzhou and Linxia Prefectures, standardized scores 77

2.2 Percentage female pilgrims (2012–2014) and female illiteracy in Lanzhou and Linxia Prefectures 80

2.3 Gansu Hajj rates (2006–2014) and per capita gross product 81

2.4 Xinjiang Hajj rates (2012–2014) and Muslim percentage 82

2.5 Ürümqi Hajjis (2005–2014) by ethnicity and gender 83

MAP

2.1 Important cities of China's Hajj belts 72

TABLES

2.1 Muslims and Hajj pilgrims by gender and prefecture in Gansu 75

2.2 Socioeconomic characteristics by prefecture in Gansu 76

2.3 Hajj rates and female participation in Lanzhou and Linxia Prefectures 78

2.4 Demographic characteristics of Lanzhou and Linxia Districts 79

2.5 Correlates of Hajj rates and female participation in Lanzhou and Linxia Prefectures ($n = 15$) 80

Acknowledgments and Note on Transliteration

This book owes much to the generosity of colleagues and friends who have provided insightful comments on the topic of pilgrimage from both historical and theoretical perspectives. The contributors to this volume were invited to submit a study on an aspect of Muslim pilgrimage in particular historical and social contexts, based on their expertise. In attempting to rise to this challenge, the chapters presented here explore themes on pilgrimage with a focus on specific localities, shrines, mosques, or Mecca, where Muslim identities through ritual traditions continue to be reinvented in complex and porous ways. We would like to thank all the contributors, the anonymous reviewers, and especially Elaine Maisner and series editors Carl W. Ernst and Bruce B. Lawrence at the University of North Carolina Press for making this work possible, to the benefit of current and future researchers. We would like to thank Mehrnaz Eizadyrad for help with copyediting. Finally, special thanks are owed to Nile Green and Karen Ruffle, who read the manuscript and offered helpful comments.

The present volume adopts a system of transliteration for Arabic, Persian, and Turkish based loosely on that used in the *International Journal of Middle East Studies* (*IJMES*), with some modifications and eliminating all diacritical marks except when transliterated passages from the original text are included, and American Library Association–Library of Congress (especially for chapters 2, 5, and 12, which include Chinese and Urdu). With the aim of appealing to nonspecialists, the recurring words "Hajj," "'Umra," and "Muharram" appear as capitalized English words. "Imam" is also used as it appears in English dictionaries. While we adopt the Arabic word *"ziyara"* for the volume, we do not privilege such transliteration over other linguistic expressions in their vernacular forms. As the following chapters demonstrate, variation in the use of the term *"ziyara"* carries plural understandings of pilgrimage. Finally, all years in the text relate to the Common Era unless otherwise stated.

Muslim Pilgrimage in the Modern World

Introduction

BABAK RAHIMI AND PEYMAN ESHAGHI

The Hajj represents one of the most significant ritual observations for Muslims. Traveling long distances through various routes and gathering in multitude in Mecca, Muslim pilgrims perform traditions that date back to the first time the Prophet and his followers observed the Hajj on the morning of the fourth day of the eleventh month in the Islamic calendar in 629 C.E.[1] Such traditions encompass several interconnected rites, many of which are symbolically referenced to Abraham and his son Isma'il, who, following Prophet Adam, are believed to have rebuilt the cubical stone structure Ka'ba, the symbolic focal point of the Hajj.[2] Such traditions have varied in practice and entailed complex meanings, such as circumambulation, incubation, or drinking the water from the well of Zamzam. Similar to other obligatory traditions such as *salat* (prayer), the Hajj rituals are inherently compulsory undertakings incumbent on every Muslim, at least once in a lifetime. The undertakings implicate commemoration and covenant with God, whose blessing is sought during the performances, thus rendering meaningful the world and beyond.[3]

Ritual observations are reenactments of an expression of devotion in historical time. As a living tradition with a long history of intricate performances, the Hajj is the medium for expressing a set of repetoires codified by norms and conflicts in which camaraderie and competition prevail in shaping Muslim identities. As one of the largest annually performed pilgrimage rites in the world, the Hajj puts complex social forces on display — that is, affective ways pilgrims undergo change in social relations across local and global settings. Paradoxically, such social changes that heighten already fluid identities consolidate the social realities of pilgrims. Social dynamics for performing the Hajj entail various dimensions but, by and large, are tied to mundane factors, many of which entail stratified practices, such as gaining prestige, status, or material prosperity, especially on the return home. Departure and return to a perceived home is central to pilgrimage. A returning pilgrim stages piety through varying degrees of social relations specific to the locality where the pilgrim returns. The locality heightens how prosaically a returning pilgrim can be received by family, friends, neighbors, and coworkers, allowing social integration across local and global settings, although hardly in an identical way.

In broad terms, pilgrimage is an assemblage of fluid identities and connectivities. Crucial to these connectivities is what qualifies pilgrimage to emerge as a recognizably ritual tradition. People perform pilgrimage in complex interconnectivities. And they do so with various motivations, ostensible or implicit; at times what claims to be the intention for ritual observation may contradict other competing motivations—conscious or otherwise, worldly or spiritual.[4] Muslim pilgrims may perform the Hajj not only as a quest for redemption, informed by the desire for penitence and salvation, but also for recognition as participants within a larger or localized Muslim community.[5] When the Hajj is observed, subjectivity changes—though not always in life-changing ways—according to a constellation of performances across class, gender, national, and racial practices that make pilgrimage possible in the first place. And yet such subjectivity is perpetually contingent upon processes of stratification and territorialization that render them possible despite porous conditions.

Pilgrimage is also a public ritual event. As a communal phenomenon, the Hajj is one of the most visible displays of rites, increasingly made visual with the spread of digital media within postcolonial contexts. Along with ʿUmra (a minor pilgrimage to Mecca that can be performed at any time of the year), the Hajj has served as a confluence of several rituals—some of which as rites of passage—undertaken as a way of making piety public and salvation a matter of collective recognition. It is in the course of the Hajj that the Muslim *umma* becomes visible and also visualized through ritual performance, hence transformed into a public body, as millions of pilgrims gather to circle the Kaʿba in a counterclockwise direction. Given its obligatory salience, the Hajj combines both earthly and spiritual significance *toward* and *at* a sacred site in reliving an experience lived by other Muslims in the past. Reliving such experiences also entails divergent backgrounds in terms of class, ethnicity, gender, race, and national origin; meanwhile, such divergences in social practice can be reified in the context of local and especially regulative policies in what Robert Bianchi has called "an affair of the state."[6] The state-led institutionalization of pilgrimage operates in supervising the pilgrims, coordinating their travels, and investing in Hajj-related facilities—including holy sites—according to competing notions of local and transnational governance and politics. The Hajj displays the intersection of state and local governance in the use of administrative-bureaucratic strategies and mechanisms over the performances in what Saud al-Sarhan calls "Hajj management."[7]

The use of the word "variation" perhaps best describes how the Hajj is performed as a public ritual. The array of shared practices also reflects the extensive and overlapping ritual traditions associated with Muslim pilgrimage, commonly known as *"ziyara"* (or *"ziyarat"* in Persian, Urdu and Sindhi). The term in its Arabic roots refers to the action of "visitation," a temporary outing to a blessed place associated with a pilgrimage site, mostly a tomb or a gravesite. In fact, one may argue that the Hajj is a form of the performance of grave visitation, as discussed in chapter 1.[8] *Ziyara* traditions are wide and complex. They can include visitation to the tomb of holy figures as well as to living persons, traces left behind as a promise of a messianic return, animals, trees, stones, or relics; even dreams can be considered pilgrimages. They can take place at home, in a neighborhood, at work, and even at war—violence can reconfigure pilgrimage as a profound experience. This rough sketch of *ziyara*, which will be expanded in the following discussion, gives us a sense of the complex ways we can understand Muslim performances of pilgrimage. It also gives us an understanding of *ziyara* that cannot render a uniform identity in terms of an Islamic sameness. If anything, the sociohistorical trajectory of such diverse practices, through dispersed local and translocal settings of performance, lay out the relative social meanings of pilgrimage. The contingent practices may as well operate as sites for interventions and displacement of a reified conception.

So, if variation in practice does not define pilgrimage, what, then, identifies Muslim pilgrimage? And what specifically qualifies its unique manifestation in the "modern world"? This book presents studies that seek to understand the linking of variations in Muslim pilgrimage to modernity as a sociohistorical human condition. *Muslim Pilgrimage in the Modern World* emphasizes the study of pilgrimage by Muslims of diverse backgrounds not as a "religious ceremony" or merely an obligatory practice with soteriological dimension nor a cultural inscription of religious meaning but as interpretation of self and other in the world through ritual as both discourse and practice. This description generates a notion of the expression "in the Modern world" as multiple ways of being or becoming modern in accord with specific localities, though always connected with the translocal, where identities are performatively enacted. Here, the spatial "in" signifies a metaphoric indication of inclusion within a space, a condition or perhaps a position(ing) within social limits. Here, modernity reveals complex modes of self-understandings in complex relation with others in a distinct locality, experienced and imagined in the world and beyond.

The studies in this volume are also informed by a conception of pilgrimage that inherently views "ritual" as sociohistoricaly situational and yet deeply interpretative. The sociohistorical diagnosis, in particular, draws on themes of cultural mediation and embodiment in connection with a set of institutions that grow out of complex conditions of transnational capitalism linked to various forms of governance over ritual life. Yet within such conditions, there is creativity of action generated by different modes of articulating and negotiating one's situationality, which underlines the interpretative dimension wherein various pilgrimage rituals emerge. In what follows, our aim is to examine key terms and concepts related to "Muslim pilgrimage" and, in so doing, reflect on experiences and historical boundaries through which Muslimness become open to continual reconstruction in shifting social terrains.

"Muslim Pilgrimage": Between Hajj and *Ziyara*

We begin with a basic postulate that "pilgrimage" is a concept with semantic roots in a Euro-Christian past.[9] By this we do not mean that the term is exclusively "Western" and that it does not entail a sociological reality but that, as a discourse, it carries its own history and discipline with a propensity to be universalized to define a distinct human activity. Along with universalizing terms such as *religion* and *ritual*, there is a complex historical context through which "pilgrimage" has emerged as a concept of inquiry, scholarly or otherwise, particularly in the late nineteenth century, during which the field of religious studies became institutionalized at universities in western Europe and North America. Such institutional processes cannot be disentangled from particular linguistic and cultural milieus. As Dionigi Albera and John Eade have argued, pilgrimage—though studied in a variety of academic disciplines—has been framed largely around Christianity and through an anglophone field of inquiry.[10] It is through such an implicit universality that the discipline of pilgrimage studies has developed, especially during the twentieth-century rise of universities and the growth of academic disciplines in the humanities and social sciences.

However, this historical process has not followed a deterministic scheme, as the field of pilgrimage studies has and continues to be contested with emerging studies, especially in non-anglophone academic fields. While the global domination of anglophone academia is not to be ignored, to write about "Muslim pilgrimage" from an academic standpoint would require an awareness of knowledge networks and production industries through which contemporary Islamic and religious studies have been realized. Such cultural productions involve histories of changes in discourses, variations in linguistics, and practices in academic tropes that give rise to a field in historical time, until an epistemic shift occurs in the mutual constitution of knowledge and power. Such historical analysis would also include studies of non-Muslim visitation sites as intraregional practices performed in interconnected spiritual landscapes, most famously evident in medieval and early modern Anatolia or India.[11]

Significantly, the study of Muslim pilgrimage, especially Hajj studies, has been deeply tied to such discursive fields. As Boissevain has shown, both anglophone and French academics focus on how the Maghrib underwent changes in the twentieth century, with a major shift toward the study of local politics and religious authority taking place in the 1960s.[12] While shifts indicate the unstable discursive patterns in which pilgrimage as a subject of inquiry has undergone, they also reveal social changes in the wider context of global modernity. Such shifts are indicative of the complex variations of experiences and interpretations of modernity, especially in the period after World War II. They embody social imaginaries of autonomy, freedom, and growth in the ways Muslims perceive their lives and the varieties of being (or becoming) modern through pilgrimage.[13] Pilgrimage, in other words, is both a symbolic and material site wherein Muslims redefine themselves in a context of modern sensibilities.

In line with the said theoretical observation, the present volume does not seek to define "Muslim pilgrimage" but instead offers ethnographic accounts of diverse Muslim practices identified as "pilgrimage" that share a resemblance not in the normative scheme of practices but in diverse experiences that cluster around interpretative ways to describe self and reality on interrelated local and global levels. Hence, the title "Muslim Pilgrimage in the Modern World" assumes that what manifests as Muslim pilgrimage in the modern context is inherently tied to globalizing perceptions of progress, spiritual or otherwise, which entail notions of autonomy and freedom in reformulation, negotiation, or contestation of ways of modernness. It is in these situated circumstances that we seek to provide an account of Muslim pilgrimage across various regions around the globe. Such an attempt would ultimately conceptualize Muslim pilgrimage in ambiguous terms.

Considering Islamic traditions, how pilgrimage ascribed significance as either Hajj or *ziyara* can be differentiated in terms of complex practices associated with travel, experienced and articulated through textual and visual media. Throughout history, Muslims have reflected on the virtues of Islamic cities as pilgrimage destination sites, where the grave or the remains of a saint can be visited on a yearly basis. Written works on Mecca, Medina, Najaf, Karbala, and cities of the Levant[14] have all described the virtues of pilgrimage sites, and such descriptions have hardly identified a single place as a pilgrimage destination. In such works, Muslims jurists, historians, and geographers have employed historical and geographical textual practices to articulate the legitimation and prevalence of pilgrimage at various localities—at times in the course of pilgrimage travel—with varying importance; hardly have they agreed on an exclusive number of places for pilgrimage. Books on the hagiography of grave veneration in the Muslim lands stress the diverse ways pilgrimage destination has been understood by Muslims.[15] This is particularly true for competing sects as they seek to distinguish their intrasectarian identity through pilgrimage, as in the case of *didar* rituals in Isma'ili Shi'ism, which is primarily about seeing the living Imam and discourages visitation of Twelver shrines.[16] Such multiplicity in devotional practice can certainly be identified in various Shi'i and Sunni[17] devotional texts and guidebooks on how to fulfill pilgrimage and observe all the required ritual etiquettes.

The diversity of pilgrimage traditions has inspired Muslims to produce and consume textual accounts about Hajj and other sites of pilgrimage, making it one of the most popular literary genres in Islamic history. These diaries provide us with invaluable information about different aspects of non-Hajj veneration traditions, particularly the visitation of saints. The genre of travelogue (*rihla*), for example, has included a range of references to numerous sacred places and objects as well as diverse forms of pious rituals associated with shrines and other visitation sites. And yet such diverse forms of piety have also been considered highly contested acts of exclusion.[18]

Since the middle period of Islamic history (945–1503), a polemical legal tradition has existed against non-Hajj pilgrimage and the veneration of saints, most popular in North Africa, Levant, and Anatolia. Jurists such as Ibn Taymiyyah (1263–1328) saw an inherent tension between the Hajj—as the only legitimate pilgrimage to Islam's most holy city, Mecca—and *ziyara*, since such practices contradicted the unity of God and associated earthly substance with intercession and reverence for shrines with divine transcendence. The forces who oppose veneration of saints underwent a resurgence in subsequent revivalist movements, especially with the rise of Wahhabism—a self-proclaimed "unitarian" (*tawhidi*) movement founded by Muhammad ibn 'Abd al-Wahhab (1703–92) in the eighteenth century—

as well as twentieth-century movement known as Salafism.[19] Although these trends have faced critical objection from most Muslim branches, the Salafi demolition of tombs and shrines, along with attacks on pilgrims, became most pronounced with the rise of ISIS in Iraq and Syria between 2014 and 2017.[20] Meanwhile, anti-shrine campaigns have also been implemented in secular political contexts, such as in Soviet-era Central Asia in the 1980s, when Islamic practices, especially in their popular form, were institutionally marginalized.[21]

In their complex, individual, or communal manifestations, Muslim pilgrimage traditions go far beyond the Hajj as specific rituals performed in the beginning of the seventh day of Dhu al-Hajj. The *ziyara* comprise a complex set of practices that are mostly performed as visitation rites, though what is visited varies in location and performance.[22] Considering that *ziyara* roughly translates to "visitation," pilgrimages are observed by Muslims of various branches. Ranging from *mawlid*, celebrations of the Prophet's birth date, which can include visitation to the Prophet's tomb, to his household's tomb, and even to Christian and Jewish shrines, *ziyara* can parallel and also simulate the Hajj, especially in the form of circumambulation rituals as performed at a variety of shrines from North Africa to Asia. Among common features are gift giving and the consumption of food, especially sacrificial meat for blessing and health. Significantly, *ziyara* can involve symbolic and material practices unique to the visitation tradition, including a distinct material culture of paraphernalia and devotional ceremonies that change in historical contexts.

Ziyara has several explicit features. First, the so-called secondary Islamic pilgrimages can differ in performance according to how they are carried out in the ritual process. Such an assortment of performances ranges from visiting the shrine of Sufi saint Abu al-Hasan ash-Shadhili (1196–1258) in the Humaithara valley in Egypt's eastern desert, to visiting a Coptic church in Zeitun, a suburb of Cairo, where Muslim women visit the site of Mary's apparition. Pilgrimage could occur where canonical discourses seem least present, although Islamic jurisprudence provides flexibility for the shaping of judgment and behavior, especially when gaining sanctification (*baraka*) in mundane settings connected with visitation. In other words, what defines *ziyara* is less about how Islamic the performance can be and more about different ways pilgrims of diverse background perceive, undertake, express, and internalize the performances, especially if such processes transgress normative-scriptural boundaries of Islam. It is such polyvocality, informed by multiple resources and symbols and applied by various actors and groups, that registers *ziyara* as a stream of discourses and practices, ranging from popular to official, from ordinary to the supernatural.

Second, due primarily to its polyvocality and its inclusive and wide-ranging observations, *ziyara* is cross-confessional. The process of *ziyara* encompasses non-Muslims as well. This is particularly true of Sufi sanctuaries, visited and revered by Muslims and non-Muslims alike. In India, Sufi sites such as Hayder Shaykh in Malerklota, Punjab, serve as communal locations where Muslim and Hindu devotees congregate for devotional observations.[23] As Sophia Rose Arjana has argued, this is also the case for Shi'i shrines at intra-Muslim pilgrimage sites.[24] In Lucknow, India, makeshift shrines built as replicas of Imam Husayn's tomb in Karbala, known as *ta'ziya* in North India and Pakistan, are revered and visited by Hindus and some Sunni Muslims.[25] The comparative anthropological studies in Dionigi Albera and Maria Couroucli's edited volume demonstrate the persistence of Jewish, Christian, and Muslim participation at "shared or mixed sanctuaries" in the eastern Mediterranean, where devotional practices bolster the cohabitation and intersection of Abrahamic traditions that date back to the medieval period.[26]

The third factor, though interrelated with what has already been discussed, is contestation. Depending on the location of performance, *ziyara* involves multidirectional practices, and such multiplicity accordingly entails the possibility of contestation over the range of competing claims. Contestations can be about competing devotional practices marked by vying motivations and social objectives in the course of pilgrimage or, in its extreme case, the destruction of shrines led by vying groups. This is particularly true in certain multiethnic regions such as Afghanistan and Pakistan, where popular shrines have served as public sites of sectarian conflict based on the Sunni–Shi'i divide, primarily enhanced since the Iranian Revolution of 1979. Such contested sites should be viewed in light of the importance of local histories and regional politics, especially advanced by state actors and reformists who may perceive *ziyara* as a deviation from what they understand to be true Islam.

This point is most pertinent in the case of the Arabian Peninsula, where the early nineteenth-century Wahhabi campaigns focusing on the destruction of shrines reshaped the *ziyara* landscape of the region in ways visible, ironically in their invisibility, to this day. Revivalist movements can have a long-term impact on how *ziyara* changes across the globe. As Yeoh Seng-Guan demonstrates, in Malaysia, "state-induced institutional changes," promoted by Islamic revivalism through education, have significantly changed the magical and mystical tradition, known as *Kirama*, among Malay Muslims since 1970s.²⁷ Meanwhile, shrine destruction has also seen the marginalization of *ziyara* in certain regions for its popularity along gender, class, and ethnic lines. The confluence of revivalist movements—especially Sunni Islam and twentieth-century state building in the Persian Gulf region and in the Levant with the rise of the Islamic State (ISIS) in 2014—has led to considerable transformations in *ziyara* traditions.

The fourth aspect is space. Even if the act of visiting takes the form of a dream or a visual journey, the act of visitation, in its multiple manifestations, is inherently associated with spatialized practices. Visitation as *mazarat* in its Arabic medieval form or as *ziyaratgah* (place of visitation) in its Persian form reveals a complex ordering of space wherein the act of visiting as reenactment becomes realized. What reveals the complexity of spatialization is the dynamic role of multiple factors that range from economics to gender to cultural practices—that is, forms of praxis that construct social relations in ritualized mediation between memorial and spiritual realization. Such practices emphasize the social phenomenon of pilgrimage in the ways space is (re)structured or in what can be called "place-making"—as a trajectory of shared, though hardly stable, meaning in distinct spatial domains.

Place-making can become manifest at any localities where the spiritual can attain religious significance for a household, a group, a community, or a state apparatus. The emergent sanctuary formation can also take form alongside or within other consecrated sites, where commemorative or celebratory assemblies take place on a calendarial basis. An ordinary site can crystallize into a shrine with a temporal sighting of a holy vision, an apparition that could gain physical permanency through recurring visitations and social recognition. For example, a vision of Fatima, the daughter of the Prophet, by a young boy during the Muharram mourning ceremonies in remembrance of the martyred Imam Husayn, the grandson of the Prophet, at a mosque in the Arab neighborhood of Bushihr, Iran, can in a matter of a few days transform into a shrine within the mosque, where pilgrims, as far as Iraq, visit for blessing or *baraka*.²⁸ Places of visitation can be multilayered and situated within other building complexes, such as mosques, where the body of a deceased saint could also be buried. *Ziyara* sites are permeable places, where earthly desires and spiritual transcendences are (re)enacted through locally specific expressions ranging from festivals and dance to music and chants.

The assigned symbolic importance of sanctuaries, shrines, mausoleums, and other *ziyara*-related sites brings to light the in-between, liminal realities

Introduction 9

in the interplay between this and other world(s). While less global than Hajj, *ziyara* can be encompassing, wide ranging, and, in terms of what the pilgrim encounters, an alternative experience to the routine practices of everyday life. In Sufi traditions, with a long history of spiritual guides and reverence for Sufi masters, saintly intercession plays a central role in the way earthly space interacts with the spiritual realm. The shrine marks a liminal identity in an earthly-spiritual merging at a distinct locality. The notion of "Ka'ba of the heart" stretches the Hajj into a mystical performance of internalized sacredness.[29] The "local" in *ziyara* of the tomb of a saint, as argued by Amira Mittermaier, hardly signifies a bounded place. Rather, in the course of pilgrimage and, by extension, experiences such as dreams, miracles, and healing associated with the site of pilgrimage, space becomes the "in-between-ness" of the earthly-spiritual domain that interrupts the everyday as it reorders reality in alternatively imagined and felt ways.[30]

Equally important are visitations that involve interaction with the deceased. To perform *ziyara* is to traverse into an alternative, liminal domain, primarily of the dead. In its Turkish and Persian versions, the *dargah* is constructed over the grave of a revered Sufi saint and presents a threshold or portal that opens up the temporal-earthly to the spiritual world. The way through, within which the divine presence is inscribed in terms of threshold, identifies *dargah* as a place of intercession, where the burial site of a saint is celebrated as a way to reach the spiritual in festive performances, such as music, songs, and illumination with candles. Devotion to a shrine, in this sense, is less about disciplined prayer and more about the carnival-like practices closely linked to the memorial of a saintly figure and in connection with spiritual regeneration. Likewise, the theme of spiritual regeneration stresses variation and at times contradictory intentions—incentives and desires in making pilgrimage.[31]

Fifth, and closely related to space, is how the sacred is fused with materiality. Together with other obligatory and nonobligatory rituals, *ziyara* traditions have included a range of practices that revolve around shared and, at times, competing notions of venerated space in material settings. In varied sociogeographic landscapes, at times even mobile in technological domains, Muslim communities have been peppered with shrines, sanctuaries, mausoleums, tombs (*turbas*), and sites of apparition, where bodies, artifacts, ghosts, and footprints of the Prophet and his descendants leave spiritual traces on the earthly ground. Even in the Hijaz regions of western Saudi Arabia, where shrines, burial sites, and historic places have been demolished, beginning with the Wahhabi sack of Karbala in 1801 and

1802, the Green Dome, where the tomb of the Prophet of Islam in Medina is located, remains a major pilgrimage site, observed after the Hajj pilgrimage.[32] These traces may appear in the form of sensations, visions, trances, or technological mediations, such as photos or films that form material realities of spiritual experience in what Oleg Grabar has described as "commemorative structures"—complex arrangements of relations between space, memory, and the sublime.[33]

In exploring commemorative structures, we can consider intricate material practices that make pilgrimage possible as a performative process. The Shrine of the Cloak in Qandahar, Afghanistan, is a site of *ziyara* where a cloak, believed to have been worn by the Prophet, lies inside a mosque, serving as a memorial to the Messenger of God. To visit the cloak is not merely to view a holy object but to encounter an intimacy with the Prophet, whose life, remembered in the act of visitation, remains the ideal model of piety for Muslims.[34] Such intimacies in the course of pilgrimage demonstrate the powerful role of memorial practices, conceived through the consumption, exchange, and giving of sensorial objects in a larger pilgrimage landscape representing the spiritual dreamworlds.

It is no wonder that *ziyara* is often associated with the purchase, sale, and reselling (or gifting) of trinkets, amulets, souvenirs, prayer beads, prayer stones (*turba* or *muhr*), ornaments, healing potions, and perfume at the local market or inside a shrine. The mutual confluence of pilgrimage and the economic activities, especially in terms of makeshift and permanent bazaars in the vicinity of pilgrimage destinations, has been historically complex and widespread.[35] The gifting of objects, devotional or otherwise, has provided an occasion for pilgrims to engage with the complex network of reciprocity economy. Such a gift economy, as Marcel Hénaff has shown, affirms social bonds and recognition, public connections that, one can further argue, pilgrims can renew with the status of *za'ir* and ultimately cultivate social mobility.[36] Likewise, the divine is re-sanctified in material objects that are intimately linked with other ritual performances, such as *dhikr*, a tradition of remembrance of Allah observed not only by Sufis but also by other Muslims during *ziyara* and also Hajj. During pilgrimage, or in fact during any form of social practice, the material embodies agency, a fluid matrix of objects containing and relaying emotions that render memory essential to the experience of visitation.

As for the sixth feature, *ziyara* is about the vernacular. From East Asia to North Africa, from Central Asia to the Middle East, Muslim pilgrims have traveled short or long distances to marked tombs, graves, houses, or natural places in local settings in what Arjana describes as "vernacular structures" of apparently mundane significance.[37] For the most part, such marked sites appear in the form of relics, graves, monuments, or shrines that present mystical and at times magical domains where the dead and the living can communicate in local settings. In its messianic form, the blessed local site, where the Mahdi has appeared or promises a return, connects the present with a radically open future. Due to the focus on intercession in ordinary situations, which the person undergoing spiritual change experiences, the relationship between the familiar and the local, the resident and the paranormal, remains intimate. The shrines of Sufi saints in Uighur China, for example, are often unmarked in the desert field but fused into the geographic landscape in the form of supernatural forces, as pilgrims visit and leave offerings for healing. These local shrines present a kind of visitation practice that permits the ordinary to carry extraordinary powers at a distinct locality with its marked vernacular appearances.

Finally, networks of cooperation and trust are what make pilgrimage possible as a local and potentially translocal phenomenon. In this light, the political cannot be dissociated from the associational processes. Recent scholarship, for example in the francophone academia, has produced studies on the relationship between social capital and the political aspects of shrine formation in (post)colonial contexts of regions in the Middle East and North Africa. The ways in which a shrine's popularity declines or rises depends on various network factors, including the role of family ties in promoting a saint, as shown by El Ayadi, Rachik, and Tozy in urban and rural Morocco.[38] The anthropological work of Danielle Provansal shows the important role women play in local pilgrimage in Algeria, where visitation to saintly shrines is perceived as a woman-specific activity in redefining their social position in the context of gender power relations and shifting urban and rural settings.[39] Likewise, the popularity of *mukams* (from the Arabic *maqam*) as female-saint shrines in Sylhet, Bangladesh, has primarily depended on active Sufi networks in the promotion of the status of a woman's spiritual status to the level of sainthood.[40] How a specific shrine is associated with gender signification, say of a female saint, is subject to microsocial ties and intricate performances of authority.[41]

However, authority is not just about social capital but also about financial capital and the ways in which investment in certain pilgrimage practices such as shrines can lead to the spread of distinct traditions in a local or national setting. In Iran, *imamzadahs*—shrines of mostly descendants of imams—have sprouted since the establishment of the Islamic Republic in 1979 largely due to a growing religious tourist industry coupled with semi-private and state involvement in the promotion of devotional Shi'ism in Iranian urban and rural life.[42] Likewise, in Jordan, the rebuilding of mausoleums, including those of the Companion of the Prophet, by King 'Abdullah and his son, the current monarch, has led to renewed conceptions of Islamic sanctified territories. Such renewal of sacred spaces has also elevated the importance of the mausoleums into cultural heritage sites for the Jordanian tourist industry, which caters to world travelers and Jordan's growing tourist industry.[43] In the case of Hajj, historically speaking, the economic activities revolving around pilgrimage have been extensively global and intricately regulated. In precolonial southeast Asia, as Eric Tagliacozzo has shown, for example, the Hajj played an important role in maritime economic activities across the Indian Ocean, which required various regulative measures over financial transactions related to transregional travel.[44] In the colonial period, European powers, especially the Dutch, introduced new regulative measures that involved not only financial transactions for transportation costs but also data collection on Hajj pilgrims throughout the nineteenth century.[45] Pilgrimage is an economy, and the Hajj and *ziayara* are no exceptions.

To explain the multifaceted life of pilgrimage, one tends to employ the metaphor of a "network" and cognate terms such as "nodes" and "interlinkages" to better illustrate the porous set of social practices that identify pilgrimage. And it is precisely because of this fluidity of relations, as explained earlier, that making typologies in defining "Muslim pilgrimage" can be a challenge. The difficulty of classification, though not exclusive to pilgrimage studies, is particularly problematic when boundaries between *ziyara* and Hajj collapse through practice in ritual contexts. In intricate ways, the two overlap in both symbolic and material terms. As a substitute for the Hajj, *ziyara* to a local graveyard—known as "the poor person's Hajj"—serves as a closer geographical replacement for those who might not be able to physically or financially travel to Mecca. In what Hamid Algar has called "the relativisation of the Ka'ba," shrines and mausoleums in Bulgaria, Morocco, Senegal, and India have provided alternative devotional spaces for traveling devotees.[46] While at times such sites, including Sufi lodges and sanctuaries, have rivaled Mecca, they have served as substitutes, or even replicas of Mecca—original copies with distinct significance of their own. In his study of pilgrimage in Central Asia, Thierry Zarcone described such sites as "second

Mecca," or substitutes to Hajj that reconstruct the pilgrimage experience at a distinct locality, where economic, political, and spiritual strength can be reproduced in place of Mecca.[47]

Equally important to discuss is how certain *ziyara* traditions can be observed during Hajj, such as visiting the grave of an imam or reciting a *fatiha* prayer for a deceased saint or family member.[48] Let us call this interrituality. The performance of certain prayers evokes the *ziyara* in Hajj. Similarly, trips to Hajj may also include a visit to a shrine in another country, as in the case of Senegalese pilgrims who, on the way back from Mecca, stop in Fez, Morocco, to visit the Sufi lodge of Sidi Ahmad el Tajani.[49] As Katia Boissevain has argued, the element of substitution underscores a deep intercession between Hajj and *ziyara*, which defies a simplified separated study of the two forms of "Muslim pilgrimage": modern or otherwise.[50]

Though inseparable, there are yet distinctions between *ziyara* and Hajj, perhaps not in their classification but in their family resemblance. The Hajj is exclusively meant for Muslims and also observed at a designated calendarial time. Moreover (and more importantly), as a canonical tradition, Hajj is preferred over *ziyara*, which is deemed a deviation in terms of *bida'* (innovation) or *shirk* (idolatry) by certain Muslims—in particular, Salafi Sunnis. However, we argue that these distinctions are not about substance but about the degree to which a distinct pilgrimage tradition is privileged over another. How Hajj differs from *ziyara* is effectively a matter of interpretation about what can be included as a visitation practice, rather than a normative definition of what constitutes Islamic pilgrimage. The attempt to make typologies based on theological content would therefore require a definition of Muslimhood built exclusively around canon and dogma, which is—at least in idea—beyond the scope of an academic enterprise as presented in this book.

Seen from this critical interpretative perspective, a multidimensional approach would be foremost in order for a wide-ranging study of Muslim pilgrimage. Looking at pilgrimage through a multidimensional lens would embrace an array of practices and divergent ways of giving account to Muslim pilgrimage in the broader modern context of what Eric J. Hobsbawm described as the "international standardization" of lived experience.[51] In what follows, we provide a tentative thematic outline of Muslim pilgrimage by which the present volume is conceptualized. Our aim is not to provide a typology based on a system of classification but to delineate key family resemblances on a set of shared polythematic markers that render "Muslim pilgrimage" possible for discussion in an academic venue.

The Modernity of Muslim Pilgrimage

If histories of Muslim pilgrimage in their varied and competing forms have always been contested and reconfigured through practice, then how can we historically distinguish different forms of Muslim pilgrimage? In other words, what is unique to "modern Muslim pilgrimage" that would enable us to define it in distinction from "pre-modern Muslim pilgrimage"? And if there is a defining feature (or features), how can such a definition help us better understand being modern, Muslim or otherwise, in the world?

Here we attempt to narrate a shared set of thematic markers that portray a configuration of Muslim pilgrimage and its modernity in relation—contentious or otherwise—to rationality and technology. Such a portrayal also provides thematic features that have been historically unprecedented: First is the key practice of travel in association with distinct technologies as a central theme in how pilgrimage can be described though not defined. By "travel," we refer to human movements as situated practices performed in a changing context of distinct frameworks of mobile action. People travel for various purposes, and they do so in locally situated frameworks that inform their decisions. Yet particularly in its pre-nineteenth-century mode, which involved complex nodes of social relations across wide geographies, travel for the purpose of performing pilgrimage across long distances—to the Arabian Peninsula or to any other geographic place that contributes to "being Muslim" as a social process—was hardly viewed as an ordinary experience.[52] In its "modern" form—the nineteenth century and beyond—more accessible, efficient, speedy, and centralized travel became a social experience involving complex networks of governance, private agencies, and civic associations. The modernity of travel—of which Muslim pilgrims avidly partook, especially in the nineteenth century—constituted the limits of overlapping practices of global commerce, international transportation, tourism, and colonial networks.[53] Cultural expressions of travel—through memoirs, diaries, and travelogues—have also been produced through an expanding printing market and reading public, especially since the nineteenth century.

The institution of pilgrimage as travel is essentially a form of self-negotiation. In broad historical terms, pilgrimage has always encompassed departure, arrival, and, most importantly, a return journey. Depending on the specific case, it has primarily been at arrival when new social, gender, or class identities are renegotiated (though at times disputed by competing actors) with the acquired title of "Hajji" (male) or "Hajjia" (female).[54] Whether going by land, ship, auto, or air, Muslim pilgrims are involved in varied forms of interactions in the course of travel and return—that is, if the traveler has the financial and physical means to do so. Historically speaking, the privileged status, prestige, and social influence, especially when tied with class and gender, have been contingent on the various modes of travel. Depending on the locality where the pilgrim begins his or her travels, status gained from pilgrimage has become less prestigious in regions where travel is least expensive and more accessible to the local population.

However, status can be earned by demonstrating how well one is able to access, negotiate, circumvent, and ultimately overcome complex networks that govern local or translocal pilgrimage connections, highlighting a "modern" experience in the relation with socio-technological and governmental ways of doing travel. Because of increasing regulation over the Hajj by local and national agencies, particularly the Saudi government since the second half of the twentieth century, the Hajj status has undergone a different kind of change. In its postcolonial form, the Hajj would gain new symbolic capital not because of the hardship of travel, as was evident in the pre-nineteenth-century era, but because of the social influence, with claims on bureaucratic and regulative processes ranging from acquiring a passport or visa, or reserving a highly sought-after airline ticket. The aspect of status is tied to the second feature, capital, flowing as a global process and ranging from financial to symbolic. Capital is paramount to the experience of travel in pilgrimage. Pilgrimage entails economic status that in turn enhances one's spiritual capital. In historic terms, such capital has been less about the possession of material goods associated with the site of pilgrimage and more about the accumulation of generosity, piety, and care for the public good, which would defy greed and wealth for the private domain. The displayed capital is made visible, shared, and consumed, in the form of gift giving and the sacrifice of an animal on the return home.

In its modern context, capital has been reconstructed in emergent social ties and status, which have affected how pilgrimage has been institutionalized through state and civic organizations. Since the mid-twentieth century and the decline in the number of destitute pilgrims—those who cannot afford pilgrimage but manage to travel anyway, only to face difficulties at arrival, a result of Saudi Hajj regulations—pilgrimage has seen a bolstering of economic and social status within wider social practices.[55] It is important to note that, by and large, this aspect has depended on the locality to which the pilgrim, male or female, returns to claim his or her new social identity. In various contexts, pilgrimage and its social capital formations have played a key role, especially during the return phase of the journey, when a renewed status becomes recognized based on material and symbolic importance.

In the case of *ziyara*, the reproduction of status for female and male members of a community, especially on their return from a pilgrimage, has revolved around the enhancement of distinct status identity related to the symbolic significance of the pilgrimage site—that is, the material and spiritual power associated with the saint—as observed by Eickelman in his study of shrines in Boujad, Morocco.[56] In Twelver Shiʿi Islam, social status for *ziyara* of a shrine of imam is reserved, as noted in the official title of "Karbalayi" for someone who has visited Karbala, Iraq, where Husayn, the grandson of the Prophet, is buried, or "Najafi" for someone who has visited the shrine of ʿAli ibn Abi Talib, the Prophet's cousin and son-in-law, in Najaf, Iraq. Status displays a distinct social mobility that both maintains and generates frameworks of identity by which actors can situate themselves in relation to their social settings. Such situated relations also involve material and symbolic significance of an imagined pilgrimage site that informs varieties of capital gains, including economic ones, in mostly urban settings. The key issue here is that in its modern context, Muslim pilgrimage has seen a major shift in changing status formations in competition or intersection with other status identities, such as secular ones based in governance, education, or the private sectors. These processes have been ambivalent, and yet include an integral role in redefining Muslim identities in an increasingly governable network of pilgrimage management.

Increasing fragmentation of identity leads to the third and more central feature: experience. Undoubtedly, all forms of pilgrimages involve experience, but pilgrimage in its modern context involves technological configurations in sensing space and time, self, and other in what Marshall Berman famously called the "experience of modernity."[57] By the mid-nineteenth century, as most Hajjis traveled from European colonies to Arabia, pilgrimage travel underwent significant changes in what can be described in terms of a rationalization of movement across time and space. Although the experience of pilgrimage travel has always involved transportation technologies, including the use of domesticated camels across Afro-Eurasian caravan routes, which expanded in the early modern period, the emergence of steamship, locomotive, automobile, and airplane introduced a globalizing experience of travel that changed perceptions of time and space.[58]

Nevertheless, more central to perceptual changes in Muslim pilgrimage has been the development of complex regimes of discipline, regulation, and surveillance in its colonized form in the birth of a "modern" conception of distant travel under British and French imperialism beginning in the mid-nineteenth century.[59] As shown by Eric Tagliacozzo, Valeska Huber, and Robert R. Bianchi, Hajj travel, especially since the second half of the nineteenth century, underwent major globalizing changes. These transformations included the governing over of pilgrim bodies by global health regimes; the institutionalization of disinfection and medical centers to prevent the spread of disease; and the formation of what Bianchi calls "Hajj bureaucracies," under the control of the Saudi state apparatus, to oversee the influx of international travelers to Mecca.[60] In its "modern" sense, the Hajj is a disciplinary enterprise of complex practices of governance.

In addition to the context of globalizing regimes of control and regulation, the modernity of Muslim pilgrimage has hardly been divorced from the experience of modernness in its various sociocultural and economic contexts, ranging from national to diasporic settings. Although questions remain as to how and when travel becomes "sacred" or how pilgrimage remains distinguished, if at all, from touristic experience, as argued by Erik Cohen, the unique attributes of modern Muslim pilgrimage continue to be fused with global processes that have led to distinct understandings of religiosity in what Arjun Appadurai has described as a contradictory world of flows and structures.[61] Such contradictory realities experienced by Muslims, whether performing pilgrimage or not, is contingent on transnational dynamics, in which anxieties of distance, fatigues of mobility, and desires for arrival at shifting notions of home and homeland constitute a new global reality of (uneven) interconnectivity.

If anything, the modern experience, with its inherent challenges to how religion is imagined in everyday life, entails the fragmentation, though hardly the waning, of the worldly and the spiritual. Pilgrimage to Mecca can still ignite a spiritual awakening, as it did for Malcolm X in 1964, but with the accelerated access that transcontinental air travel brings, so can pilgrimage become transformed into a touristic experience in proximity to a sacred site, as in the Saudi implementation of the ongoing construction of upscale shopping malls, luxury hotels, and leisure spaces in Mecca.[62] Meanwhile, in its reverse form, a tourist destination such as the Hagia Sophia Museum in Istanbul, Turkey, can fulfill a traveler's desire for a spiritual experience as a commercialized tourist site or as a repository of the remains of a bygone Byzantine Christian imperium.[63] In its globalizing form, the modern Muslim pilgrimage experience is about the building up of a meaningful world, but one that is intrinsically tied with globalization of experience in its diasporic, national, and transnational forms.

What "meaningful world" is constructed through pilgrimage? While pilgrimage in Islam does not necessarily imply a mere "journey," Muslim pilgrimage traditions have combined a set of individual and collective experiences of sacred and mundane travel. The experience of *visitation* offers a key reference that implies a transformative quest for spiritual truth. The quest concerns the highest form of self-discovery, a voyage of inner passage unfolding in spiritual states or stages through which pilgrims undergo in the course of visitation. The experience of travel, either physical or spiritual, also entails transitional processes, thresholds through which an intermediate state of being between home and the sacred site is the manifestation of an otherworldly dimension. Consecration of a place is therefore a manifestation of the sacred in doing pilgrimage, or in what Mircea Eliade famously described as "theophany": a threshold space of revelation where human experience undergoes a radical change.[64]

Nevertheless, as Victor Turner famously explained, there is "organization and discipline" in the way the liminal experience of pilgrimage as a social process is attained.[65] That is, there is structure in the ways pilgrimage rituals and relics connect with a large body of Islamic practices and revolve around historical contexts and mythologies of extraordinary people, holy figures, or messianic characters, which embody the most spiritual dimension of the religion. In pilgrimage lies spiritual histories that entail economies and material cultures built around experiences of travel, arrivals, visitations, and eventual departures toward home, economies and cultures that are shaped in shifting historical and social contexts. In "modern" terms, Muslim pilgrimage practices are reflections of an increasingly interconnected set of relations and, accordingly, their entailed experiences, which span over space and time across the globe.

In its global context, pilgrimage interconnectivity also reflects intricate ways of grappling with conflicts over ideals and practices to (re)define Islam through devotions and performances charged with spiritual importance. Modern pilgrimage can be described in this sense as increasing opening spaces of interpretation—multivocal sites wherein aesthetic, moral, political, and spiritual frameworks of action become pronounced across temporal and cultural settings. Edith and Victor Turner famously argued for the liminal and *communitas* nature of pilgrimage—that is, the practice of separation from structures of mundane daily life, during which direct experience of the sacred becomes possible. Distinct from everyday life, pilgrimage draws boundaries between the mundane and the extraordinary, a liminal realm where in various performances of Hajj, such as males dressing in *ihram*, a reversal of reality is made in the reordering of lived time and space in a symbolic attempt to prepare for this-worldly death.[66]

Separation from daily life can entail other social processes. Pilgrimage can also comprise the reification of conflict. Contestation over sacred and secular discourses and practices related to pilgrimage rites could occur between competing Muslims who vie for access, resources, and status in locally situated ways.[67] As argued by John Eade and Michael Sallnow, pilgrimage can be viewed as public forums of contestation in structured modes of social relations, as competing discourses and practices provide meaning to individuals and communities performing pilgrimage as a ritualized practice.[68] What remains unique to pilgrimage is not an overarching universality of ritual action, as argued by Turner, but practices contingent to sociocultural contexts that become manifest in uneven and indeterminate ways. In its modern manifestation, such indeterminacies have multiplied and proliferated across time and space while globalizing certain norms and practices that undermine standardization in complex ways.

The key issue here is the degree of contention in its modern contexts, as conflict and competing notions of Muslimness articulated through pilgrimage have widened across the globe since the nineteenth century. Throughout Islamic history, contentious debates and competing attributions have emphasized how pilgrimage rites and their theological repertoires and semblance of praxis can mark competing claims to identity and authority.[69] In its modern form, as Emilio Spadola further elaborates in his study in this volume (chapter 10), pilgrimage now continues with "a lengthy history of multipolarity and multiplicity of practice, piety, and authority within the Muslim world." The multidirectional aspect demonstrates some of the ways in which that pilgrimage characterizes a porous reality through which such ritual performances, even when under attack, serve as desire for singularity of identity in claims over politics with a global reach while also serving local and national interests with multiple agendas.

To articulate a definition of "Muslim pilgrimage in the modern world" would therefore begin and end in a nondefinition, which would be best described as a set of thematic trajectories of what is perceived as pilgrimage practices. Such trajectories do not define but ascribe modernity to Muslim pilgrimage that continues to undergo change in the era of global capital, with religion facing increasing commodification in the marketplace of standardized competition.

The Structure of the Volume

The present volume aims to expand on these complex features of Muslim pilgrimage practices in their modern particularities through a thematic approach. As a result of an overconcentration on the Hajj rituals, many traditions of Muslim pilgrimage that embody such combined liminal and contentious dynamics have been marginalized in various studies, although numerous anthropologists and sociologists, especially in non-anglophone fields, have underscored the importance, vastness, and diversity of non-Hajj pilgrimage traditions.[70] Our hope in this collection of essays, though with the least intention of striving to offer a comprehensive study, is to shed light on several themes related to Muslim pilgrimage practices and the ways in which they have been maintained or undergone change with the reconstruction of the pilgrimage tradition with respect to changes in historical, geopolitical, and technological realities. *Muslim Pilgrimage in the Modern World*, therefore, aims to provide a set of thematic accounts of the histories, traditions, and practices of Muslim pilgrimage in their diverse forms, and also examine current attempts to reconstruct rituals in their changing sociocultural, political, embodied, and technological frameworks.

Divided into three parts, this book provides eleven case studies, each with a focus on a theme related to the notion of "modern pilgrimage." In the first part, "Rethinking Muslim Pilgrimage," four contributors offer theoretical and empirical studies on the role of history and politics with an eye on transnationalism, broadly speaking, defined as intensified awareness and interactivity of social networks in the context of receding economic, cultural, and political boundaries. The objective in this section, which focuses mostly on Hajj, is to discuss the underlying historical sociological processes, intertwined with the political realities, with which pilgrims reinvent identity across the world. In the second part, "Embodiment, Memory, and Materiality," the discussion shifts to the theme of corporeality and materiality, showing that the complex relationship between the local and the translocal lies in experiential practices that cultivate memory and are affectively reproduced through materiality.

The four essays in this section explore the translocal by focusing on material cultural processes embedded in a globalized setting. The transnationalism of Muslim pilgrimage is further elaborated in the third section, "Communication, (New) Media, and Space," where the remaining three essays focus on the theme of media practices and communication paradigms in the reconstruction of Muslim ritual cultures of pilgrimage, mostly in their non-Hajj manifestation. In these essays, the contributors examine how ritualized religious experience is transformed through changing technological practices. In this final part, contributors also provide ethnographic analysis on the role of technology in changing Muslim pilgrimage to redefine the "modern" as a historical experience of ritual spirituality.

History, Politics, and Transnationalism

As a rite of passage marked by travel, pilgrimage is the reenactment of redrawing space across vast territories. In historical time, pilgrims carry on the task of redrawing boundaries of home and sacred site through ritual performances that transgress geographical boundaries, dissolving the concepts and practices of a bounded space of dwelling beyond the familiar social linkages of daily life. Since the rise of territorialized nation-states in the early modern period and as a result of the increased flow of capital, labor, slavery, migration, technology, and colonial practices, transnationalism has signified a growing weakening of the nation-state. However, such weakening has seen a simultaneous growth of national consciousness, perhaps in reaction to globalization, which are tied to local and governmental practices that seek to solidify the territoriality of the "nation-state." The apparent paradox is marked in the way globalizing, border-transcending processes reconfigure national boundaries. The transnational continues to persist within the national context marked by the emerging diasporic, migratory, cosmopolitan, and communicative-technological spaces.

In the case of religious rites such as pilgrimage, politics enters not only in the practice of transgressing geographical boundaries—as pilgrims attain translocal senses of belonging in competing discourses and practices over religious ideals as equally important diverse modern practices are appropriated—but also in the institutionalization of regimes and policies to manage and govern the rituals and pilgrims who perform them. The role of the state on both the local and the national level is undeniable, but so is the role of transnational political enterprises. In historical terms, the case of nineteenth-century European colonial powers serves as an intriguing example of an institutional attempt to control cholera during Hajj season in regions such as India and Southeast Asia so as to prevent Western societies from contamination, hence solidifying national boundary.[71] An approach of considering pilgrimage as a "transnational" phenomenon suggests that the "national" continues to play a key role in the economic, cultural, and political influences that operate globally.

As a tradition of long-distance travel, however, the Hajj embodies a universal ideal of faith that transcends local boundaries. Such an ideal entails a spiritual cosmopolitanism in varied ritual practices. The ihram ritual clothing, for example, which involves both men and women wearing white garments as a symbol of purity and unified wholeness, serves as a way to cast aside individuated perception in place of a universal fellowship. Responding to the race consciousness of his American identity, Malcolm X describes his Hajj experience with fellow (white) Muslims in the following words: "We were *truly* all the same (brothers)—because their belief in one God had removed the 'white' from their *minds*, the 'white' from their *behavior* and the 'white' from their *attitude*."[72] As a spiritual awakening—particularly of the sort that Malcolm X experienced just months prior to the landmark Civil Rights Act of 1964—Hajj strips away ethnicity, race, and national identity, with each pilgrim, female and male, rearranging individuated life for an integrated community of shared morality.

But such an ideal has historically been in tension with earthly affairs, that is, regimes of governance that have sought to control the universality of Hajj. Until the early twentieth century, the Hajj travel was intrinsically linked with decentralized networks of governance across vast regions, especially as transregional travel routes expanded after the Mongol conquests in the thirteenth century. Not until the 1950s, however, would Hajj undergo a comprehensive regulatory expansion under the Saudi government, which had taken over the Hijaz in 1925 and had initiated Hajj reforms in 1926. Today, the experience of Hajj is mostly a product of postwar Saudi modernization: construction of shopping malls, luxury hotels, and landmarks that have made Mecca (and Medina) into what Juan E. Campo describes as the "radical transformation of Hajj sacred landscape."[73] While air travel and other forms of transportation technologies, including information technologies, have underscored the globalization of pilgrimage, Saudi state projects to streamline and manage the flow of pilgrims into its territorial state have enhanced the national infrastructure schemes. In addition, government policy has put in place Hajj quotas, which, in part, have been adopted in line with diplomatic relations with other nations as well as state ideology.

The paradox here encompasses both the globalization of the Hajj—in the construction, for example, of massive hotel structures that accommodate thousands of pilgrims from around the world—and, simultaneously, the process of nationalization in fostering Saudi state power through massive national construction projects. In his 1964 travel diary, famed Iranian intellectual Jalal Al-i Ahmad cringed at the fast pace of Saudi modernization in reconstructing Mecca and Medina, even making Ka'ba, as he jokingly remarks, out of "reinforced concrete."[74]

With a critical eye, Al-i Ahmad would add the following: "There is no alternative but to internationalize these shrines, Mecca, Medina, Arafat and Mina, to place them under the management of a joint council of Muslim nations and to remove them from Saudi Arabia control. The revenues must come from income generated by the Hajj. Instead of Saudi Arabian police there must be guides from every nation. Legitimacy must be granted to the special customs each sect."[75] This passage is remarkable not just for articulating an international ideal of Hajj governance but also for renewed its claim over legitimacy in reference to Islam's multiple identities. Al-i Ahmad's call for emancipating Hajj from the grip of Saudi rule is a telling narrative of a Muslim desire for an Islamic cosmopolitanism that has remained a mere dream since perhaps the time of the Prophet. Echoing nineteenth-century pan-Islamism, the underlying concern of Al-i Ahmad's call is a demand for a progressive movement of Islamic universality, a movement in which transnationalism would play an integral role in shaping the modern Muslim identity through the Hajj tradition.

It may seem ironic to speak of Hajj as transnational while considering the origins of the ritual as a local shrine in pre-Islamic Arabia. That shrines such as Ka'ba are local sacred sites, however, does not exclude their translocality. In its pre-Islamic period, Mecca represented a regional, nevertheless translocal, shrine for accommodating several deities, including Jesus and Mary, that attracted pilgrims and merchants alike, as it was a major trading town at the crossroads of Afro-Eurasian caravan routes.[76] In its early Islamic period, Hajj brought pilgrims from the Arabian Peninsula, and later, as Islam spread throughout Africa and Asia, the shrine city gained significant religious and political prestige, bringing pilgrims from faraway lands, a process that spread with the Islamization of Southeast Asia after the thirteenth century. Equally significant were *ziyara* performances at sites of apparition in the fusion of local economies, cultures, and politics of the shrine with translocal networks, leading to the crystallization of economic and religious cultures across time and space. What emerged out of the complex local and translocal symbiosis were multiple Muslim identities throughout history, closely tied to diverse rituals, with interpretative frameworks for shaping solidarity, however contentious in practice.

This is the argument that Brannon Wheeler proposes in chapter 1 of the present volume. In "Sacrifice and Pilgrimage: Body Politics and the Origins of Muslim Pilgrimage," Wheeler focuses on the relationship between sacrifice and pilgrimage, arguing that the origins of Hajj lie in the gift-giving rituals associated with burial sites in the form of sacrifice, which predate Islam. In an archaeologically and textually informed study, Wheeler underscores the economic and religious significance of pre-Islamic Kaʿba to the shrine landscape of the Arabian Peninsula, with Mecca as a major graveyard for prophets who made pilgrimage to the city. Standing stones (such as the Black Stone) signified funerary monuments, and Kaʿba itself represented a "tomb marker."

The importance of the funerary performances and sacrificial rituals, mostly of domesticated animals, associated with the pre-Islamic pilgrimage to the Mecca sanctuary, Wheeler argues, is evident in early Islamic Hajj performances. Pilgrimage linked with sacrifice in respect to the tomb, as in the case of the Prophet Muhammad's sacrifice and distribution of animal body parts among pilgrims in his farewell pilgrimage at Mecca, represents a reinvention of older traditions that carry the themes of regeneration of communal identity through animal sacrifice. The significance of Islamic sacrificial performance, however, lies in the construction of a "new world" cosmogony and an eschatological reconstruction of locality as a cosmic opening of a new reality. The camel sacrifice by Prophet Muhammad, Wheeler argues, represents a performance of body politics, as the flesh of the camel is distributed among Muslims. The ritual, reenacted into the modern era, provides an opportunity of transregional magnitude for pilgrims to renew bonds through animal sacrifice, a process that would enable them to identify with a Muslim identity in the course of the performances—particularly in the consumption of ritual food. In this ritualized form, identity is regenerative, and the role of the performances is marked as the vehicle for the renewal of translocal regeneration.

Rites of sacrifice, however, are not limited to symbolic expression of identity in the form of a "body politic" at the pilgrimage site, where the arrival and visitation journey take place. Moving to the contemporary era, in his detailed study of Chinese government control over Hajj, Robert R. Bianchi draws attention to complex workings of local and other governmental agencies that make the Hajj travel possible in the first place (chapter 2). In the case of Chinese Muslim pilgrims, who have grown in size since 1992 and are separated by ethnic group across China, ability to participate in the Hajj has depended on the pilgrimage quota negotiated between Beijing and the Saudi government, although there are also cases of "illegal" travel through third countries. Hajj participation also depends on Beijing's distribution of quotas among various Chinese Muslims, with the Hui of the western provinces more favored because of their history of resistance to the central government, whose strategy is to provide religious benefits, such as the Hajj, as a way to attain support and greater legitimacy and stabilize the various provinces along ethnic and religious lines.

Along ethnic and gender lines is the formation of economic and social networks that empower one group of Muslims against another for more advantageous Hajj allocation. The role of literacy among females in performing Hajj, for example, provides an understanding that accessibility to state regulation over pilgrimage has considerably little to do with existing cultural and social capital connected with local economies in urban settings. The key point that Bianchi proposes with regard to Chinese Hajj regulation is the state construction of Chinese identity in relation to economic, demographic, and ethic factors in changing rural and urban relations. The regulative process, Bianchi argues, is uneven, but so is the Chinese government's attempt to balance recognition at home and abroad for providing religious benefits to its ethnic minorities. It is worth noting that for Bianchi, identity formation in the course of the Hajj begins before any religious performance takes place in Mecca—that is, in the complicated network of state regulations, local networks, and demographic landscapes tied to the global processes in which the Chinese government seeks to participate and gain legitimacy. A major feature of Chinese Hajj experience is Beijing's strategic policy use of Hajj as a way to participate in what Bianchi calls "Islamic Globalization," an interrelated set of changes that integrate Muslims into a globalized domain of connectivity.

Similar to Bianchi's study of Chinese Hajj as a transnational process closely tied to national projects, Paulo G. Pinto's study of Muslim pilgrims from Brazil begins with the local-national experience and the capacity to shape meaning and identity through competing Muslim groups in transnational sites of interconnectivity (chapter 3). Pinto provides insight into another Muslim minority in a geographical context in which Islam is also relatively marginal but mostly with an urbanite identity and roots from the Middle East. But in the Brazilian case, conversation to Islam has introduced an intriguing example of a distinct form of what Pinto calls "globalizing oneself," as new converts with new Arabic names perform Hajj or ʿUmra as a way to claim religious identity distinct from non-converts of Middle Eastern descent. In studying various Muslims groups and sects in Brazil—particularly competing groups, such as the Shi'i and Salafi—Pinto argues how Hajj, on the rise since 2000 and organized through private and Islamic institutions such as mosques, has redefined Muslim Brazilian identities that, while transcending local groups, are intimately linked with sacred sites visited through transnational travel.

Pinto also draws attention to the importance of *ziyara* and its material cultures, which will be discussed in more detail in the following section, as important means of forging a transnational Muslim identity—at times a contentiously sectarian one—in the Brazilian context, though with globalized implications. Muslim pilgrimage traditions, he argues, have facilitated the globalization of "religious imagination" among Muslims in Brazil while reinforcing heritage cultures of distinct Muslim groups—particularly in the case of *ziyara* performances—but are doing so by long-distance travel to countries of origin, such as Syria. In what he calls "codification of Islam," Pinto is keen to show that religious identity in the Hajj performance is realized through conscious rethinking of Islamic practices and forms of sacred living, which pilgrimage provides an opportunity to reinvent. The possibility of politics lies in the negotiated ways identity is ritually reconstructed through local and global processes.

The notion of identify reconfiguration through ritual is further examined in the study of American Muslims' Hajj experience by Sophia Rose Arjana and Rose Aslan. As Arjana and Aslan show in their study of Muslim American Hajj narratives (chapter 4), the experience of pilgrimage is hardly monolithic, as American pilgrims shape competing perceptions and hence interpretations of Islam in reference to the politicization of religion in the United States and Saudi Arabia. Studying diverse female and male pilgrim narratives, including converts to Islam, Arjana and Aslan delineate both spiritual and mundane practices of Hajj, including the experience of shopping for gifts and souvenirs that demonstrate a multidimensional set of practices. Differences in class, gender, and race entail different perceptions and experiences of Hajj among American Muslims. While Hajj brings a multitude of Muslims together in shaping a transnational political community of *umma*, in practice, pilgrimage to Mecca concurrently involves the reproduction of different identities and, hence, shaping of competing experiences and interpretations of Islamic identity based on gender, nationality, capital, and racial background. The politics of Hajj is the collective expression of (uneven) differences of pilgrim identities specific to local and national contexts.

Embodiment, Memory, and Materiality

In *A Season in Mecca: Narrative of Pilgrimage*, the Moroccan scholar 'Abdellah Hammoudi describes his pilgrimage experience at the mosque of Mecca in the following words:

> What, then, was this enclosure I had entered and could not violate by leaving, lest I fail to do what was expected? The enclosure took place in rules, laws and specific changes in appearance that ordered its approach, that prepared for harmony with the "sacred-forbidden" territory of mosque of Mecca. The mosque of Mecca, called a Haram, a sanctuary, shares with the one in Medina this unique quality. The body—when it forgoes its limits, the clear configuration bestowed on it by tailored clothing—projects itself into a transforming time and space. I could feel it becoming a shifting territory of sacredness even before arriving at the limits of Mecca's sacred-forbidden spaces. I felt once again that I was approaching the unknown and I struggled against the old feeling of fear. Perhaps Mecca's Haram waiting for me at the end of the road would take me over in a way I could not predict. My body, divested of its habitual contours, might be absorbed in bits and pieces, or dissolve as if sucked in by the Holy Mosque.[77]

There is something deeply intimate about Hammoudi's personal account. As a critical observer of Saudi control over the Hajj, in what he describes as the "Hajj government," which in effect has profoundly shaped modern Muslim pilgrimage, Hammoudi shares here an emotive experience of pilgrimage that highlights the transformation of the pilgrim's body through the sacred space.[78] The relationship between affective experience and spatial enclosure of the sacred marks a dynamic emotive process, which is not limited to a metaphoric transfiguration. In an intricate way, regulations over how to behave at a sacred site is experientially fused with spiritual territoriality. The spiritual is the bodily site articulated in sacred enclosure.

In an important way, Hammoudi's description brings the body as the central focus of the pilgrimage experience. It is the (male) body of the narrator and the materiality of how his body is represented in the public that "projects" spatial reality of a sacred kind. Yet the body and its limited projection in the spatial order is also about habitual delineations, a remembering of an intense experience that allows the narrator to become one with the pilgrimage experience as an encountered physical space. It is in the process of memory and its textual or visual rearticulation that the enclosure can attain a reality of social substance.

Hammoudi's account provides an intriguing example of the intersection between regulative structures of ritual space and perceptual experiences embedded in bodily practices. The relationship between an inner sense of spirituality and outer substance is marked in his description at the mosque of Mecca in a fluid transformation that allows for a ritual experience of embodiment—a way of inhabiting a lived encounter to shape agency. Though the body, as Drew Leder has described, can "disappear" in the fading of consciousness of everyday life in distress or forgetfulness, the body in Hajj opens up, projecting outwards, interrupting the routines of life.[79] What the Hajj body reveals is a significant site of experience, a site wherein an individuated experience is able to affectively embody a sacred territory as a universal ideal and, at the same time, as a specific geographic locale.

Hammoudi's account expands the theme of this volume from the historical and political realities of pilgrimage to an embodied conception of Muslim pilgrimage. Such a shift in focus would identify pilgrimage as an experiential process, a theme that was equally explored by Wheeler, Pinto, and Arjana and Aslan in the previous section. As a social construct, the body of the pilgrim is not a passive object of ritual enactment but an active agent in constructing perceptions of self and the world. The body is also situated in shifting environments that, in connection with the materiality of everyday life, highlight the practice of emotions expressed in aesthetic, cultural, and memorial mediums of communication.

In *Sensational Religion: Sensory Cultures in Material Practice*, Sally M. Promey argues that the body, associated with sensation, is intrinsically linked with images that foster meaning in changing social contexts.[80] Taste, desire, vision, dream, or even ecstasy in the course of the pilgrimage experience require a material presence, even if implicitly evident, blurring the imagined boundary between subject and object, between pilgrim and the materiality of pilgrimage. The mutual composition of the pilgrim's perception of his or her experience, as described by Hammoudi in the earlier passage, and perceived material realities, ranging from the mosque to *ihram* clothing, is indicative of the role of the body as a perceptual process of self-construction, though always situated in a sociohistorical setting. The material aspect involves essential attributes in sensations and expressions that reconfigure social identity and status, as elaborated in the previous section. And they do so in a web of economies and modes of communication in primarily opening up material arenas, such as markets, for wider social interaction on both local and global levels.

Pilgrimage experiences such as travel or dreams therefore entail material significance.[81] From this view, religious experience becomes realized in what

Paulo G. Pinto, following Eickelman and Piscatori, calls "objectified" expressions of religious traditions, which accentuate the codified discourses and practices associated with the spatial and temporal processes of pilgrimage.[82] As material traditions, pilgrimage identifies a marketplace where ideas are fused with material goods. Practiced not only by merchants, clerics, state officials, and soldiers, but also by ordinary pilgrims who have been a familiar sight on the roads to Mecca and other major pilgrimage destinations, Muslim pilgrimage traditions have always constituted sites of materiality in the consumption, production, and exchange of artifacts, souvenirs, technologies of communication, and bodily consumption of food. The also serve as a form of material culture, in the production of social identities based on class, gender, ethnicity, and race. The prominence of material culture, regardless of its form and practice, is particularly evident in grave-visiting rituals. Somewhat similar to Hajj and to pilgrimage performances in Mecca and Medina, *ziyara* entails a symbolic order of ritualized interment in the use of shrouds, burial vaults, headstones, and, most importantly, decorative shrines, where pilgrims expect connection with the spiritual through the aestheticized material forms.

Material objects associated with pilgrimage reveal forms of values or immaterial norms embodied in sociophysical sites that accommodate, transport, travel, and settle in multiple experiential sites. Materiality also reveals ways of social interaction around objects, artifacts, or relics; and such forms of sociability entail economies, cultures, and politics that revolve around geographies, affects, and symbols of shrines. In what Nile Green has called the "architecture of sainthood," shrines comprise physical and symbolic networks, bound in symbols and affects between text and body of the saint represented as a revered tomb.[83] Shrines, tombs, and graves as places of visitation constitute changing material infrastructures that set a relational context between things and pilgrims. Such infrastructures also signify institutionalized practices that include collections and commoditized objects for those who acquire, borrow, rent, or even steal, continually subject to repossession. The boundaries of pilgrimage possession are always provisional.

Objects of pilgrimage culture are laden with meaning, and exchanging and consuming them entails embodied experiences. In *The Life of Things, the Love of Things*, Remo Bodei identifies the subjectivity of objects in ways humans perceive their built material life through aesthetic and experiential depictions.[84] From luxury goods to objects of everyday use, materiality reveals a human world of ideas, values, and sensations in re-creating lived reality in alternative ways. Material cultures of pilgrimage, in particular, communicate new sensations of objects and perceptions, which, as embodied practices, enable pilgrims to experience pilgrimage as a series of sensations that connect and convolute the material with the supernatural. The material culture of pilgrimage conjoins the realm of "objects" and "spiritual" in which the actualization of pilgrimage is made possible.

The inclusion of materiality in line with embodied practices would suggest an account of Muslim pilgrimage that requires a different way of looking at the world of objects. Such a focus would examine histories, memories, and cultures of pilgrimage objects such as carpets, coins, compasses, maps, engravings, paintings, monuments, roads, roadside inns (caravansaries), culinary objects, metal flasks, glass bottles, bronze cups, *ihram* garments, guidebooks, manuals, posters, travel books, steamship ticket stubs, souvenirs, photos, films, and videos as living experiences. Each object entails shared values designed, exchanged, and consumed for multiple purposes. Each object is intimately connected with the course of ritual performance, including the production of material and landscape sites associated with the act of pilgrimage travel: its caravan routes, automobile roads, and oceanic passages, where objects such as tents, bridges, traffic signs, and ships are made, bought, exchanged, and consumed.[85] Materiality also carries its own histories—both individual and social, but more importantly social, as objects emerge from and merge within a complex network of circulations and exchanges. Railroads and material cultures associated with transport technology—as David Walker has shown in his study of Mormon missionary and tourist activities in nineteenth-century Utah—posit sensations of spirituality and new understandings of religion.[86] The rise of Hajj pilgrimage print culture in the nineteenth century, as Barbara D. Metcalf has demonstrated, produced new forms of self-awareness and ideologies in reconstructing Muslim identity in an increasingly globalized world.[87]

The materiality of pilgrimage is a public process, and its consumption or exchange is a collective affair. Such public material displays of piety combined with living traditions of visitation of shrines and far distant sacred sites serve as a reminder of the transregional characteristics of pilgrimage, a disposition that inherently takes place in networks of relations and connections that make a locality into a regional or global event. In the materiality of spiritual culture, pilgrimage identifies changing institutions that are economized, materialized, and more importantly globalized, especially in contemporary contexts.

The chapters in this section consist of studies that extend the theme of materiality and embodiment in the cultural memories of Muslim pilgrimage.

Central to these studies is the role of perception and sensations in relation to material culture and its potential to reproduce or challenge identity in the transformation of Muslim pilgrimage in shifting localities. The relationship between ways of perceptions and materiality is explored in chapter 5. In his study of an intersex *fakir* pilgrim to Sehwan Sharif, Pakistan, Omar Kasmani provides a revealing study on dream visions embedded in aesthetic and media material that reconstruct sacred space. In what he calls "occasion for engagement," Kasmani argues that *ziyara*, especially in its Sufi form, constitutes a "dialogical" interaction between material and spiritual practices of tangible and visionary qualities. One of the most intriguing arguments Kasmani offers is the role of the Pakistani state in its adoption of shrines since 1960 and reproduction of sacred space and cultures of sainthood, especially in terms of gender and regional geographies on the national level. As Kasmani shows, the underlying relationship between *ziyara* and governmentality is the embodied exchanges of material, sensory, and spiritual practices.

The role of state is further elaborated by Azim Malikov's study of shrine pilgrimage in post-Soviet southern Kazakhstan (chapter 6). In his historical and ethnographic study, Malikov shows that religious cultural revival in Kazakhstan is directly connected with state-led projects in rebuilding older and newer shrines. Along with pilgrimage tourism and production of material culture, *ziyara* in Kazakhstan has become a multilayered process, with competing actors reinventing traditions with unintended consequences. At the core of the reinvention process is the role of memory and the ways in which identities are reconstructed through the medium of pilgrimage material culture. In her study of the Syrian shrine of Sayyida Zaynab, Edith Szanto continues the study of material culture, basing it on her ethnographic study of the shrine economy and tourist industry in Syria (chapter 7). The sort of materiality that she identifies in the Shi'i pilgrimage site is the practice of gift giving, mostly inside and outside shrine space, where these bits of material spiritual culture are consumed, produced, and exchanged between inhabitants and visitors. Closely associated with hospitality, gifting is the practice of exchanging goods that can be shared, exchanged, and, above all, felt by all, including inhabitants who provide religious services at hospitality tents outside shrines. Gift exchange as a material practice also takes place between pilgrims and saints through symbolic and sensory practices inside the shrine. Ultimately, what is achieved in the distinct material culture of gift giving and circulation of goods is the formation of *communitas* and ways in which a liminal collectivity of equals could be realized.

In their study of grave visitation at the tomb of two revered Muslims in Mount Kawi (*Gunung Kawi*), East Java, Indonesia, Julian Millie and Lewis Mayo look at the complex expressive and representational features of Muslim pilgrimage in the accommodation of multiple symbolic and material traditions, including non-Muslim ones. In this ethnographic account (chapter 8), we are offered a study of the role of indigenous local practices in shaping a number of material cultural practices. Such practices are elaborated in terms of fluid boundaries marked by locals and visitors, who perform pilgrimage for legitimizing aims and a plurality of worldly and spiritual meanings. The religious materiality revealed in this study is inclusive of religious plurality, with an appeal to a wider population from different religious backgrounds.

Materiality, however, can entail conflicts over how to appropriate sacredness to grave-visiting practices by competing Muslim actors, as demonstrated in the contention between reformists and traditionalists in the initial decades of the twentieth century. Similar to the Bianchi and Malikov chapters, this chapter highlights the role of postcolonial state power in forging ahead with what they consider "correct" religious behavior regarding shrine culture, excluding practices deemed indigenously non-Islamic as they move toward "cultural normalization" in shaping national citizenship. Mount Kawi visitors, though, are content to participate in their spiritual practices among those from other religious backgrounds. As Millie and Mayo argue, there is a relationship between the fluid borders and the richness of cultural wealth that brings pilgrims together in a specific place. Here, materiality of pilgrimage perpetuates both localizing practices and globalizing patterns of nation building through a popular religion sanctioned by the state.

Communication, (New) Media, and Space

> Late that afternoon, I made more tea. Switching on the computer,
> I surfed the internet for information on how to do Hajj. On the verge of
> the most fundamental pillar of being a Muslim, I found myself an
> imposter. I didn't even have a copy of the Qur'an here in the Kingdom, let
> alone a book about how to do Hajj. At last, I found a diagram explaining
> the stages of the journey. Designed for children, it was one of the few
> explanations I could find in English. I gathered up the pages as they
> unfurled from the printer. Fat arrows depicted steps that would soon be
> mine. I read hungrily.
>
> —Qanta Ahmed, *One Thousand Roads to Mecca*, 572–73

We begin this section with a quote from the memoir of Qanta Ahmed, a British-Pakistani physician in Saudi Arabia who, in response to the death of a colleague's child, performed the Hajj in 2001. In this intriguing account, Ahmed, who lacks Islamic fluency, seeks to learn about the Hajj through the internet. How she describes her first encounter with Hajj-related information online is intriguing. "On the verge of the most fundamental pillar of being a Muslim," she writes, "I found myself an imposter." What provokes Ahmed to see herself as a pretender appears in the experience of going online and exploring the fundamentals of her faith in digital space. In this first-encounter experience with Hajj, the internet is a substitute for the Qur'an, or any other print literature, on learning how to do pilgrimage, although the internet would most certainly provide more information than the Qur'an on the Hajj. Ahmed's reclaiming of her past and social identity in Islam is being achieved through the medium of global interconnected networks, the internet, bringing about an experiential spirituality mediated in the digital space where other Muslims also participate without face-to-face interaction.

Ahmed's online encounter with the Hajj is what German sociologist Wilhelm Dilthey famously described as the "common sphere," where collective experiences in relation to information, discourses, images, texts, and events, such as Hajj, are interpreted in a shared universe.[88] The internet provides not only information but also felt encounters of interpretative significance with other Muslims who produce diagrams, guidelines, accounts, and experiences about the Hajj. In the digital space of the internet, Hajj performance becomes familiarized and accessible, leading a newcomer to consume "hungrily" for a perceived identity associated with the Islamic rites, a kind of personalization of faith made explicit in the digital space, and its ethos of constant connectivity embodied in the performance of "surfing" in a vast ocean of networked knowledge.

While material infrastructure constitutes its operational processes, technology can also be described as practices that foster ways of imagining and feeling, modes of embodiment that translate experience into alternative interpretations of self and reality. We go online to search for information and do so by embarking on an experience that leads to a perception of reality beyond the here and now, a transcendence of immaterial force. Whereas technology can be understood to serve as a "tool" for actors to construct religious experience, one can equally argue, as Jeremy Stolow provocatively suggests, that technology itself can embody religious themes related to theology, cosmology, and ethics.[89] In Ahmed's description, the internet not only provided information about Hajj but enabled her to delve into an alternative world, where she can consume the sacred in the information archived in digital space. So, she writes, "Fat arrows depicted steps that would soon be mine." In a curious way, experiences with technologies such as the internet construct perceptions of magic and power that may not be felt in the disenchanted world of modernity.[90]

Based on this account, the invention and globalizing use of the steam engine and the telegraph in the nineteenth century, for example, can be understood as the introduction of new perceptions about space and time through new forms of long-distance travel and communication. What these technologies provided was new configurations of bodily and social relations in the experience of travel and home, although manifested unevenly across the globe as a result of European colonialism.[91] Inasmuch as speed and distance had undergone considerable changes in the late nineteenth century, the new modes of communication and technology had also expanded and stretched notions of health, governance, and even ways of performing pilgrimage travel in light of the new tourism culture, spearheaded by the growth of the pilgrim population, especially in the postcolonial era.

In the information age, activities related to religion on varied forms of information technologies reenact sacred space, through which a distinct religious experience can occur. Simulation and reality, in their material sensation, become overlapped in the medium of telecommunication. Pilgrimage travelogues—in particular, their printed manifestation in the nineteenth-century age of European imperialism—testify to a new age of communication in which both Muslims and non-Muslims would produce an array of accounts of their travels to Mecca.[92] These accounts identify a new medium of experience in the sacred land where pilgrimage can no longer be observed in physical but only in virtual presence. Such virtuality is most evident on the internet, where a blending of physical and virtual space is marked in performances such as "cyberpilgrimage," which, in the words of Mark MacWilliams, allows pilgrims to "travel electronically through the same mythic imaginaire that is architecturalized in situ in the 'real' pilgrimages."[93] Religious action through technology does not attain an independent and separate realm from the "real" world but reshapes the perceived reality into a new experience, virtual, magical, or otherwise.

The chapters in this final section explore the importance of mediated practices in the ways pilgrimage is shaped in localities that are themselves reshaped by technological changes. In chapter 9, Babak Rahimi looks at the messianic pilgrimage practices of the shrine-mosque of Jamkaran, in central

Iran, believed by Twelver Shiʿi to be an apparition site of Muhammad al-Mahdi, the Hidden Imam (the Twelfth Imam of Twelver Shiʿi). As another example of an ethnographic study in this volume, Rahimi shows the relevance of materiality in millenarian rituals. More importantly, he focuses on the digital space and the role of the internet in determining how a transnational felt community of pilgrims with messianic spirituality are formed in relation to the shrine's sacred locality in popular tales and sites of miracles. The presence of digital technology, Rahimi shows, lies not just in networking—a way for members and devotees to share news, disseminate information, and organize religious or social events—but in producing distinct experiences of pilgrimage in digital space. In what he calls "digitized pilgrimage," Rahimi argues that the element of "live" in the digital experience of pilgrimage sites, including Jamkaran, underscores a fluidity between emotive presence and the site of visitation, intermingling the material with the digital in ways that cause pilgrimage to undergo a transformation of substance rather than kind. Also, as Rahimi argues, the relationship between the emotive and the virtual undergo a different form of change when the digital becomes embedded in the physical experience of pilgrimage at the visitation site. Here we can speak of the "incorporation" of digital embodiment that introduces new sensations, memories, perceptions, and relations to self and others, marked by new practices of the magical and the spiritual in the mediated experiences of shrine visitation.

Whereas Rahimi's case study on Jamkaran is concerned with the complex relationship between technology and pilgrimage in shaping solidarity, for Emilio Spadola (chapter 10), pilgrimage is a contested site over piety, authority, and identity. Emerging technologies, such as online video and social media, expose an entrenched mode of contestation in discourses and traditions of Muslim pilgrimage. The online visualization of shrine destruction by militant Salafi Muslims addresses a reformist project of renewal through purification of "un-Islamic" practices and should not be seen as distinct from pilgrimage traditions shaped in constructing or expanding shrine structures. The visualization of shrine destruction, however, also signifies a distinct communicative practice in an information era, or what Spadola calls "technical reproduction"—when technology and religion continue to fuse and redefine global modernity. Spadola traces the mass mediation of the destruction, revealing a multifaceted and conflicted Muslim pilgrimage culture. What is paramount to consider in this study is that shrines, as material-spiritual sites, embody a communicative force, and their destruction and the posting online of that destruction by militants affirms a global appeal for a single Muslim community with a single pilgrimage site, the Kaʿba.

The final study (chapter 11) by Reza Masoudi Nejad shifts attention to a different account of communicative aspects of Muslim pilgrimage. In his study of Dawoodi Bohras, a sect within Ismaʾili Shiʿism, in India, Masoudi Nejad offers an ethnographic account of a distinct Muslim pilgrimage practice that revolves around the living body of the spiritual leader of the sect rather than a physical shrine of a deceased saint. In what he describes as "fluid sacred geography," pilgrimage communicates in the very embodied spirituality of a sacred persona, whose corporeal movement serves as a moving and revered target for (mobile) visitation in the renewal of the minority community, which has been historically marginalized by the larger Sunni population. The use of communication technologies such as the internet and mobile phones to organize and coordinate movement during pilgrimage events around the spiritual leader of the sect reveals an intricate connection between technology, ritual, and community formation practices. With Mumbai as a cosmopolitan backdrop, Masoudi Nejad demonstrates a communicative feature of pilgrimage that is porous and expresses piety in the assemblage of pilgrim movement rather than mere gathering at a shrine site.

To articulate a non-definition, Muslim pilgrimage is a mobile, fluid, contested, and negotiated set of practices that undergo perpetual change in response to complex sociohistorical, economic, and political processes that define modernity as experience and interpretation. Rather than offer a unified front with a primal theoretical trajectory, *Muslim Pilgrimage in the Modern World* explores the previously explained themes in examination of different case studies. The essays rethink pilgrimage and complicate the rituals both in their Islamic manifestation and as a set of established discourses and practices in the reconstruction of modernity through religious traditions. While these essays do not seek to resolve the discussion about the nature of pilgrimage, they aim to map out changing traditions and practices that underscore ways of thinking about Muslim pilgrimage as well as ways that Muslims of diverse backgrounds perform pilgrimage in contested historical and social contexts. Though hardly a unified sense of pilgrimage, the mark of commonality here is one of shared, globally situated experiences, materialized and communicated through local places, travel routes, and mediated sites wherein pilgrimage as an increasingly globalized practice has become a manifestation of the new modern experience of the global Muslim.

Notes

1. According to the Islamic tradition, the first pilgrimage took three days to complete. It was observed after the Treaty of Hudaybiyyah (628 C.E.), when Muhammad and the Quraysh tribe agreed to the peaceful return of Muslims to perform pilgrimage at Mecca.

2. Qur'an 3:96. Ka'ba, as the focal point of the Hajj, has served as the physical manifestation of Allah's will on earth, as he commanded Abraham and Isma'il to build the shrine (Qur'an 22:26–29; 2:125–27). Though the history of the site predates Muhammad, visited by Arabs as a religious site before Islam, Islamic historical imaginary has revolved around the story of Abraham as the first and ideal Muslim associated with the Hajj.

3. Qur'an 2:200–201, 5:1.

4. Carol Delaney, "The Hajj: Sacred and Secular," *American Ethnologist* 17, no. 3 (1999): 87–109.

5. M. Abdel Haleem, "Early History and Politics: The Religious and Social Importance of Hajj," in *The Hajj: Collected Essays*, ed. Venetia Porter and Liana Saif (London: British Museum, 2013), 4; Narifumi Maeda, "The Aftereffects of Hajj and Kaan Buat," *Journal of Southeast Asian Studies* 6, no. 2 (1975): 181–82; Abdellah Hammoudi, *A Season in Mecca: Narrative of a Pilgrimage*, trans. Pascale Ghazaleh (New York: Hill and Wang, 2005), 10–23; L. P. Harvey, "The Moriscos and the Hajj," *Bulletin of British Society for Middle Eastern Studies* 14, no. 1 (1987): 22; Susan O'Brien, "Pilgrimage, Power, and Identity: The Role of Hajj in the Lives of Nigerian Hausa Bori Adepts," *Africa Today* 46, no. 3/4 (1999): 31.

6. Robert Bianchi, *Guests of God: Pilgrimage and Politics in the Islamic World* (Oxford: Oxford University Press, 2004), 70.

7. Saud al-Sarhan, "The Saudis as Managers of the Hajj," in *The Hajj: Pilgrimage in Islam*, ed. Eric Tagliacozzo and Shawkat M. Toorawa (New York: Cambridge University Press, 2016), 196–212.

8. Hajj has been described as *"ziyara bayt Allah al-haram"* (pilgrimage to the sanctified house of God). In other words, Hajj is a *ziyara*, but each *ziyara* is not Hajj.

9. See Dionigi Albera and John Eade, "Pilgrimage Studies in Global Perspective," in *New Pathways in Pilgrimage Studies: Global Perspectives*, ed. Dionigi Albera and John Eade (New York: Routledge 2017), 6–9.

10. Dionigi Albera and John Eade, "International Perspectives on Pilgrimage Studies: Putting the Anglophone Contribution in Its Place," in *International Perspectives on Pilgrimage Studies: Itineraries, Gaps and Obstacles*, ed. Dionigi Albera and John Eade (New York: Routledge, 2015), 1–22.

11. Laila Prager, "Alawi Ziyāra Tradition and Its Interreligious Dimensions: Sacred Places and Their Contested Meanings among Christians, Alawi and Sunni Muslims in Contemporary Hatay (Turkey)," *Muslim World* 103, no. 41 (2013): 55, 60–61; Joseph Meri, "Pilgrimage to the Prophet Ezekiel's Shrine in Iraq: A Symbol of Muslim-Jewish Relations," *Perspectives*, Spring 2012, 22–25; Josef Meri, "Aspects of *Baraka* (Blessing) and Ritual Devotion among Medieval Muslims and Jews," *Medieval Encounters* 5, no. 1 (1999): 55; Dominique-Sila Khan et al., "Coexistence and Communalism in the

shrine of Pirana in Gujurat," special issue, *South Asia* 22 (1999): 142, 143, 146; Nile Green, "Oral Competition Narratives of Muslim and Hindu Saints in the Deccan," *Asian Folklore Studies* 63 (2004): 224.

12. Katai Boissevain, "Studying Religious Mobility: Pilgrimage, Shrine Visits and Religious Tourism from the Maghreb to the Middle East," in Albera and Eade, *New Pathways in Pilgrimage Studies*, 94–96.

13. We borrow the notion of modernity as experience and interpretation from Peter Wagner. See Peter Wagner, *Modernity as Experience and Interpretation: A New Sociology of Modernity* (Cambridge, UK: Polity, 2008).

14. On Mecca, see al-Azraqi, *Akhbār Makka wa mā jā'a fīhā min al-Āthār* (Mecca: Maktaba al-Asadī, 2004); Muhammad Ishaq Fakihi, *Akhbār Makka* (Mecca: al-Nihda al- Hadītha, 1986); 'Ali bin 'Abd al-Qadir Tabari, *Al-Arj al-Maskī fī al-Tārīkh al-Makkī* (Mecca: al-Maktaba al-Tijāriya, 1995); Qutb al-Din Hanafi, *al-I'lām bi A'lām bayt Allāh al-Harām* (Cairo: Maktaba al-Thiqāfa); Muhammad Jar Allah Makki, *al-Jāmi' al-Latīf* (Beirut: al-Fikr, 1972); Ibn Zia Makki, *Al-Tārīkh Makka wa al-Masjid al-Harām wa-al-Madīna al-Sharīfa wa al-Qabr al-Sharīf* (Mecca: al-Maktaba al-Tijāriya, 1997); Hasan bin yasar al-Basri, *Fadā'il Makka wa Sukun fī-hā* (Kuwait: Maktaba al-Falāh, 1982); Muhammad bin Ahmad Shaybi, *I'lām al-Anām bi-Tārīkh Bayt Allāh al-Harām* (Mecca: Jāmi'a Um al-Qurā, 2007); Omar bin Fahd Makki, *Ithāf al-Warā bi-Akhbār Um al-Qurā* (Cairo: Dār al-Jayl, 1983); Shams al-Din Muhammad bin Ishaq Kharazmi, *Ithāra al-Targhīb wa al-Tashwīq ilā al-Masājīd al-Thalātha wa al-Bayt al-'Atīq* (Mecca: Maktaba al-Nazār, 1998); Zayn Al-Abidin Husayni Kashani, *Mafraha al-'Anām fī Ta'sīs Bayt Allāh al-Harām* (Tehran: Mash'ar, 2008); Muhammad bin Sabbagh, *Tahsīl al-Marām fī Akhbār al-Bayt al-Harām wa al-Mashā'ir al-'Izām wa Makka wa al-Haram* (Mecca: Maktaba al-'Asadī, 2004); Muhammd bin 'Ali Tabari, *Tārīkh Makka* (unpublished manuscript), Library of Haram, Mecca; Sayyid Muhammad Mahdi Bahr Al-Ulum, *Tuhfa al-Kirām fī Tārīkh Makka wa Bayt Allāh al-Harām* (Tehran: Mash'ar, 2004). On Medina, see Salih al-Rufai, *Ahādīth al-Wārida fī Fadā'il al-Madīna* (Medina: Dar al-Khadīrī, 2008); Jafar bin Hashim, *Akhbār al-Gharība fī-Mā Waqa'a bi-Tība al-Habība* (Cairo: Maktaba al-Khānijī, 1992); Ibn Shabbah, *Akhbār al-Madīna* (Qum: Quds, 1989); Ibn Zabalah, *Akhbār al-Madīna* (Medina: Markaz al-Buhūth wa Dirāsāt al-Madīna al-Munawwara, 2008); 'Ali bin Sultan Muhammad Qari, *Al-A'lām bi-fadā'il Bayt Allāh al-Harām* (forthcoming); Abdulbasit Badr, *Al-Tārīkh al-Shamil li-Madīna al-Munawwara* (Medina: Basr, 1993); Abdul Aziz Madani, *Al-Tārīkh al-Amīn li-Madīna Sayyid al-Mursalīn* (Qum: Amīn, 1997); Kordi Makki, *Al-Tārīkh al-Qavīm li-Makka wa-Bayt Allāh al-Karīm* (Beirut: Dār Khidr, 1999); Ibn Zia Makki, *Tārīkh Makka al-Musharrafa wa al-Masjid al-Harām wa al-Madīna al-Sharīfa wa al-Qabr al-Sharīf* (Beirut: Dār al-Kutub al-'illmiya, 2003); Shams al-Din Sakhavi, *Al-Tuhfa al-Latīfa fī Tārīkh al-Madīna al-Sharīfa* (Beirut: al-Kutub al-'illmiya, 1993); Abd al-Quddus bin Qasim Ansari, *Āthār al-Madīna al-Munawwara* (Medina: al-Maktaba al-Salaīya, 1973); Abdullah bin Abd al-Malak Marjani, *Bahja al-Nufūs wa al-Asrār fī Tārīkh Dār Hijra al-Mukhtār* (Cairo: Dār al-Gharb al-Islāmī, 2008); Muhammd Amin Puramini, *Baqi' al-Qarghad fī Dirāsa Shāmila* (Tehran: Mash'ar, 2007); Abdullah bin Muhammad Qazi, *Ifāda al-Anām bi-Dikr Akhbār Balad al-Harām* (Mecca: Maktaba al-Asadī, 1998); Muhammda bin Muhammad Bakri, *Irshād al-Zā'irīn* (Manuscript not published yet); Abdasamad bin Abdalwahhab Ibn

Asakir, *Ithāf al-Zāʾir wa Itrāf al-Muqīm fī Ziyāra al-Nabī* (Beirut: Dār al-Arqam, 2008); Shams al-Din Muhammad bin Ishaq Kharazmi, *Ithāra al-Targhīb wa al-Tashwīq ilā al-Masājīd al-Thalātha wa al-Bayt al-ʿAtīq* (Mecca: Maktaba Nazār Mustafā al-Bāz, 1998); Nuraldin Samhudi, *Vafā al-Vafā bi-Akhbār Dār al-Mustafā* (Dār al-Kutub al-ʿillmīya, 1998). On Najaf, see, for instance, Hasan Isa Hakim, *Al-Mufassal fī Tārīkh al-Najaf al-Ashraf* (Qum: al-Maktaba al-Haydarīya, 2008); Sayyib bin Tavus, *Farha al-Gharī fī Taʿīn Qabr Amir al-Muʾminīn ʿAlī bin Abītalib* (Najaf: al-ʿAtaba al-Muqaddasa al-ʿAlawīya, 2010); Muhammad bin Abbud al-Kufi, *Nazha al-Gharī fī Tārīkh al-Najaf* (Najaf: Matbaʿa al-Ghari, 1952); Jafar Khalili, *Mawsūʿa al-ʿAtabāt al-Muqaddasa* (Beirut: al-Aʿlami, 1987). On Karbala, see, for instance, Sulayman Hadi Al-Toma, *Turāth Karbalāʾ* (Tehran: Mashʿar, 2014); Khalili, *Mawsūʿa al-ʿAtabāt al-Muqaddasa*. On the Levant, see, for instance, Muhammad Hasnayn Sabiqi, *Marqad al-ʿAqīla Zaynab fī Mīzān: al-Dirāsa wa al-Tahqīq wa al-Tahlīl* (Beirut: al-Aʿlami, 1979).

15. Muhammd Hirz al-Din, *Marāqid al-Maʿārif* (Baghdad: Dār al-Kitāb al-ʿArabī, 2009); Muhammad Sanad, *Mashāhidunā wa Qubūr Ahl al-Bayt* (Sanabis: Dār al-ʿIsma, 2011).

16. See Sophia Rose Arjana, *Pilgrimage in Islam: Traditional and Modern Practices* (London: Oneworld Academic, 2017), 80–83.

17. On Shiʿi texts, see, for instance, Ibrahim bin ʿAli Kafami, *Al-Balad al-Amīn wa-al-Dārʿ al-Hasīn min al-Adʿiya wa al-Aʿmāl wa al-Āwrād wa al-Adhkār* (Beirut: al-Aʿlami, 1982); Muhammad bin Jafar al-Mashhadi, *Al-Mazār al-Kabīr* (Qum: Muʾssasiyi Nashri Islāmī, 1999); Muhammad bin Makki Amili, *Al-Mazār fī Kayfiya Ziyārāt al-Nabī wa al-Aʾimma al-Athār* (Qum: Madrisiyi Imām Mahdī, 1990); Shaykh Tusi, *Misbāh al-Mutahajjid wa Silāh al-Mutaʿabbid* (Beirut: Muʾssisa Fiqh al-Shīʿa, 1983); Muhammad Bagir Majlisi, *Bihar al-Anwār al-Jāmiʿa li-durar Akhbār al-Aʾimma al-Athār*, vol. 101, *Kitāb fī al-Mazār* (Beirut: Muʾssisa al-Wafāʾ, 1983); Muhammad bin ʿAli al-Alawi, *Fadl Ziyāra al-Husayn* (Qum: Marʿashī, 1983); Shaykh ʿAbbas Qumi, *Hadiya al-Zāʾirīn wa Bahja al-Nāzirīn* (Qum: Sibtayn, 1983); Sayyib bin Tavus, *Iqbāl al-Aʿmāl* (Beirut: al-Aʿlami, 1996); Ibrahim bin ʿAli Kafami, *Junna al-Amān al-Wāqiya wa Janna al-Īmān al-Bāqiya* (known as *al-Misbāh*) (Beirut: al-Aʿlami, 1983); Jaʿfar bi Muhammad Qhulawayh, *Kāmil al-Ziyārāt* (Najaf: Dār al-Murtadawīyya, 1937); Sheikh Mufid, *Manāsik al-Mazār* or *Kitab al-Mazār* (known as *al-Mazār al-Saqīr*) (Qum: Hizāriyi Shiykhi Mufīd, 1992); *Mawsūaʿah Ziyārāt al-Maʿsūmīn* (7 vols.) (Qum: Muʾssisa Imām Hādī, 2005); Hasan ibn Yusuf al-Hilli, *Minhāj al-Salāh fī Mukhtasar al-Misbāh* (Qum: Maktaba Allāma Majlisī, 2009); Sayyid ʿAli bin Musa Tavus, *Misbāh al-Zāʾir*; Muhammad Bagir Majlisi, *Tuhfa al-Zāʾir* (Qum: Muʾssisa Āl-alBayt li-Ihyā al-Turāth, 1995); Muhammad Baghri Mjlisi, *Zād al-Maʿād* (Qum: Jilwiyi Kamāl, 2010); Abu al-Qasim Khan Ebrahimi, *Wadī al-Salām dar Ziyārati Maʿsūmīn wa Ādābiʿān* (unpublished manuscript), http://www.alabrar.info/. On Sunni texts, see, for instance, Muhammad bin Omar Fakhr al-Razi, *Ziyāra al-Qubūr* (Qum: Zāʾir, 1997); ʿAli b. Abi Bakr Harawi, *Lonely Wayfarer's Guide to Pilgrimage: ʿAlī b. Abī Bakr al-Harawī's Kitāb al-Ishārāt ilā Maʿrifat al-Ziyārāt*, trans. Josef Meri (Princeton, NJ: Darwin, 2004); Barbara M. Cooper, "The Strength in the Song: Muslim Brotherhood, Audible Capital, and Hausa Women's Performance of the Hajj," in "Globalization?," special issue, *Social Text* 60 (Autumn 1999): 88.

18. Among most famous *rihlas* of Hajj are Ibn Jubayr, Ibn Battuta, Nasir Khusraw, Shinqiti, Muhammad Rashid Rida, Ibrahim Rafat Pasha and Nabulusi. See Ibn Jubair, *The Travels of Ibn Jubayr*, trans. Ronald Broadhurst (Noida: Goodword, 2007); Ibn Batuta, *Kitāb rihlat Ibn Batūtah: al-Musamma Tuhfa al-Nazzar fī Gharā'ib al-Amsār wa-Ajā'ib al-Asfār* (Cairo: Matbaʿat Wādī al-Nīl, 1904); Nasir Khusraw, *Safarnāmiyi Nāsir Khusraw* (Tehran: Kitābhā-yi Jībī, 1971); Muhammad al-Amīn Shinqītī, *Rihlat al-Hajj ilá Bayt Allāh al-Harām* (Makka al-Mukarrama: Dār ʿĀlam al-Fawā'id, 2005); Muhammad Rashīd Ridā, *Rihlāt al-Imām Muhammad Rashīd Ridā* (Beirut: al-Muʾassasa al-ʿArabīyah lil-Dirāsāt wa-al-Nashr, 1979); Ibrahim Rafat Pasha, *Mirāt al-haramayn* (Al-Riyād: Dār al-Marīh, 1986); Abd al-Ghanī al-Nābulusī, *al-Haqīqah wa-al-majāz fī Rihla bilād al-Shām wa-Misr wa-al-Hijāz* (Dimashq: Dār al-Maʿrifah, 1989).

19. Some of the main works in the Wahhabi approach to pilgrimage are as follows: Muhammad Nasir al-Din al-Albani, *Ahkām al-Janā'iz wa Bidaʿuhā* (Riyadh: Maktaba al-Maʿārif, 1992); Muhammad bin Ahmad Maghdisi Hanbali, *al-Sārim al-Munkī fī al-Rad ʿalā al-Subki* (Beirut: al-Riyān, 2003); Muhammd bin Abd al-Wahhab, *Kashf al-Shubahāt fī al-Tawhid* (Riyadh: Dār al-Samīʿī, 1998); Ibn Taymiyyah, *Ziyāra al-Qubūr wa al-Istinjād bi-al-*Maqbūr (Tanta: Dār al-Sahāba li al-Turāth, 1992).

20. For instance: Zayni Dahlan, *Al-Durar al-Sanīya fī al-Rad ʿalā al-Wahhābīya* (Damascus: Dār Qār Harā, 2003); Jami Sidghi Zahawi, *Al-Fajr al-Sādiq fī al-Rad ʿalā Munkirī al-Tawassul wa al-Kirāmāt wa-al-Khawāriq* (Istanbul: Işık, 1984); Hasan bin ʿAli al-Saghaf, *Al-Ighātha bi-Adilla al-Ishtighātha* (Amman: Maktaba al-Imām al-Nawawī, 1990); Sulayman bin Abdulwahhab, *al-Sawāʿiq al-Ilāhiya fī al-Rad ʿalā al-Wahhābiya* (Istanbul: Işık, 1979); Ayaz bin Musa al-Yahsabi, *Al-Shifā bi-Taʿrīf Huqūq al-Mustafā* (Ain El Tineh: Dār al-Kitāb al-ʿArabī, 1984); Abu Hamid bin Marzugh, *Al-Tawassul bi-al-Nabī wa Jahala al-Wahhābīʾīn* (Istanbul: Işık, 1976); Ismaʿil bin Ishaq Jahzami, *Fadl al-Salāt ʿalā al-Nabī* (Damascus: al-Maktab al-Islāmī, 2010); Sulayman bin Abd al-Wahhab, *Fasl al-Khitāb min Kitāb Allah wa Hadīth al-Rasūl wa Kalām al-Ulamā fī Madhhab ibn ʿAbd al-Wahhāb* (Istanbul: Işık, 1979); Zayni Dahlan, *Fitnā al-Wahhābiyya* (Istanbul: Işık, 1978); Sayyid Muhsin Amili, *Kashf al-Irtīyāb fī Atbāʿ Muhammad bin ʿAbdulwahhāb* (Qum: Dar al-Kitāb al-Islāmī, 1992); Jafar Kashif al-Ghita, *Manhaj al-Rashād li-man Arād al-Sadād* (Qum: al-Ghadīr, 2000); Mahmud Said Mamduh, *Rafʿ al-Manāra li-Takhrīj Ahādīth al-Tawassul wa al-Ziyāra* (Cairo: al-Maktaba al-Azhariya li al-Turāth, 2006); Yusouf Nobahani Shafii, *Shawāhid al-Haqq fī al-Ithtighātha bi-Sayyid al-Khalq* (Beirut: Dār al-Kutub al-ʿIlmiya, 2007); Taghi al-Din Fasi, *Shifā al-Ghirām bi-Akhbār al-Balad al-Harām* (Cairo: Maktaba al-Thiqāfa al-Dīnīya, 2008); Taqi al-Din Sobki, *Shifāʾ al-Siqām fī Ziyāra Khayr al-Anām ʿalayhi Afdal al-Salāt wa al-Salām* (Beirut: Dār al-Kutub al-ʿIlmiya, 2008).

21. See Devine DeWeese, *Shrine and Pilgrimage in Inner Asian Islam: Historical Foundations and Responses to Soviet Policy* (Washington, DC: National Council for Soviet and East European Research, 1995); Krisztina Kehl-Bodrogi, "Who Owns the Shrine? Competing Meanings and Authorities at a Pilgrimage Site in Khorezm," *Central Asian Survey* 25, no. 3 (2006): 235–50.

22. Dale F. Eickelman and James Piscatori, eds., *Muslim Travellers: Pilgrimage, Migration and the Religious Imagination* (Berkeley: University of California Press, 1990).

23. Anna Bigelow, *Sharing the Sacred: Practicing Pluralism in Muslim North India* (Oxford: Oxford University Press, 2010).

24. See Arjana, *Pilgrimage in Islam*, xxi.

25. The places where tomb replicas are displayed and maintained are known as *ta'ziya-khana* (*ta'ziya* house). For an account of *ta'ziya* and its distinct material religious context in India, see Karen Ruffle, "Presence in Absence: The Formation of Reliquary Shi'ism in Qutb Shahi Hyderabad," *Material Religion* 13, no. 3 (2017): 329–53. For Sunni visitation of Shi'i shrines, see Edith Szanto, "Sayyida Zaynab in the State of Exception: Shi'i Sainthood as 'Qualified life' in Contemporary Syria," *International Journal of Middle East Studies* 44 (2012): 285–99.

26. Dionigi Albera and Maria Couroucli, eds., *Sharing Sacred Spaces in the Mediterranean: Christians, Muslims, and Jews at Shrines and Sanctuaries* (Bloomington: Indiana University Press, 2012), 1. See also Josef Meri, *Cult of Saints among Muslims and Jews in Medieval Syria* (Oxford: Oxford University Press), 2002; Meri, "Pilgrimage to the Prophet Ezekiel's Shrine in Iraq," 22–23; Davis Howell, "Health Rituals at a Lebanese Shrine," *Middle Eastern Studies* 6, no. 2 (1970): 180; Meri, "Aspects of *Baraka* (Blessing) and Ritual Devotion," 58; Khan et al., "Coexistence and Communalism," 142, 143, 148; Green, "Oral Competition Narratives of Muslim and Hindu Saints in the Deccan," 224; Richard C. Martin, "Hajj," in *Encyclopedia of Islam and the Muslim World*, ed. by Richard C. Martin (New York: Macmillan, 2004), 533; Pamela Berger, "Jewish-Muslim Veneration at Pilgrimage Places in the Holy Land," *Religion and the Arts* 15, no. 1 (January 2011): 1–60; Bigelow, *Sharing the Sacred*.

27. Yeoh Seng-Guan, "Religious Pluralism and Pilgrimage Studies in West (Peninsular) Malaysia," in *New Paths in Pilgrimage Studies: Global Perspectives* (New York: Routledge, 2017), 68–88.

28. Babak Rahimi, "Subaltern Modernities: Mediated Experience, Ritualization and Being Modern in the Arab Iranian Community of Bushehr," in *Social Theory and Area Studies in the Global Age*, ed. Said Amir Arjomand (Albany, NY: SUNY Press, 2014), 389–414.

29. Rahimi, 260–67.

30. Amira Mittermaier, "(Re)Imagining Space: Dreams and Saint Shrines in Egypt," in *Dimensions of Locality: Muslim Saints, Their Place and Space*, ed. Georg Sauth and Samuli Schielke (New Brunswick; London: Transaction, 2008).

31. John R. Bowen, *A New Anthropology of Islam* (Cambridge: Cambridge University Press, 2012), 115.

32. The Prophet's grave is blocked off by a gold structure and black curtains, preventing the visitors to get near the tomb, which underscores the Wahhabi prohibition of visitation of graves.

33. Oleg Grabar, "The Earliest Islamic Commemorative Structures, Notes and Documents," *Ars Orientals* 6 (1996): 7–46.

34. The same is true for the Prophet's "Noble Cloak" (Hırka-i Şerif) in Istanbul, Turkey. The cloak, attributed to the Prophet, is preserved at a mosque built by the Ottoman Sultans. The cloak is put in a box and exhibited each year in the month of Ramazan. Each year, thousands of Muslims from Turkey and abroad travel to Istanbul to visit the cloak. "Cloak of Felicity" (Hırka-i Saâdet) is the name of another cloak

attributed to the Prophet, preserved in the Topkapi Palace along with many other relics attributed to the Prophet, his household, and his companions. See Aydın Hilmi, *Hırka-i Saadet Dairesi ve Mukaddes Emanetler* (Istanbul: Kaynak, 2004); Sümeyra Güldal, "Hırka-i Şerîf Camii, Din ve Hayat," *İstanbul Müftülüğü Dergisi* 1 (2007): 92–95; "Hırka-i Şerif, bu Ramazan da ziyaret edilebilecek," *Sabah*, August 27, 2017.

35. See Edith Szanto, "Sayyida Zaynab in the State of Exception: Shi'i Sainthood as 'Qualified Life' in Contemporary Syria," *International Journal for Middle Eastern Studies* 44 (2012): 288; Fariba Adelkhah, "Moral Economy of Pilgrimage and Civil Society in Iran: Religious, Commercial and Tourist Trips to Damascus," *South African Historical Journal* 61, no. 1 (2009): 40, 43, 48; Richard Kurin, "The Structure of Blessedness at an Muslim Shrine in Pakistan," *Middle Eastern Studies* 19, no. 3 (1983): 313; Narifumi Maeda, "The Aftereffects of Hajj and Kaan Buat," *Journal of Southeast Asian Studies* 6, no. 2 (1975): 184.

36. Marcel Hénaff, *Le prix de la vérité: le don, l'argent, la philosophie* (Paris: Editions du Seuil, 2002).

37. Hénaff, 16.

38. Mohammad El Ayadi, Hassan Rachik, and Mohammad Tozy, *L' Islam au quotidien: Enquête sur le valeurs et les pratiques religieuses au Maroc* (Casablanca, Prologues, Coll: Religion et société.

39. Danielle Provansal, "Le phénomène maraboutique au Maghreb," *Genève-Afrique* 14, no. 1 (1975): 59–77.

40. Alyson Callan, "Female Saints and the Practice of Islam in Sylhet, Bangladesh," *American Ethnologist* 35, no. 3 (2008): 396–412.

41. Raymond Jamous, *Honneur et baraka: les structures sociales traditionelles dans le Rif* (Cambridge: Cambridge University Press, 1981).

42. See Sabine Kalinock, "Touching a Sensitive Topic: Research on Shiite Rituals on Women in Tehran," *Iranian Studies* 37, no. 4 (2004): 665–74.

43. Norig Neveu, "La sacralisation du territorie jordanien. Reconstruction des lieux saints nationaux, 1980–2006," *Archives de sciences sociales des religions* 3, no. 151 (2010): 107–28.

44. Eric Tagliacozzo, *The Longest Journey: Southeast Asians and the Pilgrimage to Mecca* (Oxford: Oxford University Press, 2013): 63–81.

45. Tagliacozzo, 75–77.

46. Hamid Algar, "*Tarīqat* and *Tarīq*: Central Asian Naqshbandīs on the Roads to the Haramayn," in *Central Asian Pilgrims: Hajj Routes and Pious Visits Between Central Asia and the Hijaz*, ed. Alexandre Papas, Thomas Welsford, and Thierry Zarcone (Berlin: Klaus Schwarz Verlag, 2012), 118.

47. Thierry Zarcone, "Pilgrimage to the "Second Meccas" and "Ka'ba s of Central Asia," in Papas, Welsford, and Zarcone, *Central Asian Pilgrims*, 257–77.

48. This point challenges Shemeem Abbas's definition that *ziyara* is the distinct ceremony in that prayer for the deceased saints are observed. See Shemeem Abbas, *The Female Voice in Sufi Ritual: Devotional Practices of Pakistan and India* (Austin: University of Texas Press, 2002), 159.

49. Nazarena Lanza, "Pèlernier, faire du commerce et visiter les lieux saints: le tourisme religieux sénégalais au Maroc," *Routes migratoires africaines et dynamiques*

religieuses, quells enjeux sociaux? La'Année du Maghreb 11, ed. Sophie Bava and Katia Boissevain (Paris: CNRS Editions, 2014), 157–71.

50. Boissevain, "Studying Religious Mobility," 89–105.

51. E. J. Hobsbawm, *The Age of Capital: 1848-1875* (London: Weidefnfeld & Nicolson, 1975), 82–83.

52. For a historical study of Hajj and *ziyara* pilgrimage, with a focus on Central Asia, see Algar, "*Tarīqat* and *Tarīq*."

53. One important example is the train from Istanbul to Hijaz, which streamlined travel from different parts of west Asia to Hijaz. See James L. Gelvin and Nile Green, eds., *Global Muslims in the Age of Steam and Print* (Berkeley: University of California Press, 2014). Metin Hülagü, *Bir Umudun İnşası Hicaz Demiryolu* (Istanbul: Yitik Hazine, 2006); Ufuk Gülsoy, *Hicaz Demiryolu* (Istanbul: Eren, 2011); Ufuk Gülsoy, *Kutsal Proje Ortadoğu'da Osmanlı Demiryolları* (Istanbul: Timaş, 2010); Charles-Eudes Bonin, "Le chemin de fer du Hedjaz," *Annales de géographie* 18, no. 102 (1909).

54. Raymond Scupin, "The Social Significance of the *Hajj* for Thai Muslims," in *The Anthropology of Islam Reader*, ed. Jens Kreinath (1982; repr. New York: Routledge, 2012), 25–33

55. Social status encompasses ways of recognition on the collective level through key discursive practices, such as respect, honor, or the use of official titles such as "Hajji." For example, see Zain 'Abdullah's account on a pilgrim's return from Hajj in the American context, explaining the experience in the following terms: "'I was out here [vending] before they came with their stores. They see me workin' here every day. So they know that I'm not lazy. Some of them know that I made *Hajj* [pilgrimage] twice. So they give me respect for that. But I'm doing my part!' he shouts. 'I'm holding it down. They know I'm not lazy.'" Zain Abdullah, *Black Mecca: The African Muslims of Harlem* (New York: Oxford University Press, 2010), 129. See also Arjana and Aslan's chapter in this volume on Abdullah's account.

56. Dale F. Eickelman, *Moroccan Islam: Tradition and Society in a Pilgrimage Center* (Austin: University of Texas Press, 1976).

57. Marshall Berman, *All That Is Solid Melts into Air: The Experience of Modernity* (New York: Simon and Schuster, 1982).

58. Stephen Kern, *The Culture of Time and Space, 1880-1918* (Cambridge: Cambridge University Press, 1983).

59. Michael Christopher Low, "Empire and the Hajj: Pilgrims, Plagues, and Pan-Islam under British Surveillance, 1865-1908," *International Journal of Middle East* 40 (2008): 269–90.

60. Eric Tagliacozzo, "Hajj in the Time of Cholera: Pilgrim Ships and Contagion from Southeast Asia to the Red Sea," in Gelvin and Green, *Global Muslims in the Age of Steam and Print*; Valeska Huber, "International Bodies: The Pilgrimage to Mecca and International Health Regulations," in Tagliacozzo and Toorawa, *The Hajj*; Robert R. Bianchi, "The Hajj by Air," in Tagliacozzo and Toorawa, *The Hajj*.

61. Erik Cohen, "Pilgrimage and Tourism: Convergence and Divergence," in *Sacred Journeys; The Anthropology of Pilgrimage*, ed. Alan Morinis (Westport, CT: Greenwood Press, 1992); H. Aziz, "The Journey: An Overview of Tourism and Travel in the Arab Islamic Context," in *Tourism and the Less Developed World: Issues and Case Studies*, ed.

D. Harrison (Wallingford, Oxon, UK: CABI, 2001); Arjun Appadurai, *Modernity at Large: Cultural Dimensions of Globalization* (Minneapolis: University of Minnesota Press, 1996).

62. Jerome Taylor, "Mecca for the Rich: Islam's Holiest Site 'Turning into Vegas,'" *Independent*, September 23, 2011, http://.independent.co.uk/news/world/middle-east/mecca-for-the-rich-islams-holiest-site-turning-into-vegas-2360114.html.

63. For a study of the phenomenon of touristic experience transforming into a spiritual pilgrimage event, see Dean MacCannell (Dean MacCannell, *The Tourist: A New Theory of the Leisure Class* (New York: Schoken Books, 1976); Nelson Graburn, "Tourism: The Scared Journey," in *Hosts and Guests: The Anthropology of Tourism*, ed. Valene L. Smith (Philadelphia: University of Pennsylvania Press, 1977), 17–32.

64. Mircea Eliade, *The Sacred and the Profane: The Nature of Religion*, trans. Willard R. Trask (1957; repr., New York: Harcourt, 1987), 24–29.

65. Victor Turner, *Dramas, Fields, and Metaphors: Symbolic Action in Human Society* (New York: Cornell University Press, 1974), 171.

66. On the liminal character of *ihram*, see Arnold Van Gennep, *The Rites of Passage*, ed. M. Vizedom and G. Caffee (1909; repr., London: Routledge & Kegan Paul, 1960), 185.

67. Scupin, "Social Significance of the *Hajj* for Thai Muslims"; Juan Eduardo Campo, "The Mecca Pilgrimage in the Formation of Islam in Modern Egypt," in *Sacred Places and Profane Spaces*, ed. Jamie Scott and Paul Simpson-Housley (New York: Greenwood Press, 1991).

68. John Eade and Michael J. Sallnow, introduction to *Contesting the Sacred: The Anthropology of Pilgrimage*, ed. John Eade and Michael Sallnow (London: Routledge, 2000).

69. Eickelman and Piscatori, *Muslim Travellers*.

70. See, for example, the classic work of Dale F. Eickelman on the Moroccan pilgrimage center of Boujad and the significance of history in the shaping of a non-Hajj Muslim pilgrimage tradition. See also the collection of essays in Georg Stauth and Samuli Schielke, eds. *Dimensions of Locality: Muslim Saints, Their Place and Space* (London: Transaction, 2008).

71. Tagliacozzo and Toorawa, introduction to *The Hajj: Pilgrimage in Islam*.

72. Malcolm X, with the assistance of Alex Haley, *Autobiography of Malcolm X* (repr.; 1964, New York: Ballantine Books, 2015), 347.

73. Juan Eduardo Campo, "Representations of a Changing Sacred Landscape Past and Present," in Tagliacozzo and Toorawa *The Hajj*, 286.

74. Jalal Al-e Ahmad, *Lost in the Crowd*, trans. John Green (Washington, DC: Three Continents Press, 1984), 30.

75. Ahmad, 30–31.

76. Harry Munt, "Pilgrimage in Pre-Islamic Arabia and Late Antiquity," in Tagliacozzo and Toorawa, *The Hajj*.

77. Abdellah Hammoudi, *A Season in Mecca: Narrative of a Pilgrimage*, trans. Pascale Ghazaleh (New York: Hill and Wang, 2006), 123–24.

78. Hammoudi, 123–24.

79. Drew Leder, *The Absent Body* (Chicago: University of Chicago Press, 1990), 53.

80. Sally M. Promey, "Religion, Senstation, and Materiality: An Introduction," in *Sensational Religion: Sensory Cultures in Material Practice*, ed. Sally M. Promey (New Haven: Yale University Press, 2014).

81. Mittermaier, "(Re)Imagining Space," 51.

82. Paulo G. Pinto, "Pilgrimage, Commodities, and Religious Objectification: The Making of Transnational Shiism between Iran and Syria," *Comparative Studies of South Asia, Africa and the Middle East* 27, no. 1 (2007): 109–25, 110.

83. Nile Green, "Religious and Cultural Roles of Dreams and Visions in Islam," *Journal of the Royal Asiatic Society* 13, no. 3 (2003): 287–313, 303.

84. Remo Bodei, *The Life of Things, the Love of Things*, trans. Murtha Baca (New York: Fordham University Press, 2015).

85. Andrew Petersen, *The Medieval and Ottoman Hajj Route in Jordan: An Archaeological and Historical Study* (Oxford: Oxbow Books; London: Council for British Research in the Levant, 2012); Eric Tagliacozzo, *The Longest Journey: Southeast Asians and the Pilgrimage to Mecca* (Oxford: Oxford University Press, 2013).

86. David Walker, "Transporting Mormonism: Railroads and Religous Sensation in the American West," in Promey, *Sensational Religion*, 581–604.

87. Barbara D. Metcalf, "The Pilgrimage Remembered: South Asian Accounts of the *Hajj*," in Eickelman and Piscatori, *Muslim Travellers*.

88. Wilhelm Dilthey, "The Construction of the Historical World in the Human Sciences," in *Dilthey: Selected Writings*, ed. P. Rickman (Cambridge: Cambridge University Press, 1914).

89. Jeremy Stolow, "Introduction: Religion, Technology, and the Things in Between," in *Deus in Machina: Religion, Technology, and the Things in Between*, ed. Jeremy Stolow (New York: Fordham University Press, 2013), 10.

90. Alfred Gell, "Technology and Magic," *Anthropology Today* 4, no. 2 (1988): 6–9.

91. See Michael Adas, *Machines as the Measure of Men: Science, Technology, and Ideologies of Western Dominance* (Ithaca, NY: Cornell University Press, 1989).

92. See Umar Ryad, ed., *The Hajj and Europe in the Age of Empire* (Leiden, UK: Brill, 2016). For a European account of Mecca, see, in the same volume, Ulrike Freitag, "Heinrich Freiherr von Maltzan's 'My Pilgrimage to Mecca': A Critical Investigation," 142–54.

93. Mark MacWilliams, "Virtual Pilgrimage to Ireland's Croagh Patrick," in *Religion Online: Finding Faith on the Internet*, ed. Lorne L. Dawson and Douglas E. Cowan (New York: Routledge, 2004), 227.

PART I | Rethinking Muslim Pilgrimage
History, Politics, and Transnationalism

CHAPTER ONE

Sacrifice and Pilgrimage
Body Politics and the Origins of Muslim Pilgrimage

BRANNON WHEELER

Sometime during the fifth century B.C.E., a gift of eight silver vessels was made to a shrine located at what is now known as Tell al-Maskhuta, some twelve miles west of the modern Egyptian town of Ismailiyah.[1] Today the vessels are in the Brooklyn Museum. Along with the vessels were found a number of agate stones, which may have decorated a wooden box in which the gift was transported to the shrine. Holes in the stones suggest that they may have been used as amulets prior to their gold mounting. Three of the silver vessels are inscribed with Aramaic texts, the shortest of which simply gives the recipient of the donation as "han-Ilat," or "the goddess," presumably the deity of the shrine.

Inscriptions from other locations in Syria and the Arabian Peninsula refer to "Allat" and "Lat," and the Qur'an mentions "al-Lat" as the name of a deity worshipped by pre-Islamic Arabs.[2] Herodotus, who traveled throughout Egypt in the fifth century B.C.E., writes that the Arabs worshipped a goddess named "Alilat," whom they identified with the Greek goddess Aphrodite Urania but perhaps also with Athena.

The longest inscription gives the name of the person donating the silver vessel and identifies the goddess Ilat as its recipient: "That which Qainu son of Geshem, king of Kedar, offered to Ilat."

As a tribal grouping from the northern Arabian Peninsula, Kedar is known from a number of contexts in the ancient world, including the Bible. Jeremiah 2:10, from the late seventh century B.C.E., refers to the Kedar as living at the eastern edges of the world. The oracle of Jeremiah 49:28–33, which may refer to the campaign of the Babylonian king Nebuchadnezzar against the Arabs in 599 B.C.E., mentions Kedar. Ezekiel 27:21 mentions the "princes of Kedar" as delivering sheep to the Phoenicians. Arabic sources from the early Islamic period state that the Kedar—named after one of the twelve sons of Ishmael the son of Abraham—is the tribe from which the Prophet Muhammad descends.

From the inscriptions, it is evident that the vessels were deposited at the shrine as a votive offering, brought perhaps by a group making pilgrimage to the site for the purpose of making the donation. The evidence for such votive offerings is widespread in the Mediterranean and Middle East and is not uncommon among the Arabs of Syria and the Arabian Peninsula. Other ancient shrines in the area provide documentary and archaeological evidence attesting to the common practice of pilgrimage among Arabs in pre-Islamic times.[3]

Making pilgrimage for the purpose of giving gifts or making a sacrifice to deities lives on in the Islamic pilgrimage to Mecca and to other sites linked with the Prophet Muhammad and the early history of Islam. Arabic literary sources link Islamic practices with pre-Islamic pilgrimages throughout the Arabian Peninsula and among Arabs outside Arabia.

Islam is one of the only religions that continues the regular practice of animal sacrifice. Unlike Judaism and Christianity, in which the practice has been textualized or sublimated, making sacrifice a vestige of a more primitive stage in the development of religion, Islam makes sacrifice central to the identity of individual Muslims and to the constitution of the Muslim community as a whole. It does this through the annual ritual performance of the pilgrimage to Mecca, when the Muslim world comes together to worship at what is regarded as the earth's first temple, following in the footsteps of the earliest biblical prophets, Adam and Abraham. The centrality of the temple and the animal sacrifice that accompanies the pilgrimage to this temple roots the contemporary practice of Muslims not only in the classical origins of Abrahamic religion but in the model of religion that stands at the foundations of human civilization in the Middle East.

The following pages examine the origins and early development of Muslim pilgrimage. Archaeological and other documentary evidence, taken alongside Arabic literary sources, show how a number of ancient concepts and practices were incorporated into and aligned to coincide with the life of the Prophet Muhammad. Pre-Islamic notions linked with fertility and death were used to portray the Prophet Muhammad as initiating a new world order set into the historical framework of cosmogony and eschatology.

Origins of Pilgrimage to Mecca

The ninth-century Iraqi historian Muhammad b. Jarir al-Tabari (d. 923) relates an account regarding the Ka'ba in Mecca during pre-Islamic times.

> The Tubba' and his people were idolaters. He set out for Mecca. On the way to Yemen, when he arrived between 'Usfan and Amaj, he was met

by a group from Hudhayl b. Mudrika b. Ilyas b. Mudar b. Nizar b. Ma'dd.

They said: "King, do you want us to show you an ancient treasury, which the kings before you ignored, in which is pearls, topaz, emeralds, gold and silver?"

He said: "Of course."

They said: "It is a temple [bayt] in Mecca in which its people worship and pray."

The real intention of the Hudhaylis, however, was to cause the king's destruction, for they knew that any king who treated it with disrespect was sure to die.

Having agreed to the proposal he first sent for the two rabbis [whom he had met earlier in Medina] and asked their opinion. They told him that the sole object of the Hudhaylis was to destroy him and his army: "We know of no other temple in the land which God has chosen for himself," they said, "and if you do what they suggest then you and all your men will be destroyed."

The king asked them what he should do when he got there. They told him to do what the people of Mecca did: Circumambulate the temple, venerate and honor it, shave his head, and behave with all humility until he had left its precincts.

The king asked the rabbis why they too should not perform these rites and they replied that it was indeed the temple of their father Abraham but the idols which the local inhabitants had set up around it and the blood which they shed there kept them from coming. [They concluded by remarking that] the people there are unclean polytheists.

Recognizing the truth of their advice, the king summoned the men from the Hudhayl and cut off their hands and feet before continuing to Mecca. He went around the Ka'ba, sacrificed, shaved his head and stayed there for six days, sacrificing animals, which he distributed to the people, and giving them honey to drink.[4]

Subsequent to this incident, Ibn Ishaq reports that Tubba' had a series of dreams instructing him to cover the temple with woven palm branches and then special fine cloths from Yemen. He is said to have ordered the local inhabitants to keep the temple clean, forbade blood and dead bodies from the area, and made a door with a lock and key for the Ka'ba.[5] A pre-Islamic poem cited by Ibn Ishaq claims that Tubba' made the pilgrimage barefoot, bringing with him two thousand Mehri camels, which he sacrificed and fed to the people there.⁶ Abu Hurayrah reports that the Prophet Muhammad said the Tubbaʿ king was the first person to put a cover (*kiswa*) on the Kaʿba, and Abu ʿArubah al-Harani relates that the first thing ever given to the Kaʿba was this covering.⁷

Arab historians record the giving of gifts to the Kaʿba and the sanctuary in Mecca by other pre-Islamic kings. In his collection of accounts of pre-Islamic history, Ahmad b. Abi Yaʿqub al-Yaʿqubi (d. 905) mentions that ʿAbd al-Muttalib, the paternal grandfather of the Prophet Muhammad, uncovered the treasury of the Kaʿba when he was digging for the well of Zamzam.⁸ According to Yaʿqubi and others, the treasure discovered by ʿAbd al-Muttalib included swords and other weapons, armor, and two golden gazelles. Ahmad Ibn Saʿd (ca. 784–845) reports, on the authority of Ibn ʿUmar, that ʿAbd al-Muttalib used the golden gazelles to make doors, a lock, and keys to protect the Kaʿba.⁹

In his wide-ranging history, Abu al-Hasan ʿAli al-Masʿudi (d. 956) describes how the Sasanian king Sasan b. Babak put two golden gazelles, swords, and some other gold into the well of Zamzam.¹⁰ Ibn al-Kalbi relates that it was the Iranian king Babak b. Sasan who buried weapons and other jewelry at the site of the Kaʿba, and a number of accounts attribute the burial of these and other objects to pre-Islamic Arab kings and the Jurhum, who are said to have inhabited Mecca in the time of the Prophet Ishmael.¹¹ The eleventh-century historian Muhammad b. Ahmad al-Biruni (d. 1048) claims that this ancient tradition of giving gifts to the Kaʿba was continued by ʿAbd al-Muttalib and later by caliphs such as ʿUmar b. al-Khattab.¹²

These examples show that the Kaʿba and the surrounding Meccan sanctuary were understood to be like other temples in the ancient Near East. The donation of votive offerings to temples and shrines is attested in the Arabian Peninsula and surrounding regions. An Assyrian inscription mentions the king of South Arabia putting gems and spices in the foundation of a temple built for the celebration of the New Year's festival.¹³ Weapons, armor, and war trophies, along with slain animals and representations of animals, were buried at ceremonial locations at Janussan and at other locations in northern Arabia.¹⁴

Many of the votive offerings link hunting, sacrifice, and pilgrimage to the site of the burial at the sanctuary. A South Arabian king is recorded as having offered twenty-five gazelles for the rebuilding of a temple and fortress in the city of Shabwah.¹⁵ Descriptions of ritual hunts include the distribution of the quarry's meat at the site of the sanctuary, a ceremony sometimes marked by the offering of the horns of the animal to the site. Ninth-century writer al-Jahiz reports that the horns from the ram offered by Abraham instead of his son Ishmael used to be hung from the Kaʿba.[16] A hunting ritual from the Hadramawt casts the head hunter in the role of the ancient priest-king who circumambulates the cultic rocks of the sanctuary before and after the hunt.[17]

The discovery of relics offered to a sanctuary in these accounts parallels the discovery or installation of relics at the establishment of places of pilgrimage in other contexts. Accounts of the recovery of the True Cross, for example, narrate how the location of the relic marks the place on which the Roman state built the Jerusalem church as part of a larger pilgrimage route through Palestine, Sinai, and Egypt.[18] Linking the establishment of cities and shrines to pilgrimage and the distribution of sacrificed or hunted animals is found in ancient Egypt, Cambodia, China, and Rome.[19]

Sacrifice and Tombs

Pilgrimage sites are often places for the burial of the dead, and the rituals of pilgrims are closely associated with those used for funerary practices. Numerous examples of pre-Islamic practices linking pilgrimage, sacrifice, and visitation of the dead are attested in the Arabian Peninsula and the desert regions bordering the settled areas of the Fertile Crescent. Safaitic inscriptions mention sacrifices to different deities—including a number to Lat, Ilat, and Ruda—offered on behalf of dead relatives.[20] Herodotus (3.8–9) describes an Arab practice of smearing blood on standing stones. Arab caravan cities, such as Hatra and Palmyra, were built around places of sacrifice and pilgrimage. The precincts of these sites were bounded by places of sacrifice around the cities.[21] In the Negev and Sinai, standing stones arranged in ritual patterns marked special areas near pre-historic settlements.[22]

A fifteenth-century compilation of historical traditions related to Mecca, attributed to Taqi al-Din Ahmad b. ʿAli al-Makki (d. 1429), describes how in pre-Islamic times, the territory of the Meccan sanctuary was demarcated by standing stones.[23] Yaqut b. ʿAbdallah al-Hamawi (d. 1229) claims that the erection of such standing stone markers was used throughout the Arabian Peninsula to indicate the boundaries of a sanctuary or place of pilgrimage and sacrifice [hima].[24] An inscription from the south Arabian sight of Itwat describes a series of ritual rules to be observed by pilgrims attending the first fruit and animal sacrifices.[25]

A first-century Nabataean inscription in Wadi Ram mentions the burial of a camel at a tumulus tomb built for the father.[26] The burial of camels at human tombs is found at tumuli graves near a number of sites in the Arabian Peninsula, including Mleiha, al-Dur, Jabal al-Buhais, Jabal Emalah, Hafit, Baat, Beles, and Raybun. These burials may be related to those at the Nabataean necropolis of Madaʾin Salih, the tumuli graves near Taymaʾ, and the rock-pile graves in Wadi al-Turba. The burial of the camels and horses indicate that they were sacrificed before being interred next to the human graves. It is possible that the sacrifices performed at these tombs were linked with pilgrimages and other rituals common in the religious fairs and markets of the Hijaz and capital cities of southern Arabia. A text inscribed on a tomb in the Wadi Ghabr of the Hadramawt identifies the person buried next to a camel.[27]

Literary sources also attest the connection of pilgrimage and sacrifice to burials and funerary rituals. In his heresiography, twelfth-century Iranian scholar Muhammad b. ʿAbd al-Karim al-Shahrastani (d. 1153) mentions the "*baliya*," a camel or horse tied to the grave of its deceased owner or hamstrung and left for dead.[28] Other Arabic sources report that mounts and other domesticated animals were slaughtered at the site of the grave and then either burnt or preserved by being stuffed with grass.[29] Sometimes the meat of the sacrificed animal was eaten as part of the ritual funerary meal (*walima*). Later, visitors to the tomb would perform sacrifices on behalf of the dead. Jahiz reports incidents in which hundreds of camels or all the available young camels and sheep were sacrificed at the tomb of martyrs.[30] In his *Kitab al-Aghani*, tenth-century Arab historian Abu al-Faraj al-Isfahani (d. 967) relates the sacrifices of camels at the tombs of relatives and at standing stones (*ansab*), marking burial sites of well-known people.[31]

Sacrifices and votive offerings in connection with pilgrimage to shrines is well attested in ancient South Arabia. Not unlike the items of treasure said to have been offered to the Kaʿba in Mecca, bulls and camels of gold are mentioned as offerings to certain shrines and places of pilgrimage and sacrifice in Sabaean inscriptions.[32] Qatabanian inscriptions mention statues of gold offered and installed in sanctuaries and linked with the activities of priests and kings.[33] A Himyaritic king is reported to have sacrificed seventy thousand camels in Mecca, and the offering of cult objects, weapons of bronze, and gold and various other animals—including ibex, snakes, and a mouse—are mentioned in connection with cultic activities surrounding sites of pilgrimage.[34] Horse sacrifices in Greece and India tied to burial places evince similar practices, as do certain practices among Native American peoples.[35]

Graves in Mecca

That Mecca itself was considered to be a graveyard is evident from a large number of Muslim traditions about the city and the cult site in pre-Islamic times. Syrian historian Nur al-Din al-Halabi (d. 1635) writes that there are three hundred prophets buried in the sanctuary surrounding the Ka'ba.[36] Other traditions—included in the *Akhbar Makka*, attributed to the ninth century's Muhammad b. 'Abdallah al-Azraqi—claim that there are ninety or ninety-nine prophets buried within the area bounded by the Rukn, the Maqam Ibrahim—the well of Zamzam and the Hijr.[37] In his commentary in the Qur'an, Muqatil b. Sulayman (d. 767) reports that among the ninety prophets buried in the Meccan sanctuary are Hud, Salih, and Ishmael.[38]

Muqatil also reports that there are seventy prophets buried in the sanctuary at Mecca, corresponding to the number of prophets reported by Abu Dharr, on the authority of Mujahid, to have made pilgrimage to the Ka'ba.[39] The number seventy may be related to the ancient idea that there were seventy nations in the world and that each of these nations is represented by a prophet who made pilgrimage to and was buried in Mecca.[40] Other traditions claim that Jesus, Moses, and Salih came to Mecca riding camels and that Mary the mother of Jesus made the pilgrimage to Mecca.[41] A Qadi of Mecca reports, on the authority of 'Abdullah b. al-Zubayr, that a thousand Israelite prophets made the pilgrimage to Mecca.

Various markers reported to have been established within the Meccan sanctuary are described as funerary monuments not unlike other standing stone sites scattered throughout the Arabian Peninsula and the Syrian desert. Ibn Hisham and others mention a "Rukn of the Yemenites," the "Rukn of the Banu Ghumah, and special prayers offered at a succession of "Rukn" around the Ka'ba, suggesting that in pre-Islamic times, a Rukn was separate from the Ka'ba.[42] The Rukn as a standing stone at which certain rituals associated with cultic sites, including sacrifice, were performed is attested.[43] According to a tradition preserved in al-Nasa'i, the Prophet Muhammad "greeted" (*istalama*) a certain stone upon entering the sanctuary around the Ka'ba.[44] Practices at other sites throughout the Arabian Peninsula and the greater region indicate that such standing stones and cult objects were used as markers of tombs.[45]

The Ka'ba itself resembles a tomb marker and may have been used as such in what, in pre-Islamic times, were two separate pilgrimages—the "focus" of the pilgrimage. Some scholars maintain that the Prophet Muhammad's farewell pilgrimage, especially the practice of "standing" (*wuquf*) at ʿArafat, is to be understood as uniting "Hajj" to ʿArafat and the "ʿUmra" to the Kaʿba in Mecca.[46] Hisham b. al-Kalbi (d. 819) mentions the ritual visitation of other Kaʿbas throughout the Arabian Peninsula, including Najran, Sindad (between Kufa and Basra), and al-Hawraʾ.[47] The Nabataean deity Dushares may have been worshipped as a Kaʿba-like stela, and the cubical Kaʿba-like structures found at the necropolises of Petra and Madaʾin Salih appear to have been markers of burials. Other necropolises in the Arabian Peninsula — at ʿAin Jawan, Thaj, al-Kharj and Aflaq — as well as at ceremonial burial sites further afield, attest to the connection between pilgrimage and the visitation of tombs marked by cult objects, especially standing stones.[48]

Pilgrims to the Meccan sanctuary and the rituals they perform there are also closely associated with funerals and visiting the dead. Funerary practices — including circumambulation of the tomb, wearing certain clothing and neglecting one's appearance, and stipulating specific types of prostrations and standings — closely parallel the rituals observed by the Muslim pilgrimage to Mecca.[49] Certain rites described in the so-called Manasik al-Hajj guidebooks mirror ancient customs associated with the visitation of and sacrifice at the site of tombs.[50] Covering the Kaʿba with the *kiswa* cloth is also understood in the context of ancient Near Eastern new year and funerary rituals.[51] The white cloths in which the pilgrims dress and the prohibition of other types of clothing resemble the wrapping of corpses for interment and parallel the ritual dress worn in other funerary ceremonial contexts.[52] This symbolism extends to the popular custom of pilgrims preserving their ritual garb, having been soaked in the water of Zamzam, to be used as a burial shroud at the time of their death.

Early Muslim Pilgrimage

In his collection of authoritative hadith reports, the well-known ninth-century Iraqi scholar Ahmad b. Hanbal (780–855) preserves several variants of a statement made by the Prophet Muhammad regarding pilgrimage. "Do not fasten saddles except for three [destinations]: the Mosque of the Haram, this mosque of mine [in Medina] and the Mosque of al-Aqsa."[53]

This report is found widely in collections of prophetic hadith reports and is generally understood by Muslim jurists as authorizing pilgrimage to Mecca, Medina, and Jerusalem alone.[54] For example, thirteenth-century Shafiʿi jurist Ibn Abi al-Khayr al-ʿUmrani mentions a tradition that a vow made to perform prayer in any mosque is only valid for the three main mosques of Mecca, Medina, and Jerusalem.[55]

It is worth noting that these three locations are all sites to which the pilgrimage includes visits to the tombs of prominent figures from the history of the prophets. The tomb of the Prophet Muhammad in Medina is praised as a place to visit, and such a visit is often combined with a pilgrimage to Mecca in Islamic practice.[56] In his treatise on pilgrimage, Taqi al-Din al-Subki (d. 1355)—the fourteenth-century chief Qadi in Damascus—lists the virtues of visiting the tomb of the Prophet Muhammad in Medina. It is said that on the Day of Judgment, the Prophet Muhammad will intercede and witness on behalf of those who visited his tomb in Medina.[57] The Prophet Muhammad is reported to have said that visiting his tomb is equivalent to having visited him and been one of his followers during his lifetime.[58] Prayer in the mosque built over the tomb of the Prophet Muhammad is equivalent to one thousand prayers performed elsewhere.[59] A pilgrimage to Mecca that does not include a visit to the tomb of the Prophet Muhammad in Medina is considered to be offensive.[60] The eleventh-century Maliki jurist Ibn ʿAbd al-Barr (d. 1071) relates traditions that prayer at the tomb of the Prophet Muhammad is better than prayer in Mecca and that the place where the Prophet will intercede on the day of judgment is at his tomb in Medina.[61]

Islamic pilgrimage to Jerusalem includes visiting a number of sites associated with Israelite prophets. In his eleventh-century compendium of the virtues of Jerusalem, Ibn al-Murajja encourages prayer at the mihrabs of Adam, Seth, Idris, Noah, Hud, Salih, Shem, Abraham, Ishmael, Isaac, Jacob, Joseph, Reuben, Simon, Judah, Dan, Benjamin, Caleb, David, Solomon, Jesus, Zechariah, and John.[62] The sixteenth-century pilgrimage guide of Nasir al-Din Muhammad al-Rumi describes pilgrimage to the places of Solomon, Isaiah, and the tomb of David.[63] Muslim burial sites in Jerusalem are also assigned special value. Kaʿb al-Ahbar is reported to have said that whoever is buried in Jerusalem has already passed over the "straight path" to paradise, and other traditions relate that burial in Jerusalem is equivalent to being buried in the "heavens of this earth" (*al-sama' al-dunya*).[64] In his commentary on the hadith compilation of al-Bukhari, Ibn Hajar explains that burial in the "holy land" of Jerusalem refers to places where prophets, martyrs, and saints are buried.[65]

This is also the case for the other major places of pilgrimage in the early Islamic period. Making pilgrimage to the mosque of Abraham at Khalil, where Abraham and others are said to be buried, is said to be equivalent to visiting the Garden of Eden.[66] Seventy prophets, including Moses, are said to have prayed in the mosque of Abraham, and the practice of seclusion during Ramadan (iʿtikaf) is only allowed in the mosques at Mecca, Medina, Jerusalem, and Khalil.[67] In his sixteenth-century pilgrimage guide, Ibn al-Hawrani (d. 1596) compares pilgrimage to the tomb of John the Baptist in Damascus with pilgrimage to Jerusalem.[68] The Umayyad mosque in Damascus is specified as one of only four pilgrimage destinations along with Jerusalem, Medina, and Mecca.[69] Kufa is also listed as one of the sites authorized as a place of pilgrimage: "The most distinguished mosques are the mosque of Mecca, then the mosque of the Prophet, then the mosque of Jerusalem, then it has been said the mosque of Kufa on the authority of the consensus of the companions of the Prophet and people say also the mosque of Damascus."[70]

According to numerous traditions, Adam is said to be buried in the mosque at Kufa, and all the prophets are said to have prayed in Kufa, just as they are reported to have done in Jerusalem and Mecca.[71]

Cosmogony and Eschatology

An inscription engraved on a cliff at the site of ʿUqla, about ten miles west of the cultic capital center of Shabwah, records a sacrifice made by the king on the occasion of the rebuilding of the city and central temple: "Yadaʾʿil Bayyin king of Hadramawt, son of Rabb-Shams, of the freepeople of Yuhabʿir, he who transformed and altered the city Shabwa and rebuilt in stone the temple, roofed [and] paved the fortress, when they [the temple and fortress] collapsed. They [Yadaʾʿil and his party] killed 35 bovines, 82 young camels, 25 gazelles and eight cheetahs at the fortress Anwadum."[72]

Other inscriptions from South Arabia attest to the connection between the killing of wild animals and the erection of cult objects. A Sabaean inscription on a stela erected in Maʿrib features a boustrophedon text remembering a hunt, including the weapons and methods used, by the priest-king (*mukarrib*) of Saba.[73] According to other inscriptions, the quarry of such hunts were sacred game, and the erected cult objects served as the focus for pilgrimage and special circumambulation ceremonies.[74] Similar cult objects and ritual dances were practiced to mark the offering of wild animals at the coronation of neighboring Ethiopian kings.[75]

Throughout the ancient Near East and in the larger ancient world in general, such sacrifices (of both hunted and domesticated animals) and pilgrimages were recorded as having accompanied the establishment and renewal of sanctuaries. The ancient Israelite cult, involving pilgrimages and the offering of sacrifices, is centered on the temple in Jerusalem, the building of which is the culmination of a national history recounted in the biblical account from Adam to Solomon.[76] Exodus 40:34–48 and 1 Kings 8:1–11 describes, in terms not unlike those used for the building of the temple of Baʿal, the procession of the Ark with the presence of Yahweh to be placed at the cult center.[77] Inscriptions from Gudea narrate how the temple of Ningirsu was constructed out of materials collected from all the mountains of the world. A special "Mace of the Relentless Storm" is fashioned and presented to the king symbolizing the conquests and international relations displayed by the culling of the timber and stone from the edges of the earth.[78] The *Enuma Elish* contains the epic of Marduk's establishment of the central shrine of Babylon and the creation of the city and the rest of the world around it from the remains of the dismembered body of Tiamat.[79]

As it is portrayed in the classical Islamic sources, the Prophet Muhammad's sacrifice of camels and distribution of his body parts at the culmination of his farewell pilgrimage appears to represent a ritual marking the foundation or renewal of an ancient sanctuary and place of pilgrimage. That the pre-Islamic pilgrimage centered on the place of sacrifice at Mina was linked with fertility rites is evident in the rushing to Muzdalifah after the standing at ʿArafat for the Ifadah, which used to begin with the sinking of the sun and, the next morning, with the rising of the sun.[80] The pre-Islamic Arabic deity Quzah was the god of rain and thunder, revealed at Muzdalifah in the fire on the mountain.[81] Fire, by itself or as part of a sacrifice, is found in a number of ancient cultures as a reference to the origins of civilization— that is, a gift of the gods—and to the cultivation and processing of crops and other natural resources for human society. Other pre-Islamic and early Islamic practices are similar to pagan fertility and funerary rites, and a number of rituals associated with the pilgrimage to the Kaʿba parallel Semitic rites of sacrifice and mourning signifying the resurrection of the dead and the rebirth of crops as part of the natural cycle of seasons.[82]

Mythological features from the pre-Islamic practice of sacrifice and pilgrimage as commemorations of establishing a sanctuary are incorporated into the Muslim pilgrimage to Mecca. This linking of sacrifice to fertility and funerary rituals is found in Muslim pilgrimages to other sites that, like Mecca and Jerusalem, are regarded as places where kings, prophets, saints, and martyrs are buried. Sacrificial victims are buried to "feed" the land (and the people interred there). Tombs, the burial position of the dead, and grave markers represent the rebirth and fertility of the land.[83] Muslim circumcision

Sacrifice and Pilgrimage 59

rites at the site of tombs, including horse and gun play, dancing, uncovered females, and mourning, recall the seasonal public new year and harvest festivals of the ancient Mediterranean and Iraq.[84] Pre-Islamic practices include giving drink to the dead, mourning and sacrifices to bring Baʿal back to life, and references to ritual eaters of the dead.[85]

Not unlike the rituals associated with fasting during Ramadan, Muslim rituals linked to pilgrimage and sacrifice recall ancient conceptions of the New Year. The Babylonian New Year celebration marks the return of the dead during the short period of chaos that occurs before the divine decrees for the New Year are received by the king.[86] The Qur'an refers to the "laylat al-qadr" on which the Qur'an was sent down from God to the Prophet Muhammad.[87] Fakhr al-Din al-Razi explains that on this "new year" night, God decrees rain, sustenance, and life for the following year. In his commentary on the Qur'an, al-Tabari says that on this night God decrees not only the fertility of the natural world but also the human affairs of civilization.[88] The practice of "seclusion" (iʿtikaf), usually observed during the last part of Ramadan to coincide with the laylat al-qadr, is specifically tied to the sanctuary at Mecca, both historically and legally.[89] According to various sources, the Prophet Muhammad practiced special rites of seclusion (tahannuth) during Ramadan at sites located around Mecca.[90] Muslim tradition holds that the first revelation of the Qur'an fixed the conditions of the coming year and designated the names of those who would perform pilgrimage to Mecca in that year.[91]

Muslim belief and practice locates Mecca at the origins of the natural and political worlds. ʿAʾishah, the wife of the Prophet Muhammad, is credited as having said that Mecca was the first place created on the earth: "Mecca is the city of God. He made it great and made it sacred. God created Mecca and surrounded it with angels before he created anything else in the world for a thousand years and attached to it Medina and attached to Medina Jerusalem [Bayt al-Maqdis], then he created all of the world after that in a thousand years in a single creation."[92]

THROUGHOUT THE ANCIENT Mediterranean, Mesopotamia, and among the Arabs in pre-Islamic times, each New Year marked by pilgrimage and sacrifice was regarded as a repetition of creation.[93] In Babylon, the so-called creation epic (Enuma Elish), in which the god-king Marduk constructs the central sanctuary of his capital after creating the world out of the dismembered body of Tiamat, is read in late autumn on the fourth day of the Akitu New Year's festival. Israelites made pilgrimage to Jerusalem at the same time of the year for the feast of tabernacles (Sukkot), remembering creation and

Yahweh's victories over the sea. The distribution and eating of sacrificial animals parallels these cosmogonic acts of dismemberment by the gods. Herodotus and others describe similar practices among the pre-Islamic Arabs of the Sinai, dismembering and eating raw victims dedicated to the morning star.[94]

The farewell pilgrimage and final sacrifice of the Prophet Muhammad at Mecca and its ritual repetition by later generations of Muslims represent and recall the foundations of the new world of Islamic civilization. Like other ancient Near East leaders before him, the Prophet Muhammad purifies and renews the central sanctuary of his new political order. His pilgrimage serves as an exemplum for the future commemoration of this founding. The sacrificial act remembers the cosmogonic combat and dismemberment marked by the New Year. It brings fertility to the land and establishes the city as its capital.[95]

Conclusion

Mecca is the place where creation begins, where it is commemorated and linked to the origins of Islamic civilization; it is also the place where the world will end. Medieval histories of Mecca mention the notable tombs located in the city and the virtues of those buried there.[96] The Prophet Muhammad is reported to have granted special blessings to people buried in Mecca and to those who visited the dead in the city.[97] Among the blessings is the direct intercession for the dead by the prophets buried within the sanctuary on the Day of Judgment.[98] The black stone mounted on the Ka'ba and visited by pilgrims is itself a symbol of this history—sent down from heaven, marking the replacement of Jerusalem as the direction of prayer, the place of sacrifice for all nations, and designating the spot where the world was created and will end.[99]

According to Muslim interpretation, the Prophet Muhammad's camel sacrifice was a substitute for his own body. Ibn Ishaq explains that one hundred camels were required to redeem the father of the Prophet Muhammad from being sacrificed by his father. Islamic law specifies that one hundred camels must be sacrificed in place of a human victim, and it is the price to pay for the life of an individual. Not only does the Prophet Muhammad distribute the one hundred camels to his followers, but he also distributes the hair and nails removed from his body at the conclusion of the ritual. Creation accounts from the ancient Near East and Indo-European peoples often feature the king or the first man sacrificing his own body to create civilization. The distribution of the parts directly parallels the social structure and identity of the "body politic" that emerges from and is traced back to this event, which is repeated and recalled in pilgrimage and sacrificial rituals.

It is this mythological and ritual character of the Islamic pilgrimage to Mecca that makes it so central and significant to Muslim identity and history. Like the ancient kings and prophets that came before him, the Prophet Muhammad offers himself as the foundation upon which human civilization is established. It is this act and the future resurrection of the dead at the end of time that pilgrims recall and expect when they visit Mecca and perform the rites due to the sanctuary.

Notes

1. Isaac Rabinowitz, "Aramaic Inscriptions of the Fifth Century B.C.E. from a North-Arab Shrine in Egypt," *Journal of Near Eastern Studies* 15, no. 1 (1956): 1–9.

2. Qurʾan 53:19.

3. Uzi Avner, "Ancient Cult Sites in the Negev and Sinai Deserts," *Tel Aviv* 11, no. 2 (1984): 115–31.

4. Muhammad b. Jarir al-Tabari, *Taʾrīkh al-Rusul wa al-Mulūk*, ed. M. J. de Goeje (1879–1901; repr., Leiden: E.J. Brill, 2010), 14–15; Ibn Ishāq, *The Life of Muhammad: A Translation of Ishāq's Sīrat Rasūl Allāh*, trans. A. Guillaume (Oxford: Oxford University Press, 1955), 8.

5. Ibn Ishāq, *Life of Muhammad*, 9.

6. Ibn Ishāq, 9.

7. Muhammad b. Bahādur al-Zarkashī, *Iʿlām al-Sājid bi-Ahkām al-Masājid*, ed. Abū al-Wafā Mustafā al-Marāʿī (Cairo: Majlis al-Aʿl ā li al-Shuʾun al-Islamiya, 1384), 33–34.

8. Tabarī, *Tārīkh al-Rusul wa al-Mulūk*, 1088; William Montgomery Watt and M.V. McDonald, trans., *The History of al-Tabarī: Muhammad at Mecca* (Albany: State University of New York Press, 1988), 15; Ahmad b. Abī Yaʿqūb al-Yaʿqūbī, *Taʾrikh al-Yaʿqubi*, ed. ʿAbd al-Amir Muhanna (Beirut: Dar Sadr, 1993), 18.

9. Ahmad Ibn Saʿd, *Al-Tabaqāt al-Kubrā*, ed. Muhammad ʿAbd al-Qādir ʿAtā (Beirut: Manshūrāt Muhammad ʿAlī Baydūn, 1990), 1:69.

10. Abu al-Hasan ʿAlī Masʿūdī, *Murūj al-Dhahab wa Maʿādin al-Jawhar* (Beirut: al-Jāmiʿa al-Lubnānīyya, 1965–66), 1:242; Uri Rubin, "The Kaʿba: Aspects of Its Ritual Functions and Position in pre-Islamic and Early Islamic Times," *Jerusalem Studies in Arabic and Islam* 8 (1986): 117.

11. Rubin, "The Kaʿba," 117.

12. Muhammad b. Ahmad Bīrūnī, *Kitāb al-Jawāhir fī Maʿrifat al-Jawāhir* (Hyderabad: Dāʾirat al-Maʿārif al-ʿUthmānīyah, 1355), 66.

13. Israel Ephʿal, *The Ancient Arabs: Nomads on the Borders of the Fertile Crescent, 9th–5th Centuries* B.C. (Leiden: E.J. Brill, 1982), 123–24.

14. Robert Hoyland, *Arabia and the Arabs: From the Bronze Age to the Coming of Islam* (New York: Routledge, 2002), 189, 186; A. Jamme, *Sabaean Inscriptions from Mahram Bilqis* (Baltimore: Johns Hopkins University Press, 1962), 745.

15. James Pritchard, ed., *Ancient Near Eastern Texts Relating to the Old Testament* (Princeton, NJ: Princeton University Press, 1969), 669–70.

16. Muhammad b. ʿAbdallāh Azraqī, *Akhbār Makka*, ed. Rushdī al-Sālih Malhas (Beirut: Dār al-Andalus, 1983), 156.

17. R. B. Serjeant, *South Arabian Hunt* (London: Luzac, 1976), 56–57.

18. Heribert Busse, "Jerusalem and Mecca, the Temple and the Kaʿba: An Account of Their Interrelation in Islamic Times," in *The Holy Land in History and Thought*, ed. M. Sharon (Leiden: E.J. Brill, 1988), 236–46; Stephan Borgehammar, *How the Holy Cross Was Found: From Event to Medieval Legend* (Stockholm: Almqvist and Wiksell International, 1991).

19. Paul Wheatley, *The Pivot of the Four Corners: A Preliminary Enquiry into the Origins and Character of the Ancient Chinese City* (Chicago: University of Chicago Press, 1971), 465–76.

20. G. Ryckmans, "Le Sacrifice ZBH dans les Inscriptions Safaïtiques," *Hebrew Union College Annual* 23 (1950–51): 431–38.

21. E. Douglas Van Buren, "Places of Sacrifice ('Opferstätten')," *Iraq* 14 (1952): 76–92.

22. Avner, "Ancient Cult Sites in the Negev and Sinai Deserts," 115–31; Udo Worschech, "The Burial Ground of ar-Raha al-Muʿarrajah," *Annual of the Department of Archaeology in Jordan* 44 (2000): 193–200.

23. Taqī al-Dīn Ahmad b. ʿAli al-Makki, *Shifāʾ al-Ghirām bi-Akhbār al-Balad al-Harām* (Beirut: Dār al-Kutub al-ʿIlmīyah, 2000), 1:72.

24. Abū ʿAbdallāh Yāqūt, *Muʿjam al-Buldān* (Beirut: Dār Ihyāʾ al-Turāth al-ʿArabī, 1979), 3:790, 912.

25. Mahmūd ʿAlī Ghul, *The Pilgrimage at Itwat* (London: Institute of Archaeology, 1984), 33–39.

26. Hani Hayajneh, "The Nabataean Camel Burial Inscription from Wādī Ram, Jordan," *Die Welt des Orients* 36 (2006): 104–15.

27. S. Frantsouzoff, "The Hadramitic Funerary Inscription From the Cave-Tomb at al-Rukbah (Wādī Ghabr, Inland Hadramawt) and Burial Ceremonies in Ancient Hadramawt," *Proceedings of the Seminar for Arabian Studies* 33 (2003): 251–65.

28. Muhammad al-Shahrastānī, *Milal wa Nihal* (Leipzig: Harrasowitz, 1923), 2:439.

29. E. Lane, *An Account of the Manners and Customs of the Modern Egyptians* (London: Ward, Lock, 1890; Julius Wellhausen, *Reste arabischen Heidentums* (Berlin: G. Reimer, 1897; repr., Berlin: Gruyter, 1927).

30. Yāqūt, *Muʿjam al-buldān*, 3:49.

31. Abū al-Faraj al-Isfahāni, *Kitāb al-Aghānī* (Cairo: al-Hayʾa al-Misrīya al-ʿĀmma li al-Kitāb, 1970), 1:168; Ignaz Goldziher, "le Culte des Ancestres et le Culte des Morts chez les Arabes," *Revue de l'histoire des religions* 10 (1884): 332–59.

32. *Répertoire d'Epigraphie Sémitique* (Paris: Imprimerie nationale; Paris: C. Klincksieck, 1900–19), 4193, 4142, 4145, 4143, 4144.

33. *Répertoire d'Epigraphie Sémitique*, 4102, 4232, 3902; Josef Henninger and P. Wilhelm Koppers, "Das Opfer in den altsüdarabischen Hochkulturen," *Anthropos* 37–40 (1942–45): 793–96.

34. Alfred Von Kremer, *Die Himjarische Kasideh* (Leipzig: F.A. Brockhaus, 1865); A. Jamme, *Classification descriptive generale des inscriptions sud-Arabes* (Tunis: Imp. Bascone Muscat, 1948.

35. Michael Astour, *Hellenosemitica: An Ethnic and Cultural Study in West Semitic Impact on Mycenaean Greece* (Leiden: E. J. Brill, 1976), 80–92; John M. Campbell, "Territoriality among Ancient Hunters: Interpretations from Ethnography and Nature," in *Anthropological Archaeology in the Americas* (Washington, DC: Anthropological Society of Washington, 1968), 1–21.

36. ʿAlī b. Burhān al-Dīn Halabī, *al-Sīra al-Halabīyya* (Cairo: al-Matbaʿa al-Bahīyya, 1300), 14.

37. Azraqi, *Akhbār Makka*, 2:134.

38. Qur'an 2:125. On Qur'an 2:125, see Muqātil b. Sulaymān, *Tafsīr Muqātil b. Sulaymān*, ed. ʿAbdallāh Mahmūd Shahātā (Cairo: Al-Hayʿa al-Misrīya al-ʿĀmma li al-Kitāb, 1979–88).

39. On Qur'an 2:125, see Muqātil b. Sulaymān, *Tafsīr Muqātil b. Sulaymān*.

40. Mālik b. Anas, *al-Muwattāʾ* (Beirut: Dār al-Kutub al-ʿIlmīyah, n.d.), 1:423–24.

41. Muhammad b. Ahmad b. Muhammad Ibn al-Dīyāʾ, *Bahr al-ʿAmīq fī Manāsik al-Muʿtamar wa al-Hājj ilā Bayt Allāh al-ʿAtīq* (Mecca: al-Maktabah al-Makkīyah, 2006), 54–55.

42. Muslim b. al-Hajjāj, *Al-Jāmiʿ al-Sahīh* (Beirut: Dār al-Jīl, N.d.), 1:48.

43. Henri Lammens, *L'Arabie occidentale avant l'Hégire* (Beirut: Imprimerie Catholique, 1928), 119.

44. On Nasaʾi, see ʿAbd al-Rahmān b. Abī Bakr Suyūtī, *Al-Durr al-Manthūr fī Tafsīr al-Maʾthūr* (Beirut: Dār al-Kutub al-ʿIlmīyah, 1990), 228–30. Lammens, *L'Arabie occidentale avant l'Hégire*, 141; the so-called Black Stone is reported on p. 40.

45. C. A. Burney, "A First Season of Excavations at the Urartian Citadel of Kayalidere," *Anatolian Studies* 16 (1966): 101–8.

46. C. Snouck Hurgronje, *Het Mekkaansche Feest* (Leiden: E.J. Brill, 1880), 68–124; Martijn Houtsma, *Het skopelisme en het steenwerpen te Mina* (Amsterdam: J. Müller, 1904), 185–87.

47. Ibn al-Kalbī. *The Book of Idols*, trans. Nabih Amin Faris (Princeton, NJ: Princeton University Press, 1952), 39–40; Lammens, *L'Arabie occidentale avant l'Hégire*, 128–29.

48. Richard Bowen, *The Early Arabian Necropolis of Ain Jawan: A Pre-Islamic and Early Islamic Site on the Persian Gulf* (New Haven: American Schools of Oriental Research, 1950); Oliver Lecomte, "Ed-Dur, les occupations des 3e et 4e s. ap. J.-C.: Context des trouvailles et materiel diagnostique," in *Materialien zur Archäologie der Seleukiden- und Partherzeit im südlichen Babylonien und im Golfgebiet*, ed. Uwe Finkbeiner et al. (Tübingen: Ernst Wasmuth, 1993), 195–217; Fuʾād Safar and Muhammad ʿAlī Mustafā, *Al-Hadr, Madinah al-Shams* (Baghdad: Wizārat al-Aʿlām, 1974); Rachel Hachlili, *Jewish Funerary Customs, Practices and Rites in the Second Temple Period* (Leiden: E.J. Brill, 2005), 339–44; M. Gawlikowski, *Monuments Funéraires de Palmyre* (Warsaw:

Editions scientifiques de Pologne, 1970), 27; E. L. Sukenik, "A Jewish Tomb in the Kedron Valley," *Palestine Exploration Quarterly* 69 (1945): 126–30; N. Avigad, *Ancient Monuments in the Kidron Valley* (Jerusalem: Magnes Press, 1954), 70; Donna Kurtz and John Boardman, *Greek Burial Customs* (Ithaca: Cornell University Press, 1971), 166–67.

49. Arent Jan Wensinck, "Semitic Rites of Mourning and Religion: Studies on the Origin and Mutual Relations," in *Verhandelingen der Koninklijke Akademie van Wetenschappen te Amsterdam* (Afdeeling Letterkind Nieuwe Reeks Deel, 1918), 18.1; Lane, *An Account of the Manners and Customs of the Modern Egyptians*; G.E. von Grunebaum, *Muhammadan Festivals* (New York: Roman and Littlefield, 1951).

50. Hava Lazarus-Yafeh, *Some Religious Aspects of Islam: A Collection of Articles* (Leiden: E. J. Brill, 1981), 140.

51. Wensinck, "Semitic Rites of Mourning and Religion," 78–80.

52. Victor Turner, "Death and the Dead in the Pilgrimage Process," in *Religious Encounters with Death*, ed. F. E. Reynolds and E. Waugh (University Park: Pennsylvania State University Press, 1976), 12–23; Mircea Eliade, *Shamanism* (Princeton, NJ: Princeton University Press, 2004), 184–86; Shashibhusan Dasgupta, *Obscure Religious Cults as Background of Bengali Literature* (Calcutta: University of Calcutta, 1946), 204.

53. Ahmad b. Ibn Hanbal, *Musnad* (Cairo: al-Matbaʿa al-Maymanīyya, 1895), 177, 241.

54. M. J. Kister, "'You Shall Only Set Out for Three Mosques': A Study of an Early Tradition," *Le Muséon* 82 (1969): 173–96.

55. Ibn Abī al-Khayr ʿUmrānī, *Al-Bayān fī Fiqh al-Imām al-Shāfiʿī* (Beirut: Dār al-Kutub al-ʿIlmīyya, 2002), 4:459–60.

56. ʿAdil Ahad Abd al-Mawjūd and ʿAlī Muhammad Maʿūd, eds., *Subl al-Hudā wa al-Rashād fī Sīra Khayr al-ʿIbād* (Beirut: Dar al-Kutub al-Ilmiyya, n.d.), 3:281–330.

57. ʿAli b. ʿAbd al-Kāfī Taqī al-Dīn Subkī, *Shifāʾ al-Siqām fī Ziyāra Khayr al-Anām* (Beirut: Lajna al-Turāth al-ʿArabī, n.d.), 14–15, 39–40.

58. Subkī, 29–37.

59. ʿUmrānī, *Al-Bayān fī Fiqh al-Imām al-Shāfiʿī*, 4:353.

60. ʿUmrānī, 4:354.

61. Ibn ʿAbd al-Barr, *Al-Istidhkār al-Jāmiʿ li-Madhāhib Fuqahāʾ al-Amsār wa al-ʿUlamāʾ al-Aqtār fīmā Tadammana-hu al-Muwattāʾ* (Beirut: Dār al-Kutub al-ʿIlmīyya, 2006), 2:446–52.

62. Ibn al-Murajja, *Fadāʾil Bayt al-Maqdis* (Beirut: Dār al-Kutub al-ʿIlmīyya, 2002).

63. Mircea Eliade, *History of Religions Ideas* (Chicago: University of Chicago Press, 2004), 72–73.

64. Zarkashī, *Iʿlām al-Sājid bi-Ahkām al-Masājid*, 294.

65. Ahmad b. ʿAlī Ibn Hajar, *Fath al-Bārī bi Sharh Sahīh al-Bukhārī* (Beirut: Dār Ihyā al-Turāth al-ʿArabī, 1401), 46.

66. Zarkashī, *Iʿlām al-Sājid bi-Ahkām al-Masājid*, 68, 88, 208.

67. Zarkashī, 388.

68. ʿUthmān b. Ahmad Ibn al-Hawrānī, *Al-Ishārāt ilā Amākin al-Ziyārāt*, ed. Bassām al-Jābī (Damascus: Matbaʿa al-Maʿārif, 1981), 3–27, 30–33.

69. Muhammad Zaynahum, ed., *Arbaʿ Risāʾil fī Fadāʾil al-Masjid al-Aqsā li-Ibn ʿAsakir wa Ibn al-Farkāh wa al-Maqdīsī* (Cairo: Dār al-Nadī, 2000), 62.

70. Kister, "'You Shall Only Set Out for Three Mosques,'" 24.

71. Kister, 189; Muhammad Baghir Majlisī, *Biḥār al-Anwār* (Tehran, 1887), 2:85.

72. H. St. J. B. Philby, *Sheba's Daughters* (London: Methuen, 1939), 448c, 451–52.

73. James B. Pritchard, *Ancient Near Eastern Texts Relating to the Old Testament*, 630–70.

74. A. F. L. Beeston, "The Ritual Hunt," *Le Muséon* 61 (1948): 184–85; Carlo Guarmani, *Northern Najd: A Journey from Jerusalem to Anaiza in Qasim*, ed. Douglas Carruthers (London: Argonaut, 1866), 180–92.

75. Nikolaus Rhodokanakis, *Altsabäische Texte I*, Sitzungsberichte (Österreiche Akademie des Wissenschaften. Philosophisch-Historische Klasse), 206 Bd, 2 Abh (Leipzig: Hölder-Pichler-Tempsky, 1927); G. Ryckmans, *Le religions arabes préislamiques* (Louvain: Universitaires, 1951), 326.

76. Jon Levenson, *Sinai and Zion* (New York: Harper One, 1987), passim.

77. Andrée Herdner, ed., *Corpus des Tablettes en Cunéiformes Alphabétiques Découvertes à Ras Shamra-Ugarit de 1929 à 1939* (Paris: Imprimerie Nationale, 1963), 4.6.44–59.

78. James Pritchard, ed., *Ancient Near Eastern Texts Relating to the Old Testament*, 3d ed. (Princeton: Princeton University Press, 1969), Cylinder B, 2:16–23, 5:1–9.

79. Jonathan Z. Smith, *To Take Place: Toward Theory in Ritual* (Chicago: University of Chicago Press, 1987).

80. Arent Jan Wensinck, "Arabic New Year and the Feast of Tabernacles," in *Verhandelingen der Koninklijke Akademie van Wetenschappen te Amsterdam, Afdeeling Letterkunde* (Nieuwe Reeks) (Amsterdam: Uitgave van de koninklijke Akademie van Wetenschappen te Amsterdam, 1925) 25:62.

81. Houtsma, *Het skopelisme en het steenwerpen te Mina*, 197; Snouck Hurgonje, *Het Mekkaansche Feest*, 157.

82. Lazarus-Yafeh, *Some Religious Aspects of Islam*, 42–45, 140n34; Fleming Huidberg, "The Canaanite Background of Gen. 1–3," *Vetus Testamentum* 10 (1960): 56; Granqvist, *Muslim Death and Burial: Arab Customs and Traditions Studied in a Village in Jordan* (Helsinki: Helsingfors, 1965), 53n9.

83. Samuel Curtiss, *Primitive Semitic Religion Today* (London: Hodder and Stoughton, 1902), 175, 223–24.

84. Nanno Marinatos, "Public Festivals in the West Courts of the Palaces," in *The Function of Minoan Palaces*, ed. R. Hägg and N. Marinatos (Stockholm: Svenska Institutet i Athen, 1987), 135–43; C. J. Bleeker, *Egyptian Festivals* (Leiden: E.J. Brill, 1969), 112.

85. S. G. F. Brandon, *The Judgment of the Dead: The Idea of Life and Death in the Major Religions* (London: Weidenfeld and Nicolson, 1967), 11; Huidberg, "The Canaanite Background of Gen. 1–3," 6; Astour, *Hellenosemitica*, 228–49.

86. Henri Frankfort, *Kingship and the Gods* (Chicago: University of Chicago Press, 1948), 79.

87. Qurʾan, 97.

88. Qurʾan, 97:1.

89. Wensinck, "Arabic New Year and the Feast of Tabernacles," 6n4, 18, 162.

90. Muhammad b. Ismāʿīl Bukhārī, *Saḥīh* (Damascus: Dār al-Qalam, 1981), 30:52; Muslim, *Al-Jāmiʿ al-Saḥīh*, 13:175, 177.

91. Tabarī, *Tārīkh al-Rusul wa al-Mulūk*, on Qurʾan 30:59 and Qurʾan 30:143.

92. Zaynahum, *Arbaʿ Risāʾil fī Fadāʾil al-Masjid al-Aqsā li-Ibn ʿĀsakir wa ibn al-Farkāh wa al-Maqdīsī*, 100.

93. O. E. Oesterley, "Early Hebrew Festival Rituals," in *Myth and Ritual: Essays on the Myths and Rituals of the Hebrews*, ed. S. Hooke (Oxford: Oxford University Press, 1933), 111–46.

94. Herodotus, *Historiae*, trans. A. D. Godley as *The Histories* (London: Heinemann, 1924), 3:8; Jane Harrison, *Prolegomena to the Study of Greek Religion* (Princeton, NJ: Princeton University Press, 1991), 485.

95. Lammens, *L'Arabie occidentale avant l'Hégire*, 107; Isfahānī, *Kitāb al-Aghānī*, 14:96, 15:15.

96. Azraqi, *Akhbār Makka*, 2:208; Muhammad b. Ahmad Fasi, *Shifāʾ al-Ghirām bi al-Akhbār al-Balad al-Harām* (Beirut: Dār al-Kutub al-ʿIlmīyya, 2000), 1:374–78.

97. Azraqi, *Akhbār Makkah*, 4:50.

98. Subkī, *Shifa al-Siqam fī Ziyāra Khayr al-Anām*, 138–60.

99. Fasi, *Shifāʾ al-Ghirām bi al-Akhbār al-Balad al-Harām*, 1:260.

CHAPTER TWO

The Hajj and Politics in China

ROBERT R. BIANCHI

In the last thirty years, China's Hajj has grown slowly and steadily from about one thousand pilgrims in 1992 to five thousand in 2004, ten thousand in 2007, and nearly fifteen thousand in 2015. By international standards, these are modest figures, leaving Chinese Muslims with no more than two-thirds of the pilgrimage quota normally allotted to communities of comparable size.[1] Moreover, opportunities to participate in the Hajj from China are very unequally distributed across regions, ethnic groups, classes, genders, and generations. This pattern of restrained growth and selective targeting illustrates the abiding caution that guides China's political and religious leaders as they try to foster more routine contacts between Chinese Muslims and the Islamic world, their clear preference being a series of small steps and half measures they can carefully monitor and regulate.

The government's control over Hajj traffic from China is far from complete. Pilgrimage officials estimate that one-quarter to one-third of Chinese Hajjis avoid the state-sponsored program, traveling to Saudi Arabia independently—and often illegally—via third countries, such as Pakistan, Turkey, and Malaysia. Beijing is trying to capture greater market share by expanding services and charter flights for pilgrims, but Hajj officials might stop short of creating a full monopoly if they carve out a niche for private companies offering high-end tours to luxury travelers.[2]

China's national Hajj quotas are negotiated annually between Beijing and Saudi Arabia with a tacit agreement to keep the total below international levels until the central government builds up the Hajj infrastructure and strengthens its capacity. As the government's designated agent overseeing Muslim affairs, the Chinese Islamic Association has sole legal authority for pilgrimage management. The headquarters in Beijing allocates Hajj quotas to the provincial offices, who then distribute places to local districts according to their estimates of the numbers of Muslim residents and the growing demand from registrants who sign up on long waiting lists, which often stretch for a decade or more into the future.

In recent years, the screening criteria have tightened considerably. Prospective pilgrims must be between fifty and seventy years of age. They must provide evidence of good health and good character, including political loyalty and a clean legal record. When their turn comes, they must deposit in advance the equivalent of $8,200 as a financial guarantee.

Local religious and government officials have wide discretion in applying these requirements, and there are frequent investigations into alleged favoritism and corruption, leading to several well-publicized dismissals and prosecutions for tampering with the selection process. Every year, an increasing number of provincial and local governments offer prospective Hajjis online registration and open access to all names and numbers on the waiting lists. By providing greater convenience and transparency, pilgrimage managers hope to show their concern for minimizing corruption while earning greater public acceptance of the competitive and controversial process they are rapidly building but still cannot fully control.

This chapter summarizes nationwide trends in Hajj participation and highlights important variations between regions and demographic groups. It examines the spatial distribution of hot spots and cold spots of Hajj activity, exploring their tendency to support more open or closed social worlds in which some Muslims are well-connected to the dominant non-Muslim society while others remain more isolated in minority enclaves. It also describes how China's Hajj administration creates both opportunities and barriers to collective action, which shape the interplay of social groups and governmental authorities. Finally, it offers suggestions for rethinking modern Muslim pilgrimage by explaining how the Hajj benefits from and stimulates the wider processes of globalization, which are transforming the Islamic world as a whole.

Regional and Ethnic Variations in Hajj Activity

China's Hajj services are highly skewed to the benefit of about one-quarter of the Muslim population, while leaving the majority neglected or marginalized. Year in and year out, around 65 percent of the pilgrims come from a handful of western provinces that account for only 25 percent of the total Muslim community—Gansu, Ningxia, Qinghai, Sha'anxi, Inner Mongolia, and Yunnan. These are China's most ethnically diverse regions. In these districts, most Muslims are Chinese-speaking Hui, whose communities overlap with dominant populations of Han Chinese as well as large groups of Tibetans, Mongols, Uyghurs, and many smaller minorities. These regions constitute the strategic borderlands and trade routes connecting China to Russia, Kazakhstan, Mongolia, Myanmar, Laos, and Vietnam.

In contrast to these favored zones, Xinjiang, which is home to nearly one-half of China's Muslims, accounts for just over 20 percent of the country's legally organized Hajjis. Hui residents of northern Xinjiang are far more likely to make the pilgrimage than are their Uyghur neighbors, but they, too, are clearly underserved compared to Hui Muslims in the other western provinces.

The most striking disparity in Hajj participation is not between Hui and Uyghur but between the Hui themselves—particularly between the western and eastern portions of the Chinese-speaking Muslim population. The Hui of the eastern and southern provinces are nearly as numerous as their counterparts in the interior—about one-quarter of all Muslims in China—but their share of pilgrims is less than 15 percent. Hence, the Chinese-speaking Hui of the eastern and coastal provinces, who are commonly described as the most sinicized and indigenized of China's Muslims, are no more likely to go on the Hajj than are the disfavored and disaffected Uyghurs of Kashgar and Hotan in southern Xinjiang.

Students of Hui society frequently refer to the eastern communities as the "inner Hui" and the western groups as the "outer Hui." Such distinctions highlight the contrast between eastern Muslims' greater adaptation to the cultural and political domination of the Han majority versus the western Hui history of resistance, revolt, and relative isolation. By designing a Hajj program that favors the western Hui and neglects the easterners, China's political and religious leaders are taking a calculated gamble. The ruling party-state is betting that by providing well publicized and highly valued religious benefits, they can elicit greater support from a potentially troublesome minority in governing vast provinces filled with ethnic antagonisms and national-security vulnerabilities.

Reasoning that Xinjiang is plagued by Uyghur discontent and that the coastal provinces are well secured, China's rulers view the five million Muslims of the near west as a pivotal swing group. The outer Hui compose a minority that is capable of inflicting serious harm if alienated but that can also become an indispensable partner in mediating between the Han and other ethnic groups, who often have weaker connections with one another than with their Hui neighbors.

The systematic overrepresentation of the western Hui in China's Hajj reflects their potential role as a dual bridge in contemporary Chinese statecraft, reinforcing China's still fragile national integration and promoting its burgeoning ties with the Islamic world. Chinese planners are not merely trying to unite the country's disparate regional economies into a single nationwide market; they also hope to lead an even more ambitious integration of transcontinental and transoceanic commerce throughout Eurasia and Africa. The proposed trade routes of the "One Belt, One Road" venture—Beijing's shorthand term for the Eurasian Economic Belt and the Maritime Silk Road—crisscross the major lands of the Islamic world throughout Afro-Eurasia and connect the sea lanes of the western Pacific, the Indian Ocean basin, and the Mediterranean.[3]

More than ever, China stands to gain politically and economically by portraying itself as an Islam-friendly country and as a sister civilization of Muslims and other non-Western peoples. As the United States and the European Union become increasingly entangled in civil wars and antiterrorist battles in Islamic countries, China not only publicizes the growing participation of its Muslims in the Hajj but also trumpets the leading role of Chinese workers and engineers in building the new rail lines that carry pilgrims from every country between the holy sites around Mecca itself.[4]

China's Hajj Belts: The Silk Road, the Yellow River, and the Red River

The heartland of Hajj activity in China is the north central region. The consistent hot spots of pilgrimage tend to cluster along two diagonal lines that crisscross the interior provinces, forming a giant X with its intersection at Lanzhou, the capital of Gansu Province. The line running from southeast to northwest traces the historical Silk Road and the modern rail links from Xi'an (near the former Tang dynasty capital) to Lanzhou, through the towns of Jinchang and Jiayuguan in the Gansu Pass and into the north Xinjiang districts of Hami, Ürümqi, and Karamay, near the border with Kazakhstan. The line running from southwest to northeast follows the Yellow River from the Qinghai towns of Xining and Haidong to Linxia and Lanzhou in Gansu, through the Ningxia towns of Tongxin, Lingwu, Yinchuan, and Shizuishan, and then to the upper reaches of the Ordos Bend in Inner Mongolia and the towns of Bayannur and Hohhot (see map 2.1).

Lanzhou has long served as the military and political control center of north central China and as the key base for expansion to the northwest. In recent years, several districts in the wider Lanzhou Military Region have become sites for big air force bases, for much of China's nuclear missile deterrent, and for the country's growing space program. Ambitious new projects to develop

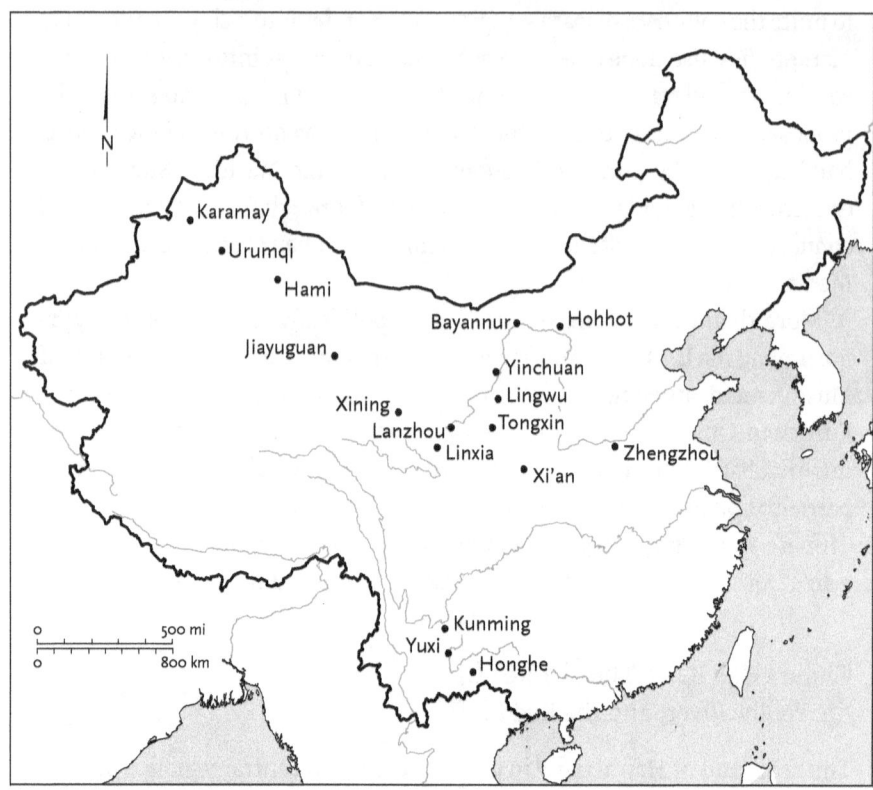

MAP 2.1 Important cities of China's Hajj belts.

and integrate the economies of "the Great West" will further strengthen Lanzhou's role as the region's leading hub of transport, commerce, and industry.

Yunnan is a secondary center of Hajj organization in the southwest. Pilgrimage is popular in the western mountain region of Dali and in the provincial capital of Kunming, but the highest rates of participation are to the south and southeast—in the town of Yuxi and along the Red River valley districts of Honghe and Wenshan near Vietnam.

All the evidence suggests that China's Hajj program is geared toward engendering support from the segment of the Muslim population that is most pivotal to the settlement and economic development of the western interior, particularly the sensitive borderlands, where interethnic relations are historically troublesome and military resources are increasingly concentrated. Lanzhou and Kunming are the northern and southern epicenters of widespread regional networks connecting the upwardly mobile commercial, farming, and professional classes of Muslims in scores of towns and rural communities that link the coastal provinces of the Han-dominated heartland with western China and with neighboring countries in Central Asia and the Middle East, South Asia, and Southeast Asia.[5]

The regional imbalances of China's Hajj program are clearly displayed in aerial photographs of the pilgrims' lodgings near the Grand Mosque in Mecca.[6] In 2014, Chinese Hajjis stayed in nine rented dormitories. Xinjiang's pilgrims occupied only two of them, Gansu Hajjis had a large building to themselves, and Ningxia pilgrims took over two smaller complexes. Qinghai Muslims occupied a building on their own plus seven floors of a nearby twelve-story structure. Yunnan pilgrims filled up eight floors of another hotel, leaving two floors each for Hajjis from Sha'anxi and Inner Mongolia. Pilgrims from the twenty-one other provinces—from Heilongjiang in the far north to Hainan and Guizhou in the south—managed to fit into the single remaining building except for a small group that had to share two floors of the Qinghai Hajjis' lodgings.

Nodes and Enclaves

China's Hajj belts are vibrant networks connecting diverse and far-flung communities, but they also contain many gaps and backwaters. It is common to see districts with very high and very low rates of pilgrimage right next to each other. Variations in Hajj participation strongly correlate with several factors that reflect the degree to which local Muslims are enmeshed in or detached from the Han-dominated societies that surround them. The more open and well-connected Muslim districts support stronger Hajj activity, whereas the more self-contained and inward-oriented districts have the lowest Hajj rates.

In general, Hajj participation is higher in districts where Muslims are a small portion of the total population and lower where Muslims are strongly concentrated or numerically dominant. In China, the Muslims who are most likely to make the Hajj are not those who are surrounded by other Muslims but those who are less conspicuous residents of urban neighborhoods dominated by Han Chinese or of mountain towns populated by other minorities who are not Muslims. Ironically, Muslims living in districts that are officially designated as Hui Autonomous areas make the Hajj less frequently than those who live elsewhere, including the Muslim residents of regions that are nominally Tibetan, Mongol, or shared by several minorities.

The sharpest division appears in the Hajj rates of urban and rural communities, but farming districts also vary widely, depending on whether they produce for the market or benefit from seasonal wages. Overall, Hajj participation correlates most positively with measures of wealth—such as per capita income and per capita gross product—and with literacy rates for both males and females. Hajj rates correlate most negatively with the percentage of the workforce engaged in agriculture and with the Muslim percentage of the total population. Population density also correlates with Hajj activity, but it does so at a slightly weaker level than do the other variables.

Female Pilgrims

Women commonly make up 50 percent or more of the Hajj delegations from most provinces, and they increasingly dominate the registration lists of future pilgrims. In many ways, Muslim women in China resemble their counterparts in other Asian countries, including Indonesia, Malaysia, and Singapore, as well as northeastern Pakistan, western Turkey, and southern Nigeria. The role of Chinese women in making the Hajj a distinctly family affair reflects their wider importance in the workforce, as business managers, and as property owners.[7] In today's China, Muslim women also have less difficulty in meeting security tests, which usually focus on men, particularly young males who are Central Asian in appearance. In Ürümqi—the capital of Xinjiang Province and the site of frequent clashes between Han and Uyghurs—the barriers to Uyghur pilgrimage are targeted primarily at men rather than women. In fact, Uyghur women in Ürümqi make the Hajj in greater numbers than do the city's Hui men.

The economic and demographic factors that encourage the Hajj in general have an even stronger effect in promoting female pilgrimage. Most variables correlate with women's Hajj rates at higher levels than with the combined rates for men and women together. Literacy is a particularly important predictor of women's Hajj activity, and the influence of male literacy often equals or surpasses the role of female literacy.

Urban-Rural Gaps in Gansu

Gansu provides many examples of the sort of regional and social disparities that shape Hajj participation throughout the country. Gansu consistently sends off one of China's largest pilgrimage groups—about twenty-five hundred a year, most of whom come from the Linxia Hui Autonomous Region, where Muslims make up a majority of the population. However, looking beyond the mere number of Hajjis to the per capita rates of pilgrimage par-

TABLE 2.1 Muslims and Hajj Pilgrims by Gender and Prefecture in Gansu

Prefecture	Population, 2010	Muslims, 2010	Total Hajj pilgrims, 2006–2014	Hajj pilgrimage rates, 2006–2014	Female percentage, 2012–2014
Lanzhou	3,616,163	120,447	2,480	2,240	52.66
Jiayuguan	231,853	3,235	66	2,349	27.27
Jinchang	464,050	4,148	69	1,591	42.86
Jiuquan	1,095,947	17,818	286	1,347	33.06
Zhangye	1,199,515	4,281	31	888	44.44
Wuwei	1,815,054	6,035	70	1,458	26.67
Baiyin	1,708,751	24,006	256	1,016	43.88
Tianshui	3,262,548	226,835	945	367	45.34
Pingliang	2,068,033	147,661	1,533	1,027	49.66
Qingyang	2,211,191	5,093	22	275	58.33
Dingxi	2,698,622	25,549	584	2,834	41.24
Longnan	2,567,718	34,396	303	849	46.34
Gannan	689,132	45,024	1,066	2,812	49.67
Linxia	1,946,677	1,093,360	13,140	1,240	42.55
Total Gansu	25,575,254	1,757,888	20,846	1,233	44.50

Source: National Bureau of Statistics of China, *Gansu 2000 and 2010 Population Censuses*; 甘肃省穆斯林朝觐报名网 (Gansu Muslim Pilgrimage Registration Network), http://www.gscjbm.gov.cn.

ticipation, Linxia residents lag behind Muslims in many other districts (see table 2.1 and table 2.2).

Compared to the provincial capital of Lanzhou, only Linxia city has a high pilgrimage rate, whereas the surrounding rural districts trail the province as a whole. The urban core of Linxia has prospered by promoting stronger trading connections between Lanzhou to the north and the Tibetan highlands to the southwest, but the city's good fortune has not spilled over to the neighboring countryside.[8] Income levels drop sharply as distance from Linxia city increases, and pilgrimage activity plummets as well.

Opportunities for Hajjahs (female pilgrims) are sharply curtailed by the relative poverty and isolation of rural life in Linxia and most other parts of southern Gansu. In contrast to the low representation of Hajjahs in the countryside, there is wide diversity in the prominence of female pilgrims in the urban districts of Lanzhou. Muslim women contribute to strong

TABLE 2.2 Socioeconomic Characteristics by Prefecture in Gansu

Prefecture	Muslim percentage	Population density per capita	Gross product per capita	Rural income	Urban income per capita	Non-agricultural workers percentage	Female illiteracy percentage
Lanzhou	3.33	1,585	30,672	4,587	15,228	52.21	12.35
Jiayuguan	1.40	79	83,214	7,865	18,791	73.81	6.64
Jinchang	0.89	52	45,374	5,953	20,396	41.82	20.31
Jiuquan	1.63	6	38,305	7,234	16,348	33.97	15.16
Zhangye	0.36	29	17,093	5,575	11,817	18.54	21.57
Wuwei	0.33	55	12,250	4,551	12,267	14.84	19.29
Baiyin	1.40	81	17,956	3,386	16,101	20.26	13.71
Tianshui	6.95	230	9,202	2,825	12,348	12.83	28.46
Pingliang	7.14	180	11,202	3,136	12,575	13.23	36.42
Qingyang	0.23	82	15,095	3,154	13,353	10.91	19.03
Dingxi	0.95	133	5,530	2,701	11,789	7.93	26.87
Longnan	1.34	95	6,020	2,299	11,216	8.14	47.08
Gannan	6.53	17	9,876	2,689	11,453	15.63	55.57
Linxia	56.17	238	5,441	2,375	8,430	9.82	60.51
Total Gansu	6.64	60	15,363	3,909	14,989	19.08	27.81

Source: National Bureau of Statistics of China, *Gansu 2000 and 2010 Population Censuses*; Lu Qingzhe, "Chinese Urban-Rural Income and Consumption in 2012," in Peilin Li, Guangjin Chen, and Yi Zhang, *Chinese Research Perspectives on Society*, vol. 2 (Leiden: Brill, 2015).

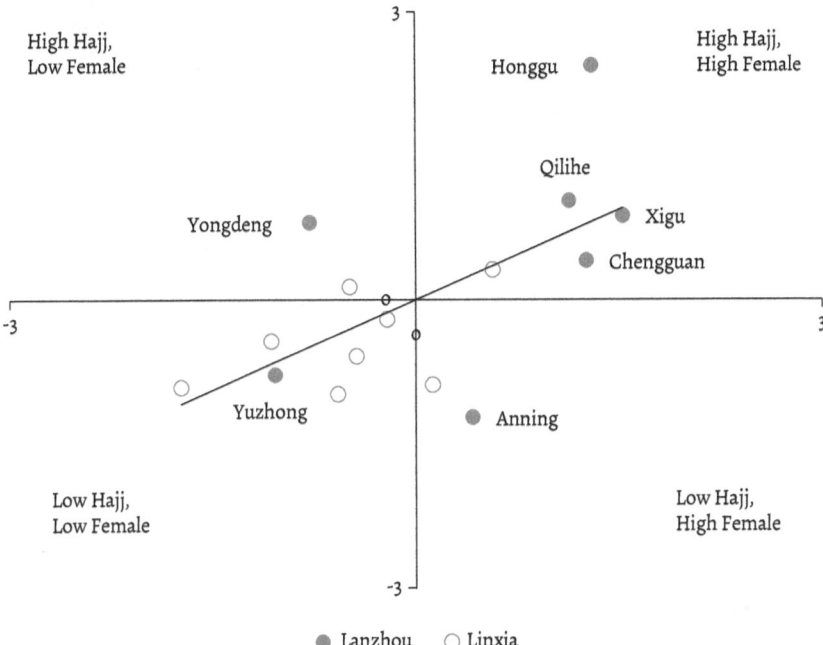

GRAPH 2.1 Hajj rates and female participation in Lanzhou and Linxia Prefectures, standardized scores.

Hajj rates in the central business and residential districts of Chengguan and Qilihe, where they regularly account for the majority of pilgrims. Female pilgrims are common in suburban Xigu and Honggu, but they are less common in working-class Anning and even more uncommon in the outlying semi-rural areas of Yongdeng and Yuzhong (see graph 2.1, table 2.3, and table 2.4).

Literacy affects Hajjah activity even more than do income and social status. The polarization of the more literate urban districts versus the less literate towns and villages is particularly dramatic (see graph 2.2 and table 2.5). Even the most basic levels of formal education make a difference in expanding Muslim women's social world, including the possibility of foreign travel for religious reasons.[9]

North of Lanzhou, Hajj rates in the towns of the Gansu corridor closely track income levels. Non-agricultural sectors such as mining, transport, and defense support both commerce and pilgrimage along the railway lines to northern Xinjiang and Central Asia. On the other hand, the mostly farming districts south of Lanzhou contain some striking examples of both strong and weak Hajj activity.

TABLE 2.3 Hajj Rates and Female Participation in Lanzhou and Linxia Prefectures

District	Hajj pilgrims, 2006–2014	Hajj rate, 2006–2014	Female percentage, 2006–2011	Female percentage, 2012–2014
Anning	37	582	43.33	42.86
Chengguan	1,060	1,953	49.10	55.25
Honggu	409	3,662	49.37	51.56
Qilihe	664	2,477	48.23	52.40
Xigu	139	2,345	50.94	49.02
Yongdeng	140	2,287	35.09	44.00
Yuzhong	31	955	33.33	54.55
Total Lanzhou	2,480	2,177	48.18	52.66
Dongxiang	2,800	1,249	33.14	39.91
Guanghe	2,884	1,442	39.02	44.79
Hezheng	810	845	28.55	30.95
Jishishan	1,199	1,117	37.47	42.08
Kangle	935	784	36.51	41.80
Linxia City	2,347	1,873	44.34	49.24
Linxia County	2,003	1,724	37.13	42.32
Yongjing	161	866	41.30	35.59
Total Linxia	13,139	1,310	37.81	42.55

Source: 甘肃省穆斯林朝觐报名网 (Gansu Muslim Pilgrimage Registration Network), http://www.gscjbm.gov.cn.

Gansu's highest Hajj rates appear in the far southwestern towns of Gannan, a Tibetan Autonomous Region bordering Qinghai. Muslim residents are small in numbers, but they are concentrated in the handful of trading centers that dominate the growing commerce between Lanzhou and Tibet. Closer to Lanzhou, the farming county of Dingxi has developed into another hot spot of pilgrimage. In a region that is widely plagued by drought and erosion, the hills of Dingxi are one of the few places where terraced agriculture produces reliable cash crops for the market. In recent years, the townsfolk of Dingxi—but not the farmers themselves—have been frequent travelers to Mecca.

The weakest Hajj activity in Gansu appears southeast of Lanzhou in the rural backwaters of Tianshui and Qingyang, near the border with Ningxia.[10] Tianshui is home to another Hui Autonomous Region—much smaller than Linxia but with a solid Muslim majority. Its Hajj rate is one of the lowest in

TABLE 2.4 Demographic Characteristics of Lanzhou and Linxia Districts

District	Muslim population	Muslim percentage	Population density	Non-agricultural population percentage	Gross product per capita	Rural income per capita	Female illiteracy percentage
Anning	7,067	2.45	2,442	72.63	24,586	7,869	5.61
Chengguan	60,350	4.72	4,000	79.84	29,524	12,381	4.29
Honggu	12,394	9.11	243	56.72	45,589	7,480	22.75
Qilihe	29,760	5.30	1,134	67.68	38,246	6,905	12.27
Xigu	6,609	1.82	831	70.79	59,123	7,587	8.77
Yongdeng	6,803	1.62	82	12.86	17,240	3,524	19.78
Yuzhong	3,608	0.83	125	7.72	19,705	3,156	20.30
Total Lanzhou	125,590	3.63	1,585	52.21	30,672	4,587	12.35
Dongxiang	249,006	87.52	194	2.69	2,785	1,814	80.27
Guanghe	222,253	97.71	409	4.01	3,901	2,542	69.36
Hezheng	106,623	57.61	193	4.81	3,999	2,230	73.50
Jishishan	119,248	50.59	259	3.37	2,942	2,011	77.67
Kangle	132,390	56.78	171	4.66	3,810	2,354	67.93
Linxia City	139,225	50.73	3,189	48.82	9,738	4,749	12.91
Linxia County	129,081	39.58	269	3.01	4,736	2,351	66.49
Yongjing	20,718	11.50	97	16.06	12,929	2,382	30.45
Total Linxia	1,118,544	57.46	238	9.82	5,441	2,375	60.51

Source: National Bureau of Statistics of China, *Gansu 2000 and 2010 Population Censuses*.

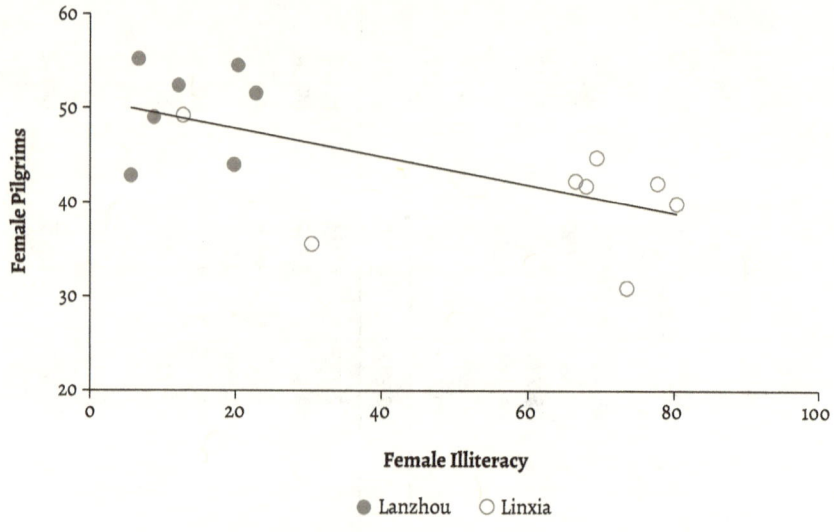

GRAPH 2.2 Percentage female pilgrims (2012–2014) and female illiteracy in Lanzhou and Linxia Prefectures. Source: National Bureau of Statistics of China, *Gansu 2000 and 2010 Population Censuses*; 甘肃省穆斯林朝觐报名网 (*Gansu Muslim Pilgrimage Registration Network*), http://www.gscjbm.gov.cn.

TABLE 2.5 Correlates of Hajj Rates and Female Participation in Lanzhou and Linxia Prefectures ($n = 15$)

	Hajj rate, 2006–2011	Female percentage, 2006–2014
Muslim percentage	−0.3340	−0.4974
Population density	0.0782	0.5428
Non-agricultural population	0.4741	0.8783
Rural income per capita	0.4731	0.8060
Gross product per capita	0.6639	0.7963
Female illiteracy	−0.4080	−0.6960

Source: Author.

the province. If Linxia is a Muslim enclave with a narrow window to the outside world through its county seat, then Tianshui's Hui district is an enclave with no window at all—except perhaps to the dry and poverty-stricken hinterland of southern Ningxia, where Muslim farmers are equally prevalent and the Hajj is similarly depressed (see graph 2.3).

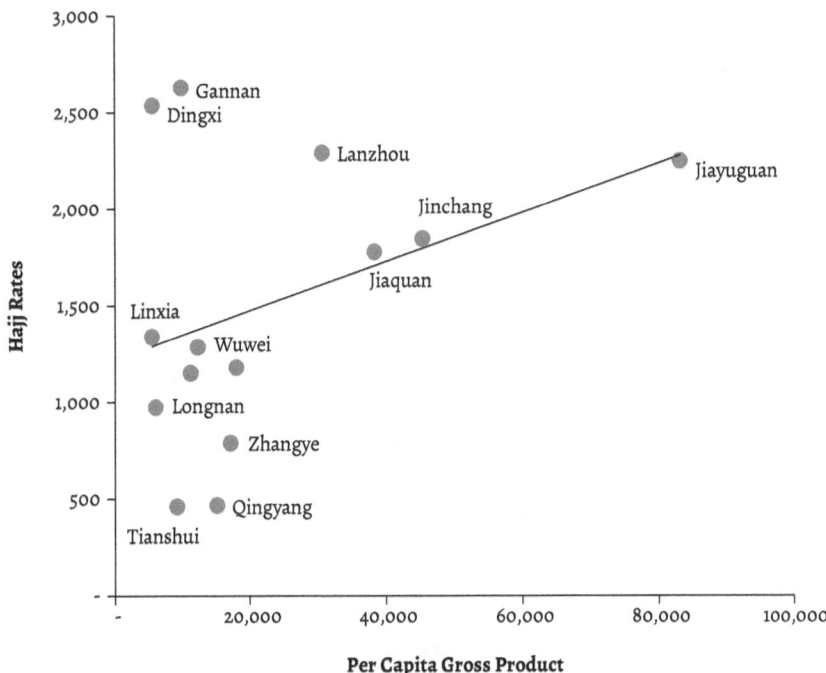

GRAPH 2.3 Gansu Hajj rates (2006–2014) and per capita gross product.
Source: National Bureau of Statistics of China, *Gansu 2000 and 2010 Population Censuses*; 甘肃省穆斯林朝觐报名网 (*Gansu Muslim Pilgrimage Registration Network*), http://www.gscjbm.gov.cn.

Ethnicity and Gender in Xinjiang

Xinjiang sends over 3,200 pilgrims to Mecca each year, amounting to a participation rate of about 350 Hajjis for every 1 million Muslim residents. This is less than half of the current national rate for China as a whole and only one-third of the international quota designated by Saudi Arabia and the Organization of Islamic Cooperation—the so-called United Nations of the Muslim world, which officially supervises global Hajj policy.

Islamic and human rights organizations around the world have long criticized China's government for imposing onerous restrictions on prospective Hajjis from Xinjiang that violate basic religious freedoms.[11] In response, Chinese authorities have begun to publicize increased Hajj services and direct charter flights from Ürümqi to Saudi Arabia. In many advertisements, government and airline officials explicitly appeal to Uyghur Muslims—particularly older married couples—pledging courteous and deferential treatment from young Han men and women who are specially instructed in

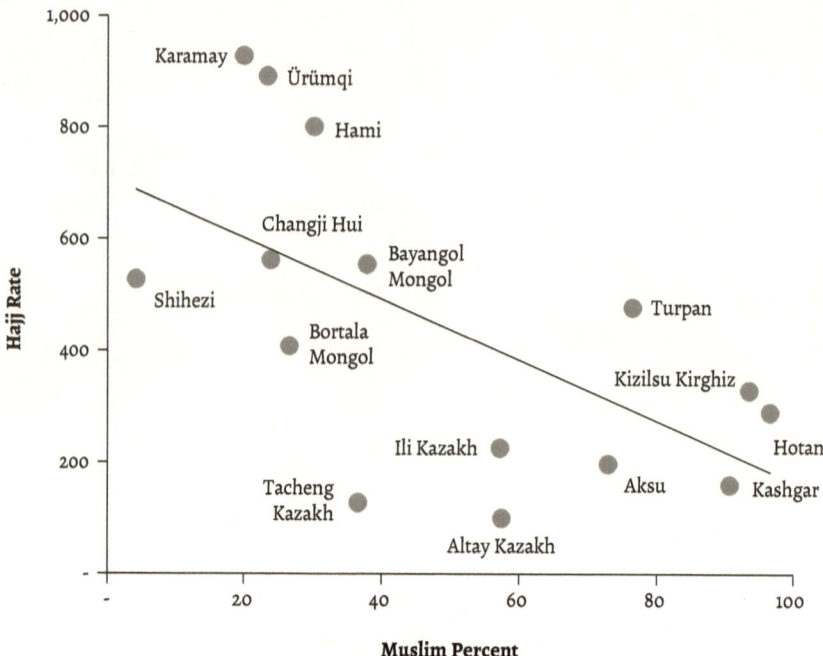

GRAPH 2.4 Xinjiang Hajj rates (2012–2014) and Muslim percentage. Source: 新疆民族宗教网, 朝觐管理办公室 (Xinjiang Nationalities and Religion Network, Office of Hajj Management), http://www.xjmzw.gov.cn.

the customs and needs of non-Han passengers.[12] In 2015, the provincial government launched an investigation of more than thirty Hajj officials in one of the Kazakh districts where friends and relatives were allegedly put at the top of the waiting list for intending pilgrims.[13]

Xinjiang's greatest Hajj activity is concentrated in the predominantly Han-populated cities of the north—Ürümqi, Karamay, and Hami (see graph 2.4). In these districts, where Muslims constitute no more than 20 to 30 percent of the residents, pilgrimage rates are close to the national average and are gradually approaching the international standard. Across the mountains to the south, pilgrimage is weakest in Kashgar, Aksu, and Hotan—predominantly Uyghur districts where residents have clashed with security forces many times over the last decade. Non-Uyghur Muslims in the Kazakh and Kirghiz areas are similarly alienated from the state-sponsored Hajj. In between these extremes, pilgrimage reaches modest but steady levels in ethnically mixed districts where state enterprises are important and where the Hui form a sizable part of the Muslim society.[14]

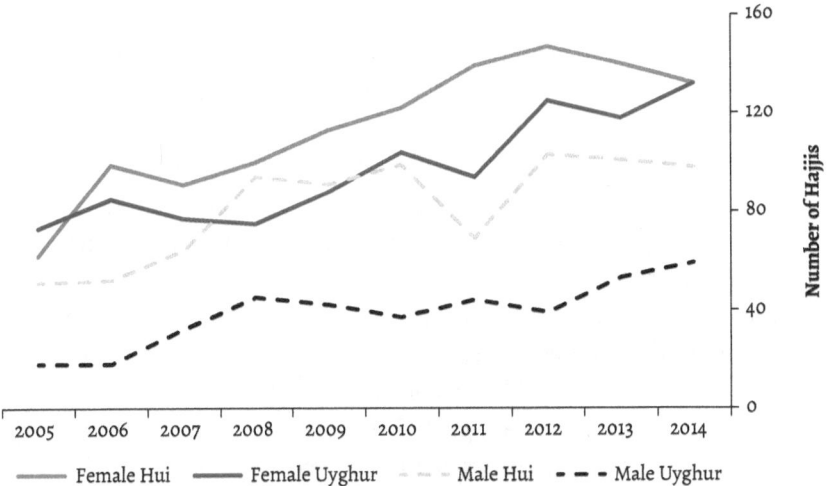

GRAPH 2.5 Ürümqi Hajjis (2005–2014) by ethnicity and gender. Source: 新疆民族宗教网, 朝觐管理办公室 (Xinjiang Nationalities and Religion Network, Office of Hajj Management), http://www.xjmzw.gov.cn.

Ürümqi's Hajj participation is notable not only because of its relative strength and growth but also because of the sharp disparities between genders and ethnic groups (see graph 2.5). The selection of Hajj candidates is increasingly skewed toward women over men. The imbalance appears in both Hui and Uyghur communities but Uyghur males are particularly disadvantaged. Between 2012 and 2014, women made up 88 percent of Hui pilgrims and 70 percent of Uyghur pilgrims.

In the aftermath of the 2009 riots, tighter controls on travel had unequal effects on genders and ethnic groups. Hui women were barely affected—in fact, their numbers increased steadily after the riots, tapering off only in the last few years. Uyghur women suffered a temporary decline, but they soon rebounded and reached near parity with the female Hui. The most serious decreases appeared among the men in both groups, but in quite different ways. The number of Hui males dropped sharply just after the violence but gradually regained its previous strength. In contrast, pilgrimage for Uyghur men was virtually frozen both before and after 2009, leaving them far behind the others.

Because Uyghurs make up about 50 percent of Ürümqi's Muslim residents, compared to 35 percent for the Hui, the ethnic and gender disparities in local Hajj rates are far greater than the aggregate numbers suggest.[15] Among the Hui, pilgrimage levels are about 1,670 per million for women and

The Hajj and Politics in China   83

1,200 for men. The rates for Uyghurs, on the other hand, are just 940 per million for women and 380 for men. Kazakhs account for about 10 percent of the Muslims in Ürümqi, but they received less than 2 percent of the district's Hajj quota.

The sharp ethnic segregation of Ürümqi's neighborhoods also influences pilgrimage activity.[16] Hajj rates are higher in the newer, more Han-dominated areas, particularly the northern district of Gaoxin, and lower in the older business district of Tianshan, where Uyghurs are most prevalent.

In general, Muslims who live in neighborhoods with heavier Han concentrations make the Hajj more frequently than do Muslims who live close to co-religionists. The effect of living outside the traditional ethnic enclaves is stronger for Uyghurs than it is for the Hui—another indication that traveling to Mecca often becomes easier for Chinese Muslims who are able to establish regular contact with Han people and their culture.

Small-Scale Pilgrimage in Henan

The province of Henan is a model of efficient Hajj management at the local level. Clustered near the southern branch of the Yellow River in China's central plain, the one million or so Hui Muslims of Henan support a small but consistent flow of Hajjis that is still quite rare in eastern China. Each year, Henan sends about four hundred pilgrims to Mecca. This level of activity is close to the average number from Ürümqi and at about the same low per capita rate as Xinjiang in general. However, it is only a small fraction of the elevated Hajj rates prevailing among the western Hui—rates that regularly reach two thousand or twenty-five hundred pilgrims per million Muslims in the north central provinces and Yunnan. Thus, even though Henan's Hajj seems impressive in the context of eastern China, it still lags far behind the growing number of hot spots where Chinese pilgrimage activity has reached two or three times the global average.

Henan's pilgrims travel together in nine buses that depart from collection points throughout the province and carry them to Beijing, where they board two charter flights for Saudi Arabia. Two-thirds of the Hajjis come from just two neighboring districts in the far north: the towns around Jiaozuo and Jiyuan on the northern shore of the Yellow River, and the provincial capital of Zhengzhou on the southern side of the river. All the other districts in Henan contain about two-thirds of the Muslim population, but they account for only one-third of the pilgrims. Hajj rates drop dramatically in Kaifeng, the former Song dynasty capital, and near the borders of the neighboring provinces of Shandong, Anhui, and Hubei.

The spatial organization of Hajj activity in Henan is quite distinct. In contrast to the broad networks of the western Hui and the sharp segregation of Xinjiang, Henan's communities appear stacked in a set of regional layers running north to south. As pilgrimage traffic traces the course of the Yellow River, the Hajj itself resembles a weakening current that loses force downstream. Moving east toward the sea, the Hajj diminishes gradually; moving south toward the lands of rice and fishing, it slows to a mere trickle. The centrally located district of Xuchang marks a threshold between the vibrant Hajj of the north and west and the negligible pilgrimage of the south and east.

The Hajj as a Collective Action Problem

The uneven organization of China's Hajj reflects the wider dilemmas of collective action that permeate Chinese society and politics. Regularly mobilizing thousands of Muslims for international travel requires great expenditures of resources and broad delegations of authority. Both the officials who enable such activities and the groups that benefit from them tend to harbor mixed feelings about the consequences.

Political and bureaucratic leaders are eager to garner support and recognition at home and abroad for providing valued public services with modern and equitable systems. But they are also worried about losing control of the processes and people involved lest they blossom into power centers that develop social roots and minds of their own.

The communities and local officials who profit from a more vigorous pilgrimage are equally ambivalent. They welcome the government's shift from indiscriminate suppression to selective sponsorship, but they know too well the traps of division and dependency that can disempower passive clients of the party-state's largesse.

Promoting the Hajj is another means of encouraging the emergence of stronger interest groups that are likely to demand greater representation and autonomy. China is similar to most countries with a growing population of middle-class Muslims who are increasingly educated and involved in world affairs. The relatively high income and status of pilgrims makes them deeply invested in preserving existing institutions, but their history of political exclusion and cultural marginality creates a strong desire for wider power sharing. In this sense, the dilemmas of China's Hajj typify—and perhaps reinforce—many other mounting tensions across the country.

Conclusion

The Hajj is one of several channels through which China's leaders hope to negotiate a gradual opening to the modern mainstream of the Islamic world. In addition to sponsoring pilgrimage, state agencies are discussing a host of projects in Islamic banking and finance as well as special economic zones to boost investment and trade with Muslim countries. Educational exchanges are sending Chinese students to Islamic universities and bringing Islamic modernists to teach in China. China's most important multinational alliance—the Shanghai Cooperation Organization—is planning to include key regional powers, such as Pakistan, Iran, and Turkey. An increasing number of Chinese scholars and diplomats are describing world religions—especially Islam—as valuable resources for enhancing China's "soft power" in global politics. In China's academic journals and mass media, discussions of "geo-politics" and "geo-economics" now include frequent references to "geo-religion."[17]

The developmental processes that have stimulated the Hajj and other Muslim pilgrimages are the same forces that have transformed the Islamic world as a whole. Economic growth and technological advances have spurred rapid urbanization, higher education, and greater consumption among the middle class, women, and youth. Those groups, in turn, have created demand for elected governments to increase public services and accountability. In all regions of the world, we have seen the spread of international regimes regulating world commerce, migration, health, and crime. Today's pilgrimages are an integral part of the larger process that I describe as "Islamic Globalization"—interconnected changes in economics, politics, religion, and diplomacy that are propelling an increasing amount of Muslim countries into the middle ranks of world power.[18]

By promoting the Hajj and other pro-Muslim projects, Chinese leaders seek to benefit from Islamic Globalization in several arenas at the same time. Domestically, they want to garner support from Chinese Muslims while suppressing religious dissenters and separatists. In Muslim countries, they expect broader commercial and diplomatic influence along the continental and maritime Silk Roads of Afro-Eurasia. And in great power politics, they hope to show that China can rally the rest of the non-Western world behind demands for a more inclusive international system.[19]

China's leaders join a long line of authoritarian regimes and colonial rulers that also tried to use pilgrimage to bolster crumbling political systems. In the past, such efforts usually backfired against both Muslim and non-Muslim governments. Similar policies are even less likely to succeed in the future because the modern Hajj is inextricably tied to means of empowerment that are within the grasp of Muslims everywhere—widely shared access to information and action that make universal ideals of freedom and equality more urgent and realizable than ever.

Notes

1. Robert R. Bianchi, *Guests of God: Pilgrimage and Politics in the Islamic World* (New York: Oxford University Press, 2004).
2. Robert R. Bianchi, "Hajj by Air," in *The Hajj: Pilgrimage in Islam*, ed. Eric Tagliacozzo and Shawkat Toorawa (New York: Cambridge University Press, 2015).
3. Robert R. Bianchi, "Silk Roads and Great Games: Prelude to Global Governance or Great Power Conflict?," *Journal of Middle Eastern and Islamic Studies (in Asia)* 8, no. 4 (2014): 43–62.
4. Deng Shasha, "China-Built Light Rail Whisks 1 Million Hajj Pilgrims to Mecca in Saudi Arabia," *Xinhua*, November 20, 2010, 1.
5. Ma Ping, "The Structure of Social Networks of China's Hui Muslims," *Journal of Hui Muslim Minority Studies* 69, no. 1 (2008): 5–10.
6. Chinese Hajj Workgroup, "Information on the Lodgings of Each Region's Pilgrims in Mecca," *Chinanet News*, September 11, 2014, 1, http://news.china.com.cn/zhuanti/cjzl/2014-09/11/content_33479625.htm.
7. Robert R. Bianchi, "Islamic Globalization and Its Role in China's Future," *Journal of Middle Eastern and Islamic Studies (in Asia)* 9, no. 4 (2015): 33.
8. Jing Xu, "Study on Evolution of Spatial Structure of Pan-Linxia Economic Zone," *International Journal of Financial Research* 5, no. 2 (2014): 142–50.
9. Emily Hannum and Jennifer Adams, "Girls in Gansu, China: Expectations and Aspirations for Secondary Schooling," in *Exclusion Gender and Schooling: Case Studies from the Devoloping World*, ed. Maureen A. Lewis and Marlaine E. Lockheed (Washington, DC: Center for Global Development, 2007), 71–98.
10. Sharna Nolan, Murray Unkovich, Shen Yuying, Li Lingling, and William Bellotti, "Farming Systems of the Loess Plateau, Gansu Province, China," *Agriculture, Ecosystems and Environment* 124, no. 1–2 (2008): 13.
11. Unrepresented Nations and Peoples Organization, "Majority of China's Muslims Still Cannot Make It to Mecca," UNPO press release, October 29, 2007.
12. Gao Bo, "State Trips Cater for Xinjiang Pilgrims Heading to Mecca," *China Daily*, April 14, 2015.
13. Gao Bo, "Mecca Pilgrimages Face Tighter Control to Prevent Corruption," *China Daily*, January 22, 2015.
14. Stanley Toops, *Demographics and Development in Xinjiang after 1949* (Washington, DC: East-West Center, 2004).

15. Anthony Howell and C. Cindy Fan, "Migration and Inequality in Xinjiang: A Survey of Han and Uyghur Migrants in Urumqi," *Eurasian Geography and Economics* 52, no. 1 (2011): 119–39.

16. Song Li, Xiaolei Zhang, Shoushan Li, Hongru Du, and Lingyuan Zhang, "Multi-Ethnic Residential Segregation in Urumqi, China, 1982–2010," *Sociology Study* 3, no. 10 (2013): 744.

17. Xu Yihua and Zou Lei, "Geo-Religion and China's Foreign Strategy," *China International Studies* 1, no. 26 (2013): 26.

18. Robert R. Bianchi, *Islamic Globalization: Pilgrimage, Capitalism, Democracy, and Diplomacy* (Singapore: World Scientific, 2013).

19. Bianchi, "Islamic Globalization."

CHAPTER THREE

Pilgrimage and Transnational Religious Imagination in the Muslim Communities of Brazil

PAULO G. PINTO

Pilgrimage—understood as a journey toward a place that contains or embodies a specific source of sacred power[1]—became a significant practice among Muslims in Brazil in the last decade of the twentieth century, when a growing number of faithful engaged in travels to holy places in various parts of the Muslim world.[2] Brazil has no Islamic holy places or shrines in its territory; therefore, Brazilian Muslim pilgrimage has always been about a pilgrimage abroad, usually to the Middle East or North Africa.[3] Several factors concurred to enable the development of pilgrimage as a regular religious practice in the Muslim communities in Brazil.

A major factor was the opening of Brazilian society to transnational and globalized cultural trends.[4] This phenomenon was connected to Brazilian immigration to Europe and the United States in the 1980s, neoliberal economic reforms in the 1990s, and the new diplomatic engagement of the Brazilian state in international arenas—including the Middle East—in the 2000s.[5] Economic factors were also important, as the stabilization of the economy and the adoption of a strong currency, the real, in 1994 made international travel accessible to many Brazilians for the first time in decades, allowing many Muslims to travel in the form of pilgrimage by their own means. Parallel to that, many Islamic institutions began to use funding from Saudi Arabia, Iran, or the Gulf countries to sponsor tour groups of Brazilian Muslims to pilgrimage to the holy sites in Saudi Arabia, Iran, or Iraq.

In order to demonstrate the impact of pilgrimage practices in the Muslim communities in Brazil, I will analyze here the practices and discourses that are invoked by pilgrimages in their various stages of execution, from the preparation of the journey to the telling of stories to the showing of pictures after the return of the pilgrims. This analysis will show how these practices and discourses have led to the reconfiguration of the religious identities of Brazilian Muslims within the framework of the transnational religious imaginations that were created through pilgrimage. While Dale Eickelman and James Piscatori correctly point out that "travel is pre-eminently an act of imagination," we could add that in the case of the Muslims in Brazil,

89

the pilgrim's travel also produces and shapes various forms of religious imagination—that is, the capacity to mobilize ideas, images, and references to objects and places in order to give symbolic reality to spheres of religious belonging that lie beyond the local religious communities[6]—which affect the way he or she understands, lives, and connects to Islam.[7]

I will also focus on how pilgrimage allows codifications of Islam, which can be described as normative definitions of the religious tradition as a specific set of textual and ritual references that circulate in transnational arenas to be appropriated by the Muslim communities in Brazil. This process articulates the local realities of Muslims in Brazil with the religious landscape of globalized Islam. Those who performed pilgrimage to holy places considered central to the Islamic tradition acquired religious symbolic capital, which gave them religious distinction in their communities of origin.[8] In some communities in Brazil, such as Rio de Janeiro and Curitiba, this religious distinction was translated into religious authority, allowing the emergence of religious leaders who reformed the religious practices of the community according to codifications of Islam that circulated in transnational religious circuits.

The Religious and Cultural Dynamics of the Muslim Communities in Brazil

Before analyzing the practices of pilgrimage by Muslim communities in Brazil, we need to understand their sociocultural context. Beginning in the late nineteenth century, Brazil's Muslim population was formed by successive waves of migration from the Middle East (Syria, Lebanon, and Palestine) and by the conversion of Brazilians. The number of Muslim immigrants arriving from the Middle East increased considerably after the 1970s, outnumbering their Christian counterparts. Among the Muslims themselves, there is a great diversity of interpretations and forms of living Islam, as they comprise Sunnis, Druze, 'Alawis, and Shi'i.[9] The Muslim communities in Brazil are mostly urban, and according to the 2010 national census, the largest ones are located in São Paulo, Foz de Iguaçu, Curitiba, São Bernardo do Campo, Brasília, and Rio de Janeiro.[10]

The first Islamic institutions in Brazil were charitable societies, created in the 1920s and 1930s. The oldest was the Muslim Charitable Society (Sociedade Beneficente Muçulmana) of São Paulo, founded in 1929. While this institution was clearly Sunni, it aimed to be a reference for all Muslims in Brazil. However, Druze and 'Alawis created their own institutions in other parts of Brazil. Already in 1929, the Druze Charitable Society (Sociedade Beneficente Druziense) was created in Oliveira, Minas Gerais, and in 1956 it was transferred to Belo Horizonte, the capital city of the province. In 1931, the 'Alawi community in Rio de Janeiro created the 'Alawi Charitable Society (Sociedade Beneficente Alauíta), later renamed 'Alawi Muslim Charitable Society (Sociedade Beneficente Muçulmana Alauíta). During the 1950s and 1960s, other charitable societies were founded by Sunni Muslim communities throughout Brazil. With funding from Egypt, the Muslim Charitable Society of São Paulo built Brazil's first mosque—named simply Brazil Mosque (Mesquita Brasil)—between 1946 and 1960.[11]

Between the 1970s and the 1990s, the availability of funding from Saudi Arabia and Iran, which have competed for influence in the Muslim world since the Iranian Revolution in 1979, as well as from Jordan and the Gulf countries allowed Muslim communities and institutions to build mosques in Curitiba, Foz do Iguaçu, Paranaguá, Rio de Janeiro, Belo Horizonte, São Bernardo do Campo, Campo Grande, Cuiabá, Brasília, and other cities in Brazil. While the majority of these mosques were Sunni, the increasing number of Shi'i immigrants that arrived in Brazil after the 1970s and the establishment of transnational links with Iran led to the creation of Shi'i religious institutions and the construction of Shi'i mosques and *husayniyya* in São Paulo, Foz do Iguaçu, and Ponta Grossa.

The same period saw the creation of Islamic institutions dedicated to the spreading of Islam and the certification of halal products in São Paulo and its periphery.[12] These institutions have had an important role in the development of pilgrimage practices among Muslims in Brazil since 2000, as they used part of their resources to sponsor pilgrimage trips to the holy sites in the Middle East. These institutions also worked as mediators between the Muslim communities in Brazil and transnational sponsors, gathering funding from several embassies of Arab countries, as well as from private Islamic institutions in the Middle East, to pay for Brazilian Muslims to pilgrimage during Hajj or 'Umra.[13]

In 1979, FAMBRAS (Federation of Muslim Associations of Brazil; Federação das Associações Muçulmanas do Brasil) was founded in São Paulo. In its role as an overarching organization that speaks for the various Muslim communities in Brazil, FAMBRAS has a large number of affiliates, although there are some Muslim institutions and communities in Brazil that are not related to it. In addition to conducting several activities aimed at spreading Islam throughout Brazil, it serves as an important agency for the certification of halal food for export through its branch Cibal Halal.

FAMBRAS is also recognized by many sectors of the Brazilian state, such as the Ministry of Foreign Affairs, as an institution that represents the Muslims in Brazil as a collectivity. This "official" recognition makes FAMBRAS an actor in the slow process of reconfiguration of Brazilian national identity since the adoption of multiculturalism as a guiding principle for state social and cultural policies in the 1990s. FAMBRAS's partnership with the state, including its role in the export of halal products, allows it to present Muslims as a group to be recognized as a distinctive but integral part of Brazilian society with transnational links to the Muslim world.

In 1987, CDIAL (Center for the Spreading of Islam in Latin America; Centro de Divulgação do Islã na América Latina) was founded in São Bernardo do Campo, also centering its activities on the spreading of Islam in Brazil and certification of halal products. Also in the 1980s, a branch of the Saudi-based WAMY (World Assembly of Muslim Youth; Assembléia Mundial da Juventude Islâmica) was established in São Bernardo do Campo, centering its activities on mobilizing Brazilian Muslims to engage in ritual practices, such as Ramadan fasting, and collective activities, such as Islamic campouts, Muslim Youth meetings, or Islamic conferences, both in Brazil and abroad. In 1999, the more recent of these Islamic institutions, the Islamic Center in Brazil (Centro Islâmico no Brasil), was created in São Paulo. The center is a Shi'i institution dedicated to the spreading of Islam in Brazil and the certification of halal products.[14]

In 2005, the Supreme Council of Theologians and Islamic Affairs of Brazil (Conselho Superior dos Teólogos e Assuntos Islâmicos do Brasil) was created in an attempt to unify and homogenize the normative religious discourse of the Muslim communities in Brazil. This effort at creating a unifying body of Muslim religious authorities in Brazil can be seen as a response by religious specialists to the growing religious role of the Islamic institutions linked to halal certification. Despite its ambition, the council remains clearly Sunni in its composition and thus has influence in only part of the Muslim communities in Brazil.

With its privileged dialogue with the Brazilian state, FAMBRAS helps push the notion of multiculturalism beyond the racialized boundaries within which it is usually understood in Brazil. However, we should refrain from seeing FAMBRAS activism, as well as that of any of the other Islamic institutions, as weakening idealized notions of Brazilian national identity. On the contrary, these Islamic institutions try to expand notions of "Brazilianess" in order to incorporate the transnational connections that are inscribed in

Brazilian Muslim identities through pilgrimage practices and various forms of religious imagination.

This can be seen in the efforts of these Islamic institutions to present Brazilian identities as part of the transnational Islamic arenas created by pilgrimage. All groups sponsored by these institutions to perform Hajj or 'Umra carry Brazilian flags and banners that affirm their presence as Brazilian Muslims in Mecca and Medina. Therefore, by presenting the transnational connections created by pilgrimage as a projection of Brazilianess in global arenas, rather than its relativization by the incorporation of foreign elements, the activism of FAMBRAS contributes to the reimagining of Brazilian national identity through processes of globalization of the Muslim communities in Brazil, while remaining within the discursive limits of the Brazilian national ideology as fostered by the state.

Parallel to the constitution of Islamic institutions, the construction of mosques gave more visibility and prominence to the religious aspect of Muslim institutions, especially in relation to their function as spaces of sociability for the community. This process gave a new impetus to the conversion to Islam of Brazilians without Muslim ancestry. Conversion started to become visible, albeit still a very discreet phenomenon, during the 1990s. Many of the first converts were attracted to Sufism, and most Sufi communities were organized during this period in both Rio de Janeiro and São Paulo.

There are four Sufi communities with a significant number of members: the *tariqa* ("path" in Arabic, often translated as "Sufi order") of the Shadhiliyya Yashrutiyya (Chazulia Yashrutia), which was created in São Paulo by Palestinian, Lebanese, and Syrian immigrants in the 1960s; the *zawiya* ("Sufi lodge" in Arabic) of the Naqshbandiyya Haqqaniyya in Rio de Janeiro, which was created in 1996; the *tekke* ("Sufi lodge" in Turkish) of the Khalveti Jerrahi order in São Paulo, which was created in 1992; and the Muridiyya, which has a significant number of followers among the Senegalese immigrants in Rio Grande do Sul, who created a Murid *daira* ("Sufi lodge" in Wolof) in Caxias do Sul.[15] There are other Sufi *tariqas* in Rio de Janeiro, São Paulo, and the northeast—such as the Tijaniyya, the Ganduziyya, the Naqshbandiyya Khalidiyya, the Mariamiyya, the Shadhiliyya, and the Shadhiliyya 'Alawiyya—but they have very few followers.[16]

In the 1990s, mosques became the main centers for conversion to Islam.[17] At the same time, Salafi interpretations of Islam became dominant in the religiosity of Brazilian converts, for the movement's pedagogical preaching and emphasis on a literal reading of the sacred texts allowed them to affirm their religious knowledge without referencing the cultural traditions that shaped the Muslim identities of Middle Eastern immigrants and their descendants.[18] In the 2000s, the Tablighi Jamaat began to gather followers among the Brazilian converts to Islam, for its preaching on the emulation of the Prophet's exemplary life appealed to them as a way to embody a religious self with unambiguous Islamic correctness while avoiding the doctrinal debates and cultural variation of the religious practices that thrive among the Muslims of Middle Eastern origin.[19]

Conversion to Islam created new opportunities of globalizing oneself, as converts often engage in the study of Arabic and perform pilgrimage to Mecca; to the holy cities of Iraq and Iran in the case of the Shi'is; to India and Pakistan in the case of the Tablighis; or to Turkey, Cyprus, Algeria, or Senegal in the case of some Sufis. A few others even go to live some years in the Middle East, usually studying Arabic and Islam in the centers of religious learning of Egypt, Syria, Saudi Arabia, and Iran. Thus, as I have argued elsewhere, conversion to Islam in contemporary Brazil can also be understood as a form of "conversion to globalization," as it allows the agents to integrate transnational cultural horizons into their sense of self and to experience and position themselves as active participants in global arenas through their religious identity.[20]

While conversion to Islam is connected to processes of globalization of Brazilian selves, with the converts often adopting Arabic names, donning Middle Eastern or North African attire, and incorporating Arabic words and sentences into their everyday interactions with Muslims (and sometimes even non-Muslims), it also includes processes of "creolization" of Islam in local cultural and biographical contexts.[21] By the middle of the 2000s, conversion of Brazilians to Islam became an established part of the religious life of the Muslim communities of Rio de Janeiro, São Paulo, Salvador, Recife, Fortaleza, Porto Alegre, and, on a smaller scale, Curitiba.

The phenomenon of Brazilian conversions was not the only path taken by Muslim communities to ensure their continuity in Brazilian society. Since the 1980s, there has been a religious revival among the descendants of Muslim immigrants from the Middle East. While the 1960s and 1970s were marked by a steady decline in religious practices and involvement with community affairs by the generations born in Brazil, the 1980s marked a slow emergence of religious revival among Brazilian Muslims of Middle Eastern descent.

This context of religious revival among Brazil-born Muslims of Middle Eastern descent and the growing presence of Brazilian converts also changed pilgrimage practices, broadening their scope and enhancing their importance in the religious life of Muslim communities in Brazil. Until the 2000s, very few Muslims from Brazil had performed pilgrimage to the holy sites in the Middle East. The high cost of international travel meant that only the more affluent of the members of the Muslim communities could do it. Some people combined visits to relatives in Syria, Lebanon, or Palestine with pilgrimage, doing it individually or, more often, with groups from those countries.

The Hajj—as both the main pan-Islamic pilgrimage and one of the pillars of Islam—is a shared reference of pilgrimage among Muslims in Brazil, irrespective of their affiliation to specific traditions within Islam. In a lesser way, due to its voluntary and optional aspect, the 'Umra has a similar function of putting Mecca and Medina in the center of the pilgrimage practices and religious imagination of the Muslims in Brazil. It is common for Sunnis and Shi'is in Brazil—and 'Alawis and Sufis in a much less frequent way—to have done or to be planning to do one of these two pilgrimages.

In terms of public discourse, it is an established consensus among the Muslims in Brazil that the status of the Hajj as one of the pillars of Islam puts it at the top of the hierarchy of pilgrimages. As a logical conclusion, the 'Umra is often referred to as the most important of the other pilgrimages. Among both the Brazilian Salafis, who are a large part of the converts, and the Sunni Muslims born in Brazil, 'Umra is the only pilgrimage besides the Hajj that is recognized as religiously valid and practiced. The Tablighis, who are also present among the Sunni Brazilian converts, often combine pilgrimage to Mecca and Medina with minor pilgrimage to Tablighi centers in India and Pakistan, with the latter being seen as a spiritual preparation to the former, with no possible comparison in terms of religious importance between them.

While, Shi'is, 'Alawis, and Sunni Sufis recognize the religious supremacy of the Hajj, they tend to relativize it in their own hierarchy of pilgrimages. To the Shi'is, the holy sites in Iraq (Najaf and Karbala, but also Samarra and Kazhimiyya) and Iran (Qum and Mashhad) are also centers that define and shape the sacred geography of the Islamic revelation. Some Shi'i pilgrims even consider the experience of pilgrimaging to these places to be more fulfilling than the Hajj, subverting the pan-Islamic hierarchy through embodied notions of *baraka* (grace/blessing/sacred power). Similarly, 'Alawis tend to pilgrimage to saintly shrines in Syria, or even to the holy shrines in Najaf, Karbala, Qum, and Mashhad, rather than perform the Hajj.

The Sunni Sufis in Brazil also tend to value the intensity of the experiential dimension of the pilgrimages to the center of their *tariqa*, which usually houses the tomb of the founding saint, in Algeria, Cyprus, Turkey, or Senegal, over the fulfillment of a religious obligation in the Hajj. Therefore, while the Hajj occupies the highest rank of the hierarchy of pilgrimages in terms of its religious prestige as a pillar of Islam, its canonical pan-Islamic status is often relativized or subverted in experiential terms by some pilgrims whenever it is compared with other pilgrimages that express the sectarian, mystical, or devotional traditions to which they are attached.

Muslim Pilgrims from Brazil: Globalizing Selves in Transnational Arenas

The pilgrimages that have been more often performed by Muslims in Brazil are the ʿUmra and the Hajj. Among the Shiʿis, pilgrimages to the holy sites in Iraq and Iran have also been an important practice. Also, since the 1960s, members of the ʿAlawi community in Rio de Janeiro have been combining visits to relatives in Syria with pilgrimage to the tombs of saints and *shaykhs* in the coastal mountains of Syria. Before 2000, the performance of pilgrimage created a sharp religious distinction in relation to the majority of Muslims in Brazil, enhancing the religious status of those who performed it. The pilgrims also brought back many objects that were considered to be charged with the sacred power/grace (*baraka*) of the holy place that they visited. Thus, Zamzam water, dates from Medina, and miniatures or images of the Kaʿba were brought back and given to friends and relatives, creating circuits of distribution of pilgrimage blessings within Muslim communities.

From Syria, the ʿAlawis brought back green ribbons, which were thought to carry the protective and blessing powers of the *baraka* of the ʿAlawi saints and *shaykhs*. These ribbons were wrapped around the wrist of those who received them, creating a personal connection between them and the ʿAlawi sacred figures and holy sites in Syria. This personalization of the links between the ʿAlawi community and the holy sites in Syria helped keep the ʿAlawi identity among the generations born in Brazil.[22]

During this period, some embassies of Arab countries paid pilgrimage trips to religious authorities in order to gain some influence in the Muslim communities in Brazil. Thus, in 1972, after having performed the Hajj, the ʿAlawi *shaykh* of Rio de Janeiro, Hassan Ahmad Safatli, went in pilgrimage to Najaf and Karbala, in Iraq, by the invitation of the Iraqi embassy in Brazil.[23] The embassies of Saudi Arabia, Kuwait, and Libya also sponsored pilgrimage trips of Muslim religious leaders in Brazil, usually to Mecca and Medina. In the 1980s, the Iranian embassy also sponsored pilgrimages of Shiʿi religious leaders to holy sites in Iraq, Iran, and Syria, as well as Mecca and Medina.

Living or studying in Middle Eastern countries such as Syria, Lebanon, Jordan, Egypt, Iran, and Saudi Arabia also enabled Muslims from Brazil to do pilgrimages during the 1990s. Brothers Sami and Munzer Isbelle, businessmen in their forties born in Rio de Janeiro to a family of Syrian immigrants, did the 'Umra several times and the Hajj twice (1993 and 1995) while studying at the Islamic University in Medina between 1993 and 1996.[24] They see these pilgrimages as both a major existential experience and the fulfillment of their religious duties as Muslims. They went to the Hajj with a group of other Latin American students from the Islamic University, sharing the hardships of not having any support organization. Sami noted the following: "At that time it was very rare to have groups from Latin America, and we were students, so we faced many hardships. We slept in a school that had an agreement with the university, but sometimes we had to put a mattress on the sidewalk and sleep in the street."[25] For them, these difficulties added meaning to the Hajj, for, according to Sami, "The Hajj means facing difficulties to show your commitment to God; it is not just a trip." According to Munzer, "The main concern [in the Hajj] is to do everything right; even the spiritual dimension is overshadowed by this."[26]

Despite the concern created by the correct fulfillment of the normative prescriptions in the performance of the Hajj, the two brothers also vividly recalled its experiential aspect. "During the Hajj you are in the very places where unfolded the history of Islam, of Prophet Abraham. Everybody, from all places and cultures, is there with the same purpose of worshiping God. . . . 'Arafat is the only place [during the Hajj] where all pilgrims are together doing the same thing. There you are reminded of the Judgment Day, when all humanity will be together in front of God." The ritual reconstruction of the Islamic sacred history, from the divine revelations that formed Islam to the revelatory "vision" of its eschatological conclusion in Judgment Day, shaped the experiential dimension of the Hajj for these Brazilian Muslims as being part of a larger community, the *umma*, that share a destiny inscribed in the divine plan for mankind. The emergence of this existential connection to the sacred history of Islam created the urge for them to put into practice the religious knowledge that they were acquiring in their studies in order to "correct" what they saw as deviations from the straight path. Munzer summarized this point by saying, "Today the Muslims are very numerous, but there is a lot of ignorance. You could see in the Hajj that many people did not know the basic principles of Islam. So, you have to have patience and remind people to be fearful and respectful of God." Back in Brazil, this urge translated into activism in the Muslim Charitable Society of Rio de Janeiro (Sociedade Beneficente Muçulmana do Rio de Janeiro), which, with the help of other members, resulted in a transformation of its purpose from transmitting the cultural traditions of Middle Eastern immigrants to the generations born in Brazil to spreading Islam through Brazilian society.

According to Sami, this activism was fostered by their personal experience in both the Islamic University and the pilgrimages to Mecca, for, in his words, "We were already engaged with the affairs of the mosque [in Rio de Janeiro] before going to Medina. Of course our knowledge of religion increased there [Saudi Arabia], but also we came back with a different personal connection to Islam. Because of that we had the responsibility of sharing our knowledge with the Muslims and non-Muslims in Brazil." Their status as former students of the Islamic University in Medina and Hajji, together with their active involvement with the institutional affairs of the Muslim community in Rio de Janeiro, allowed them to successfully spread the *salafiyya* as the dominant form of codification and understanding of Islam in this community. It is easy to see how their pilgrimage led to the acquisition of religious authority; the development of more "objectified" understandings of Islam, in this case identified with the *salafiyya*; and a personal engagement in the life of the community, which resulted in the spreading of new forms of religious codification among its members.[27]

After 2000, the scope of pilgrimage practices changed considerably in Brazil. Islamic institutions that worked with certification of halal products for export, such as CDIAL, FAMBRAS, and Centro Islâmico no Brasil, or that had close relations with embassies of the Arab countries, such as WAMY, began to gather funding or use part of their profits from halal certification to sponsor pilgrimage trips. This institutional sponsorship, together with the declining costs of international travel, helped transform pilgrimage into a more common practice, albeit one still restricted to a small minority, among Muslims in Brazil. According to FAMBRAS, it sponsored 124 Brazilian pilgrims to perform the Hajj between 2011 and 2015.[28]

Among the groups being formed to carry out the different forms of pilgrimage (Hajj, ʿUmra) were privately organized groups and those sponsored by the Islamic institutions. The institution-sponsored groups usually had between ten and twenty pilgrims, whereas the private groups had between five and ten.[29] These groups sometimes included men and women, with gender segregation being respected in all aspects of the pilgrimage. All groups, both Sunni and Shi'i, had a *shaykh* to accompany and guide them through the rituals and holy places of the pilgrimage.[30]

Nowadays, the Islamic institutions contact the mosques and communities with which they have ties and announce the number of places available for receiving their sponsorship for pilgrimage. Then, each community chooses who will go on pilgrimage, and the Islamic institution helps them get their Saudi visa. As the number of Muslims in Brazil who do the 'Umra or the Hajj is quite low, between 100 and 150 people a year, the Saudi embassy does not impose any quota or restriction on the number of visas it can issue to Brazilian pilgrims.[31]

The criteria for selecting those who will receive sponsorship are locally decided, but they do not differ much from one community to another. In the Muslim community of Rio de Janeiro, the priority for receiving sponsorship for pilgrimage was given to those who could not do it with their own resources, those who were active members of the community, those who showed a good level of knowledge about Islam, converts, and those who could not go previously due to delays or problems with their visa. According to FAMBRAS, only those who "can prove that they do not have financial conditions to travel" are eligible to be sponsored for the Hajj. Candidates must fill out a form on the website of the institution and wait for the analysis of their application.[32]

Throughout my fieldwork with the Muslim communities in Brazil, I noticed pilgrims' conspicuous habit of showing pictures in social media and distributing souvenirs. The pictures gave visual evidence of the stories narrated about the pilgrimage as well as the direct contact that the person had with the sources of sacred power and blessings. By doing so, they produced forms of distinction that enhanced the religious status of those who were showing them within the local Muslim community. This production of religious distinction is very effective due to the small number of people who perform pilgrimages among the Muslims in Brazil.[33]

Indeed, I could see in the pilgrimages that I accompanied that the performance of the rituals or the visitation of holy places is as important as the visual record of these acts through filming and taking pictures. Sometimes devotional acts are fully staged and posed in order to be well recorded on camera, and an act or a place that is not recorded is often regretted as having lost part of its purpose, for it could not be properly shared with those who did not come on the pilgrimage, as a pilgrim from São Paulo told me in Najaf during the pilgrimage of *arba'in* in 2013. This visual codification of the pilgrimage experience is also connected to the intense participation of Brazilian Muslims in a global online culture, as the pictures are posted on social media; thus, the experience is shared and re-signified through virtual interaction with other Muslims, as well as non-Muslims, around the globe.

The objects brought as souvenirs from the pilgrimage have a more complex symbolic configuration, depending on their use as gifts or as personal objects of the pilgrim. To the pilgrim, these objects work as concrete mnemonic devices that encode the experiential dimension of pilgrimage. They can evoke the actual places and objects that engendered religious experiences in the pilgrim, or they can work as general metaphoric substitutes for the whole pilgrimage. Thus, miniature replicas of the Kaʿba, which is the material focus and a dominant symbol of the pilgrimage to Mecca, was a souvenir that almost all pilgrims I interviewed brought back from the Hajj or the ʿUmra.[34] Sometimes a representation of the Kaʿba is chosen because of the experiential meanings attached to it. A thirty-year-old journalist in Rio de Janeiro who did the Hajj in 2013 said that he bought a miniature of the Kaʿba that had a miniature of the Qurʾan inside it and an edition of the Qurʾan that had a Kaʿba-shaped cover because, in his own words, "The thing that marked me the most was going inside the mosque and seeing the Kaʿba."

When used as gifts, souvenirs from pilgrimage strengthen the personal connection between the receiver and the pilgrim due to their value as concrete metaphors of the pilgrimage. Thus, the thirty-year-old journalist also bought several teacups with the image of the Kaʿba painted on it "as gifts for family and friends." These gifts can also create a circuit of distribution of grace or blessings (*baraka*) due to their proximity or contact with the holy places. Thus, another pilgrim—a thirty-nine-year-old teacher from Rio de Janeiro—brought from the ʿUmra several *tasbih* (prayer beads) as gifts, which, as he specified, "will bring protection and blessings to those I love, for I bought them in Mecca and rubbed them on the tomb of Prophet Muhammad, peace be upon him, in Medina."

The value created by the symbolic or material connection between the objects and the holy places that they evoke can also be translated in the monetary exchanges of the market. Many women bring from pilgrimage clothes, perfume, and makeup, which they sell to other Muslim women in Brazil. Some men also bring *tasbih*, books, *galabiyya* (traditional Middle Eastern menswear), and *taqiya* (head cover). These products are often seen as having greater religious value than those that are simply imported from other places in the Middle East.

The Brazilian pilgrims who performed the pilgrimage to Mecca and Medina in the last years recalled a structure of experience that was similar to the one described by the Isbelle brothers in relation to their pilgrimage nearly twenty years before. No doubt this is in part the result of the socialization of the Brazilian Muslims in the Salafi religious framework that is dominant in most Muslim communities in the country. All the interviewees described a high level of anxiety to perform correctly all rituals during the Hajj, in tandem with the joy and awe of being in the very places where divine revelation took place. A thirty-three-year-old Brazilian convert from Rio de Janeiro who did the Hajj in 2013 summarized this ambivalent experience in this way: "Mecca is your goal, and you are taken by the fact that you are in a place chosen by God as soon as you arrive there. But it is also a very aggressive, rough place; it demands everything from you."

In contrast, Medina is always narrated with affection, as a place where one can feel the presence of the Prophet. The same pilgrim narrated his experience at Medina as follows: "When you arrive at Medina, it feels as if you are being embraced. I felt better at the Prophet's Mosque in Medina than in Mecca, despite the emotion of having seen the Ka'ba. The Prophet's Mosque was the place where I felt more in peace in all my life." The feeling of the presence of the Prophet and the establishment of an existential connection to him is a recurrent theme in the narrative of the Brazilian pilgrims when they describe the experiential dimension of the 'Umra or the Hajj.[35]

The embodied certainty of having established a connection with the Prophet was described as a vivid sensorial memory by Hassan, a sixty-five-year-old Brazilian convert from Recife who did the Hajj in 2011.[36] In his words, "Being in Medina was wonderful; you could feel the presence of the Prophet. . . . What I really remember was the scent of perfume, of incense. It marked me. I still can smell it every time I remember the Prophet. It makes me certain that he is with me." For many pilgrims, the establishment of an experiential connection to Islamic sacred places or concrete symbols, such as the figure of the Prophet, gave these things an existential dimension, inscribing them in their lives and even their own sense of self.[37] This process induced reconfigurations of their own selves according to what they started to perceive as the tenets of Islam from their pilgrimage experience. Thus, Fernando, a thirty-three-year-old convert from Rio de Janeiro, said, "After doing the Hajj, I tried to improve my religious life. I have been a Muslim for ten years, but only now I decided to learn Arabic in order to read the Qur'an in its original version. I always thought that it was not necessary to move away from my identity. I am Fernando, carioca, *flamenguista*.³⁸ But now I know that I need to be in contact with the source of Islam."

This example shows how the experience of pilgrimage led to the reconfiguration of the religious self of some Muslims in ways that articulated it with spheres of religious belonging that lay beyond the local community, broadening the scope and the limits of their religious imagination and giving an experiential content to abstract notions, such as that of the *umma*. Of course, this effect of pilgrimage is neither universal nor homogeneous among Muslims in Brazil, with some of them acquiring a clearer understanding of their religious and cultural specificity as Brazilian Muslims. For example, a forty-one-year-old convert from São Paulo, who did the Hajj in 2012, told me, "Of course when you go to the Hajj you understand Islam better; you become in contact with the source of religion. But not everything you see in Mecca and Medina is what you should follow. It is just their understanding of Islam, and some things are just wrong. So, not everything we do here is wrong, and if they adapted things to their society, we can adapt to ours."

The effects of pilgrimage on the religious imagination also differ when we take into account the Shiʿi community or the Sufi groups in Brazil. While the sacred geography of the majority of Sunni Muslims, in particular those who follow Salafi codifications of Islam, has only one center—Mecca and Medina—Sunni Sufis, Sunni Tablighis, ʿAlawis, and Shiʿis have a multicentered sacred landscape. Therefore, the pilgrimage practices of Muslims in Brazil create discrete albeit partially overlapping sacred geographies, which have their intersection in the spaces of the Hajj.

The members of Sufi communities often go on pilgrimage to the main *zawiya* (Sufi lodge), which is usually where the main *shaykh* lives or where the founding saint is buried. Thus, since the 1990s, some members of the *tariqa* Shadhiliyya ʿAlawiyya in São Paulo have gone on pilgrimage to Algeria in order to be initiated by the *shaykh* of the main *zawiya*.³⁹ Similarly, members of the Khalveti Jerrahi order in São Paulo have gone on pilgrimage to the main *tekke* (Sufi lodge) in Turkey, and members of the Nashbandiyya in Rio de Janeiro have gone on pilgrimage to Cyprus either to receive the teachings and blessings of *shaykh* Nazim while he was alive or to receive his *baraka* after his death.

The members of the Muridiyya who can afford the costs of international travel go on pilgrimage to Touba, Senegal, to celebrate the Gran Magal, the festivity that marks the exile of *shaykh* Ahmadou Bamba, the founder of the brotherhood, during the French colonial occupation of Senegal. Almost all pilgrims are Senegalese disciples, but in 2014 one Brazilian convert did the pilgrimage to Touba. The Murids also engage in the practice of re-creating the pilgrimage to Touba in diasporic settings, gathering to celebrate the Gran Magal. Since 2013, the *daira* (Sufi lodge) of Caxias do Sul serves as the center of this celebration in the state of Rio Grande do Sul, and hundreds of members of the Muridiyya who live elsewhere in the state travel there for the Gran Magal. Thus, while there is no Islamic sacred site in Brazil, the Muridiyya doctrine that "Touba is everywhere" allows its followers to create the idea of a sacred space through the enactment of pilgrimage practices during the Gran Magal.[40]

To Shi'is in Brazil, the sacred geography of Islam has a multiplicity of centers that, while they do not deny the religious supremacy of Mecca and Medina, make it less absolute. Therefore, they consider Najaf and Karbala in Iraq and, in a lesser way, Qum and Mashhad in Iran to be holy places toward which the religious imagination of the Shi'i is drawn and from where discourses, images, and practices that shape and demarcate Shi'ism as a transnational imagined community spring. While the Shi'i have organized collective pilgrimages to Mecca and Medina since the early 2000s, pilgrimage to specific Shi'i holy places were usually made together with visits to family in the Middle East.

It was only in December 2012 that the first group of pilgrims sponsored by the Centro Islâmico no Brasil traveled to perform the *arba'in* pilgrimage to Najaf and Karbala in Iraq and, later on, to Mashhad and Qum in Iran. Group members who lived in São Paulo included Nasser, the thirty-six-year-old president of the Centro Islâmico no Brasil, who was born in Iran and of Iraqi descent; 'Ali, a thirty-five-year-old Brazilian convert to Islam, born in the northeast of Brazil; and Hajja, a fifty-year-old Lebanese woman. I accompanied this group throughout the whole pilgrimage to the holy places in Iraq and Iran during December 2012 and January 2013.

Najaf, which was the first stop in the pilgrimage, occupies a central place in Shi'i religious imagination and cosmology as a location where key events of religious history unfolded—including Adam's expulsion from Eden, the landing of Noah's ark, and the martyrdom of Imam 'Ali—and where the protagonists of these sacred dramas are buried. The symbolic role of Najaf in the organization of a Shi'i cosmology was didactically explained by the president of the Centro Islâmico no Brasil when he described the importance of the shrine of Imam 'Ali: "Here are buried the one who created humanity [Adam], the one who re-created it [Noah], and the one who did a revolution that made humanity enter in a new era ['Ali]." As he finished his explanation, during which he noted that Najaf got its name from the fact that it was the first hill that appeared after the water of the Flood receded, the Brazilian convert exclaimed: "This is a very ancient land! We are standing were all history started!" While Najaf cannot compete with Mecca or Medina in terms of primacy in the history of Islam, the discourses mobilized during the pilgrimage of *arbaʿin* put it in the center of the history of humanity, which is also part of the sacred history of the divine plan of the creation.

When the group arrived at Karbala, after walking half the distance from Najaf over two days, the group of pilgrims from Brazil went directly to the shrine of Imam Husayn. Once inside, the group dispersed with the crowd, each one trying to touch the silver grilles of the tomb while making their personal prayers and addresses to the Imam. Some people screamed, "Labayka ya Husayn!" (At your call, Oh Husayn!) Others grabbed the silver screen around the tomb and kissed it or rubbed it with their hands, their body, or pieces of cloth to get as much *baraka* as possible. When we met afterward, all members of the group were clearly moved by the experience. Hajja expressed well how the intensity of the emotional experience in the shrine engaged the sense of self of the faithful into individualized reflexive religious practices by saying that she spent the night praying in the shrine because "today I felt the call of the Imam. I had to stay close to him."

In a similar way, the Brazilian convert expressed the existential connection he established with the figure of Imam Husayn through his experience in his tomb by saying, "I did what I had to do here. I came to answer the call of the Imam, and now I can go home because he is with me. I feel his presence in my heart." The intense experiential dimension of the *arbaʿin* pilgrimage, together with the repositioning of Najaf in the religious imagination of the pilgrims, enticed comparisons with the pilgrimage to Mecca and Medina. After returning from Karbala to Najaf, Hajja exclaimed, "There were at least 7 million pilgrims here! In Mecca they only have 2 or 3 million. . . . That shows the strength of the call of the Imams. The Sunnis have no *baraka*." ʿAli responded, saying, "I did the Hajj and I felt nothing. Here you can feel the presence of the Imam [Husayn]; he is alive in your heart. I was in Medina reciting the *fatiha* in front of the tomb of the Prophet when a stupid Wahhabi came and started screaming that I was doing something wrong. Why? Can't I pray in front of my Prophet? That's why the Hajj is just an obligation, without emotion." These comparisons subvert the traditional religious hierarchy that put the Hajj, which is identified with Sunni or, more specifically, Wahhabi control over the holy sites in Mecca and Medina, above all pilgrimages. Using the intensity of religious experience as the measure for the strength of holiness in pilgrimage, these pilgrims reshape the sacred geography of Islam within the framework of Shi'i religious imagination, displacing Mecca and Medina in favor of Najaf and Karbala.

The construction of these Shi'i-framed sacred geographies shows an enhanced consciousness of being part of a transnational religious community by the pilgrims from Brazil. This is expressed by the desire to inscribe the Shi'i community of Brazil in the sacred landscape defined by pilgrimage. While walking on the road between Najaf and Karbala, where groups and individuals were carrying the flags of their countries, Nasser said, "We should have brought a Brazilian flag with us; otherwise nobody will know that we exist. Next time we must do it!" However, the sense of belonging to a transnational religious community can also bring an enhanced consciousness of one's distinction and specificity within it. After having seen the various ritual performances of Iranian, Arab, and Turkish pilgrims in Najaf and Karbala, with their different rhythms, languages, songs, and gestures, 'Ali said, "I will compose a samba in honor of Imam Husayn. Then, the next time we will do *ziyara* (pilgrimage/ritual salutation of a sacred figure) in our way." Hajja reacted negatively to this affirmation, saying, "This is not possible. It is a lack of respect. The samba is not suitable to do *ziyara*." 'Ali insisted, saying, "Why not? Every people put their songs and their dances in the *ziyara*. You just need to look at it. Just because they are from a Muslim society is it OK? It makes no sense. Either we take their songs out, or I can use the samba without any problem."

From this debate, we can see that the Brazilian convert aimed to inscribe not only the presence but also the cultural difference of the Shi'i community in Brazil into the sacred landscape defined by pilgrimage, because he understood that all other pilgrims were doing exactly that with their ritual performances. On the other hand, the Lebanese pilgrim, despite having been living in Brazil for decades, could not see the religious constructs of Iranian, Turkish, or Arab Muslims as being cultural products in the same way as a samba honoring Imam Husayn. Thus, the processes of globalization and creolization unleashed by pilgrimage are unevenly distributed among pilgrims, with the converts being more sensible to the cultural specificities of religious practices, creating a creative tension of disagreements and debates that define the dynamics of the religious imagination of Muslims from Brazil.

Conclusion

This analysis showed how pilgrimage practices among Muslims in Brazil affected their religious imagination in discrete historical, cultural, and religious contexts. Until the 2000s, pilgrimage was restricted to religious authorities, meaning that anyone else who did it gained enormous religious distinction and cultural capital, which could be translated into forms of religious authority. This was the case of the Isbelle brothers, who had their religious imagination transformed by their studies and pilgrimages in Saudi Arabia and, once back in Brazil, gained enough religious status and authority to successfully transform the religious codification of the Muslim community in Rio de Janeiro, fostering a Salafi understanding of Islam among the members of the community.

With the increase in the number of pilgrims in the 2000s, due largely to the sponsorship of pilgrimage trips by Islamic institutions linked to the certification of halal products, sometimes in partnership with Arab embassies or private Islamic institutions in the Middle East, pilgrimage helped increase the globalization of the religious imagination of Muslims in Brazil, allowing them to articulate their religious identity in larger religious spheres of belonging. However, the exposition to global arenas of religious performance can also enhance the consciousness of the cultural background of all religious codifications, leading to the affirmation of one's cultural specificity as compatible with a globalized Muslim identity. This trend is most present among converts, albeit reaching only a small minority among them.

While the ideal of Islamic unity dominates the discourses of the pilgrims, the distinct circuits of pilgrimage that are demarcated by the various Islamic traditions generate discrete sacred geographies that ground distinct and, sometimes, divergent forms of religious imagination. Even when these holy cartographies overlap, they have incompatible topographies and incongruent configurations of the centers and peripheries inscribed in them. Therefore, we can say that pilgrimage practices have produced a growing complexity of layers and circles of belonging and experience, contributing to the pluralization of the ways of being Muslim in Brazil.

Finally, despite its small size and peripheral position in the Islamic world, the ethnographic account of pilgrimage practices among Muslims in Brazil reveal processes that can illuminate important aspects of contemporary Muslim pilgrimage. The main one is the reconfiguration of the religious self through its experiential inscription in larger arenas of religious experience and belonging. These arenas can have local, regional, or national dimensions, as is the case with pilgrimages to saintly tombs in Muslim-majority countries, or transnational and globalized characteristics, which is the case for Brazilian Muslim pilgrimages but also, in a more general way, for pilgrimages such as the Hajj or *ziyara al-arbaʿin*.

The transformation of the religious self often implies adherence to a specific codification of Islam or, at least, reconfiguration of previous understandings and forms of living one's Muslim identity. Therefore, this process can be seen as a form of "conversion," which is often grounded in the religious experiences enticed by the pilgrimage practices and the sense of greater closeness to the realm of the sacred that they provoke in the pilgrims. In this sense, Muslim pilgrimage participates in the constitution of both the "public affirmation of belonging" and the "interiority" that Clifford Geertz aptly identified as the defining aspects of contemporary religion.[41] Therefore, looking at the sacred journeys of Brazilian Muslims, we can see how contemporary Muslim pilgrimages structure experiential journeys of the religious self in globalized settings.

Notes

1. This definition encompasses both pan-Islamic pilgrimages, such as the Hajj, and those that are specific to certain groups, such as the *ziyara al-arba'in* among the Shi'is or devotional visitations (*ziyara*) to saintly tombs and shrines.

2. The ethnographic data analyzed here were gathered during several periods of fieldwork among the Muslim communities of Rio de Janeiro, São Paulo, Curitiba, Foz do Iguaçu, Porto Alegre, and Recife, Brazil, from 2003 until 2015. During this period, I accompanied a group of Shi'i pilgrims from São Paulo to the holy sites in Iraq and Iran for the *ziyara al-arba'in* in 2012–2013. I thank CNPq and FAPERJ for the grants that made this research possible.

3. This is not the case in all of Latin America, for there are Islamic pilgrimage sites in Argentina. The older one seems to be the 'Alawi shrine of *Cheij* (*Shaykh*) Ahmad Mahrij (other forms of his name in Arabic and Spanish are Ahmed Mehrej, Ahmad Mehry, Amado Mirih, and Tio Hamito) which is located in a rural cemetery in the province of Santa Fé. The shrine is visited by 'Alawis, Sunni Naqshbandi Sufis, and even some Catholics who seek the blessings of this 'Alawi saint. The Sunni Sufis linked to the Rabbani branch of the Naqshbandiyya also have built four replicas of *shaykh* Daghestani's tomb, which is located in Damascus, Syria, in the dergahs (Sufi lodges) of San Lorenzo, Glew, Mendoza, and Mallin Ahogado. These replicas demarcate an Islamic sacred topography that covers a large part of Argentina, enticing pilgrimage practices that are limited to the members of these Naqshbandi Sufi communities. See Silvia Montenegro, "Alawi Muslims in Argentina: Religious and Political Identity in the Diaspora," *Contemporary Islam* 12, no. 1 (2018): 23–38. I thank the anthropologist Silvia Montenegro (CONICET—Argentina, Universidad Nacional de Rosario) for calling my attention to *Cheij* Ahmad's shrine as well as to the four replicas of *shaykh* Daghestani's tomb. I also thank Silvia for the joint fieldwork we did at the Naqshbandi Rabbani community in El Bolson, Argentina, in 2018.

4. "Globalization" can be defined as discrete processes of increasing intensity of the exchanges and connections between societies around the globe, with multiple economic (market integration, neoliberal policies), cultural (transnational cultural

connections, new social imaginaries), and political (challenges to the nation-state, new nonstate, or suprastate actors) dimensions. I am interested here in the cultural dimensions of these processes in Brazilian society and how the Muslim communities were affected by them and also contributed to creating them through their transnational religious imaginaries and practices, such as pilgrimage.

5. Many of the first Brazilian converts without Arab or Muslim family background entered in contact with Islam or converted while living in the United States or Europe.

6. This definition builds on Benedict Anderson's idea of "imagined communities." Benedict Anderson, *Imagined Communities: Reflections on the Origin and Spread of Nationalism* (London: Verso, 1991). Dale Eickelman and James Piscatori had previously stressed the importance of various forms of travel, including pilgrimage, in the shaping of Islamic religious imaginations. Dale Eickelman and James Piscatori, eds., *Muslim Travellers: Pilgrimage, Migration, and the Religious Imagination* (Berkeley: University of California Press, 1990).

7. Dale Eickelman and James Piscatori, preface to Eickelman and Piscatori, *Muslim Travellers*, xii.

8. Pierre Bourdieu, *Outline of a Theory of Practice* (Cambridge: Cambridge University Press, 1997), 171–83.

9. While ʿAlawis define themselves as part of Shiʿism and are recognized as such by other Shiʿis, for the sake of readability, the "Shiʿi" will be used in this chapter to refer only to the Twelver or Jaʿfari Shiʿis.

10. The demographic census of 2010 puts the number at 35,167 Muslims in Brazil (Instituto Brasileiro de Geografia e Estatística, http://ibge.gov.br/home/estatistica/populacao/censo2010/caracteristicas_religiao_deficiencia/default_caracteristicas_religiao_deficiencia.shtm). Muslim religious authorities speak of 1 to 2 million Muslims in the country. Raymond Delval estimated the number of Muslims in Brazil to be 200,000 in 1983 (Raymond Delval, *Les Musulmans en Amérique Latine et aux Caraibes* [Paris: L'Harmattan, 1992], 201). In 2011, the Pew Forum estimated the 2010 Muslim population of Brazil to be 204,000 ("Table: Muslim Population by Country," January 27, 2011, http://www.pewforum.org/2011/01/27/table-muslim-population-by-country). Based on my ethnographic knowledge, I consider that plausible estimates for 2016 could range between 100,000 and 200,000 Muslims in Brazil.

11. From the 1940s to the 1960s, before the emergence of funding from Saudi Arabia, Iran, and the Gulf countries, Egypt was the main source of funding for Muslim religious institutions. This policy of funding religious institutions aimed to establish Egypt as the main reference in the Muslim world, adding economic patronage to the religious prestige of al-Azhar mosque/university. Initiated by the Egyptian monarchy, this policy was continued by Nasser, who added a nationalistic layer to it, also funding the creation of departments of Arabic language in universities in Brazil, Argentina, and Chile. A remnant of this policy is the fact that until 2005, most Sunni *shaykhs* in Brazil were Egyptian, usually with degrees from al-Azhar.

12. Brazil is the third largest exporter of halal meat in the world. Therefore, halal certification generates large revenues for these Islamic institutions. All halal products are exported, making it impossible to find them in the Brazilian market despite the presence of Muslim communities in the country.

13. For sponsoring the Brazilian Hajj pilgrims in 2015, FAMBRAS partnered with the Zayed Charitable Foundation; the Islamic Affairs and Charitable Activities Department; the Dubai Charity Association; and the Dar Al Ber Society, all based in the United Arab Emirates (http://fambras.com.br/blog_port/?p=551).

14. CDIAL and WAMY are Sunni institutions. FAMBRAS was founded by a Shi'i businessman but has a generic Islamic religious orientation within the limits of Sunni religiosity.

15. The Senegalese immigrants started to settle in Caxias do Sul in 2011, and an organized Murid community emerged in 2013. The community reached three thousand members at its height, but the economic crisis since 2014 led to the dispersion of its members, who went to other places in Brazil, or to Chile, or returned to Senegal. I thank Renan de Araujo Rodrigues, graduate student in anthropology at the Universidade Federal Fluminense, who did fieldwork research with the Senegalese Murids in Brazil for his master's thesis in 2015, for sharing his data about the Muridiyya.

16. *Tariqa* refers to three distinct, albeit complementary, religious realities: (1) the mystical path toward the Divine reality/truth; (2) the rituals, doctrines, and models of mystical experience of a particular Sufi tradition; and (3) the social organization of this tradition into patterns of power relations and community life. For an overview of the Sufi communities in Brazil, see Mario Alves da Silva Filho, "A Mística Islâmica em Terræ Brasilis: o Sufismo e as Ordens Sufis em São Paulo" (master's thesis, Pontifícia Universidade Católica de São Paulo, 2012), 111–62.

17. For an ethnographic account of converts to Islam in São Paulo and Campinas, see Cristina Maria de Castro, *The Construction of Muslim Identities in Contemporary Brazil* (Lanham, MD: Lexington Books, 2013). For an ethnography of the pedagogical role of sermons among Muslims in Rio de Janeiro, see Gisele Chagas, "Preaching for Converts: Knowledge and Power in the Sunni Community in Rio de Janeiro," in *Ethnographies of Islam: Ritual Performances and Everyday Practices*, ed. Baudoin Dupret, Thomas Pierret, Paulo G. Pinto, and Kathryn Spellman-Poots (Edinburgh: Edinburgh University Press, 2013).

18. The *Salafiyya* is an Islamic reform movement that emerged in the nineteenth century, preaching a return to the "original" Islam of the Prophet and his companions as it was codified in the sacred texts of the Qur'an and the Hadith. In the twentieth century, some trends of the *Salafiyya* were influenced by the stricter literalism of Wahhabi interpretations of Islam, due to the growing influence of Saudi Arabia throughout the Sunni Muslim world.

19. The Tablighi Jamaat was created in India in 1927 with the aim of making Muslims return to the "correct" practice of Islam through the emulation of the Prophet's example. This movement spread throughout India and Pakistan and became globalized through the South Asian diaspora in Europe, the Middle East, and the Americas.

20. Paulo G. Pinto, *Islã: Religião e Civilização, Uma Abordagem Antropológica* (Aparecida: Editora Santuário, 2010), 219; Paulo G. Pinto, "Conversion, Revivalism and Tradition: The Religious Dynamics of Muslim Communities in Brazil," in *Crescent over Another Horizon: Islam in Latin America, the Caribbean, and Latino USA*, ed. Logroño Narbona, Maria del Mar, Paulo G. Pinto, and John Tofik Karam (Austin: University of Texas Press, 2015), 111.

21. On creolization as the constant production of local-global hybrids, see Ulf Hannerz, *Transnational Connections: Culture, People, Places* (London: Routledge, 1996).

22. Interestingly, these ribbons worked as markers of the religious boundaries between the ʿAlawis and the other Muslims in Brazil, but not between them and the larger Brazilian population, for attaching protective ribbons from the church of Nosso Senhor do Bonfim (Our Lord of Bonfim) in Salvador, Bahia, to the wrist is a widespread custom among Brazilian Catholics and followers of African Brazilian religions, occurring even among non-believers and members of other religions.

23. I thank Muna Omran—granddaughter of *shaykh* Hassan Safatli, associate professor of the Graduate Program in Literature at the Universidade Federal Fluminense, and researcher of the history of the ʿAlawi community in Brazil—for sharing the documents pertaining to this trip, including an itinerary handwritten by *shaykh* Safatli and the letter from the Iraqi embassy inviting him to visit the "Islamic centers" (*Marakiz al-Islamiyya*) in the country.

24. For them, the Hajj did not include the visit of the holy places in Medina, because they were living there and used to go to these places as part of their everyday devotions.

25. Sami Isbelle, interview with the author, Muslim Charity Society, Rio de Janeiro, May 14, 2014.

26. Munzer Isbelle, interview with the author, Muslim Charity Society, Rio de Janeiro, May 14, 2014.

27. The process of religious objectification aims to produce self-contained systems based on decontextualized principles. It resembles what Max Weber defines as the processes of "rationalization" of religion. See Dale Eickelman and James Piscatori, *Muslim Politics* (Princeton, NJ: Princeton University Press, 1996), 38; Max Weber, *Economy and Society* (Berkeley: University of California Press, 1978), 439–51.

28. "FAMBRAS organiza viagem para o Hajj 2015," accessed December 20, 2015, http://fambras.com.br/blog_port/?p=551.

29. In 2015, a group of sixteen pilgrims was sponsored to perform the Hajj by FAMBRAS. In 2014, the same institution sponsored a group composed of eight Brazilian pilgrims, one Cuban, one Paraguayan, and one Haitian to perform the ʿUmra. "FAMBRAS organiza viagem para o Hajj 2015"; "Muçulmanos brasileiros realizam a UMRAH com apoio da FAMBRAS," accessed December 20, 2015, http://fambras.com.br/blog_port/?p=257.

30. The Arabic word *shaykh* is used by both Sunnis and Shiʿi in Brazil to refer to their religious leaders.

31. This yearly estimate was given to me by FAMBRAS and Centro Islâmico no Brasil.

32. "FAMBRAS organiza viagem para o Hajj 2015."

33. According to an estimate of the president of the Centro Islâmico no Brasil, when considering all kinds of pilgrimage, the number of pilgrims does not exceed 150 per year. The main pilgrimages are the ʿUmra and the Hajj, with the Shiʿis also doing pilgrimages to the holy sites in Iraq and Iran during ʿashura and arbaʿin.

34. For the concept of "dominant symbol," see Victor Turner, *The Forest of Symbols: Aspects of Ndembu Ritual* (Ithaca, NY: Cornell University Press, 1967), 30–32.

35. It is tempting to attribute this central role of the figure of the Prophet in the pilgrimage to the holy places of Saudi Arabia to influences from the Christian cul-

tural context in which Brazilian Muslims live, besides the Christian background of most Brazilian converts to Islam. However, this would be a culturalistic oversimplification of a more complex phenomenon, for devotion to the figure of the Prophet is widespread throughout the Muslim world and structures the experiential dimension of the ʿUmra/Hajj to many people who were born Muslims in Muslim-majority societies. I heard very similar considerations about the "kind" aspect of Medina, and how feeling the presence of the Prophet and being in connection with him was the most striking part of pilgrimage, from Pakistani and Syrian pilgrims returning from the Hajj in 1999 and 2000.

36. Hassan converted to Islam from Catholicism in 2001. He is the oldest convert of the Muslim community in Recife. Until 2014, he was the only member of the community, besides the *shaykh*, to have done the Hajj.

37. This process allows these symbols to be infused with experiential meanings in a way that is analogous to what Gananath Obeyesekere describes as the configuration of *personal symbols*. Gananath Obeyesekere, *Medusa's Hair: An Essay on Personal Symbols and Religious Experience* (Chicago: University of Chicago Press, 1981).

38. *Carioca* designates people who are born in the city of Rio de Janeiro; *flamenguista* designates a fan of Flamengo, a popular soccer team from Rio de Janeiro.

39. Filho, "A Mística Islâmica em Terræ Brasilis: o Sufismo e as Ordens Sufis em São Paulo," 147.

40. I thank Renan de Araujo Rodrigues for sharing these data about the Muridiyya in Brazil.

41. Clifford Geertz, *Available Light: Anthropological Reflections in Philosophical Topics* (Princeton, NJ: Princeton University Press, 2000), 167–86.

CHAPTER FOUR

Red, White, and Blue
American Muslims on Hajj and the Politics of Pilgrimage

SOPHIA ROSE ARJANA AND ROSE ASLAN

In the 2014 PBS documentary *Sacred Journeys: Hajj*, Anisa Mehdi, a Canadian Muslim journalist, takes her viewers on the pilgrimage known as Hajj with a group of Muslim Americans from Boston. The pilgrims come from diverse backgrounds, and all of them have different reasons for going. Although the Hajj is a sacred journey, pilgrims deal with mundane as well as sensitive issues. Amira Qureishi—a California-born feminist-leaning Muslim chaplain at Wellesley College—expected to have an uninterrupted spiritual experience. But when visiting a mosque in Medina, she finds herself restricted to a separate room for women, which prevents her from viewing the main part of the mosque, which has important religious significance for Muslims. When describing her experience about the gender segregation, Qureishi bursts into tears, caught between the emotions of love and frustration. Viewers watch her struggle to keep her cool and strive for a deep experience while grappling with the gender discrimination that is embedded within the very structure of Saudi society. We follow the ups and downs of Qureishi and the other Boston pilgrims during their stay in Medina, shopping in the malls of Mecca and participating in Hajj rituals. The documentary offers a taste of how American Muslims experience Hajj and highlights the numerous challenges they face traveling as Americans in Saudi Arabia and encountering fellow Muslims from around the world.

In this chapter, we examine the travel narratives of several Muslim Americans who have made the journey to Saudi Arabia for the annual ritual of Hajj. In addition to building on the scholarship that exists regarding American Muslims on Hajj, we hope to provide some insights into the different ways in which they experience the journey. Although an obligatory pillar of Islam, only Muslims with the financial and physical ability to do so perform Hajj. This chapter explores some of the issues presented by U.S. society, particularly economic privilege, that affect the Hajj experience. In the United States, there are numerous Muslim communities exhibiting great diversity in terms of sect, racial and ethnic identity, and politics. Our contribution provides a glimpse into representatives of a few of these communities, which we hope will be both enlightening and provocative. While providing an overview of the logistics of how American Muslims arrange their trips, the chapter provides insight into the core experiences of pilgrims, with a focus on the written narratives of four converts.

Since 2001, Islam's visibility in the United States has grown exponentially. Much of the attention has been focused on political Islam and its relationship to the Cold War, American empire and petro-economics. Over the past fifteen years, scholars have produced numerous studies of Islam for public consumption. Reza Aslan's *No God but God: The Origins, Evolution, and Future of Islam* and Omid Safi's *Memories of Muhammad: Why the Prophet Matters* are two books that offer sound and readable reflections on the history, theology, and practices of Islam.[1] Muslim subjects have also entered popular culture with works such as Sandow Birk's graphic rendition of the holy text in *American Qur'an* and Marvel's most recent superheroine, Ms. Marvel/Kamala Khan, created by G. Willow Wilson.

Scholarship focusing on American Muslims includes Zareena Grewal's monograph *Islam Is a Foreign Country: American Muslims and the Global Crisis of Authority* and Sohail Daulatzai's book on African American Islam and political liberation, *Black Star, Crescent Moon: The Muslim International and Black Freedom beyond America*.[2] Still, far less attention has been placed on the study of American Muslims than on other subjects within Islamic studies thanks to several factors, including the low population of Muslims in the United States (2 percent), the importance of the Arab states due to petro-economics, and the continued focus on political Islam.

Among the topics in Islam in America that are under-studied, American Muslims and their experience of Hajj has received practically no attention. There are no monographs and few academic articles on the topic apart from a short encyclopedia entry in *Encyclopedia of Muslim-American History*.[3] Select ethnographic studies include passing references to Hajj. One example is Zain 'Abdullah's excellent study *Black Mecca: The African Muslims of Harlem*, in which a male Hajj remarks, "Some of them know that I made Hajj [pilgrimage]. So they give me respect for that."[4] The lack of studies focusing on Americans on Hajj leaves many college instructors to rely on the experience of Malcolm X, documented in his autobiography (coauthored by Alex Haley) and in the Spike Lee film based on the autobiography. Malcolm X's transformative experience is iconic, a lesson in the hope Islam provides for racial and political justice. The story of Malcolm X fits perfectly into the Turnerian model of pilgrimage, in which the pilgrim is transformed by the experience of *communitas* and returns to his or her regular life a changed person.[5] However,

Hajj is not life changing for everyone, a fact pointed to by several scholars. For this reason, a broader perspective on the topic is needed, one that is attentive to the myriad of social factors that influence one's pilgrimage experience.

Muslims in America

Muslims have had a presence in the Americas since before the founding of the republic. The earliest report is of Estevanico (also known as Estevan), a Moroccan Muslim slave who accompanied a Spanish expedition on the Colorado River in 1527.[6] It is probable that other Muslims were present on the ships of European explorers who landed in the Caribbean and in South, Central, and North America. With the growth of agricultural industry in the Americas, enslaved Africans—many of whom were Muslim—were brought to work on plantations, in factories, and in other white-owned businesses. Scholars have started to uncover the lives of some of the Muslims from this era. South America had maroon communities, which included escaped Muslim African slaves.[7] In North America, African Muslims were observed performing *salat* and writing in Arabic. These lost histories are only now being recovered by such scholars as Matthew Restall, Samory Rashid, Michael Gomez, and Thomas Parramore.[8]

American Muslims had an early presence in several urban centers, including New York City, Philadelphia, and Boston, as well as in less populated areas, such as the Midwest and the American West. Interestingly, the oldest community buildings are not located on the East Coast but in the Midwest. Cedar Rapids has the second-oldest mosque in the country (the oldest, in North Dakota, burned down in the 1970s). Muslims have also been part of the history of the Southwest and Rocky Mountains. Nabil Echchaibi, a scholar of religion and media at the University of Colorado in Boulder, founded a project that explores the history of Islam in the western region of the United States.[9] Among the stories this project has uncovered are those about the early Sufis of Montana and a Muslim (who happened to be a Hajj) who was hired to explore a camel route from New Mexico and Arizona to California.[10]

Today, American Muslims are small in number, accounting for about 2 percent of the population, a number that is growing but still represents a minor community within the U.S. cultural landscape. The largest demographic of Muslims is African American, with immigrants following and white converts making up the smallest number. Members of all these various groups go on Hajj, in some cases with others from their community and in other cases alone or with family members. What happens while on Hajj—the travel arrangements, accommodations, and company pilgrims keep—is the focus of the second part of this chapter.

Muslims, American Privilege, and Social Capital

American Muslims are not a cohesive, unified community. There are Sunni, Shi'i, African American, Indo-Pakistani, Arab, Indonesian, Persian, Salafi, traditionalist, and progressive Muslims, as well as individuals who are "unmosqued" (who do not attend a mosque because they cannot find one that is accessible or relevant to their lives) and those who are "Supermarket Muslims," leading secular lives except for the holiest month of the Islamic calendar and practicing a "casual" brand of Islam.[11] All these factors affect the experience of those who undertake the journey to Mecca. In particular, we are interested to discover how American exceptionalism and social privilege affect the experiences of some American Muslims who go on Hajj.

Americans are wealthier than the vast majority of Muslims who go on Hajj. The average income of someone from Indonesia, the world's largest Muslim country, is smaller than the average income of a U.S. American by a factor of fifteen.[12] Muslims from less wealthy countries, which include the majority of the world's Muslims living in Asia and Africa, often undertake Hajj when they are older, spending their life's savings on the journey. In some cases, local religious authorities allow a "substitution Hajj" because the cost is so out of reach. For most Americans, the Hajj is not the result of a lifetime of saving funds, or the culmination of a lifetime of waiting, because they can afford to undertake the journey earlier in life.

American Muslims may also be influenced by the cultural practices of exceptionalism and privilege that characterize U.S. society. Jasbir K. Puar describes these practices, or orientations, as being reflected in the "narratives of excellence" that run through American identity, resulting in economic and class divisions like the ones seen among pilgrims on Hajj.[13] These elements of U.S. culture run directly against Islamic teachings on human equality, economic fairness, and social justice, and Hajj as an experience may be complicated by the contradictions between American practices and the religious values many Muslims hold. How this influences the experience of Hajj is an important question, in part because the pilgrimage to Mecca is meant to bring the Muslim closer to God and more conscious of the ethical imperative that the Prophet left humans to "show their heart, their spiritual education, the control of the ego and the blossoming of faith, dignity, goodness, nobleness of soul and, for coherence's sake, commitment among their fellow human beings in the name of their principles."[14] American Muslims must negotiate these religious beliefs within the current milieu, a reality that includes options for Hajj featuring first-class air travel, luxury hotels, and other experiences that are not available to the vast majority of pilgrims who undertake the journey.

Social capital is often described as a product of the social structures in society and the actions of individuals within it, allowing for the achievement of social goals through certain actions, behaviors, and, in the case of religion, rituals.[15] As Coleman describes it, "Like other forms of capital, social capital is productive, making possible the achievement of certain goals that in its absence would not be possible."[16] Hajj is an important producer of social capital due to its prominent role in Islam. Hajj is for many "the religious apex of a Muslim's life."[17] Pilgrims come from vastly different backgrounds, which makes the question of social capital an interesting one because its use varies greatly depending on the individual. As one scholar puts it, "The impact of Hajj on individual aspirations and identities varies greatly and depends on a host of factors, including the status, motives, education, and gender of the pilgrim involved, and the local Islamic context from which he or she departs."[18]

The Hajj creates social capital in the form of a gained status as a "Hajji" (male) or "Hajjia" (female). In some cases, this newly gained status helps social actors negotiate their community better. As one study of Nigerian pilgrims argues, "Rather than enjoying more uniform conduct according to a set of universal and authoritative beliefs, increased travel to Mecca in this case has served to authorize and perpetuate very local practices and beliefs which have long been condemned as un-Islamic."[19] American Muslims also grapple with these issues of orthodoxy, status, and social capital. However, they experience Hajj differently, often within pilgrim communities that are American and European and apart from their fellow Muslims from Asia, Africa, and the Middle East. The question we turn to now is, How does this affect the American Muslim experience of Hajj?

The Logistics of Hajj

While Hajj is a strenuous five-day ritualized pilgrimage, 'Umra takes only a few hours to complete and can be done many times by pilgrims staying in Mecca. In the United States, preparing for Hajj is quite simple, and the facilities offered to Western Muslims are luxurious compared to those afforded to pilgrims on smaller budgets. Whereas Muslims in Muslim-majority countries must wait their turn to go on Hajj because of the quota imposed by Saudi Arabia and might only be allowed to go once in their lifetime, Muslim Americans are permitted to go every five years. In the twenty-first century, Hajj was performed annually by up to twelve thousand Muslim Americans out of 2.5 million pilgrims from around the world; and in 2013, fourteen thousand Americans went on Hajj.[20]

Pilgrims must first choose a travel agency, as it is very difficult to procure a pilgrimage visa without help. There are numerous routes that pilgrims choose, including (1) joining a Hajj group from their local mosque if available, which offers the added bonus of the possibility of traveling with friends and making friends from the same city or location; (2) signing up for a trip with a well-known religious leader they respect and admire, who leads the tour through a travel agency; (3) using a travel agency recommended by friends or family members; or (4) conducting extensive online searches and making use of Hajj tour review websites, such as HajjRatings.com. Many potential pilgrims are able to find a trustworthy tour group or travel agency by visiting HajjRatings.com, which is run by a group of volunteers in an undisclosed location. The website covers Hajj companies from around the world, but most ratings seem to focus on tour companies from North America and the UK. Because there are numerous people trolling the website and writing negative reviews, it can be difficult to find accurate ratings of certain Hajj groups, but based on the ratings and extensive reviews, there seems to be a consensus for when a company is doing a decent job or failing its clients. A handful of companies stand out as being high quality, well organized, and helpful, while others have a number of unfavorable reviews, which accuse them of being crooks and complain about the terrible accommodations, logistical difficulties, and preferential treatment for high-paying pilgrims. Hajj might be a spiritual journey, but the companies that arrange the trips make a profit from their services and may find ways to cut corners to the detriment of their customers. At the same time, the logistics of putting together a Hajj tour and pleasing hundreds of customers/pilgrims among millions of other pilgrims is one of the most difficult logistical challenges for travel agencies. Some agencies have mentioned that they are unable to provide a "stress-free experience," which is a challenge, as Americans in general have exceedingly high expectations for travel facilities, stemming from a "customer is always right" attitude.[21]

Because of strict visa regulations, the Saudi Arabian Ministry of Hajj allows only a select list of Muslim-owned travel agencies based in the United

States to offer their services to American Muslims. The majority of American pilgrims book packages at five-star hotels, with economy packages offered for four-star hotels. Tour agencies offer various options to pilgrims, such as hotels that are close to the holy mosques in Mecca and Medina, VIP tent accommodations near Jamarat in Mina, and add-on package tours to nearby cities such as Amman, Jerusalem, and Cairo. A deluxe Hajj package booked from a reputable travel agent in Pakistan costs between $4,900 and $6,800. In Egypt every year, ten thousand pilgrims are lucky enough to win the Hajj lottery, which is subsidized by the government, includes round-trip airfare and rooms in three- or four-star hotels, and is worth between $3,000 and $5,000.[22]

One of the best-known U.S.-based Hajj companies is Dar El Salam Islamic World Travel (DES), which has offices in New York, Florida, Texas, California, and Canada. DES was established in 1985 and claims to have served thousands of clients and to have representatives in more than thirty cities around the world. As scholars can be a big draw for specific Hajj packages, DES has a page on its website that lists some of the scholars who lead its Hajj tours. These scholars include many prominent Muslim leaders (almost all of them men) based in the United States, such as Khalid Latif, Yasir Qadhi, Muzammil Siddiqi, and Mohamed Magid Yasmin Mogahed. Their presence guarantees that the company will draw large numbers of clients and has most definitely helped cement Dar El Salam's reputation as one of the most popular U.S. Hajj tour companies. However, DES is not cheap; it offers only luxurious packages for the well-off, beginning with its deluxe package and then increasing in price with its super-deluxe package and finally its executive program. Hajj packages start at $9,100 for the most basic trip of more than two weeks; the super-deluxe package is about $13,000, and the executive package is $15,500.[23]

A more reasonably priced Hajj tour agency, Al-Manasik, has received high ratings and reviews on HajjRatings.com and provides comfortable packages for middle-class American pilgrims. Al-Manasik's packages start at $7,995 and increase to $10,995 for a more luxurious package. Prices for packages always go up with room choice; the numbers given here reflect the price for a package trip that puts pilgrims in rooms with three other people of the same sex. Tour agencies like Al-Manasik place less importance on tour leaders and more on providing comfortable and organized tours. Al-Manasik often recruits American students studying in Saudi Arabia or local guides who are fluent in English to lead its groups instead of well-known Muslim American scholars. Pilgrims pay significantly more money to be placed in a triple or double room. The prices of packages differ based on four- or five-star accommodations or an apartment in the suburbs, the hotel's proximity to the sacred sites, and the location and size of tent accommodations in Mina and 'Arafat.[24]

Once pilgrims register with a tour agency and pay a hefty deposit, they must send the necessary documents through the travel agency to receive a Hajj or 'Umra visa. Men with "Muslim" names face few difficulties receiving a visa, but women and converts have more obstacles in meeting the visa requirements. All converts to Islam must submit a copy of their *shahada*, or document of conversion, notarized by an Islamic center with their visa application to ensure their genuine conversion to Islam. Male pilgrims receive independent Hajj or 'Umra visas, but women receive visas that list a *mahram*—a male relative or their husband—as their travel companion and guardian. All women under the age of forty-five must be accompanied by a *mahram*; women forty-five and over can travel alone within a group but must submit a notarized letter from their husband, son, or brother giving them permission to go on pilgrimage. Unmarried female converts have the biggest problem getting a visa because they generally lack a Muslim *mahram*, and their non-Muslim male relatives would not be able to accompany them to Mecca, as non-Muslims are not allowed inside the sacred cities. Female converts are sometimes able to get a visa to travel with a Hajj group, but typically they must be married and travel with their husband.

Before going on Hajj, pilgrims often attend classes at their local mosque on the rituals and etiquette of Hajj and 'Umra or take an online class and watch informational videos online. They also collect the required ritual Hajj items, borrowing them from friends who have already gone on Hajj, ordering them online, or receiving them as part of their Hajj tour package. Men must acquire an *ihram* garment, which consists of two white towels and open-toed shoes. Although women do not have to wear a specific garment, they often buy special outfits for Hajj, including all-white cotton dresses and scarves, which are available from online Islamic clothing stores. Pilgrims also purchase useful travel items for the intense journey, such as portable hooks for hanging items in the bathrooms; pain medication; money belts to protect their valuables from thieves; umbrellas for men, who are not allowed to wear anything on their heads during Hajj; unscented shampoo, conditioner, and lotion (the wearing of scents is forbidden during Hajj); and guidebooks for Hajj and 'Umra rituals.

Muslim American Hajj Narratives

Although we have a handful of Hajj narratives from American pilgrims from the twentieth century, we have hundreds, if not thousands, of narratives available in published form as well as in blogs, Twitter, Tumblr, Facebook, Snapchat, and other social media outlets from the twenty-first century.[25] Earlier American Hajj pilgrims—such as Malcolm X, who made his pilgrimage in 1964—focused primarily on spiritual awakenings and social issues, and these topics are still at the forefront of many modern American pilgrim narratives. Additionally, modern American pilgrims encounter and discuss challenging situations brought on by modernity. Examples include the destruction of historical mosques and other sacred heritage sites in Mecca and Medina to make way for renovations, new hotels, and luxury malls; technology embedded in religious rituals, such as a Hajj metro line, traffic lights in the ritual walk between Safa and Marwa in the Grand Mosque of Mecca, and a golden clock tower that looms above the Grand Mosque of Mecca; the ubiquity of cell phones and selfies; and constant connection to the world through the internet. While pilgrims often make the intention to detox from technology and from their lives back home, they find that Mecca and Medina are not immune to modernity; as a result, they often struggle to connect with their Creator and focus on worship while surrounded by modern technology and materialism.

Although much more research needs to be done on the many Muslim American pilgrimage narratives available, this study closely examines the writings of four American pilgrims, three of whom went on Hajj in the twenty-first century and one who went on Hajj in the 1990s.[26] All four are converts to Islam who offer exceedingly different perspectives on Islam and their experience of the Hajj. The four were chosen either because they are widely known among Muslim Americans and beyond or because they have a unique take on the Hajj.

One engaging online Hajj narrative is by Amina Wadud, a well-known Muslim scholar. Wadud is an African American convert to Islam, best known for her work on gender in Islam. Wadud has written several widely read books, including *Qur'an and Woman: Rereading the Sacred Text from a Woman's Perspective* and *Inside the Gender Jihad: Reform in Islam*. In 2010, Wadud went on Hajj on her own (without a *mahram*) with an American tour group. Her scholarly background and expertise in Islam were instrumental in her insightful observations, which were often critical, reverent, and scholarly. Wadud blogged on a regular basis while she prepared to go on Hajj, during Hajj, and upon her return.

Even before she reached Mecca, Wadud immediately began to feel connected with other pilgrims, starting during her layover in the Paris airport: "I am with them. They are with me and we are part of what will eventually swarm to three million persons!"[27] As soon as she reached the Jeddah airport, Wadud described the chaotic process of entering through Saudi Arabian customs. She shuffled from window to window trying to figure out what she needed to do to go through customs and eventually resorted to speaking English to ensure that the government employees would treat her more respectfully than pilgrims from developing countries.[28] Wadud used English throughout her journey in Saudi Arabia in the hope of receiving preferential, or at least decent, treatment from storekeepers, government employees, and others.

Wadud writes in detail about getting from the airport to the hotel, describing the logistical nightmare and haphazard and dirty state of the bus.[29] She praises the beauty and magnetism of the Haram (the area around the holy cities) and of her fellow pilgrims, but she is careful to point out gender discrimination and segregation. She notes that "priority seating on the first floor of the Haram is given to the men, with male and female security guards shuffling women out of their spots to give way to men, creating men's sections in a way that is more intrusive or abrasive than what I've observed and practiced everywhere else here." Women are restricted to sitting in certain locations in the mosque, and she notes that the gender police (whom she refers to as the "guardians of the 'this sacred space is too sacred for you women, so give it up to the men'") vigilantly watched out for what they considered to be inappropriate gender interactions.[30] Being a Muslim feminist, Wadud is deeply perturbed by the favoritism for male pilgrims she sees in Mecca. Despite the euphoria she experienced, she is aware that Mecca is not a spiritual utopia.

The self-published Hajj narrative *Mecca and the Hajj: Lessons from the Islamic School of Hard Knocks*, from 2006, is by Jane Straitwell, a white American convert. Straitwell provides an almost too honest look at the Hajj, including the negative and positive aspects of her journey. Having converted to Islam primarily because of her hate for president George W. Bush, Straitwell went on Hajj soon after becoming Muslim to learn more about her newly embraced religion. In her book, Straitwell comes across as a naive, cynical, and pampered woman, focused on indulging herself and her anxieties. At the

FIGURE 4.1 Religious souvenirs, Mecca (photograph by author).

beginning of her book, written in diary form, Straitwell writes of her many doubts about whether she should go on Hajj, as she was turned off by the Imam who held classes at the mosque on Hajj; by the thought of wearing a headscarf for an entire month, which would give her a headache; and by the fear of losing her new job.[31] She struggled with the headscarf, calling it "my freaking Hajj Halloween costume on my freaking head."[32] While on Hajj, Straitwell had to deal with an incompetent tour agency, culture shock, and numerous challenges to her comfort zone. At times, she would see her fellow pilgrims as obstacles on her spiritual journey. When beginning her circumambulation around the Ka'ba, Straitwell expressed, perhaps ironically, that although the pilgrims were there to engage in the pilgrimage rites, it seemed to her that "their ulterior motive for being there was just to smush poor sweet me."[33] More often than not, Straitwell seems to be disappointed and upset by her newfound coreligionists for not living up to her interpretation of Islam through the lens of American exceptionalism and white feminism.

Straitwell did not appear to interact with many non-American pilgrims, looked down on many of them, and made conjectures about their lives without speaking with them: "I never saw so many Indonesian Muslims in my life. Many of them looked really poor, like peasants. I wondered if so many of them came as a result of the tsunami. . . . Three out of four people here look like lowly peasants. . . . The image of 500,000 airborne African and Indonesian peasants is staggering."[34] Being in a foreign land with Muslims from exotic places gave her a magical feeling, but she maintained her standards by staying at a four-star hotel.[35] Like many American pilgrims, Straitwell was fascinated by the clothing worn by pilgrims from around the world and called it the "Mecca fashion parade."[36] Using toilets was also a challenge for her, and she avoided using squat toilets as much as possible.[37] As for the tent city in Mina, she considered it to be the "Girl Scout camp from hell!"[38] On numerous occasions, Straitwell was inconvenienced by non-Western lower-class pilgrims. At one such time, while stuck on the tour bus, she complained that she wanted to pray outside but could not, as many pilgrims were camped out outside the bus.[39] She was constantly on a search for conveniences she was used to in the United States, such as ice cream and donuts and Western-style toilets, and she whines about having had to spend six hours in the "dirt-poor, third-world section in Arafat," as if she barely survived rubbing shoulders with those she considered lower than herself.[40] Her description of the "poor" pilgrims is cringe-worthy; for instance, she refers to the "poor schmucks" who sell "pathetic little objects on pathetic little blankets."[41]

Straitwell had numerous encounters with Muslim men that left a bitter taste in her mouth. Once, when trying to pray in al-Safa, a man told her she could not pray where she was, and she called him a "rude chauvinist pig."[42] Her encounters with Muslim men and women over gender issues show how women are held to different standards. Whereas male pilgrims seldom mentioned being lectured to or chastised for the way they were acting, Straitwell records countless interactions where this occurred. Straitwell's response to these people was "Get over it, I'm never going to change. Let's form a truce, 'I'll act more lady-like and you take your mind out of the gutter.'"[43] Straitwell evidently enjoyed getting into pointless debates with men about her interpretation of religion, randomly engaging male pilgrims in discussions on this topic. Once, she instigated a debate with a male pilgrim about the legitimacy of Amina Wadud leading mixed prayers in New York and was shocked and mortified when he spoke out against it. Her response to a Sudanese pilgrim was to insult his entire country by claiming that Sudan is a country where "a million women were raped."[44]

The Hajj narratives from female pilgrims offer a very different take on Hajj than that of the male pilgrims, revealing the many ways in which women are treated differently in the Saudi Kingdom. At the same time, Straitwell's attitude reveals her persistence in upholding her interpretation of Islam as the only correct version despite being a brand-new convert, not unlike the strident Wahhabi perspective on religion.

While most pilgrims write about Hajj in a primarily reverent modality, Michael Muhammad Knight, in *Journey to the End of Islam*, approached his Hajj with his own biases and perceptions of Saudi Arabia. Before going on Hajj, his Muslim girlfriend, who had previously been on 'Umra, told him that Mecca was a "really beautiful place in the middle of a really ugly place. I wish it could have been somewhere else," and Knight adopted this approach for his own Hajj ordeal.[45] Knight's narrative weaves between critiquing the Saudi government and its Wahhabi ideology, giving historical backgrounds on the rituals and sacred spaces, and ruminating on the feelings and emotions that arose during his pilgrimage.

The tent city in Mina is organized by nationalities, with North American, European, and Turkish pilgrims sharing the same area in a relatively nice part of the vast temporary city. Knight describes staying in tight accommodations in the tent city of Mina as like being at summer camp. Since he had signed up for a luxurious Hajj package, he was plied with refreshments and three square meals a day.[46] Knight describes his section as a "gated community"; outside the gates, he would encounter beggars and sub-Saharan Africans, but inside he mingled with Rolex-wearing Pakistani American uncles.[47] Knight was aware of his privilege and savored the comfort of his trip, although he tried to make up for it by helping other pilgrims during his Hajj.

After finishing his 'Umra and getting his head shaven, Knight did not share a spiritual revelation with his readers. Rather, he blatantly states that "for the time being, I wasn't a pilgrim anymore, just a dude in Mecca at a 5-star hotel with breakfast and dinner buffets and internet access, and I could cut my nails and wear blue jeans again."[48] Knight juxtaposed his experiences inside the spiritually potent al-Masjid al-Haram with the neighborhood located directly outside the mosque. He ate at the Burger King, where the cash register displayed "Holy Mosque Have It Your Way." The surreal experience of eating a Beef Royale combo meal next to the most sacred Muslim space in the world was not lost on Knight. He noted, "It was easy to feel like the Haram had lost something in the modern era, landing somewhere between the Stone Age and Saudi Disney, but it wasn't all gone. . . . The real was still there, and I hope that I could unlock it, insha'Allah, if I was willing to get weird."[49] In Medina, Knight also complained about the materialism that was prevalent in the city. "I stayed away from the Prophet's mosque surrounded by Starbucks and KFC and Hardee's, but can we even call it the Prophet's Mosque? Did anyone really think he'd [the Prophet] want it that way? When 'Ali bought Fatima a gold necklace, the Prophet called it a necklace of fire, so she sold it and bought freedom for slaves with the money. But the Saudi kings thought of themselves as heirs to the other enshrined bodies. . . . It wasn't the Prophet's Mosque, not anymore."[50] Similar to many modern Hajj pilgrims, Knight was attracted to the spirituality of the Grand Mosque while disgusted by the materialism that surrounded him throughout the holy city of Mecca. He was attuned to Saudi hypocrisy, witnessing displays of piety side by side with displays of extravagance and preferential treatment for wealthy pilgrims.

Knight's narrative contains a plethora of critiques of the Saudis and their treatment of sacred spaces connected to the Prophet Muhammad and other early Muslim figures. On his trip to the Mountain of Light (Jabal al-Nur), where the Prophet Muhammad first received the Qur'anic revelation from God, Knight found the site in disarray and full of litter. He posited that the neglect indicated the Saudi government's disapproval of pilgrims visiting the site.[51] Despite his attempts to pray and meditate at the Cave, he found the rush of the people and crowds to be tiring, explaining, "I only thought of the people fighting for a chance to sit there, expecting some magical power from the spot, and my own hypocrisy, since I had only added to the crowd. Maybe the Saudis were right in discouraging visits to this place, since it seemed to bring out the superstitious bullshit side of religion."[52] Knight was constantly reminded of what he saw as Saudi hypocrisy during his trip to Mecca and Medina: while visiting the Jannat al-Baqi cemetery in Medina, he kept noticing signs and warnings against practices that Saudis disapproved of, especially around the graves of the imams. He tried to understand the Saudi perspective, but he ultimately concluded that "they [Saudis] ruined it by installing shaykhs and religion cops to harass everyone."[53] Knight is often let down by his high expectations for experiencing heightened spirituality on his Hajj, only to be disappointed in his own self as well as fellow pilgrims and the actions of the Saudi government.

Another widely distributed Hajj narrative is that of Michael Wolfe, who, like Knight, is a white male convert to Islam. As one of the first widely distributed books on Hajj by an American (other than Malcolm X), Wolfe's book *The Hadj: An American's Pilgrimage to Mecca* has a devotional tone. His narrative conveys his piety during his journey, but his status as an American and, perhaps even more importantly, as a man reveals his perspective and privilege. The first half of the book is concerned with his long-term stay in Morocco, and the second half focuses on his Hajj journey. Throughout the book, Wolfe shows his particular interest in his fellow travelers as being exotic, especially people wearing "traditional" clothing. Wolfe is constantly struck by the shared humanity of the pilgrims as well as their differences as revealed in their traditional clothing.

Once Wolfe began his Hajj and donned the *ihram* garment, he was greatly affected, noting that "the uniform cloth defeats class distinctions and cultural fashion. Rich and poor are lumped together . . . looking like penitents in a Bosch painting. The ihram is as democratic as a death shroud."[54] Whereas Knight goes back and forth, giving historical background, snippets of conversations with people, and his own take on the sites and rituals, Wolfe narrates information given to him without much of his own perspective. Wolfe was constantly in a state of awe of the religious structures, people from foreign lands, and new rituals that he encountered on a frequent basis. Wolfe encountered few problems and, because of his status as a well-known American Muslim convert, was presumably treated very well by Saudi officials.

As previously noted, male and female pilgrims experience Hajj differently, and male pilgrims hold much more privilege because of their gender. Both Wolfe and Knight went on pilgrimage on their own, without female relatives, and thus were completely separated from the female pilgrims and had barely any interaction with them. Knight describes the women as almost invisible and remarks that they appeared to disperse to their own spaces in mysterious ways. Wolfe seemed to have had few brushes with women; almost all the people he mentions encountering during his journey were men. Wolfe describes the communal experience of wearing *ihram* without taking into consideration that women were not dressed in the same way. At the same time, Knight was highly aware of the privilege he received as an American on a VIP Hajj package and as a man. He often tried to use his privilege to assist other pilgrims, such as women trying to pray in tight places, but still felt some guilt for the amount of privilege he had in comparison to that of many of the pilgrims around him. Wadud was aware of the privilege she had as an American, although she was less privileged than the male pilgrims due to her gender. Because she can speak Arabic and pass for an Egyptian, she can switch between identities depending on the situation. Wadud experienced a sense of unity with the pilgrims around her, especially the women she met as they prayed together and challenged the status quo by refusing to stick to the dedicated women's area. In contrast to Wadud's often humble demeanor, Straitwell was unaware of her many privileges and suffered as a consequence. Because of the challenges and culture shock she faced throughout her trip, Straitwell gained little from her Hajj and returned bitter and resentful of her newly embraced religion.

Despite the different backgrounds of the four Muslim authors discussed here, there are a number of themes that they all took note of during their Hajj: (1) they were fascinated by people's traditional clothing outside of Hajj and appreciated seeing all the male pilgrims donning the white *ihram* garment; (2) they underwent a form of culture shock from being in Saudi Arabia, a country whose norms and values are the polar opposite of those in America; (3) they were enthralled by their interactions with people from around the world, although they had instances of discomfort due to their inability to communicate and their perception that their personal space was invaded; and (4) they all had a mixture of positive and negative experiences, at times undergoing intense feelings of reverence and ecstasy at the Kaʿba combined with disgust when observing the commercialization of the Hajj, the commodification of religion, the lack of organization and cleanliness, and the cruelty of the religious police toward anyone who deviated from normative Wahhabi doctrine and practices. Most notably, male pilgrims have much more privilege than female pilgrims, who are faced with constant vigilance and chastisement by the religious police and mosque guards.

Conclusion

Upon arrival home from Hajj, American pilgrims, like their fellow Muslims around the world, are feted by friends. Muslim communities will hold Hajj parties for pilgrims, where friends and family celebrate their new status as Hajji or Hajjia. At these gatherings, pilgrims are asked to narrate their Hajj experience, focusing on the spiritual lessons. In Mecca and Medina, pilgrims spend a part of their time shopping for gifts, picking up items like prayer beads, dates, perfume, incense, prayer rugs, copies of the Qurʾan, Islamic books, headscarves and *abayas* (dresses) for women, *thawbs* (robes) and hats for men, and other items available from vendors in the many malls, street stalls, and markets of the two cities. Most importantly, pilgrims obtain large plastic containers containing water from the sacred Zamzam spring in Mecca. Apart from sharing their Hajj with fellow Muslims, Muslim Americans who are involved in interfaith engagement are often invited to speak about their Hajj experience at churches, synagogues, and other religious communities. Muslim Americans Hajj pilgrims have been sharing stories of their experiences for many decades, and their journeys on Hajj offer a window into one aspect of their ritual lives.

Muslim pilgrims from around the world go on Hajj every year (and ʿUmra throughout the year) to engage in a communal experience of fulfilling one of the five pillars of Islam. While wealthy Muslims from both non-Western and Western countries uniformly enjoy a luxurious Hajj vacation, many pilgrims from less privileged backgrounds endure much more difficult Hajj journeys with few luxuries. Even the most reasonable Hajj trips for Muslim American pilgrims are somewhat equivalent to VIP pilgrimage trips for pilgrims from non-Western countries, which means that almost all Americans who go on Hajj have access to facilities and accommodations that few Muslims from developing countries have. Despite the fact that Islam brings them together into the *umma*, or imagined Muslim community, and that they perform the same rituals, pilgrims have different experiences of Hajj based on their nationality, financial means, preconceptions, and personalities.

Notes

1. Reza Aslan, *No God but God: The Origins, Evolution, and Future of Islam* (New York: Random House, 2005); Omid Safi, *Memories of Muhammad: Why the Prophet Matters* (New York: HarperOne, 2010).

2. Zareena Grewal, *Islam Is a Foreign Country: American Muslims and the Global Crisis of Authority* (New York: NYU Press, 2013); Sohail Daulatzai, *Black Star, Crescent Moon: The Muslim International and Black Freedom beyond America* (Minneapolis, University of Minnesota Press, 2012).

3. Maria F. Curtis, "Hajj," in *Encyclopedia of Muslim-American History*, ed. Edward E. Curtis (New York: Facts on File, 2010).

4. Zain Abdullah, *Black Mecca: The African Muslims of Harlem* (New York: Oxford University Press, 2010), 125.

5. Mark MacWilliams, "Virtual Pilgrimages on the Internet," *Religion* 32, no. 1 (2002): 325.

6. Abdin Chande, "Islam in the African American Community: Negotiating between Black Nationalism and Historical Islam," *Islamic Studies* 47, no. 2 (2008): 222.

7. Samory Rashid, "Toward Understanding America's Islamic Legacy," *Islamic Studies* 38, no. 2 (1999): 353.

8. Matthew Restall, "Black Conquistadors: Armed Africans in Early Spanish America," *Americas* 57, no. 2 (2000): 171–205; Matthew Restall and Jane Landers, "The African Experience in Early Spanish America," *Americas* 57, no. 2 (2000): 167–70; Samory Rashid, *Black Muslims in the U.S.: History, Politics, and the Struggle of a Community* (New York: Palgrave Macmillan, 2013); Michael A. Gomez, "Muslims in Early America," *Journal of Southern History* 60, no. 4 (1994): 671–710; Thomas C. Parramore, "Muslim Slave Aristocrats in North Carolina," *North Carolina Historical Review* 77, no. 2 (2000): 127–50.

9. Elena Draper, "CU Boulder Team Breaks Ground on Research on Rocky Mountain Muslims," *Denver Post*, January 27, 2011.

10. *Sacred Lines: Muslims in the Mountain West*, Center for Media, Religion and Culture, November 27, 2013, https://www.colorado.edu/cmrc/2013/11/27/sacred-lines-muslims-mountain-west.

11. Jane I. Smith, *Islam in America* (New York: Columbia University Press, 1999), 21.

12. "GDP Per Capita (Current US$)," http://data.worldbank.org/indicator/NY.GDP.PCAP.CD.

13. Jasbir K. Puar, *Terrorist Assemblages: Homonationalism in Queer Times* (Durham, NC: Duke University Press, 2007), 5.

14. Tariq Ramadan, *In the Footsteps of the Prophet: Lessons from the Life of Muhammad* (New York: Oxford University Press, 2007), 197.

15. Andrew Greeley, "Coleman Revisited: Religious Structures as a Source of Social Capital," *American Behavioral Scientist* 40, no. 5 (1997): 588.

16. James S. Coleman, "Social Capital in the Creation of Human Capital," *American Journal of Sociology* 94 (1988): 98.

17. Reza Aslan, introduction to *One Thousand Roads to Mecca: Ten Centuries of Travelers Writing about the Muslim Pilgrimage*, ed. Michael Wolfe (New York, Grove Press, 1998), xiii.

18. Susan O'Brien, "Pilgrimage, Power, and Identity: The Role of Hajj in the Lives of Nigerian Hausa Bori Adepts," *Africa Today* 46, no. 3/4 (1999): 13.

19. O'Brien, 34.

20. Curtis, "Hajj," 223; Mas'ood Cajee, *American Hajj* (Department of State, International Information Programs, 2014).

21. Curtis, "Hajj," 226.

22. "10,000 Muslims Win Hajj Lottery Packages," *Cairo Post*, April 3, 2015, http://thecairopost.youm7.com/news/144593/inside_egypt/10000-muslims-won-in-Hajj-lottery; Abdel Razek Al-Shuwekhi, "13,000 Pilgrims Arrive in Saudi Arabia for Hajj: Tourism Ministry," *Daily News Egypt*, September 22, 2014, http://dailynewsegypt.com/2014/09/22/13000-pilgrims-arrive-saudi-arabia-Hajj-tourism-ministry/.

23. Home page, www.darelsalam.com.

24. Home page, www.almanasik.com.

25. During the 2015 Hajj, Snapchat dedicated a channel for pilgrims to share their Hajj experiences, and Snapchat users around the world were exposed to the Hajj through this medium. See "Watch SnapChat's Live Story from Mecca during the 27th Night of Ramadan," *Ummah Wide*, July 13, 2015, https://ummahwide.com/watch-snapchat-s-live-story-from-mecca-during-the-27th-night-of-ramadan-aef20e1d8d50.

26. Amina Wadud, "Hajj Journal—Makkah Experiences," *Religion Dispatches*, November 2, 2011, available at http://www.patheos.com/resources/additional-resources/2011/11/amina-waduds-hajj-journal-makkah-experiences-11-02-2011; Amina Wadud, "Hajj Journal—On the Plains of Arafat," *Religion Dispatches*, November 3, 2011, available at http://www.patheos.com/resources/additional-resources/2011/11/amina-waduds-hajj-journal-on-the-plains-of-arafat-11-03-2011; Jane Straitwell, *Mecca and the Hajj: Lessons from the Islamic School of Hard Knocks* (Berkeley, CA: Straitwell Travel Books, 2006); Michael Muhammad Knight, *Journey to the End of Islam* (Berkeley,

CA: Counterpoint, 2009); Michael Wolfe, *The Hadj: An American's Pilgrimage to Mecca* (New York: Atlantic Monthly Press, 1993).

27. Wadud, "Hajj Journal—Makkah Experiences," 3.
28. Wadud, 4.
29. Wadud, 6.
30. Wadud, 7.
31. Straitwell, *Mecca and the Hajj*, 14.
32. Straitwell, 33.
33. Straitwell, 30.
34. Straitwell, 31–35.
35. Straitwell, 50.
36. Straitwell, 52.
37. Straitwell, 54.
38. Straitwell, 85.
39. Straitwell, 90.
40. Straitwell, 91.
41. Straitwell, 101–2.
42. Straitwell, 45.
43. Straitwell, 65.
44. Straitwell, 90.
45. Knight, *Journey to the End of Islam*, 198.
46. Knight, 324.
47. Knight, 365.
48. Knight, 255.
49. Knight, 263.
50. Knight, 312.
51. Knight, 270.
52. Knight, 273.
53. Knight, 300.
54. Wolfe, *The Hadj*, 156.

PART II | Embodiment, Memory, and Materiality

CHAPTER FIVE

Pilgrimages of the Dream
On Wings of State in Sehwan Sharif, Pakistan

OMAR KASMANI

> He came for me and said, "Child." I said, "Yes, *baba*." He said, "Do you wish to do *ziyara*?" I said, "Yes, I wish to do so." And what *ziyara* he made me do!
>
> —AKRAM

Every time Akram narrated his_her story of pilgrimage to Sehwan Sharif in Sindh, Pakistan, s_he would return to a richly detailed dream sequence from his_her childhood. For it was in a dream that Akram first performed *ziyara*, that is to say a pilgrimage or a viewing of a holy relic, place, or person. In time, this pilgrimage of the dream would turn out to be the blueprint for an eventual journey to Sehwan prompting an intersex child to abandon home and family.[1] But what had first captured the imagination of the nine-year-old was a winged creature that unfailingly appeared on the sky each time Akram retired for the night. Baffled by the vision of the returning bird, Akram would share the contents of the dream with his_her mother. It was of no significance, she would say, dismissing its recurrence as an ordinary nightmare. Years later, however, having arrived in the pilgrimage town, Akram would come to the understanding that the bird in question was indeed a royal falcon (*shahbaz*), whose incessant appearance in the dream was in fact a premonition of a journey that s_he was to eventually undertake in pursuit of the falcon-saint of Sehwan, Lal Shahbaz Qalandar (d. 1274).[2]

That journeys to holy sites are divinely sanctioned, that saints are found through dreams, or that believers are called to saints' shrines in waking visions is hardly news when it comes to pilgrims' accounts of places of pilgrimage. But not always do dreams and visions simply occur. Often they are evoked by the tactical exercise of sleeping on hallowed ground, like that of shrines and cemeteries; they are invited, also anticipated, through intimate exchanges with Sufi bodies and persons; and, in some cases, they are enabled and intervened in via processes of the state.[3] To illustrate how the relationship between saints and their devotees comes to be mediated through offices of the state is particularly relevant to this discussion given that since the early

1960s, religious endowments in Pakistan have been administered under the bureaucratic structures of the state within the framework of the Ministry of Religious Affairs and the Auqaf Department.[4] Under this new order, saints' shrines were no longer considered private holdings and their tombs not always deemed familial inheritance.

If public administration of shrines changes the physical experience of a saint's place—for example, through urban redesign of devotional centers and architectural modifications in shrine space—its stake in the shrine's symbolic aspects must not escape our attention.[5] In her evocative work on dreams at Egyptian shrines, Amira Mittermaier has highlighted the importance of apprehending the correspondences between physical aspects of shrine-space and its dialogical counterpart, dream-space, without which, she has argued, any understanding of saints' places is incomplete at best.[6] For example, one of the four ways in which shrines and dreams are interrelated, she explains, is that dreams transport dreamers to specific shrines.[7] Following in her footsteps, I attend to dreams, pilgrimages, and pilgrimages of the dream, but in this case to illustrate the ways in which the Pakistani state's interest in saints' places exceeds its material dividends. What this suggests is that such intervention also comes to shape the contours of the places' imaginal and dialogical spheres, where imagination does not stand for something arbitrary, unreal, or fictive but points instead to its sensorial, creative, and visionary potentials.

Dreaming the saint is not what is novel in Akram's story of pilgrimage. What is remarkable is the manner in which Akram's dreams correspond to the specific imaginary of the saint and the contemporary trajectory of the shrine of Sehwan in its post-nationalization period. What this means is that in discussing the scope of governmentality—that is, a tactical arrangement, in this case of saints, shrines, and pilgrimages—we ought to make conceptual room for the charismatic reserve and symbolic resourcefulness of saintly figures and settings, of which the state as medium not only partakes but also *disposes*, sometimes through affective means, guiding spiritual as well as embodied exchanges between subjects and saints of the state.[8] Akram's dreams are therefore better read in tandem with wider social and co-constitutive processes, like a mediatization of the saint of Sehwan. Since its public takeover in 1960, Sehwan's shrine has benefited from conditions that enable and promote access to its charismatic reserve through a systematic and tactical proliferation of texts: songs, legends, fairs, films, and images, as well as dreams. To illustrate this point, I first present Akram's sequenced account of the dreams, one of many that were narrated to me on several occasions during fieldwork.⁹ This particular one was audio-recorded in November 2013. I then turn to a brief survey of the changing life and times of Sehwan since the nationalization of shrines in Pakistan.¹⁰

The Dreams of Akram

There is a precise sequence to the dreams that would eventually lead a young Akram from his_her village in the Punjab in search of an enigmatic saint. There is also an order of events and places through which Akram would eventually come to understand that the destination his_her dreams were pointing toward was in fact Sehwan. However, what had first set into action this geography of visions and destinations was indeed a film song.¹¹ More interestingly, the song feature and its opening lines are interlaced in Akram's telling of dreams, revealing a fascinating confluence of the lyrical with the visual.

> At night, we used to play an [audio] cassette, the people of the village would play [a song]: *Shahbaz kare parwaz te jane raz dilan de* (Shahbaz goes into flight; for known to him are the secrets of the heart!) . . . I would listen to it . . . and while listening to it I would fall asleep. In the morning, when the mullah would give the call for prayer, in the early hours a dream would come to me: there is a garden and in it I would go. The fruits that are unripe and green, those I would pick and place them in the folds [*jholi*] of my long shirt. When I would put it in the *jholi*, a gardener would come to me. As the gardener approaches, he asks, "What is it in your *jholi*?" He asks me thrice. The first time he asks what is there in my *jholi*, I remain quiet. Then a second time he inquires, "Child, what is it?" I know that I have stolen it, I have plucked the unripe fruit. And in his hand is a stick. I am afraid that he might just hit me! What can I tell him that I have stealthily picked the fruits? He asked me once, and then again, when he asked me the third time, I lay open like this and there they had turned red! Oh! I picked the fruit while it was green, how did it turn red? The dream would come to me there in the village, as I would sleep at night. . . . How is it that the green fruit I picked has turned red, I would wonder!

Akram's dream was a recurring one. And while s_he was keen to figure it out, Akram's mother would routinely disregard its significance. Unbeknownst to Akram at the time was the significance of the fruits' turning red. If *Shahbaz* (royal falcon) of the saint's three-part title referred to his miraculous flight corresponding with the inaugural vision of the bird at night, the word *Lal* (ruby) emphasized his hardened jewellike rank among saints. *Lal* was also red, the color associated with the saint of Sehwan. The turning red of the fruit, as Akram would narrate it to me years later in Sehwan, was one among many signs that the *ziyara* s_he was being prepared for in the dream was that of Qalandar. But this s_he had not known then. After a year of its recurrence, Akram went to his_her mother again, more perturbed than ever. This time, however, she explained that certain offerings were due at saints' places and shrines in Akram's name and that she had forgotten to make those in time. The incessant dream, she now told Akram, was in fact a reminder. According to Akram, the dream of the garden lasted a full year before it finally stopped. In a final dream, however, the same gardener who had questioned him_her on the matter of the fruits made an offer.

> The same gardener, the one from the first dream, he said, on the last day, "Child, do you want to do *ziyara*?" I said, "Yes, *baba*, I would like to do *ziyara*." He says, just take the straight road; we go ahead to do *ziyara*, and on the way we find a *sabil* [vessel] of water. I drink water from the *sabil*; having drunk from it I go farther to perform *ziyara*. As I go for *ziyara*, I cross a door, then another; as I walk through the third one, I see a man sitting, two men are sitting. . . . Him on this side, and him on the other, in the center is the fire. He rises, and speaks to me, the one who has this much of a beard, white in color. Such is the light of his beard, and what of his face can I tell you! He came for me and said, "Child." I said, "Yes, *baba*." He said, "Do you wish to do *ziyara*? I said, "Yes, I wish to do so." And what *ziyara* he made me do! Then I performed the *ziyara* like this: as I see, my sight falls first on his rosary, the one that is turning, it gives off a great light, then my sight moves toward his face, then I see the clouds, half of it lies behind me, half ahead of me, in the middle is the image.
>
> I wonder, who this *wali* is, who is this man? I must find him. In my heart is this: "Shahbaz goes into flight; known to him are the secrets of the heart," I want to be a *murid* [disciple] of the one, I want to serve the one who knows the secrets of the heart.

Akram's dream is also an account of a first *ziyara* as much as the dream is the very space in which the *ziyara* occurs. But even though s_he performs *ziyara*—an imaginative pilgrimage if you will—the holy persons of the dream and the destinations s_he journeyed to or to which s_he was being called were unknown to Akram at the time. *Ziyara* is commonly translated as "pilgrimage" and refers to a merit-earning act of visiting or journeying to a revered site. But *ziyara*, as the dream in question reveals, is both the journeying to and the viewing of that revered site, relic, or person. In other words, one does *ziyara* just as much one can be at a *ziyara*.

Furthermore, while *ziyara* specifically and literally refers to the *what* of the pilgrimage—that is, the act of visiting a holy site—it also implicates the *where* of it in that it refers to the space in which the interaction between the pilgrim and the object of veneration takes place. More often than not, pilgrimages are studied as collective and communal experiences that involve specific places and occur within a ritually prescribed frame of time (for *ziyara* as social process).[12] My interest, however, is to highlight its dialogical features and maintain that *ziyara* in the context of this discussion is better understood as *occasion for engagement*, where occasion is not simply an event but an active force that effects engagement, encompassing its tangible, sensory, and imaginal forms. In other words, *ziyara* occasions as much as it is the occasion for engagement, whereby a pilgrim comes into contact with powerful persons and places in spiritual as well as in embodied ways, whether such affective engagements are to take place in material or visionary settings, in prescribed time or extended over a lifetime, in collectives or by oneself. Hence, *ziyara* as occasion embraces pilgrimages of the dream as well as sustained dialogical pursuits that are not restricted by the sequence of ritual time or waking life.

While journeys of the dream are for dreamers and believers a fully valid alternative to physical travel,[13] Akram's *ziyara* in the dream would be followed by a second *ziyara*, this time compelling the eleven-year-old Akram to leave home and travel in pursuit of the then unknown and enigmatic saint in flight. "As I described this [*ziyara*] to my mother, the dream was forgotten. When the dream was lost, my head started to turn such that I cannot tell you. I stepped out of my home and told my mother, 'Shahbaz goes into flight; known to him are the secrets of the heart; we shall meet if we live; try and forget me if I die! My soul has become such, my mother, that I cannot stay home for five more minutes!'"

The veiled messages of the dream offered little direction to Akram's journey as s_he made his_her way away from home to a saint's fair in Faisalabad city. Once the fair was over, s_he boarded a bus to Lahore and arrived at the city's most prominent shrine complex, the Data Darbar. It was here that Akram first found mentorship with a *malang* (fakir, dervish).[14] When a full year had passed and on a day when countless other *malangs* had gathered for another saint's festival in Lahore, Akram's *malang*-mentor revealed his plans to take leave for yet another destination, advising the young Akram to return home. A bus had already been arranged to take a party of *malangs* to the saint's fair in Sindh, but Akram it seemed was not invited. As the mentor spoke of his plans to travel to Sehwan, an audiocassette could be heard playing in the background. This was the very song Akram had listened to back in the village, causing on this occasion the entire party of *malangs* to rise and chant slogans. But Akram sat and wept.

> Where is Lal, I wondered; if indeed Shahbaz flies and known to him are the secrets of the heart, where are you, then, and why don't you know the secrets of my heart? As I cried, the *malang* asked me, "Child, what has happened to you?" I asked him, "*Baba*, where are you going?" The *malang* said, "Have you heard this cassette?" to which I said yes! The *malang* told me that he had received an invitation to this saint's *shadi* [wedding]; an invitation, and to the saint's wedding he was going! . . . [I thought,] I must go there then, come what may! I did a courageous thing and with *baba* I arrived [in Sehwan].

As the party arrived in Sehwan, they camped in a quiet setting known as Lal-bagh (Lal's garden), a wooded grove on the outskirts of Sehwan associated with the saint himself. It was then that figures of the dream would become comprehensible to Akram. As a young child, Akram had struggled to make meaning of the winged creature, the green fruit that would turn red in the dream sequence of the garden, and who exactly was the gardener that had led Akram to the *ziyara* of the luminous persons? Here in the garden, Akram met a resident fakir who had made it his duty to tend to the trees of the saint's grove. As the pilgrimage came to a close and fakir bands prepared for their onward journeys, Akram decided to settle down in the garden of his dreams, never to return.

> I told him [the *malang*-mentor], "I have arrived where I was meant to come. May Allah keep you and make you happy; I wish to remain here, you may go if you like." He asked me, "Why?" I said to him that this place has been approved for me. I had seen a garden in my dream, so the garden came in front of me. And the *baba* [saint] that I had seen in the image between the skies, the same *baba* is here. And so, my child, I came from there to here.

At the time Akram narrated the events of the dream to me, s_he was already an established fakir in Sehwan, almost fifty years of age. The setting in which the narration took place is a fakir dwelling (*astanah*), which Akram has established in Lal-bagh at the exact spot where s_he had first arrived with the party of *malangs* (see figure 5.1). Throughout the year and especially at the time of the annual fair, Akram would open up his_her garden dwelling to visiting fakirs and pilgrims from across the country. Akram described the precise features of this place in alignment with images from the dream. The picking of the fruits in the garden, s_he explained, were a premonition for an eventual *astanah* in the garden of the saint (Lal-bagh), and the very setting of the first pilgrimage of the dream—the crossing of the three thresholds, the placement of the water-dispensing vessel, and the organization of space around a fireplace—finally came to be mirrored in his_her fakir dwelling. "The dream that had come there [in the village], I had found," Akram remarked with an air of accomplishment. "My dream had come true; my dream was now in front of me!"

That disciples come to be initiated in dreams, or that dreams offer glimpses of future events, is relevant to this discussion.[15] Equally important is the idea that dream visions have potential material consequences, especially in instances when relics of the dream are transformed into meta-relics beyond the dream.[16] Attending to such consequences means to read not only the event of the dream itself but also its afterlife. Akram's dreams and the destinations to which such visions were pointing are significant precisely for the reason that at an age when intersex and gender-variant children in Pakistan are known to seek and be sought by transgender gurus, Akram was tending toward a different futurity.[17] Akram's ascetic lifestyle and his_her private residence in a fakir dwelling instead of a life among local trans* communities and networks are outcomes of the dreams s_he had once received and the pilgrimages s_he dutifully pursued as a consequence of those visions. Moreover, while Akram's pilgrimage may have been inaugurated in dreams, it has spanned both dream-space and shrine-space: it has involved visions and waking encounters, encompassed corporeal and mystical labor typical of fakir careers, and has included in the folds of its itinerary other saints' places as well as saints' fairs.[18] What must not be forgotten, however, is that Akram's pilgrimages, the first one of the dream and the subsequent travel to Sehwan, are concurrent with a period when saints and their places were being adopted by the Pakistani state, their annual fairs were being systematically promoted, and the material and symbolic resourcefulness of shrines were being reevaluated.

Saints of the State

A countrywide survey of religious endowments (*waqf* properties) was first carried out in the early 1950s. This, as is argued, was done in lieu of the

FIGURE 5.1 A view of Akram's dwelling in Lal-bagh. Kasmani © 2012.

political and economic resourcefulness of saints' shrines as well as the routinization of power such sites and private holdings had traditionally enabled for groups and individuals claiming to be its inheritors, caretakers, and custodians.[19] It was the Waqf Properties Ordinance of 1961 that eventually set the seal on the public administration of saints' shrines. While a provision was made for the maintenance of private *waqfs*, under the new order all nonprivate endowments that were not solely charitable could validly be taken into the hands of the state.[20] This meant that shrines of celibate saints like that of Qalandar in Sehwan, which in the absence of any direct descendants could not be deemed private inheritance, came to be adopted by the Pakistani state.

While Sehwan's reputation as a place of pilgrimage is long-standing and its historical significance cannot be ignored, its countrywide profile has been bolstered since its public takeover in June 1960.[21] Before the 1960s, official Sindhi publications hardly mentioned the saint or his shrine in Sehwan.[22] This absence is remarkable in that other saints of Sindh (especially Shah Abdul Latif Bhittai, Sachal Sarmast, and Shah Inayat) are regularly featured during this period, with their annual feasts and festivals marked by dedicated special editions. Such a change makes it plausible to suggest that Sehwan acquired a national prominence in tandem if not solely as a result of the public takeover of its shrine.

In the summer of 1969, the folk-devotional song "O Lal meri," customarily performed by female pilgrims at the shrine premises, was musically arranged for a Punjabi film by legendary music director Ashiq Hussain and sung by Noor Jahan, the most iconic female singer in the country. So impactful was this cultural import that soon after, not just Punjab but the rest of the country was abuzz with its chorus: "dam-a-dam mast Qalandar" (every breath is intoxicated with Qalandar). It remains to this day one of the widest-known tributes to the saint of Sehwan. The song was featured twice in the same film, setting a trend in Punjabi films of the time.[23] These films projected Qalandar in his capacity to fly turning one of his minor miracles (*karama*) into a widely recognizable image: the flying falcon-saint. Following the saint's debut appearance on film, similar song features portray how a female protagonist in distress is rescued by a falcon-saint in his winged form, his help invoked by performing a *dhamal* (ritual drumming), sometimes filmed at the shrine itself. The song of Akram's dream—"Shahbaz Goes into Flight"—belongs to this trend, and the returning bird in Akram's dream participates in this new pictorial and lyrical imagery of the saint. Akram's case is also telling because his_her childhood coincides closely with the first decade of the nationalization of shrines. Hence, by the time Akram had arrived in the city, a steady stream of state patronage had already put Sehwan on the cultural map of Pakistan; the little-known place in Sindh had begun to attract a new and distinctly urban public from the Punjab; and contours of its mausoleum were being replicated in print and reproduced on film. In addition, improved road and rail networks in the coming years would mean that the falcon-saint of Sindh would travel far and wide on the wings of the state.[24] Today, after over fifty years of nationalization, Sehwan enjoys a steady traffic of visitors every weekend, and its annual fair attracts more than half a million pilgrims, making it one of the largest gatherings of devotees in the country.[25] It is for such reasons that an otherwise individual pilgrimage to Sehwan is better situated in wider processes of a proliferation of new imaginative texts surrounding the saint of Sehwan.

Saints' shrines, as Nile Green has illustrated in his discussion of seventeenth-century Awrangabad, are at once literary and real places.[26] In other words, texts illustrating the minor miracles and the charismatic status of a saint in question have "little practical use without a shrine at which the blessing of the saint could be accessed."[27] Similarly, adopting saints in

Pilgrimages of the Dream 141

Pakistan cannot be read independent of the state's efforts to popularize them. In this regard, it has been argued that nationalization of religious endowments in Pakistan has come with an added impetus to turn saints and saints' places into revenue-making entities for the state.[28] However, the direct and steady investment in shrines, beyond the maintenance and upkeep of mausoleums, has also involved a wider circulation of saintly lives and legends through a variety of texts and media—biographical literature, news features, devotional songs, religious posters—thus broadening the appeal of their annual fairs as well as improving access to sites of pilgrimage.[29] The case of Akram opens up possibilities to read how the interest and interventions of the Pakistani state, in enabling access to shrines and furthering pilgrimages to saints' places, has produced outcomes that exceed its material infrastructures and tangible dividends and foster a spatialization of saints and their charisma in particular through the realm of the imaginary—that is, dreams, images, visions, and visitations, especially when it comes to its nonmale subjects.[30]

As major saints' feasts and fairs (*'urs*) came to be hosted by the state, they were systematically turned into elaborate settings at which the state could stage its new symbolic role, placing itself where a spiritual custodian once stood—that is, as a mediator facilitating contact between the saint and the devotee, thus also gaining legitimacy for its own authority.[31] This also meant that annual events like the *'urs* were newsworthy. In the case of Sehwan, special *'urs* editions of Urdu and Sindhi newspapers from the 1960s onward were accompanied by reportage of the fairs covering not only their annual rites and ceremonies but also the various legends, miraculous accounts, and feats associated with the saint, enabling like never before a mass dissemination of hagiographic knowledge around the saintly figure.[32] In a study of the Data Darbar of Lahore, Strothmann has argued that a state sponsored *'urs*, with its speeches, commemorative pamphlets, annual brochures, literary conferences, and music recitals, served as an ideal opportunity to "rewrite" saints' biographies.[33] Such rewriting in the context of Sehwan has involved more architectural measures: the gradual but systematic fading away of the shrine's Hindu character involves an effort to discipline an ambiguously regarded antinomian mystic into a sharia-compliant saint of the state. Similarly, a privileging of Sehwan's Sufi character over its pre-Islamic and Shivaite heritage reveals how a public institution like the Auqaf Department participates in the larger project of reimagining the saint through a remodeling of the place of the saint, which among other things helps prioritize certain claims to the site over others.[34]

The historical transformation of living Sufis into posthumous saints involves more often than not an interest in Sufi spaces, institutions, and networks, and especially the establishing of pilgrimages.[35] The current-day implications of a patronage of deceased saints and pilgrimages to their places in Pakistan follow what Green has identified as the "architecture of sainthood" in that it enshrines the holy through creating new linkages between the image of the Sufi, the body of the saint, and the sites where it can be accessed.[36] In enabling while also guiding and regulating such access, the state finds itself a place within this architecture. The constant renovation of Sehwan's shrine since the 1970s, including its elaborate redesign from the 1990s until its latest remodeling in 2013 and the ongoing expansion of the shrine complex, tells the story of its growing importance as a place of pilgrimage; it also reveals the continued faith of the state in the shrine's economic worth and symbolic value.[37] Not just that, but extremist and anti-state groups' targeting of Pakistani shrines, including the suicide attack in Sehwan in February 2017, makes it disturbingly clear that saints' places are regarded as projects of the state. While the material, financial, and political stakes of the state are more or less evident with regard to its aim to nationalize religious endowments, dreaming subjects like Akram offer us a rare insight into other and less ordinary forms of investment in saints and shrines of the state.

Conclusion

The visionary aspects of Muslim religious experience offer valuable ways in which saintly dreams and pilgrimages of the dream (like those of Akram) may be explained.[38] Particularly illuminating is Amira Mittermaier's engagement with the intersections of dreams and shrines and the ways in which her scholarship offers to expand the discussion of the social sphere to include an "Elsewhere."[39] How believers mediate relationships with deceased saints or, for that matter, *jinns* helps us push open our analytical scopes.[40] Thus, in attending to pilgrimages of the dream, we privilege the visionary, affective, and imaginal dimensions of *ziyara*, but the material and tangible conditions that sustain such experiences of pilgrimage are not to be forgotten.

Dreams of and from saints in Pakistan, as has been illustrated, sometimes come to be configured and intervened in by wider political processes, making complex the material and imaginal spaces of pilgrimage, or occasions of intimate interactions between saints and their devotees. Put differently, the vitality of studying pilgrimage does not lie simply in questioning the religious experience of pilgrims, nor does it rest solely in sites to which such journeys are directed; the study of pilgrimage in the modern Muslim world is also a study of its increasing governmentality. By this I mean that as much as it is imperative that we rethink pilgrimage so as to better encompass its material as well as imaginal dimensions, affectful dispositions of governance cannot be overlooked either: tactics, techniques, and motivations of the state that also shape and govern pilgrims' journeys and experiences, the administrative, infrastructural, and symbolic forms these take, and the various means and media through which material and imaginal encounters—that of pilgrims with saints and their places—come to be arranged.[41]

My interest in putting the personal and the particular in conversation with the greater story of nationalization of saints and their places stems from my discontent that the conversation on change in religious institutions in Pakistan has concentrated on its material, political, and economic motivations, whereas its symbolic, visionary, and affective aspects come rarely under scrutiny. On the one hand is the claim that the state's drive to modernize shrines has included an impetus to secularize them.[42] On the other hand stands the argument that the state's effort to secularize the consciousness of its citizens has met with unexpected results in that the Pakistani state has emerged as the paradoxical promoter of popular Sufism, which it had initially set out to reform and from which it draws its own legitimacy.[43] If turning annual saints' feasts into public holidays, rendering superfluous the role of the custodian, providing medical treatment facilities at sites otherwise associated with ritual healing, and listing and describing shrines in state-sponsored tourism booklets constitute a formal emancipation, we ought also to ask questions that interrogate the ways in which the state's interest and interventions are aimed at more symbolic returns. To this end, I have argued that in making room for itself at sites of saint veneration and in disturbing conventional structures of authority, the Pakistani state has invariably imagined for itself a charismatic role, fostering for its subjects a hope for innovative possibilities of imagining themselves in relation to saints of the state. Individuals like Akram are drawn to Sehwan on the promise of the state, their journeys enabled through a reception of crisscrossing texts: songs, dreams, and architecture that continually rewrite saints and their places. The long story of Akram's pilgrimage to Sehwan is therefore incomplete without speaking of the greater dispositions of governance that make saintly figures in Pakistan ever more accessible.

Notes

1. Intersex as well as feminine-identified gender-variant individuals assigned male at birth (also *hijra, khwaja-sira, transgender*) are regarded as neither men nor women in Pakistan and are commonly described as the third sex/gender in South Asia. It is for this reason that throughout the text, I refer to Akram in fluid genders as per his_her own practice. I prefer to use "his_her" instead of the more standard "his/her" and "s_he" instead of "s/he." My use of the underscore (_) is aimed at conveying the range and the fluidity of possible identifications that involve one's sex and gender and to avoid an emphasis on choice or an either/or with the use of the forward slash (/). The name Akram echoes the gendered character of the name by which my research partner was known in the field.

2. Lal Shahbaz Qalandar is the popular reference for Sayyid 'Uthman Marwandi (1162–1274 C.E.), whose shrine draws fakirs and ascetics from across the country to Sehwan, Pakistan's most important center of pilgrimage. He is said to belong to the original thirteenth-century band of qalandars, or antinomian mystics that Ahmet Karamustafa has characterized as anarchistic, carefree individuals who were critical of established authority. See Ahmet Karamustafa, *God's Unruly Friends: Dervish Groups in the Islamic Later Middle Period, 1200–1550* (London: Oneworld, 2006). For more on Qalandars, see *MIFS Newsletter* 5 (2010–11): 2–4.

3. Amira Mittermaier, "(Re)Imagining Space: Dreams and Saint Shrines in Egypt," in *Dimensions of Locality: Muslim Saints, Their Place and Space*, ed. Samuli Schielke and Georg Stauth (London: Transaction, 2008), 60; Katherine P. Ewing, *Arguing Sainthood: Modernity, Psychoanalysis and Islam* (Durham, NC: Duke University Press, 1997).

4. The stated aims and objectives of the Auqaf Department, subject to the Ministry of Religious Affairs, Government of Sindh, include the management of shrines and mosques, providing pilgrim facilities like community kitchens and rest houses. The state also strives to generate revenue from *waqf* properties through work contracts, rents, and leases, which is mainly used for purposes of maintenance and reconstruction of old shrines and other religious endowments.

5. Samuli Schielke, "Policing Ambiguity: Muslim Saints-Day Festivals and the Moral Geography of Public Space in Egypt," *American Ethnologist* 35, no. 4 (2008): 539–52.

6. Amira Mittermaier, *Dreams That Matter: Egyptian Landscapes of the Imagination* (Berkeley: University of California Press, 2011); Amira Mittermaier, "Dreams from Elsewhere: Muslim Subjectivities beyond the Trope of Self-Cultivation," *Journal of the Royal Anthropological Institute (N.S.)* 18 (2012): 247–65; Mittermaier, "(Re)Imagining Space," 48.

7. Mittermaier, "(Re)Imagining Space," 53. The other three ways: dreams move shrines, dreamers are moved to visit shrines, and shrines shape dreams.

8. I refer to Foucault's notion of the art of governance, albeit in a limited sense, where government is not so much a question of imposing laws but of disposing things and employing tactics and techniques so that certain ends may be achieved by means of such an arrangement. Michel Foucault, "Governmentality," in *The Foucault Effect: Studies in Governmentality*, ed. Graham Burchell, Colin Gordon, and Peter Miller

(Chicago: University of Chicago Press, 1991): 87–104. "Affect" is used here in the sense of an inchoate force of encounter and extension, which is registered through sense and bodily effects. See also Deborah Gould, *Moving Politics* (Chicago: University of Chicago Press, 2009).

9. The greater material for this study draws from the researcher's doctoral dissertation, titled "Of_f the Lines: Fakir Orientations of Gender, Body and Space in Sehwan Sharif, Pakistan" (2016). It was funded by the German Research Foundation (DFG) and supervised under Dr. Hansjörg Dilger at the Institute of Social and Cultural Anthropology, Free University of Berlin. The ethnographic data quoted in this work was collected during several fieldworks lasting twelve months between 2009 and 2013. A different, initial draft of this work was read at the conference "Pakistan: Parallel Narratives of the Nation-State at the South Asia Institute," University of Heidelberg, in December 2014.

10. For change in religious institutions in Pakistan, see Jamal Malik, "Waqf in Pakistan: Change in Traditional Institutions," *Die Welt des Islams* 30, no. 1/4 (1990): 63–97.

11. For more on the dialogic of the lyrical and the political, see Omar Kasmani, "Audible Specters: The Sticky Shia Sonics of Sehwan," *History of Emotions—Insights into Research* (blog), October 2017, https://www.history-of-emotions.mpg.de/en/texte/audible-spectres-the-sticky-shia-sonics-of-sehwan.

12. In his analysis of pilgrimage to Jhok Sharif, Michel Boivin has described *ziyara* as a social process whereby discrimination and not equality in the experience of pilgrimage is the very means through which social hierarchies are maintained. See Michel Boivin, "Guthe Sufi Centre of Jhok Sharif in Sindh (Pakistan): Questioning the Ziyarat as Social Process," in *South Asian Sufis: Devotion, Deviation and Destiny*, ed. Clinton Bennett and Charles M. Ramsey (London: Continuum, 2012).

13. Mittermaier, "(Re)Imagining Space: Dreams and Saint Shrines in Egypt," 60.

14. The word *malang* is sometimes used interchangeably with fakir as its Punjabi variant. However, there are *malangs* who distinguish themselves from fakirs but offer little or no explanation. My own impression is that being a *malang* involves stricter forms of sexual abstinence.

15. Katherine Ewing, "The Dream of Spiritual Initiation and the Organization of Self: Representations among Pakistani Sufis," *American Ethnologist* 17 (1990): 56–74; Nile Green, "The Religious and Cultural Roles of Dreams and Visions in Islam," *Journal of the Royal Asiatic Society* 13, no. 3 (2003): 291.

16. Mittermaier, "(Re)Imagining Space," 51; Finbarr B. Flood, "Bodies and Becoming: Mimesis, Mediation, and the Ingestion of the Sacred in Christianity and Islam," in *Sensational Religion: Sensory Cultures in Material Practice*, ed. Salley M. Promey (New Haven, CT: Yale University Press, 2014), 473. The dream of the Egyptian Sufi al-Busiri (d. ca. 1296) is enshrined in a text titled *Qasidah burdah sharif*. According to its preface, the poem was written at a time when the Sufi suffered from paralysis. On an occasion when the Prophet visited him in a dream, al-Busiri recited the poem and was duly cured, receiving the Prophet's robe as a reward. Describing this text about a relic as "meta-relic," Finnbarr B. Flood has pointed to its reputation for healing through recitation as well as ingestion.

17. For more on *hijra* life in South Asia, see Claire Pamment, "Hijraism: Jostling for a Third Space in Pakistani Politics," *Drama Review* 54, no. 2 (2010): 29–50; Gayatri Reddy, *With Respect to Sex: Negotiating Hijra Identity in South India* (Chicago: University of Chicago Press, 2005); Serena Nanda, *Neither Man nor Woman: The Hijras of India*, 2nd ed. (Toronto: Wadsworth, 1999).

18. Mittermaier, "(Re)Imagining Space: Dreams and Saint Shrines in Egypt"; Mittermaier, *Dreams That Matter*; Omar Kasmani, "Of_f the Lines: Fakir Orientations of Gender, Body, and Space in Sehwan Sharif, Pakistan" (PhD diss., Freie Universität, Berlin, Department of Political and Social Sciences, 2016); Omar Kasmani, "Of Difference and Discontinuity: Gender and Embodiment among Fakirs of Sehwan Sharif," *Oriente Moderno* 92, no. 2 (2012): 439–57.

19. See Malik, "Waqf in Pakistan."

20. Linus Strothmann, *Managing Piety: The Shrine of Data Ganj Bakhsh* (Karachi: Oxford University Press, 2012), 55.

21. For Sehwan's Shivaite past, see Michel Boivin, *Sindh through History and Representations: French Contributions to Sindhi Studies* (Karachi: Oxford University Press, 2008); Annemarie Schimmel, *Mystical Dimensions of Islam* (1975; repr., Lahore: Sang-e-Meel, 2003). Historians as well as Sindhi nationalists contend that Sehwan's shrine is part of a larger history of Sufi sites coinciding with or replacing at times already existing sites of Shiva veneration. The shrine of Qalandar in Sehwan is known to stand at the site of the once sacred Shiva temple.

22. This is observable in *Nayin Zindagi* and *Mehran*—two prominent state-run journals published by the Information Department, Ministry of Information and Broadcasting, Sindh and the Sindhi Adabi Board, respectively.

23. The Bokhari brothers who directed and produced the film were devotees of the saint of Sehwan and regular pilgrims at the annual fair. At least six films between 1969 and 1975 featured songs in praise of the Qalandar of Sehwan.

24. Special *'urs* trains, like the Jhule-Lal Express, were also initiated to facilitate the annual journey of pilgrims connecting Sehwan with Lahore, the capital of Punjab. German filmmaker Martin Weinhart collaborated with German ethnologist Jürgen Wasim Frembgen, whose ethnographic narrative of the pilgrimage to Sehwan led to the making of the film *Der rote Sufi: Rausch und Ekstase in Pakistan* (2011). Frembgen, who also appears in the film, accompanies the pilgrims on a train journey to Sehwan. Jürgen W. Frembgen, *At the Shrine of the Red Sufi: Five Days and Nights on Pilgrimage in Pakistan*, trans. Jane Ripken (Karachi: Oxford University Press, 2011), originally published as *Am Schrein des roten Sufi: Fünf Tage und Nächte auf Pilgerfahrt in Pakistan* (Frauenfeld: Waldgut Verlag, 2008).

25. For an account of the fair, see Frembgen, *At the Shrine of the Red Sufi*.

26. Nile Green, *Indian Sufism since the Seventeenth Century: Saints, Books and Empires in the Muslim Deccan* (New York: Routledge, 2006).

27. Green, 35–36. In a study of the seventeenth-century shrines of Awrangabad, India, Nile Green has pointed toward the dual spheres in which saintly places existed, spanning their discursive and material dimensions.

28. See Malik, "Waqf in Pakistan"; Linus Strothmann, *Managing Piety: The Shrine of Data Ganj Bakhsh* (Karachi: Oxford University Press, 2016). The Auqaf Department

collects pilgrim donations (in boxes placed at the shrine) and draws income from land leases, from shop rentals, and by contracting services at the shrine premises. The department claims to be the only "self-income-generating department." Auqaf Department website, accessed June 3, 2014, http://sindh.gov.pk/dpt/usharzakaat/. For an account of the distribution of shrine revenues and the economic dimension of a Sufi shrine in Lahore, see Strothmann, *Managing Piety*, chaps. 5, 6.

29. See Jürgen W. Frembgen, *The Friends of God: Sufi Saints in Islam; Popular Poster Art from Pakistan* (Karachi: Oxford University Press, 2012).

30. Omar Kasmani, "Women [Un-]like Women: The Question of Spiritual Authority among Female Fakirs of Sehwan Sharif," in *Devotional Islam in Contemporary South Asia: Shrines, Journeys and Wanderers*, ed. Michel Boivin and Remy Delage (Oxon: Routledge, 2016).

31. Alex Philippon, "An Ambiguous and Contentious Politicization of Sufi Shrines and Pilgrimages in Pakistan," in Boivin and Delage, *Devotional Islam in Contemporary South Asia*.

32. The Sindhi language *Daily Ibrat* (published in Hyderabad) in the 1960s, for example, started to report the 'urs at Sehwan in great detail.

33. Strothmann, *Managing Piety*, 57.

34. Kasmani, "Of_f the Lines." During the shrine's repairs under the Auqaf Department in 1974, its doorbells and a Shiva Lingam–like object, customary of Hindu places of worship, were removed from the shrine's premises. More recent years have witnessed a struggle over the saint's doctrinal persuasion. While historians like Michel Boivin have highlighted his Isma'ili heritage, many sayyids in Sehwan today emphasize that the saint was indeed Shia but of the Twelver creed.

35. Blain Auer, "Intersections between Sufism and Power: Narrating the Shaykhs and Sultans of Northern India, 1200–1400," in *Sufism and Society: Arrangements of the Mystical in the Muslim World, 1200–1800*, ed. John Curry and Erik Ohlander (New York: Routledge, 2012).

36. Green, *Indian Sufism since the Seventeenth Century*, 51.

37. See also Szanto, this volume. Its rise to fame is also attributed to Zulfikar 'Ali Bhutto's (d. 1979) ascent to power, who was a devotee of the saint.

38. Green, "Religious and Cultural Roles of Dreams and Visions in Islam."

39. Mittermaier, "(Re)Imagining Space"; Mittermaier, *Dreams That Matter*, 249.

40. See Anand Taneja, *Jinnealogy: Time, Islam and Ecological Thought in the Medieval Ruins of Delhi* (Stanford, CA: Stanford University Press, 2018); Naveeda Khan, "Of Children and Jinns: An Inquiry into an Unexpected Friendship during Uncertain Times," *Cultural Anthropology* 21, no. 6 (2006): 234–64.

41. See Bianchi, this volume; Foucault, "Governmentality"; Szanto, this volume.

42. Malik, "Waqf in Pakistan."

43. Philippon, "Ambiguous and Contentious Politicization of Sufi Shrines and Pilgrimages in Pakistan," 174.

CHAPTER SIX

Shrines and Pilgrimage in Southern Kazakhstan

AZIM MALIKOV

The cult of saints and shrines—such as the reverence of *mazarat* or *kesene* (in Kazakh terminology)—plays an important role in Islamic ritual cultures of Central Asia. While there are no formal sanctification procedures and no official list of saints recognized in the Islamic world, the general consensus among scholars is that the cult of saints and shrines in Central Asia maintains a vibrant life. However, in spite of ongoing research, the subject is still under studied.[1]

Historically, the scholarly field of saints and shrines in Central Asia has undergone several changes. During the Soviet period (1917–91), ethnographers studying the cult of saints (*aulie* in Kazakh terminology) attempted to prove their mythological content and link them to pre-Islamic ideas of Central Asian peoples.[2] Although it is possible to agree on some common themes, even the preliminary study of shrine features indicates that these belief structures have sources in the pre-Islamic past and in Islamic cultural traditions. The visitation rites to shrines, particularly as a major feature of the sacred sites and depending on the region and the cultural context, maintain both general and indigenous traits.

I define pilgrimage as a journey that individuals or groups undertake based on religious inspiration to a place perceived as sacred. As Samuel George Frederick Brandon described, "Pilgrimage involves three factors: a holy place; attraction of people to this place; a specific aim, i.e., to obtain some spiritual or material benefit."[3] In light of the ongoing debate on pilgrimage, it is important to determine whether visitations of shrines, and related practices such as adoration or veneration, entail solely a religious dimension. This chapter aims to analyze the complex material culture of shrines and pilgrimage in southern Kazakhstan, with its characteristic variety of shrine types. Attention is also given to various emerging forms of pilgrimage, which has acquired a place in the region in connection with changes in society, culture, and religion at the end of the twentieth century and continued into the twenty-first century.

Southern Kazakhstan is home to three provinces in Kazakhstan. In this chapter, I analyze data from two provinces: South Kazakhstan and Qyzylorda.[4] Scientific material from the central oasis region of Transoxiana—such as the Tashkent, Bukhara, and Samarkand Provinces of the Republic of Uzbekistan and Tajikistan—was used for comparative analysis.[5]

The core question addressed in this study is approached using three types of sources. The first type consists primarily of oral traditions, recorded during field trips to the region. Secondary sources are also necessary to deal with the history and ethnography of southern Kazakhstan, written primarily by Soviet scholars, especially post-Soviet local Kazakh scholars. The shrines themselves form a source of material culture from which one can not only draw an architectural understanding of the shrines but also observe everyday rituals in their everyday settings.

I argue that the process of religious revival in post-Soviet Kazakhstan has its own distinctive indigenous element, manifested in the reconstruction of existing shrines and the creation of new sites. The shrines' veneration in Kazakhstan is connected with various factors, such as manifestation of religious identity, cult of ancestors, and group identity for descendants of sacred lineages, such as *Khuja* and *Sayyid*. Factors such as religious tourism and state policy on identity formation have also played a significant role in promoting shrine veneration in the post-Soviet period.

Kazakhstan is a multiethnic society with several dozen ethnic groups, including Germans, Dungans, Kazakhs, Kyrgyz, Russians, Tajiks, Tatars, Turkmens, Ukrainians, Uyghurs, and Uzbeks, representing many different religious, language, and cultural identities. Major ethnic groups are Kazakhs, Russians, and Uzbeks. The most densely populated region of Kazakhstan is the South Kazakhstan province (now a Turkistan province), with a total of 2.8 million, nearly one-sixth of the national population.[6]

Turkistan is a major urban center in southern Kazakhstan. According to local tradition, three pilgrimages to Turkistan are equivalent to one Hajj to Mecca. Such discourse of piety is known also in relation to the Bukharan shrine of Bahavaddin Naqshband.[7] Some scholars propose that this tradition was "invented" by local Muslim clergy because, particularly in the Soviet period, only a very few could perform pilgrimage to Mecca; therefore, local clergy recommended replacing Hajj with visitations made to local shrines.[8]

The Turkistan region of Kazakhstan has always been the religious center of the country, where most of its holy sites are based. Many *Khuja* of various lineages and ethnic affiliations are concentrated in this region.[9] Traditionally, Kazakhs belong to the religious trend of Muslim-Sunni Islam of the Sufi variation. South Kazakhstan traditions differ in some ways from those of Central Asia.[10] Popular Sufi-inspired forms of Islam have predominated in Central Asia from the time of its spread by Sufi missionaries among the Turkic peoples.[11]

The Saints and Shrines of Southern Kazakhstan

According to Islamic tradition, Muhammad is the greatest and the final Prophet in the Abrahamic line. Particularly in Sufi Islam, the prophetic tradition is carried forward by "spiritual guides and guardians such as *walis* ('friends' of God), each assigned with a specific territory of the world to watch over human beings in the World."[12] The culture of saints, an important feature of Islamic history, has always been a popular phenomenon, primarily led by common people who identify as followers of Sufi masters. In historical terms, the origin of the cult of saints was a peculiar synthesis of pre-Islam and Islamic traditions.[13] Saints arose "to satisfy (at least) two needs—the need for an emotionally richer religion, and the requirements of social structure."[14]

Charismatic figures appeal to spirituality, piety, and supernatural power (*qasiet* in Kazakh terminology), qualities that identify them as saints. In saints, people seek ways to resist illness, misfortune, war, and so on. Saints, as mediators between people and God, have the spiritual and worldly power to overcome injustice and punish the guilty. A popular belief is that saints can grant devotees blessings and provide them hope, consolation, and protection against evil. There are differences in the status of the various saints from the perspective of Muslim communities in Central Asia. Saints become defenders of devotees against physical deformity or diseases provoked by evil spirits. People have relied on saints in their search for divine truth and spiritual gratification.

In broad terms, the cult of saints in the Muslim world is complex. Although as a monotheistic religion, Islam rejects the worshipping of mortal creatures, Muslim traditions in Central Asia view saints and their spiritual powers as a medium to prevent estrangement between humans and the sacred. For the realization of such a union, pilgrims accordingly attribute miracles (*karamat*) to saints. Legendary tales about saints, revered by local populations and known across regions, speak of different forms of miracles. As a key miracle site, pilgrims visit a saint's grave and perform rituals associated with the grave as a source of miracles. This attribution of supernatural authority to a person accentuates the uniqueness of a saint—unique, that is, to the pilgrims—and enhances connection through the saint with Muhammad, his family, noble followers, and other deceased or living saints. Therefore, the cult of saints reflects a practice of honoring the sacred, associated with saints and their descendants.[15]

Sufi figures, whose descendants are still living, make the specific category of the saints. Among Kazakh and Uzbek communities, there are some in the descent group of Khuja who interpret the shrines as their symbolic capital. As Lapidus explains, "Holy lineages inherited powers transmitted by spiritual and/or genealogical descent from an earlier saint or from the Prophet himself. The descendants of a famous saint constituted a holy community based on inheritance of his spiritual qualities and lineage ties."[16] What the genealogies (nasab-nama) of some sacred lineages "make clear is that the present genealogical charters of some Khuja communities typically emphasize descent from an intermediate saintly figure."[17] For a Khuja devotee, a shrine is first of all a place of memory, the memory of an ancestor's dwelling in history.

A look at the shrines in the Turkistan region indicates that they are connected with both the relics of a pre-Islamic past and Muslim religious traditions.[18] In recent years, the number of local shrines, especially those of saints-ancestors, have been on the rise. Ancient cultures of reverence are also present. Kazakhs respect the mountain peaks—Aulie-bastau, Kazy-gurt, Jylagan-ata—as well as the lakes, rivers, and springs. An object of reverence might be a single tree in the steppe. There are a number of ancient hills, burial mounds called *"oba"* (sites of honoring "ancestor" spirits), and other revered objects that can be linked to ancient religions of nature. A traveler, encountering a tree, ties a piece of cloth to a branch with the hope that all secret wishes will be realized.[19] Moreover, there is often a shared understanding of which place is sacred, although the sacred status of some sites can be contested by certain communities.

Sites of worship share similarities with those in neighboring regions and even those in other regions of the Muslim world, but some shrines with distinctive local peculiarities also exist. The reason is ambiguity and uncertainty of the sacred status of shrines, as different legends about a saint entail a variety of cultic practices. The interpretation of the cult of saints in the eastern and western areas of Kazakhstan does not coincide with that in the southern areas, which have been historically connected with sedentary centers of Central Asia and more Islamized than other regions of Kazakhstan.[20]

Kazakhstan scholar Ashirbek Muminov has suggested a distinct typology of shrines and has singled out eight types of *mazarat* in relation to a revered saint. His proposal entails two features in the classification of *mazarat*, such as "the degree of popularity and repute" and "the composition of unit"— that is, a set of different objects around a shrine.[21] A number of shrines in the contemporary southern province of the Republic of Kazakhstan were dedicated to the holy persons in the household of the Prophet, who were venerated as saints: first and foremost, his cousin and son-in-law, 'Ali; his wife, Fatima; and, especially in the Turkistan region, the grandson of 'Ali—

Muhammad Hanafiya, the legendary preacher of Islam among nomads of Dasht-i Kipchak.[22] The cult of 'Ali was also popular in other regions of Central Asia, namely the Bukhara, Samarkand, and Surkhandarya provinces of Uzbekistan,[23] Khorezm, and the Ferghana valley. Others who are also revered include 'Abdudjalil-bab, Ishak-bab, Ukasha-ata, and other Sufi leaders. Moreover, some shrines are built for *shahids*—martyrs of Islam—highlighting variants of shrines across Central Asia, which by and large depend on local traditions fused with local sociopolitical settings.

Muslim Saints: Manifestations and Features

Since pilgrimage traditions have gained prominence in relation to their regional, historical, or geographical specificity, the hierarchy of saints for devotees varies according to where they are revered. Meanwhile, as mentioned in various textual sources, many sacred places are connected to a specific revered saint and popular among certain communities in the pre-Soviet period. Five levels of saintly hierarchy can be differentiated: saints who are venerated in one village, saints who are popular among the population of several villages, saints who are regionally important, saints whose shrines are venerated throughout Kazakhstan, and saints whose shrines are venerated throughout Central Asia. Today, Khuja Ahmad Yassevi is by far Kazakhstan's most popular saint across Central Asia.

Sufi orders such as Yassaviya, Qadyriya, and Naqshbandiya have played an important role in the spiritual life of Central Asia in the pre-Soviet period. The inhabitants of almost all these settlements had a spiritual leader, or *ishan* ("they" in Persian). Historically, the heads of the Sufi brotherhood were highly respected; for centuries, their graves were places of pilgrimage. Also, descendants of saints controlled many Sufi shrines as a source of revenue for their families. Frequently, descendants of several "holy groups" struggled for possession over a shrine. Written sources and oral biographies of famous saints and stories about their miracles still exist. Many places of worship are associated with names of revered saints mentioned in the genealogies of Kazakh and Uzbek tribes. Saints such as Bakhauddin Naqshband and Khuja Ahmad Yassevi were singled out in one Kazakh variant of "Alpamys" mystics.[24]

The veneration of saints is common throughout Central Asia but varies from one region to another. The pilgrimage in the Syr-Darya River region is quite specific to the locality, and its ritual factors mark the close coexistence of settled and nomadic populations in the pre-Soviet period. In historical terms, most ethnic Kazakhs belong to one of three *zhuz* (hordes). While these Kazakh tribal confederations are regarded as the Black Bone (*qarasiiyek*), the Khuja and the Tore (the offspring of Chingiz Khan) are considered honor groups belonging to the White Bone (*aqsiiyek*). Accordingly, the Khuja and Tore groups are not included in the numerous Kazakh genealogies (*Qazaq shezhiresi*).[25] In the nineteenth century, the most famous and noble lineages of Khuja in the Turkistan region consisted of various groups: descendants of Sayyid Ata; descendants of the third son of Caliph 'Ali, Muhammad Hanafiya; and descendants of Khuja Ahmad Yassevi. Kazakh-speaking Khuja had a special nickname for each lineage, which is still in use. For other examples, consider Khurasan Khuja or descendants of Khurasan Ata or Abdujalil Bab, Duvana Khuja, and Qilishti Khuja.[26] Some of these nicknames were originally given to one of the male ancestors and, over time, became Khuja group names. Khurasan comes from the name of a historical region in the southern part of Central Asia, northern Afghanistan, and Iran.

During the Soviet period, many shrines and some mosques were destroyed. Mullahs (jurists) were subjected to repression, and performance of pilgrimage was prosecuted as a consequence of Soviet secularization. The Soviet policy had dramatic consequences for Khuja in Kazakhstan. Many in these communities lost their property and, accordingly, their source of income. Additionally, in many areas, Khuja communities lost their culture, values, and privileged rights. During this critical period, reverence for holy places and the practice of *ziyara* were identified by Soviet ideologues as "one of the most widespread of all religious survivals" among Muslims in Soviet Central Asia.[27] For the most part, though, making Hajj was severely restricted in Soviet times. The official Soviet Muslim Board of Central Asia and Kazakhstan dissociated itself from the culture of saints and shrine pilgrimage. In fact, "the board issued several fatwas against such practices, condemning them as *bid'a*, heretical innovations in belief and practice."[28] Shrines were important targets for those who claimed Islamic orthodoxy and were also used by Soviet secularist campaigns to marginalize religion.[29]

But this did not eradicate pilgrimage culture from Central Asia. In the Soviet period, famous shrines continued to be visited by large pilgrimage populations from various parts of Central Asia, usually under the guise of tourism.[30] In this period, famous shrines gained dual functions, serving both as public museums for secular purposes and as venerated holy places frequented by pilgrims as tourists. Meanwhile, the local population continued to perceive the sacred tradition of written sources as their "true" Islam.[31] Yet orthodoxy would undergo change as official Islam was weakened by almost seventy years of state-led secular policies.

The Shrines and Religious Policy in Post-Soviet Kazakhstan

In the context of state and religion relations in post-Soviet Kazakhstan, state control over religion gave way to full-fledged reforms, which provided freedom of religion.[32] Known as the "Muslim Renaissance" in Central Asia, the period marked an unprecedented revival of religious traditions.[33] By 1991, twenty Muslims from Kazakhstan made Hajj, and by 2014, that number increased to five thousand.[34] In 1989, there were only fifty-nine mosques in Kazakhstan. In 2012, the total number of mosques in Kazakhstan increased to 2,288, and in 2017, to 2570.[35] The regional presence of the religious landscape should also be noted. A significant number of mosques (about eight hundred) are located in the country's southern regions: Turkistan, Jambul, Almaty, and Qyzylorda provinces.[36] Foreign actors played a salient role in religious revival in Kazakhstan. In the first decade of independence, radical Islam—largely financed by such countries as Egypt, Pakistan, Saudi Arabia, and Turkey—became increasingly active, vying for influence over traditional Islam in Kazakhstan.[37]

An important milestone in state management of religious affairs began with the adoption of new religious law in 2011. According to the Law on Religious Activity and Religious Associations, the Republic of Kazakhstan affirmed the right of all citizens to freedom of conscience, specifically recognizing the historical role of the Islamic Hanafiya School in the development of the cultural and spiritual life of Kazakhstan. But this specific law did not stop the state from requiring religious organizations to register with the state. Since 2011, the number of religious organizations has dwindled, as all groups are officially required to register with the state. The latest development has given way to a new perception of a "moderate peaceful Islam."[38] In this context, defining state policy toward Islam and shrines specifically identified a "type of religious nationalism in Kazakhstan, where the religious figure of a saint became mixed with modern nationalism."[39]

In post-Soviet Kazakhstan, the following discourses in the relation to shrine culture became prominent: state ideology, Wahhabi, and various sectarian and local traditions. Local traditions are presented through their indigenous expression in the form of descendants of sacred lineages and revival of shrines, together with the innovations in ritual and custom that have appeared with such inventions. These traditions also include literary publication on saints and shrines, and organizing the fests at the holy sites.[40] For Khuja lineages, the shrines are important as sacred places that not only connect them with their ancestors but give them high status in the eyes of the larger community as the descendants of saints. In many ways, renovation or reconstruction of the shrines has had a significant impact, including reverence for ancestors and a special status among peers in society.

The question of status brings us to the theme of Kazakh religious identity, a source of debate among scholars. "Whether the Kazakhs are Muslims or whether it is the ancestral rituals with elements of Shamanism which are inherent to them, are also questions that are present in the daily lives of the Kazakhs."[41] Some Kazakh scholars propose that among Kazakhs, "Islam is practiced at a superficial level in everyday life and is closely connected with pagan rituals."[42] Other scholars argue that practices formerly labeled "shamanist" should in fact be an expression of Kazakh Islam.[43] In most cases, Muslim identity in post-Soviet Central Asian countries "did not extend to feeling solidarity with the broader Muslim world."[44] Currently, under the impact of strengthening ties with Muslim countries, websites promoting the unity of the global Islamic society, and the increase in the number of Kazakhs performing the Hajj, the number of people embracing the Islamic identity are slowly growing.

The Soviet legacy of institutionalization of religious life had some impact on Nazarbaev's government policy. There are two structures that regulate religious concerns: the Spiritual Administration of Muslims of Kazakhstan (SAMK) and the Agency for Religious Affairs of the Republic of Kazakhstan.[45] This was later transformed into a committee consisting of the Ministry of Culture and Information, and in 2016, the Ministry of Religious Affairs and Civil Society was created.[46] By the decree of President N. Nazarbaev, the Ministry of Religious Affairs and Civil Society of the Republic of Kazakhstan was renamed the Ministry of Public Development of the Republic of Kazakhstan in June 2018. A committee on religious affairs was formed within the ministry.[47]

The way that embodiment as pilgrimage practice is imagined by the state is performed through distinct policies and rituals. The policy to promote or manage a well-known shrine plays an important role in shaping pilgrimage. The authorities of Kazakhstan put posters in place to set recommendations and rules of pilgrimage or visitation of graves at cemeteries and *mazarat*. The rules emerging from such policies vary and can include prohibition of pilgrims in the embodied ways they engage with shrine space. These include rules related to stepping or lying on the grave, crying loudly, caressing or kissing the gravestone, and burning candles or lighting a fire near the grave. Other rules include prohibitions against consuming food, smoking, tethering animals, and laughing or making jokes near the grave. According to these regulations, pilgrims are also not allowed to lay cloth or ribbon on the grave of saint. It is recommended, for example, to simply pray and offer donations. Passages from the hadith about grave visitation are then cited, as a way to solidify state authority over deeds of piety.

While the Spiritual Administration of the Muslims of Central Asia and Kazakhstan had developed similar recommendations during the Soviet period, the construction of large shrines dedicated to past leaders of the Kazakh tribes became a new phenomenon in post-Soviet Kazakhstan. One can observe a reconstitution of lineage-based identities, in large part by local initiative. As Edward Schatz notes, "The ru and *zhuz*-based genealogies experienced a revival as traits that distinguished ethnic Kazakhs from the nontitular citizens of independent Kazakhstan."[48] This is when locals began to glorify tribal heroes and emerged "to emphasize the role of particular lineage segments in Kazakh history."[49] Based on my ethnographic study, in Qyzylorda Province, the descendants of the Nayman tribe erected a shrine in honor of Tolegetay Sadir Nayman (who lived in the seventeenth century), and a funeral repast (*as*) was held for him.[50] The architectural complex of Tolegetay Sadir Nayman shrine strongly differs from other Islamic shrines of Central Asia. Eight cone-shaped columns of red are established near the shrine, symbolizing eight clans of Naymans. But apart from that, a mausoleum for one of the Islamic saints was built nearby. The architecture of this shrine shows an attempt to connect the ideas of honor to the ancestors and worship of Sufi saints. At the same time, the shrine serves as a symbol of tribal solidarity and the identity of Kazakh naymans. In northern Kazakhstan, one can observe the renovation of shrines with the support of state funds and private business donations (including donations from rich Khuja or Quzha families). Data from this part of Kazakhstan confirms state involvement at the local level, with varying degrees of religious legitimacy.[51] According to my ethnographic findings, today the Khuja have a certain number of ancestral shrines in southern Kazakhstan, which are financed by Kazakhs, who do not claim sacred authority through lineages but revere Khuja with various lineages.

An imported religious ideology from Saudi Arabia, Wahhabi opposition to shrine pilgrimage was introduced to Kazakhstan in the post-Soviet period. Today, certain groups in Kazakh society, such as in Tajikistan, deny the "rightfulness" of the institution of sainthood in Islam.[52] Religious freedom of the first decade of independence led to growth in the number of nontraditional religious and pseudo-religious doctrines and sects in Kazakhstan. A new movement, Ata Zholy (The Way of the Forefathers), was formed within the Islamic framework in Kazakhstan in 1997 (founder Qydyrali Taribaev). Ata Zholy was an organization that advocated a return to Kazakh Islamic traditions, such as pilgrimage and ancestor veneration.[53] Followers of Ata Zholy undertook *ziyara* to shrines in order to come in contact with spirits of the ancestors (*aruah*, from the Arabic *arwah*) and obtain their personal blessing. Ata Zholy made a good business out of these pilgrimages, receiving a steady income. In 2009, a court ruled to forbid Ata Zholy due to the damage it caused to the mental and physical health of its members in the Republic of Kazakhstan. Experts consider that the people who adhered to the sect were exposed to psychological violence, which led to suicide or serious health concerns.[54] However, the life-threatening activities of this movement went far beyond Kazakhstan, into Russia, Belorussia, and Kyrgyzstan.[55] In recent years, the state has sought to strengthen control over the religious landscape of the country. By January 1, 2011, there were 4,551 religious organizations in operation in the country; after completion of the re-registration on October 25, 2012, that number dropped sharply to 3,088.[56] On May 16, 2018, deputies of Parliament approved a draft law on religious activities and religious associations.

Pilgrimage and Rituals

There is a specific set of ideas that define rituals. One can argue that rituals are culturally constructed and take place in specific place and specific times; they are repetitive, symbolic, and meaningful for individual participants and organizations.[57] Traditions of ritual visitation associated with shrines have been transformed over the last hundred years. One of the important sources for *ziyara* are the Sufi traditions. At the beginning of the twentieth century, Sufi *dervishs* made pilgrimage to well-known shrines in Central Asia. However, they were soon prohibited, and the attempt to revive the Sufi pilgrimage tradition disappeared in the early Soviet period.[58] The tradition was never successfully revived.

Shrines can be understood as important carriers of social memory. The values and attitudes of various social groups, projected on them, are indicators of this shared memory. A shrine caretaker who recites *suras* of the Qur'an for pilgrims and provides detailed narratives of the saint's life often also manages the shrine. There is also the role of print media. The prevalence of shrines in Kazakhstan has led to demands for manuals and books that provide details on the location of shrines and the lives of the saints buried there. Many shrine catalogs have been published in post-Soviet Kazakhstan, including those of Turkistan and southern Kazakhstan as a whole.[59] As Schwab has explained, "The practice of reading shrine catalogues in post-Soviet Kazakhstan is connected with the creation of a moral community."[60] Memory is central to such moral community.

In the post-Soviet period, *ziyara* has become a multidimensional phenomenon under the influence of geography and local tradition, in line with religious views. For a devotee, *ziyara* is a series of ritual performances steeped in religious motifs that require to be remembered, so as to preserve the essence of the experience; for others, it is a rational choice to visit a shrine as a way to find solutions for ordinary yet vital problems that could be solved through the interference of a respected saint, whose place they visit. A Muslim saint is a mediator, miracle worker, healer, and warrior of the faith. And it is in such mediation where memory is (re)constructed, but only through the revered saint. *Ziyara*, then, is about the power of *baraka* (spiritual force) provided by saints and passed to their graves. Memory is an important force in the production and reproduction of such power. Pilgrims choose places, objects, and past events that help them construct memory through the visitation practice.

In Central Asia, Islam tightly interlaces with numerous features of pre-Islamic beliefs among Kazakhs. These beliefs can be described in terms of shaman spells (*baksi*) and, at the same time, can be found in sermons of Muslim Ishan. Devotees venerate shrines related to the names of Muslim saints and their graves. At the same time, revered stones, trees, and springs, though apparently unrelated to Islam, can be prayed at, and a sacrificial offering can be made against diseases and barrenness. Pilgrims visit shrines in the context of regional culture and ecological peculiarities. Some shrines are visited midweek (Wednesdays and Thursdays) and also on Fridays; others open for visitation during certain seasons. As Schwab describes, "Many Kazakhs who otherwise do not engage in regular Islamic practice will pay the caretaker (*shyraqshy*) at a saint's shrine to recite the Qur'an for them and to say a supplication afterwards."[61] *Ziyara* is a multidimensional practice.

Kazakhs preserve customs and beliefs related to cattle breeding, which were passed from one generation to another: the patron (*pir*) of horse breeding is Qambar-ata or Jylkyshy-ata; of sheep breeding, Shopan-ata; of cattle breeding, Zengi-baba; and of goat breeding, Seksek-ata.[62] In local traditions, even the bones of horses, sheep, and camels are endowed with a supernatural property and considered to be amulets, like the horns of argali, ibex, and sheep—frequent objects on the graves of saints.[63]

Shrines and Pilgrimage in Southern Kazakhstan

Cult of Saints in Current Kazakhstan

One of the most important contemporary Kazakh religious practices is the tradition of ancestor spirits (*aruahs*). Ritual observations for ancestor spirits is expressed not only in prayers performed in memory of ancestors but also at the *mazarat*, or tombs of the ancestors. The traditions of devotion to the founders of the Kazakh tribes and family lines provide a basis for the cult of saints. There are various types and features of pilgrimage, depending on the number and type of participants, whether individual, family, or group; on duration, whether long or short term; and on seasonality, whether year round or for religious holidays.

According to widespread belief in Central Asia, pilgrimage to well-known *mazarat* is equivalent to pilgrimage to Mecca. For many pilgrims in Central Asia, one has to visit all shrines in his or her vicinity before performing the Hajj. According to some, the location of a *mazarat* has a positive aura, and visiting the place and drinking its holy water is a good way to strengthen and heal various parts of the body. Such motivation may be related to a variant of rationalization of faith and traditional practice. These pilgrims may follow, at least in the short term, the ritual traditions when visiting *mazarat*, as pilgrims can engage in prayer recitation at the grave or observe a ritual feast.

In the course of pilgrimage, attitudes toward a shrine change. Most pilgrims perform visitation to fulfill a personal need, but not all pilgrimage activities are about individual needs. One of the indispensable features of pilgrimage to *mazarat* is the presence of a keeper, known as *shiraqshi* or *shaykh*, who looks after a shrine. In a situation in which a *shaykh* considers himself to have connections with a saint associated with a shrine or a number of other well-known holy figures from the past (real or imaginary), a *mazarat* becomes more of a place to visit an intermediator to a saint. Besides holding the title of a *shaykh*, such a person also maintains a status of special "saint" estate and title of Khuja or Ishan, signifying a noble genealogy with claims as an inheritor of the sanctity where he protects (*baraka*).

As for pilgrimage rituals, they are often understood as relatively constant sequences of performances with particular forms of rites of passage, which, broadly speaking, emphasize the ways pilgrims experience rituals so as to accomplish particular social, natural, or cosmic goals. Besides the shared sacred places, each tribe or settlement has its own holy site, which is located in proximity to the community. Visitation can involve an individual experience or a group activity. Pilgrimage includes the circumambulation of the site and a prayer near the sacred site. Pilgrims touch the grave, the tombstone, its threshold, the entrance door, and the frame of the *mazarat*. Other objects of reverence include the lamps and the trees, which are stroked over the face and eyes. Pilgrims also tie pieces of cloth to trees or poles, perform the ablution in holy wells or springs, and slaughter animals. There are also patron saints of clans and tribes, whose tombs are located near the tombs of famous saints; this is believed to testify to the sacred identity of the tribe or clan ancestors.[64]

The rainmaking rite (*tasattyk*) —which originated from the ancient concepts of Turkic peoples about "rain stone" (*djede tash*) — still remains in some places, though this shaman ceremony has been penetrated by Islam. Usually, *tasattyk* was organized at a river or canal, in the house yard, or at the road, for the people to eat the sacrificial food. It is a rule that the blood of a sacrificed animal must flow into the running water. In southern Kazakhstan, *tasattyk* is carried out at *mazarat*, and the blood of a sacrificial animal is dug into the ground. A mullah or any participant of the rite prays, asking Allah and ascendants to give rain, well-being, and health to all those present. As a rule, *tasattyk* is made on Thursday or Friday, because these days —especially Friday —are regarded as "Muslim honorable days."[65] The choice for pilgrimage of a shrine is connected with a certain hierarchy of saints revered by the local population. Depending on the condition of the place or the importance of the shrine, donations are made for maintaining the shrines and helping the poor.

Khuja Ahmad Yassevi Shrine

The main shrine of Turkistan is the mausoleum of Khuja Ahmad Yassevi, dating back to the twelfth century.[66] Amir Timur (1336–1405) ordered the erection of the grandiose mausoleum over the grave of the famous Sufi teacher in honor of the defeat of the Golden Horde in the late fourteenth century. The whole necropolis consists of the mausoleums of Rabiya Sultan-Begim (fifteenth century), Kazakh khan Esim (seventeenth century), and other burials formed around the mausoleum of Khuja Ahmad Yassevi. There are construction projects for Sufis and the cult of Yassevi, such as a *chill-yakhana* (retreat room) and a bath that still remain to be completed. The most important shrine is the Khuja Ahmad Yassevi, a center of national and international pilgrimage. Thousands of pilgrims visit the shrine throughout the year, and the shrine receives a large number of tourists from the region and different parts of the country.

Pilgrimage is complex and contradictory, and it does not always have a clearly felt and expressed set of motivations and concepts. For some, pilgrimage is "a good God-pleasing deed" (*sawab*). Others are more receptive to

Islamic stories about the deeds of a great saint, his miracles, and references to well-known religious figures. But sacred events from Islamic tradition are perceived as sacred in a temporal context. This aspect is best reflected in pilgrim activities related to the need to visit *mazarat* for everyday problems as a standard and repeated form of visitation practice in Central Asia. Such pilgrim activities include visiting for the purpose of remedying infertility, curing ill health, and resolving personal and family issues. For this kind of pilgrim, the glory of "powerful" *mazarat* is more important than understanding the origin of its "power."

Besides the mausoleum of Khuja Ahmad Yassevi, the population honors the graves of his close relatives: his father, Ibragim-ata; his mother, Karashash-ana, in Sayram; his daughter and son-in-law, Gaukhar-ana and 'Ali Khuja, in Turkistan. Those Khujas who consider themselves to be descendants of Khuja Ahmad Yassevi and other Sufi saints reside in Turkistan. Khujas of the Turkistan region consist of two linguistic groups: Uzbek-speaking and Kazakh-speaking. Nowadays, Khujas who claim to be descendants of Khuja Ahmad Yassevi live in various countries of Central Asia. According to my observations, the shrine of Khuja Ahmad Yassavi in Turkistan is the general place of worship for some families of Khujas from Kazakhstan and Uzbekistan who suppose themselves to be descendants of Khuja Ahmad Yassevi. Some families speak only in Uzbek, and other families of Khujas speak native Kazakh. The shrine of Khuja Ahmad Yassevi is, for all of them, a symbolic place of the belonging to the sacred lineage.[67] Thus, it can be claimed, Khuja Ahmad Yassevi's cult has transnational lines.

It is interesting to observe the enthusiasm through which modern Kazakhs have embraced Khuja Ahmad Yassevi as a "Kazakh national saint," over whose shrine they appear to have complete control.[68] However, there are ethnic components in the course of pilgrimage. For example, Rabiya Sultan Begim (d. 1485) was the great-granddaughter of Amir Timur (1394–1449). Now the cult of Amir Timur and his descendants are most popular among the Uzbekistan population and also among a certain part of the Uzbek community in Kazakhstan. The local Uzbek population that visits her grave reveres Rabiya's mausoleum. Kazakh pilgrims from different areas of Kazakhstan visit the tomb of Khuja Ahmad Yassevi and those of the Kazakh khans Esim-khan and Ablay-khan. However, Rabiya's mausoleum does not enjoy similar popularity among them. While this is not mentioned in the official history of Kazakhstan collected in shrine catalogs published in post-Soviet Kazakhstan, the influence of the official history on the formation of a pantheon of holy sites is important to note.

The performance of pilgrimage involves a series of stages. Long before the journey begins, it is necessary to make *niyat* (intention). Rules of a *ziyara* include *tau etu*, or *tawapetu* (from the Arabic *tawaf*, meaning "prayer custom"), expressed most often when contact is made by palms on the forehead. Women have to enter with their hair covered.[69] During *ziyara*, it is necessary to spend the night near a *mazarat*. The main feature of the pilgrimage process is to pay one's respects to the tomb of Arystan-bab—Khuja Ahmad Yassevi's teacher—and only then arrive in Turkistan.[70] In the 1990s, pilgrims were forced to request lodging for the night from locals; today, pilgrims stay at the modern hotel complex constructed in post-Soviet period.

In my fieldwork, I observed a group of Kazakh pilgrims who visited Khuja Ahmad Yassevi's mausoleum. In the course of pilgrimage, they stopped for a prayer at the grave of Kazakh Ablay-khan (d. 1781), without having passed the grave of Khuja Ahmad Yassevi. This implies the importance of the cult of the Kazakh rulers (Chengizids) for this group of pilgrims (Tore), who are possibly descendants of Chengiz-khan. Here we should note location of residence. Descendants of master 'Abd al-aziz Tabrizi live in the village of Qarnak (Atabay) near Turkistan.[71] They also visit the mausoleum of Khuja Ahmad Yassevi, where the cauldron made by their ancestor is stored. For them, the cauldron is a symbol of their historical roots and cultural identity.

I met different groups of pilgrims at the shrines, including families and groups of pilgrims who had organized their trip from other regions. There were also recently married couples, who came to Khuja Ahmad Yassevi's mausoleum seeking blessings. The pilgrims wore different forms of attire, including Kazakh national dress as well as casual wear and European wedding outfits. Kazakh national dress is an important marker for some pilgrims as an expression of ethnic and cultural Kazakh identity. Soviet-era heritage was noticeable in the clothes of the newlyweds, though the influence of modern Western culture was also noticeable among some pilgrims.

For the last twenty-five years, the social composition of pilgrims has changed. Travel agencies organize trips to the holy sites, especially to Khuja Ahmad Yassevi's shrine, where, according to my research, youth and women participation has also increased. Motivation for pilgrimage also drastically varies. There are those who desire to participate in a religious holiday, pray at a holy site, or yearn to recover from physical illnesses; there are those who seek prosperity for themselves and their family. Some perform charitable work or pray for forgiveness of committed sins, while others express gratitude for the benefits received from above, as a result of a previous pilgrimage.

They show devotion in order to find meaning in life, and they do so either individually or with others.

Khuja Ahmad Yassevi's history is provided as proof of the early Islamization of Kazakhs. The process has been an important cultural indicator of a country with ancient pre-Islamic roots and national traditions based on Islam. The president of the Republic of Kazakhstan, Nursultan Nazarbayev, considers Yassevi to be the spiritual founder of the Turkic people. In his opinion, the process of interference of Tengrist and Muslim cultures is connected through Khuja Ahmad Yassevi. At the same time, the mausoleum of Yassevi is a symbol of Kazakh statehood.[72] Here, the local and the national fuse in symbolic ways.

The shrine of Khuja Ahmad Yassevi has emerged as a major focus of Kazakh-Turkish cooperation, symbolizing close communications between Kazakhstan and Turkey.[73] In recent years, the Turkish Religious Foundation (TDV) in Turkistan, in the name of Khuja Ahmad Yassevi, has built a mosque and a social complex. The foundation of another mosque, which will be built on the campus of Khuja Ahmad Yassevi International Kazakh-Turkish University, was laid in April 2015. The construction is being financed by private donations of philanthropists and undertaken by the TDV. This is one of the most advanced projects in Turkistan.[74]

Ukasha Ata Shrine

Ukasha-ata *mazarat* is approximately twenty-five kilometers from Kentau city, near the Karatau Mountains. Twenty-two meters long, the tombstone on the burial place of Ukasha-ata is one of the largest in Kazakhstan.[75] According to legend, Ukasha-ata was an Arab warrior who spread Islam among the Turkic tribes. At first, the locals saw an enemy in him. Being a very devout man, Ukasha-ata did not miss any *namaz* (prayers), and when praying, he did not take notice of his surroundings. While performing prayers one day, Ukasha-ata was cruelly beheaded. The head flew away twenty meters, leaving a bloody trail. Legend says that the tombstone covers the whole distance of every drop of Ukasha-ata's blood. According to oral tradition, as the head rolled away, it fell down a well, later turning up in Mecca.[76] This legend connects the holy site in Kazakhstan with Mecca, sacred to all Muslims, and emphasizes Islamic features of the shrine as well as the relativization of the Ka'ba. In this case, though, it is not the Ka'ba that has been merely relativized but the shrine of Ukasha-ata that has been transformed into Ka'ba.

The name Ukasha is connected with the name of the associate (*ashab*) of the Prophet Muhammad—'Ukasha bin Mihsan Al-Asadi.[77] Historical data demonstrates that Ukasha ibn Mikhsan had never been to Central Asia. Researchers assume that he was buried somewhere in the Middle East. There are shrines containing the name of Ukasha in the Ferghana Valley and the Balkh region of Afghanistan.[78] The local *shiraqshi* of the Kazakh shrine of Ukasha-ata, while emphasizing special uniqueness of this holy place, insists that Ukasha-ata's cult is purely local. According to him, Ukasha had been fighting in these regions and was buried here.[79]

In 1986, the Ukasha-ata *mazarat* was destroyed as a result of Soviet-led anti-religion campaigns. The *mazarat*, however, was rebuilt in the early 1990s. The newly built *mazarat* is expansive and accommodates a deep natural well, ruptured on a rock with a spring, located near the *mazarat*. Legend says that water appeared in the moment of Ukasha-ata's death and that it has a special health-giving quality. The population of the Turkistan region has revered the sacred well of Ukasha-ata and its medicinal waters. Based on popular belief, only people with a pure soul can consume the holy water. Most pilgrims fail in bringing the water back with them because their buckets either break or spill over during their trip home. This serves as a test of how people can purify their souls and whether God hears their prayers. Pilgrims coming to the shrine in search of a miraculous cure drink water and tie a piece of cloth to a long wooden stick. The long stick is installed on a hillock of stones near the well with water. This shrine is so popular that many pilgrims from other places in Kazakhstan (Taraz, Almaty, Turkistan, and so on) and even Uzbekistan (Tashkent Province) also visit. According to my data, most pilgrims are women, who come to visit the saint and pray in order to receive his patronage. In addition, the saints' shrines attract pilgrims because of their supposed healing properties. Making a wish, pilgrims bind a cloth ribbon to a nearby bush or branches. Similar beliefs also persist in different parts of Central Asia.

Similar to other communities in Central Asia, Kazakh pilgrimage rites include circular walks around a shrine. Pilgrimage performances also involve prayers at the shrine. There are also embodied practices associated with *mazarat*, such as touching various objects, including a grave, gravestone, door, threshold, or lintel. Blessing can also be attained by touching trees. The same hand that has touched such sacred objects can touch other parts of the body, particularly the eyes; ablution by water from a "sacred" well can also be important, as is the ritual of animal sacrifice, for its blessing can be shared among the community.[80]

Conclusion

This study indicates the complex and multidimensional phenomena of pilgrimage performed in the veneration of the saints, including contradictions of notions and motifs of the local population toward *mazarat* except in the cases of the shrines legalized by the state—for example, the mausoleum of Khuja Ahmad Yassevi. Today, the spread of Islamization among the population is entangled with the growth of pilgrimage to holy sites in southern Kazakhstan.

In the contemporary era, the reconstruction of shrines is related to issues of identity and the cultural revival following the collapse of the communist regime and its secularization campaigns. In some cases, shrines have attracted people who had no prior relationship to a sacred place. New experiences to establish a genealogical connection to shrines, often for political (legitimacy), economic (profit), or social (status) reasons, is a unique feature of the post-Soviet period. The newly built shrines in the post-Soviet era provide people with a place for religious meditation, while combining it with the traditional Kazakh cult of ancestors. The synthesis of the cult of Muslim saints and the cult of ancestors of the Kazakh people can be clearly observed. In this regard, the shrines are an important element of reconstruction of identity for Khuja descent groups, affirming respect and social status among the local population.

Shrines filled the spiritual vacuum created as a result of the communist project for the secularization of Central Asia. Kazakhstan authorities, however, have used religious symbols as an anchor for political legitimacy; in doing so, symbolism and identity-shaping features of shrine cultures have greatly increased at the local, regional, and national levels. While pilgrimage has grown since the end of the Soviet experiment, the state has emerged as a key actor in the reconstruction of the largest shrines in an attempt to fuse nationalism and religion in Kazakhstan.

Notes

1. Sergei N. Abashin and Vladimir O. Bobrovnikov, *Soblazni kulta svyatikh in Podvijniki islama. Kult svýatikh i sufizm v Sredney Azii i na Kavkaze* (Moscow: Vostochnaya, 2003), 5.

2. Vladimir N. Basilov, *Kult svyatikh v islame* (Moscow: Misl, 1970), 10.

3. Samuel George Frederick Brandon, ed., *A Dictionary of Comparative Religion* (London: Weidenfeld and Nicolson, 1970), 501.

4. I would like to express my gratitude to the Max Planck Institute for Social Anthropology for scientific and financial support of my research on Khuja in Central Asia: construction and transformation of identity.

5. Azim Malikov, "Iz istorii svyatikh mest dolini Srednego Zerafshana," in *Izvestiya Kazakhskoj Natsionalnoj Akademii nauk* 2 (2010): 49–52; Abdulmamad Iloliev, "Popular Culture and Religious Metaphor: Saints and Shrines in Wakhan Region of Tajikistan," *Central Asian Survey* 27, no. 1 (2008): 59–73.

6. *Regioni Kazakhstana v 2015 godu. Statisticheskiy ejegodnik* (Astana: Komitet po statistike Ministerstva natsionalnoi ekonomiki Respubliki Kazakhstan, 2016), 26.

7. Pierre Julien, "In Quest of the Holiest Place in Central Asia," *Central Asian Survey* 4, no. 1 (1985): 116.

8. Igor Lipovsky, "The Awakening of Central Asian Islam," in *Islam: Critical Concepts in Sociology*, ed. Brian S. Turner (London and New York: Routledge, 2003), 2:316.

9. The term *Khuja* (*Khwaja, Khodja, Qozha, Khoja*), which means "master" in Persian, has been taken to imply, variously, descent from Arabs, descent from the Prophet or 'Ali, descent from the first caliphs, or descent from Islamizing saints. Devin DeWeese, foreword to *Islamization and Sacred Lineages in Central Asia: The Legacy of Ishaq Bab in Narrative and Genealogical Traditions*, vol. 2, *Genealogical Charters and Sacred Families: Nasab-namas and Khuja Groups Linked to the Ishaq Bab Narrative, 19th–21st Centuries*, ed. Ashirbek Muminov, Anke von Kügelgen, Devin DeWeese, and Michael Kemper (Almati: Daik Press, 2008), 6–33; Devin DeWeese, "The Politics of Sacred Lineages in 19th-Century Central Asia: Descent Groups Linked to Khwaja Ahmad Yasavi in Shrine Documents and Genealogical Charters," *International Journal of Middle Eastern Studies* 31, no. 4 (1999): 507–30.

10. Ashirbek Muminov, "Veneration of Holy Sites of the Mid-Sirdarya Valley: Continuity and Transformation," in *Muslim Culture in Russia and Central Asia from the 18th to the Early 20th Centuries*, ed. Michael Kemper, Anke von Kügelgen, and Dimitriy Yermakov (Berlin: Klaus Schwarz Verlag), 356.

11. Maria Eva Subtelny, "The Cult of Holy Places: Religious Practices among Soviet Muslims," *Middle East Journal* 43, no. 4 (1989): 594–95.

12. Katherine Ewing, "The Politics of Sufism: Redefining the Saints of Pakistan," *Journal of Asian Studies* 42, no. 2 (1983): 254.

13. Pedram Khosronejad, introduction to *Saints and Their Pilgrims in Iran and Neighbouring Countries*, ed. Pedram Khosronejad (Wantage: Sean Kingston, 2012), 3–12.

14. Ernest Gellner, *Muslim Society* (Cambridge: Cambridge University Press, 1995).

15. Inga V. Stasevich, "Praktika pokloneniya sakralnim objektam i predmetam v traditsionnoj i sovremennoj culture kazakhov i kirgizov (v kontekste izucheniya kulta svyatikh)," in *Tsentralnaya Aziya: traditsiya v usloviyakh peremen*. Vipusk 3. (Sankt-Peterburg: MAE, 2012), 282.

16. Ira Marvin Lapidus, *A History of Islamic Societies* (Cambridge: Cambridge University Press, 2002), 208.

17. DeWeese, foreword to *Islamization and Sacred Lineages in Central Asia*.

18. In Kazakhstan, very famous and esteemed are the saints: those also revered in official Islam: Abu Bakr, Omar, Osman, and 'Ali; warriors fallen for faith: Ishak-bab and Ukasha-ata; Sufi saints: Khuja Ahmad Yassavi, Arystan-bab, and Gaukhar-ana; the saints-ancestors of Kazakh tribes: Baydabek-ata, Domalak-ata, and Shakhan-ata; the saints-patrons of professions: Korkut, the patron of Kazakh shamans, musicians, and singers; Baba-Tukty Shashty-Aziz, the patron of Kazakh batyr; Dikan-ata, the patron

of farming; and Koshkar-ata, the patron of sheep breeding. Raushan M. Mustafina, "Obichai narodnogo islama," *Vostochnaya kollektsiya*, no. 3 (2005), 50–56. Burial places of *shahids* (died as martyrs) were also places for worshipping and religious activities, as were graves of traditional healers, who treated many people or animals and were kept in people's memory. There are also special *qadamjoi* (*qadam* means "footsteps," a place visited by a saint). While many of the saints are male, South Kazakhstan Province has a number of shrines devoted to female saints. Female pilgrimage sites are particularly amenable to the requests of girls and women. Some tombs of female saints are frequently visited—for example, the shrine of Gaukhar-ana in the Turkistan region. South Kazakhstan shrines of sacred women include those of Domalak Ana, Aysha-bibi, Karashash Ana, and Bibi Mariyam. Khamza Koktendi, *Turki teberigi Turkistan* (Almati: Kasiet Koktendi, 2008). The holy place of Aysha-bibi is especially revered by sterile women, who ask to be granted children and a good family. In South Kazakhstan, there are also shrines of warriors.

19. Mustafina, *Obichai narodnogo islama* in *Vostochnaya kollektsiya*, 56.

20. Stasevich, "Praktika pokloneniya sakralnim objektam I predmetam traditsionnoj i sovremennoj culture kazakhov I kirgizov (v kontekste izucheniya kulta svyatikh)," 272.

21. Ashirbek K. Muminov, "Svyatie mesta v Tsentralnoy Azii (vzaimodeystvie obsheislamskikh i mestnikh elementov," *MayakVostoka* 1–2 (1996): 15. By the first mentioned indication, *mazarat* may be divided into (1) well known all over Central Asia; (2) well known in one province or region; and (3) well known in only one locality. By the second indication, shrines are divided into (1) one part (only one shrine, such as a water source, a tree, or a rock); (2) two part (with an imaginary or a real grave); (3) complex (with a mausoleum); (4) with *khanaka*; (5) with a mausoleum and cemetery; (6) with a mausoleum and mosque; and (7) with a mausoleum, mosque, and madrasa with vaqf. Muminov, 15.

22. The steppe area between the Dnepr River and West Siberia.

23. Olga A. Sukhareva, *Islam v Uzbekistane* (Tashkent: izdatelstvo Akademii nauk Uzbekskoy SSR, 1960), 26–27.

24. *Alpamis-Batir, Pod redaktsiey M.O.Auezova i N.S.Smirnovoi. Izdanie podgotovili: N.S.Smirnova i T.S.Sidikov* (Alma-Ata: Izdatelstvo Akademii nauk Kazakhskoi SSR, 1961), 319–20.

25. Bruce G. Privratsky, "'Turkistan Belongs to the Qojas': Local Knowledge of a Muslim Tradition," in *Devout Societies vs. Impious States? Transmitting Islamic Learning in Russia, Central Asia and China, through the Twentieth Century; Proceedings of an International Colloquium Held in the Carré des Sciences, French Ministry of Research, Paris, November 12–13, 2001*, ed. Stephane A. Dudoignon (Berlin: Klaus Schwarz Verlag, 2004), 167.

26. Seidomar Sattaruly, *Abd ul-zhalil bab (Khorasan ata)* (Almaty: RIITS Aziya, 2007).

27. Subtelny, "Cult of Holy Places," 594–95.

28. Maria Louw, "Pursuing 'Muslimness'": Shrines as Sites for Moralities in the Making in Post-Soviet Bukhara," *Central Asian Survey* 25, no. 3 (2006): 325.

29. Devin DeWeese, "Shrine and Pilgrimage," in *Inner Asian Islam: Historical Foundations and Responses to Soviet Policy* (Washington, DC: National Council for Soviet and East European Research, 1995), 1–6.

30. Subtelny, "Cult of Holy Places," 598; Julien, "In Quest of the Holiest Place in Central Asia," 119.

31. Muminov, "Veneration of Holy Sites of the Mid-Sirdarya Valley," 356.

32. Sergey Marinin, "State Regulation of Religion in Kazakhstan: Reconsideration of Approaches," *Central Asian Security Policy* 23 (2015): 5.

33. Lipovsky, "Awakening of Central Asian Islam," 331.

34. See Gulmira Mukhtarova, "History of Kazakh Hajj," August 30, 2007, http://nm2000.kz/news/2007-08-30-1241; and Amangeldy Abdikalyk, "Over the Years of Independence, the Republic of Kazakhstan Sent about 35 Thousand Pilgrims," interview by Gulnara Adamova, September 2, 2015, http://islamsng.com/kaz/interviews/8685.

35. *Religioznie objedineniya v Kazakhstane: informatsionnij spavochnik. Astana: nauchno-issledovatelskij i analiticheskij tsentr Agenststva Respubliki Kazakhstan po delam religij* (Astana: Nauchno-issledovatelskii i analiticheskii tsentr po voprosam religii Agentstva Respubliki Kazakhstan po delam religii, 2013), 21; Ministry of Religious Affairs and Civil Society of the Republic of Kazakhstan, accessed March 30, 2017, https://www.caravan.kz/news/v-kakikh-regionakh-kazakhstana-mechetejj-i-cerkvejj-bolshe-chem-bolnic-infografika-400543/.

36. "Information about the Religious Situation in the Region," October 27, 2016, http://ontustik.gov.kz/ru/pages/informaciya-o-religioznoy-situacii-v-oblasti-o.

37. Saniya Edelbay, "The Islamic Situation in Kazakhstan," *International Journal of Humanities and Social Science* 2, no. 21 (2012): 215.

38. Edelbay, 217.

39. Ulan Bigozhin, "Religion and the Nation-State in Kazakhstan: Some Insights from Field Work in Aqkol," *CERIA Briefs* 7 (2015): 2.

40. Ashirbek K. Muminov, S. Uchastiem, Aitzhan. Nurmanovoi, and Seitomar Sattarova, *Rodoslovnoe drevo Mukhtara Auezova* (Almati: Jibek joli, 2011), 2015.

41. Saniya Edelbay, "Traditional Kazakh Culture and Islam," *International Journal of Business and Social Science* 3, no. 11 (2012): 215.

42. Ainur Kurmanalyeva, Aktolkyn Kulsaryieva, and Damira Sikhimbaeva, "The Religious Situation in Kazakhstan: The Main Trends and Challenges in World," *Applied Sciences Journal* 25, no. 11 (2013): 1615.

43. Bruce G. Privratsky, *Muslim Turkistan: Kazak Religion and Collective Memory* (London: Curzon Press, 2011). See "Bibliography of Islam in Kazakhstan" section of the following work: Simon Michael Braune, "Islam as Practiced by the Kazaks: A Bibliography for Scholars," *MELA Notes* 78 (2005), 1–17.

44. Yaacov Ro'i and Alon Wainer, "Muslim Identity and Islamic Practice in Post-Soviet Central Asia," *Central Asian Survey* 28, no. 3 (2009): 305.

45. The Agency for Religious Affairs of the Republic of Kazakhstan was established in accordance with a decree of the president of the Republic of Kazakhstan № 84 of May 18, 2011, through reorganization of the Ministry of Culture of the Republic of Kazakhstan by means of allocation of the Agency for Religious Affairs of the Republic of Kazakhstan. The agency is a central executive body in charge of state management in the field of interreligious accord, rights of citizens to freedom of religion and interaction with religious associations, and intersectoral coordination to the extent

provided by law. See https://tengrinews.kz/zakon/pravitelstvo_respubliki_kazahstan_premer_ministr_rk/konstitutsionnyiy_stroy_i_osnovyi_gosudarstvennogo_upravleniya/id-P1100000888/.

46. Nurlan Yermekbayev, "Why Kazakhstan Created the Ministry for Religious and Civil Society Affairs," November 10, 2016, http://thediplomat.com/2016/11/why-kazakhstan-created-the-ministry-for-religious-and-civil-society-affairs.

47. Government of the Republic of Kazakhstan, "Ministry of Religious Affairs and Civil Society Was Renamed the Ministry of Social Development," June 29, 2018, http://www.government.kz/en/novosti/1015185-ministry-of-religious-affairs-and-civil-society-was-renamed-the-ministry-of-social-development.html.

48. Edward Schatz, "The Politics of Multiple Identities: Lineage and Ethnicity in Kazakhstan," *Europe-Asia Studies* 52, no. 3 (2000): 499–502.

49. Schatz, 499–502.

50. Nayman was a medieval Turko-Mongolian tribe, which was later incorporated into the Kazakh, Uzbek, and Kyrgyz people.

51. Bigozhin, "Religion and the Nation-State in Kazakhstan," 2, 5.

52. Iloliev, "Popular Culture and Religious Metaphor," 61.

53. Wendell Schwab, "Islam in Print: The Diversity of Islamic Literature and Interpretation in Post-Soviet Kazakhstan" (PhD diss., Indiana University, 2011), 20, 43.

54. E. M. Smagulov, "ADR RK: Okkultnoe techenie «Ata joli» prodoljaet rabotu vo mnogikh regionakh Kazakhstana," accessed October 28, 2018, https://www.zakon.kz/4571413-adr-rk-okkultnoe-techenie-ata-zholy.html.

55. Schwab, 20, 43.

56. Sabina Seksembaeva, "Kolichestvo religioznikh obedineniy Kazakhstana posle pereregistratsii sokratilos bolee chem na tisachu," accessed November 17, 2018, https://online.zakon.kz/Document/?doc_id=31287721.

57. Jan A. M. Snoek, "Defining 'Rituals,'" in *Theorizing Rituals: Issues, Topics, Approaches, Concepts*, ed. Jens Kreinath, Jan Snoek, and Michael Stausberg (Leiden: Brill, 2006), 11.

58. Edward Bradley Reeves, "The Wali Complex at Tanta, Egypt: An Ethnographic Approach to Popular Islam" (PhD diss., University of Kentucky, 1981), 260–62.

59. Koktendi, *Turki teberigi Turkistan*; Shaydarbek Ashimuli, *Sir bojindaghi aulieler* (Almati: Atamura, 2000); Nurizat Esengeldiqyzy Baytasova, *Qabyl Bolsyn Ziyarat!* (Shymkent: Altyn Alqa, 2009).

60. Schwab, "Islam in Print," 178–79.

61. Schwab, 54.

62. Mustafina, *Obichai narodnogo islama in Vostochnaya kollektsiya*, 52.

63. Mustafina, 53.

64. Muminov, *Veneration of Holy Sites of the Mid-Sirdarya Valley*, 365.

65. Mustafina, *Obichai narodnogo islama in Vostochnaya kollektsiya*, 53.

66. Khuja Ahmad Yassavi was a famous Turkic poet and Sufi mystic. His descendants claimed that he was a descendant of the Prophet Muhammad.

67. Azim Malikov, *Sacred Lineages in Central Asia: Translocality and Identity in Mobilities, Boundaries, and Travelling Ideas; Rethinking Translocality beyond Central Asia and the Caucasus*, ed. Manja Stephan-Emmrich and Philipp Schröder (Cambridge: Open Book, 2018), 137–38.

68. Nazira. D. Nurtazina, "Religioznij turizm Kazakhstane: Istoriya i sovremennie problemi," *Sovremennie problemi servisa i turizma* 4 (2009): 25–27.

69. Nurtazina, 25–27.

70. Nurtazina, 25–27.

71. He was from Iran and made a cauldron for a shrine in 1399. In 1935, the cauldron was taken away on an exhibition to Leningrad and left in the Hermitage Museum. Only in 1989, as a result of negotiations with the authorities of the USSR, was it returned home and again solemnly established in the central hall of the mausoleum.

72. Nursultan Nazarbaev, *V potoke istorii* (Almati: Atamura, 1999), 278–79. The mausoleum of Khuja Ahmad Yassavi was pictured on the back of the banknotes of the Kazakh national currency until 2006.

73. In 2000, experts from Turkey were specifically invited to participate in the restoration of the mausoleum's original décor. Turkish president Recap Tayyip Erdoğan; his wife, Emine Erdoğan; and Kazakh president Nursultan Nazarbayev visited the mausoleum of Khuja Ahmad Yassevi in Turkistan on April 17, 2015, praying there with Turkistan head of religious affairs Mehmet Gormez.

74. Davut Han Aslan and Duygu Bozyigit, "Turkey-Kazakhstan Relations: An Overview of Mutual Relations since the Collapse of the Soviet Union," *Kwartalnik Naukowy Uczelni Vistula* 4, no. 42 (2014): 141.

75. See Azim Malikov, "Svyatilishe Ukasha-ata v yujnom Kazakhstane i ego analogii v Tsentralnoi Azii," in *Izvestiya Natsionalnogo tsentra arkheografii i istocnikovedeniya* 2 (2015): 55–63.

76. Koktendi, *Turki teberigi Turkistan*, 106.

77. *The Translation of Meanings of Sahih al-Bukhari*. Arabic-English. Vol. 7. Translated by Muhammad Muhsin Khan (Riyadh: Darussalam, 1997), 387.

78. Azim Malikov, *Svyatie mesta Turkestanskogo regiona: Osobennosti istorii i sovremennost in Lokalniye religiozniye verovaniya v Tsentralnoy Azii. Materiali mejdunarodnogo nauchnogo seminara* (Almati: Izdatelskiy dom Mir, 2017), 129–44.

79. Zaure Mirzakhojaeva, "Volshebniy istochnik," http://www.time.kz/articles/reporter/2018/10/23/volshebnij-istochnik.

80. Raushan Mustafina, *Predstavleniya, kulti i obryadi u kazakhov (v kontekste bitovogo islama v Yujnom Kazakhstane v kontse XIX—XX vv.)* (Almati: Qazaq Universiteti, 1992), 103.

CHAPTER SEVEN

Economies of Piety at the Syrian Shrine of Sayyida Zaynab

EDITH SZANTO

Until 2011, when the Syrian Uprising began, the shrine of Sayyida Zaynab, just south of Damascus, was a popular destination for Muslims, especially Twelver Shiʿis from all over the Middle East and South Asia. Located at the center of large markets, where devotees could buy religious goods such as books and prayer beads, as well as clothing and jewelry, the shrine attracted shoppers and pilgrims of all ages and economic means. This chapter examines pilgrimage with regard to economic activities that occur at the destination—in this case, the shrine and town of Sayyida Zaynab. With regard to contemporary Shiʿi pilgrimage in Syria and Iraq, Mona Moufahim and Paulo G. Pinto have focused on gifting practices and the feeling of *communitas*, which arises from religious consumption.[1] The following analysis augments their work by drawing attention to the ways in which sacred time and space influence these practices. Specifically, during its heyday, there was an important difference between the economic activities inside and outside the shrine, where non-Shiʿi participated in buying and selling Shiʿi merchandise. Inside the shrine, gifting took precedence, while outside the shrine, consumerism took precedence. During the annual commemoration of the Battle of Karbala, however, the sacred space of the shrine spilled into the streets. There, Shiʿi communities operated hospitality tents, which welcomed the visitors who poured into the shrine town. The notion that pilgrimage is a ritualized, formal visit that demands hospitality explains the centrality of these tents during Muharram. In short, by examining various pious "economic" activities in and around the shrine, this chapter contributes to a more nuanced understanding of the ways in which space and consumerism influence religious practices and consumer relationships, particularly in the case of the Syrian shrine town of Sayyida Zaynab.

This chapter first provides a brief history of the shrine town, especially with regard to the influence of religious figures and political developments in the region. Second, it examines the geographical distribution of economic activities in the shrine town. Third, it augments Mona Moufahim's tripartite typology of gifting practices by comparing social relationships with regard to space—that is, inside versus outside the shrine. The perspective on pilgrimage, which this chapter offers, emphasizes the demands religious and social relationships make on individual believers. These demands include hospitality, which, similar to the way in which Louis Massignon envisioned the practice, intensifies and needs to be met during Muharram, when the entire town transforms into a Bakhtinian carnival.² The main argument this chapter presents is that there are two economic modes at play in the shrine town. The relationships outside the shrine at times other than Muharram are governed by their monetary utility, while those inside the shrine are representative of hospitality, approximating a religious version of Marcel Mauss's concept of gifting.³

The Shrine and Town of Sayyida Zaynab

The Syrian shrine town of Sayyida Zaynab, which is located approximately fifteen kilometers south of Damascus, is considered one of the most important Shi'i shrines of the family of the Prophet Muhammad. Zaynab was the granddaughter of the Prophet and the daughter of Imam 'Ali and Fatima. She witnessed the Battle of Karbala, where her brother Husayn was martyred on 'ashura, the tenth day of the Islamic month of Muharram, in 680 C.E. Zaynab is credited with keeping Shi'i sm alive by initiating ritual mourning gatherings in memory of Husayn.⁴ It is unclear whether Zaynab is actually buried in Syria. Shi'is accept that she is buried in Syria, whereas Egyptian Sunnis hold that she is buried in Egypt.⁵

Though the shrine does appear in historical records, it was not always as prominent as it became in the last quarter of the twentieth century.⁶ In the first half of the twentieth century, the shrine benefited from the tireless efforts of Sayyid Muhsin al-Amin (d. 1952), the *mujtahid* (Shi'i jurist) of Damascus, who raised funds for renovations and authored numerous works to promote Shi'ism in Syria and to attract Shi'i pilgrims to Syrian shrines. Nevertheless, before 1948, when Palestinian refugees settled in the area, it was little more than an unimportant shrine in the midst of farmlands and olive groves. In 1967, Golani internally displaced persons (IDPs) were settled just to the north of the Palestinian camp. As both Palestinians and Golani Syrians were Sunni, the town remained largely Sunni until Shi'is coming from Iraq began to settle there in the 1970s.

Many of the first Shi'is were *ulama*, seminary students, and professionals. Some of them were exiled because of their affiliation with the Shi'i Da'wa Party. Others were exiled because they were suspected of Iranian descent.⁷

Afghan clerics and seminary students had been living in Karbala before being deported following bloody clashes between Shi'is and the Ba'th military in in Karbala in the 1970s.[8] The shrine of Sayyida Zaynab gained such prominence at that time that when 'Ali Shariati died in France in 1977, his body was flown to Syria and was buried in a small graveyard just north of the mausoleum.

In 1973, Sayyid Hasan Shirazi (d. 1980) was the first to establish a seminary in the shrine town of Sayyida Zaynab.[9] Since then, many others have built Shi'i institutions, including seminaries and hospitals that helped attract religious students, refugees, and visitors to Sayyida Zaynab. The shrine maintained its status as an important pilgrimage destination throughout the 1970s and 1980s, when the Iraqi Shi'i shrine towns of Najaf and Karbala became inaccessible, first because the Iraqi government feared the growing Shi'i opposition and later because of the Iran-Iraq War. Thereafter, the Iraqi shrines remained inaccessible due to sanctions and continuing violence. Hence, many Shi'i visited the shrine town of Sayyida Zaynab instead.

The Syrian government joined the effort of clerics to promote Twelver Shi'ism in Syria because the 'Alawite ruling elite wanted to identify as Shi'i. Throughout the 1970s and 1980s, Syrian president Hafez al-Asad faced staunch opposition by the Muslim Brotherhood, which accused him of being a non-Muslim. Asad responded by obtaining a fatwa from Sayyid Musa al-Sadr, the founder of the Amal Movement in Lebanon, which declared 'Alawites to be Shi'is and therefore Muslims.[10] This religious tactic helped Asad consolidate a fruitful alliance with Shi'is in Lebanon and the Islamic Republic of Iran. These warm relations led to mutual economic and military aid, as well as the rise of religious tourism.

Twelver Shi'is have been and continue to be a small minority in Syria. After 2003, hundreds of thousands of Iraqi Shi'i refugees came to Syria from Iraq. During the July 2006 war between Lebanon and Israel, another hundreds of thousands of "visitors" arrived from Lebanon. On a much smaller scale, there were also Shi'is from the Arab states on the Persian Gulf, such as Kuwait, Bahrain, and the eastern parts of Saudi Arabia, and Shi'is from South Asia. Iraqi refugees tended to be poor. By contrast, the religious tourists that flocked to the shrine town during religious holidays and summer months brought cold hard cash. This flow of cash, as well as the religious legitimacy it brought, ensured that the Syrian government would smile benignly at the flourishing of religious tourism. According to Shin Yasuda, approximately three million Shi'i religious tourists visited Syria annually.[11] Of these, the vast majority came from Iran; others arrived from Lebanon,

Iraq, Turkey, South Asia, and the Persian Gulf countries; and a small minority came from Europe and North America.

The Geography of Religious Tourism

The main road, which connects the shrine town with Damascus to the north, cuts Sayyida Zaynab into two halves. During its popularity, the western half was largely Sunni, though South Asians, Afghans, and some Iraqis lived there as well. The eastern half was largely Shi'i. The Sunni areas were further divided into two areas: the Palestinian camp to the south, established in 1948, and the Golani settlement to the north, built after 1967. The Golani neighborhoods were considered more liberal, relatively inexpensive, and tolerant of outsiders, which is why some South Asian, Afghan, and Iraqi Shi'is lived there. The widest street in this area was Hijera, a market famous for its low-priced wares, clothes, and grocery stands.

The main road of Sayyida Zaynab was lined with Iranian, Iraqi, and Yemeni restaurants; smaller local eateries, juice stalls, and pastry shops; and a variety of shops. To the west of the main road stood two predominantly Shi'i areas: an Iraqi neighborhood along Shari'a al-'Iraqiyin (Iraqis' street) and an Iranian area called Suq al-Iraniyin (Iranians' market), which consisted of a market surrounded by hotels. The Iraqi area to the north was considerably more conservative than Hijera, where women wore colorful scarves and dresses. Walking along the Shari'a al-'Iraqiyin, women usually wore the Iraqi abaya or a black overcoat and often a face veil. Stores on the Iraqi street had Iraqi names and carried Iraqi merchandise, such as Iraqi nationalist symbols and Iraqi food, and from there, agencies sold bus tickets to Baghdad, Najaf, and Karbala. To the north, an unused and closed-off park and bus station separated the street of the Iraqis from the shrine. South of the shrine, the Iranian area was made up of hotels and markets geared toward working-class, elderly, rural, and religious tourists. The Iranian market impinged onto the Palestinian area nearest to the shrine. The Suq al-Iraniyin carried religious items such as posters of Shi'i religious leaders, prayer carpets, prayer beads, *turba* (baked clay pieces that Shi'is use in prayer), scarves, and funerary linen.

Iranian pilgrims often stayed in Sayyida Zaynab for approximately a fortnight and split their time between the shrine of Sayyida Zaynab, the two Shi'i religious sites in the old city of Damascus, and the markets.[12] Shi'is from the Gulf typically came for a couple of months in the summer to escape the heat, to visit the shrine, and to attend summer classes at the seminaries. These

Arabs spent their money on religious items they could not obtain in the Gulf, such as books, CDs, pictures, and decorative items. The Iraqis, who usually settled for years before either returning to Iraq or migrating westward, did little shopping—religious or otherwise)—due to a lack of money. Iraqis that arrived before 2003 usually integrated a little better than those who came later. Some Iraqis, similar to some Iranian Iraqis, Afghans, and South Asians, worked as vendors and were occasionally sought after as salespeople because of their linguistic abilities. After 2007, new legislation made it increasingly difficult for Iraqis to stay and work legally. This forced them to either become day laborers or work in jobs that paid little and did not use their skills.

Economic Relations in Sacred Space

In her study on Shi'i pilgrimage and religious gifting, Moufahim identifies three types of gifting: supplication, soteriological, and liturgical.[13] All three are related, and individual practices can fall into more than one category. Moreover, it is significant that all three types occurred at the shrine demarcating sacred from ordinary space, wherein these practices did not occur to the same extent.

Supplication gifts are usually small gifts distributed at the shrine. The gifts are typically bought outside the shrine and then brought into the shrine for the express purpose of distributing them. For instance, Shi'i women commonly distributed candies or incense at the shrine of Sayyida Zaynab in gratitude for answered prayers. This was part of the practice of making religious vows, or *nadhr*, among Shi'i women, wherein women promise to donate particular items or perform specific rituals if their wishes are granted.[14] These women typically distributed milk out of gratitude for the recovery of a sick child or the successful delivery of a healthy infant. Women also distributed small gifts at the shrine before their wishes were fulfilled. Some distributed lit incense and asked those to whom they handed the incense to help pray for a loved one in need. By doing so, they created a ritual community that tied believers to one another and to the saint.

Moufahim describes soteriological gifts as doing good deeds and praying on someone else's behalf. Soteriological gifts can overlap with supplication gifts, as in the case of handing out incense and asking others for prayers. Her third type, liturgical gifts, consists of prayer-related items, such as scarves or prayer beads, which pilgrims believed to be endowed with blessings because they were acquired at or near the shrine. Inside the shrine, there was only one store, whose inventory was reduced and then moved to a small room in 2008. The store sold predominantly liturgical items, such as prayer beads, but also books by Ayatollah Khamenei and his sympathizers. There was a seasonal stand, which was affiliated with the Lebanese Hezbollah movement and sold calendars with Hezbollah's insignia, as well as CDs and DVDs of sermons by Hassan Nasrallah. Unofficially, there were third parties, such as poor women, who informally peddled incense and religious bijoux. Customers were less likely to haggle with these poor women because buying small items from them concurrently constituted acts of charity (*sadaqa*).

Besides Moufahim's threefold typology, I would add another form of exchange: that between the saint and her visitors. While pilgrims may donate money or items to the shrine, visiting Zaynab does not always require bringing elaborate gifts to be shared with other pilgrims. Some may simply tie a ribbon to the gilded latticework that encases the tomb as part of making their vow.[15] Visitors usually hang on to the grid and kiss it. The shrine fosters an affective economy aside from a gifting economy. When they leave or before entering, visitors may drink water from the fountain by the eastern exit. Other Shi'i shrines in Najaf and Karbala are similarly furnished with drinking fountains. Some believe that this water comes from the saint and will heal them. In these practices, the circulation of goods, emotions, and water produces a sense of pious *communitas*. It erases class and ethnic distinctions, cements the relationship between the saint and her devotees, and emphasizes religious unity and human needs.

Inside the shrine, visitors were mostly Shi'i. The shrine had a special area for Sunni men, which was accessible only from the main road, not from inside the shrine. Services at the prayer hall were carried out by representatives of Hezbollah and Iran's Ayatollah Khamenei. Outside, religious authority was shared on a wider basis. The Sadrs, Shirazis, and other scholarly and politically involved families ran hospitals, seminaries, and offices, where they openly challenged the views of Khamenei and Hezbollah.[16] In contrast to the vendors in the markets outside the shrine, the vendors inside the shrine complex were presumably Shi'is.

Does this mean that the circulation of goods inside the shrine produced a sense of *communitas*? More generally, how did the different national and sectarian groups relate to one another? The relationships that customers and vendors had outside the shrine differed sharply from the relationships between the pious inside the shrine. Outside the shrine, many of the vendors were not Shi'i but Sunni. They were Palestinian, Syrian, and Kurdish, while the buyers tended to be Iranians, Arabs from Gulf countries, and

Shi'is who were living in the West. Because of their religious and ethnic differences, the sellers were mainly interested in their clients as consumers; they were not invested in the *communitas* their products might induce. In my interviews, Palestinians and Kurds in Sayyida Zaynab expressed a strong dislike for Iraqis and a preference for Iranians. They bluntly admitted that the reason for their fondness for Iranians was their money. Iranians were lucrative customers who bought merchandise and then left the country. Iraqis were often poor and did not come to Sayyida Zaynab as pilgrims but as asylum seekers. This meant that they did not splurge on luxury items or unessential products in the touristy markets. Rather, they vied for jobs with locals, accepted lower wages, and thus constituted a threat to locals' livelihoods and employment opportunities. Iraqis were disliked by Syrians because their large numbers caused a housing shortage, which drove up rental and real estate prices. In addition, they saw them as a corrupting force, as Iraqi women added to the number of prostitutes. On an ideological level, Iraqis replaced Palestinians as the neediest refugees in Syria, diverting social and political attention, pity, and sympathy. Iraqis, in turn, worked in the markets and were divided when it came to Iranian customers. While they all recognized that Iranian funds were the reason the shrine town's economy thrived, some distrusted Iranians for nationalist reasons. In short, outside the shrine, relationships were defined by their economic utility.

Concurrently, there were factors that undermined *communitas* at the shrine. For one, the circulation of goods was not always voluntary. In other words, theft was a Hajj problem, particularly in 2006, when the crisis in Iraq reached new heights. This made devotees suspicious of one another and undermined their mutual goodwill. Second, the shrine's prayer hall was ideologically controlled by the Lebanese Hezbollah movement and Ayatollah 'Ali Khamenei. Their books were sold at the bookstore inside the shrine compound, and their donation boxes were circulated. Hezbollah's military might was displayed in posters near the Shi'i prayer area (or *musalla*) to the east of the shrine. Those who disagreed, such as the followers of Ayatollah Sadiq Shirazi, whose brother founded the first seminary in Sayyida Zaynab, or those who followed the Iraqi nationalist aspiring cleric and militia leader Muqtada Sadr felt left out. In fact, the Shirazis and some Sadrists purposefully avoided praying at the shrine on Fridays at noon. Instead, they formed their own circles for mourning rituals at the back of the shrine's courtyard during Muharram. They also sold their materials, including books and CDs, in their own bookstores. By encouraging their followers to not partake in the Friday prayer at the shrine, the Shirazis and the Sadrists undermined *communitas*.

Welcoming the Guests of the Saint

As noted in the introduction, pilgrimage in Arabic is *ziyara* and literally means "visitation." Someone who performs a pilgrimage is a visitor, or *za'ir*. The acts of visiting and providing hospitality, as Louis Massignon explains, are sacred duties.[17] These acts of kindness, mercy, and piety carry religious reward, or *baraka*, and can produce miracles.[18] Hosting guests is an act of honor and generosity, and in turn, it is a disgrace to fail at hosting and serving guests. Beyond blessing, as Dervla Shannahan points out, pilgrimage constitutes and strengthens the bonds of love.[19]

The notion that pilgrims are visitors responding out of love facilitated the cultivation of gifting relationships inside the shrine. It demarcated local Shi'i residents as hosts and short-term visitors as guests. This host-guest relationship became especially pronounced during the first ten days of Muharram, when local neighborhoods, extended families, seminaries, and other religious organizations donated their time and money and organized hospitality tents around the shrine and along the main road leading up to the shrine. For ten days, and again shortly for the *arba'in*, which marks the fortieth day after *'ashura*, hospitality tents served guests, pilgrims, and passersby tea, water, juice, sandwiches, and even *qayma*, a traditional dish of rice and a paste made of meat and beans. While guests did include some Sunnis who came to enjoy the free refreshments, those running the hospitality tents generally imagined themselves as hosts serving the guests of the saint.

There were two types of Shi'i visitors who came to visit Sayyida Zaynab during Muharram: those who traveled from abroad and those who lived nearby. They could be classified by relying on the German distinction between *Pilgerfahrt* (pilgrimage) and *Wallfahrt* (local pilgrimage).[20] Those who came from abroad were predominantly women, who arrived on buses that had to park outside the shrine town during Muharram. Those that came from Homs or Damascus included about the same number of men and women, many of whom walked; some even came barefoot.[21] Since both groups walked into town, both passed the hospitality tents, which welcomed Zaynab's visitors. These pilgrims belonged primarily to the working class. Wealthier pilgrims, such as Shi'is from the Gulf, avoided frequenting the hospitality tents.[22]

These hospitality tents temporarily extended the sacred space of the shrine, where gifting took place, beyond the actual space of the shrine and onto the streets leading up to the shrine. Around and beyond the hospitality tents, markets and vendors continued to sell their merchandise normally. The presence of the hospitality tents showed that in sacred time and sacred space, the relationship between pilgrims and Shiʻi residents who partook in the festivities was marked by the gifting relationship that bonds guests to their hosts and both to the saint.

This gifting relationship existed in a strange tension with the tourism industry. Many foreign pilgrims that came to Syria in the three decades before 2011 came with the help of travel agencies. Shin Yasuda explains that the establishment of these religious tourism agencies was part of Syria's economic agreement with Iran and has proven extremely profitable for both.[23] Near the shrine of Sayyida Ruqayya and the Bab al-Saghir cemetery, for example, pilgrims provided income to Sunni merchants.

After 2011, the relationships of gifting and hospitality exemplified by Muharram hospitality tents largely ceased to exist. Instead, Shiʻi fighters from Iraq and Iran now travel to Sayyida Zaynab in order to serve the saint by defending her (and to further Iranian interests in Syria). Their slogans include, "At your service, oh Zaynab!" (*Labbayka ya Zaynab!*) and "Zaynab will not be captive twice!" (*Lan tusba Zaynab marratayn!*). By defending Zaynab, her male devotees take the place of her brother, Imam al-Husayn.[24] The duty to visit Zaynab has turned, for some, into the duty to defend her.

Conclusion

Multiple conclusions can be drawn from examining pilgrimage to the shrine town. In the past, it contributed to the government's claim to legitimacy. One might, as Brannon Wheeler argues in the first chapter of this book, highlight affect or bodily senses. This chapter has examined pilgrimage as part of a gifting relationship between a saint and her devotee, though it also includes other Shiʻis during Muharram through the practice of hospitality tents. It emphasizes that relationships, including the relationships between believers or saints and the faithful, require maintenance through visiting and extending hospitality. Hospitality is a sacred duty. It is the pious basis for friendship and is a requirement for its maintenance. The fact that the Arabic term for pilgrim is *zaʾir* (visitor) further underscores this notion.

Visitors also sustain gifting practices with other Shiʻis by praying for them at the shrine or by buying them liturgical gifts inside and outside the shrine. Inside the shrine, the practice of buying resembled the practice of gifting and thus could produce a feeling akin to Turner's *communitas*.[25] During

Muharram, these gifting practices were expanded beyond the shrine to the streets surrounding the shrine through hospitality tents. The crucial difference was location: sacred versus non-sacred ground. In short, the goal of this chapter has been to examine economic activity in various locations at the shrine town of Sayyida Zaynab and to distinguish the limits of *communitas* by comparing relationships produced in differing locales.

Notes

1. Mona Moufahim, "Religious Gift Giving: An Ethnographic Account of a Muslim Pilgrimage," *Marketing Theory* 13, no. 4 (2013): 421–41; Paulo G. Pinto, "Pilgrimage, Commodities, and Religious Objectification: The Making of Transnational Shiism between Iran and Syria," *Comparative Studies of South Asia, Africa and the Middle East* 27, no. 1 (2007): 109–25.

2. Hospitality was a central concept for Massignon, who thought about Christian-Muslim coexistence in the Arab world. Hospitality "could actually encapsulate Massignon's entire concept of mysticism. Mystical consciousness is envisaged by him as a 'decentering' of one's ordinary perception, an opening to the 'stranger' or 'foreigner' who is ultimately identifiable to the Divine Host." Patrick Laude, *Pathways to an Inner Islam: Massignon, Corbin, Guenon, and Schuon* (Albany, NY: State University of New York Press, 2010), 35.

3. Marcel Mauss, *The Gift: Forms and Functions of Exchange in Archaic Societies*, trans. Ian Cunnison (London: Cohen & West, 1954).

4. Ali J. Hussain, "The Mourning of History and the History of Mourning: The Evolution of Ritual Commemoration of the Battle of Karbala," *Comparative Studies of South Asia, Africa and the Middle East* 25, no. 2 (2005): 80–81.

5. Michelle Zimney, "History in the Making: The Sayyida Zaynab Shrine in Damascus," *ARAM* 19 (2007): 695; Edith Szanto, "Contesting Fragile Saintly Traditions: Miraculous Healing among Twelver Shi'is in Contemporary Syria," in *Politics of Worship in the Contemporary Middle East: Sainthood in Fragile States*, ed. Andreas Bandak and Mikkel Bille (Leiden: Brill, 2013), 33.

6. Sabrina Mervin, "Sayyida Zaynab, Banlieue de Damas ou nouvelle ville sainte chiite?," *Cahiers d'etudes sur la Méditerranée orientale et le monde turco-iranieni: Arabes et Iraniens* 22 (1996): 149–62; Zimney, "History in the Making."

7. Marion Farouk-Sluglett and Peter Sluglett, *Iraq since 1958* (London: I. B. Tauris, 2001), 198–200, 258.

8. Laurence Louër, *Transnational Shia Politics: Religious and Political Networks in the Gulf* (New York: Columbia University Press, 2008), 196.

9. Louër, 196–97.

10. Patrick Seale, *Asad: The Struggle for the Middle East* (Berkley: University of California Press, 1995), 173.

11. Shin Yasuda, "Commitment for Strategy: Religious Entrepreneur Networks in Syrian Shi'ite Religious Tourism," *Journal of Sophia Asian Studies* 31 (2013): 35.

12. Fariba Adelkhah, "Moral Economy of Pilgrimage and Civil Society in Iran: Religious, Commercial, and Tourist Trips to Damascus," *South African Historical Journal*

61, no. 1 (2009): 39–40; Edith Szanto, "Sex and the Cemetery: Iranian Pilgrims, Shrine Visitation, and Consumer Piety in Damascus," *Syrian Studies Association Bulletin* 19, no. 2 (2014): 1–5.

13. Moufahim, "Religious Gift Giving."

14. Anne Betteridge, "Gift Exchange in Iran: The Locus of Self-Identity in Social Interaction," in "Self and Society in the Middle East," special issue, *Anthropological Quarterly* 58, no. 4 (1985): 198.

15. Gebhard Fartacek, "'Kullna miṯl baʿd'! Heilige Orte, ethnische Grenzen und die Bewältigung alltäglicher Probleme in Syrien," *Anthropos* 106, no. 1 (2011): 10–11.

16. Ayatollah ʿAli Sistani has been one of the most important religious authority figures in Shiʿism. However, his role in Syria was minor, as he operated neither a seminary nor any other kind of institution in Sayyida Zaynab. His supporters generally attended the seminaries of other scholars.

17. Yvonne Sherwood and Kevin Hart, *Derrida and Religion: Other Testaments* (New York: Routledge, 2004).

18. See Anne Betteridge, "Specialists in Miraculous Action: Some Shrines in Shiraz," in *Sacred Journeys: The Anthropology of Pilgrimage*, ed. Alan Morinis (Westport, CT: Greenwood Press, 1992), 203–7; Szanto, "Contesting Fragile Saintly Traditions," 42–47.

19. Dervla Zaynab Shannahan, "'I Love You More': An Account of Performing Ziyarat in Iraq," *Performing Islam* 4, no. 1 (2015): 61–92.

20. Gisbert Rinschede, "Forms of Religious Tourism," *Annals of Tourism Research* 19, no. 1 (1992): 57.

21. See Fartacek, "'Kullna miṯl baʿd'!," 11.

22. Kuwaiti and Saudi Shiʿis would rather attend mourning gatherings in private homes or at seminaries than remain on the streets, citing security concerns.

23. Yasuda, "Commitment for Strategy," 39.

24. Phillip Smyth, "The Shiite Jihad in Syria and Its Regional Effects," *Policy Focus* 138, February 2015, Washington Institute for Near East Policy, https://www.washingtoninstitute.org/uploads/Documents/pubs/PolicyFocus138-v3.pdf, 3–6.

25. Victor Turner, *The Ritual Process: Structure and Anti-Structure* (Ithaca, NY: Cornell University Press, 1977).

CHAPTER EIGHT

Grave Visiting (*Ziyara*) in Indonesia

JULIAN MILLIE AND LEWIS MAYO

This chapter is about the religious and spiritual observances performed at gravesites in the Republic of Indonesia.[1] Specifically, we give attention to a notable feature of Indonesian grave visiting—the fact that some of the best-attended gravesites in Indonesia attract visitors from more than one religion.[2] These sites make possible unique combinations of religious symbols and concepts that do not conform to the normative religious geographies that carry authority in contemporary Indonesia. To explore how some gravesites exert a blurring effect on religio-spiritual boundaries, we make a case study of one gravesite, namely the tomb of two Islamic heroes at Mount Kawi (*Gunung Kawi*) in East Java. This tomb attracts visitors who are affiliated with Islamic, Chinese, and indigenous Javanese religious traditions. We provide two explanations for how gravesites facilitate the weakening of borders between religions: first, pilgrims are attracted to the site because it provides opportunities for engaging in practices that have both efficacy and immediacy due to their material and sensory character; second, the site enables visitors from diverse religious spaces to be accommodated because its legitimizing narratives are multivocal and fluid. These attractions arguably outweigh any anxieties Mount Kawi pilgrims might hold about performing spiritual observances at a site shared by a number of faith groups.

The problem of materiality arises frequently in religious discourse: what role should material objects and the physical properties of places play in religious belief and practice?[3] The present volume reveals a range of Islamic responses to this question, which is unsurprising given that pilgrimage is an arena in which the relationship between sacredness and the physicality/materiality of spaces and objects appears in sharp relief. Emilio Spadola describes an Islamic ideology that associates the materiality of a gravesite with the sin of idolatry. Paulo G. Pinto reveals a contrasting Islamic evaluation of materiality: Brazilian Hajj pilgrims returning from the Holy Land bearing souvenirs, including miniature replicas of the Kaʿba. These act as "concrete mnemonic devices that encode the experiential dimension of pilgrimage. They can evoke the actual places and objects that engendered religious experiences in the pilgrim, or they can work as general metaphoric substitutes for the whole pilgrimage."[4] Omar Kasmani (quoting Nile Green) points out that from the pilgrim's perspective, an abstraction like *karamat* (proofs of saintliness) has little value without a shrine that provides a means to access them. Edith Szanto brings consumerism into the picture: the shrine of Sayyida Zaynab illustrates the varying impressions made by consumerism in a range of material practices observed at the Sayyida Zaynab shrine. All these examples suggest different responses to the question of whether materiality is a barrier or aid to religious belief and practice and to pilgrimage in particular. Mount Kawi is distinguished, we argue, by the many and complex material forms of observance a visitor can perform there and the plurality of religious meanings that these forms of observance can have.

In our opening paragraph, we referred to "normative religious geographies that carry authority in contemporary Indonesia." We speak of normative Islams in the plural because the nation's segmented Islamic community has overcome the dangers of religious difference not by reaching consensus on points of disagreement but by accommodating differences of outlook. We cannot speak of a single homogenizing Islam. Grave visiting is in fact a good illustration of how such an accommodation of difference is achieved. As we will argue, Indonesia's two largest Islamic civil society organizations, one of which is reform oriented—Muhammadiyah—and the other of which claims tradition as its founding premise—Nahdlatul 'Ulama—have different ideologies in relation to grave visiting. In coarse terms, the former claims that grave visiting is not validated as an Islamic practice by the Qur'an or the prophetic traditions, while the latter points to the same sources and identifies support for grave visiting. This dispute manifests itself in overt conflict only infrequently because Indonesian public life has never seen the establishment of the supremacy of one of these positions over the other.[5] Indonesian governments, for example, have generally refrained from influencing public conceptions of Islam in favor of one or the other. This has enabled contrasting Islamic outlooks to coexist in public settings, making it difficult to argue that there is a single normative center.

Nevertheless, normative tendencies are a feature of Indonesian Islam. There are, for example, points of consensus that are well supported across the Indonesian Islamic spectrum. Significant among these is the overlap between idealizations of contemporary citizenship and the status of monotheism as an ideological foundation of Indonesian national modernity. Although contemporary idealizations of subjectivity in the West tend not to include religious conviction, in Indonesian understandings, a modern subject is one who is monotheistic, and many Indonesians believe that monotheistic subjects should have the features attributed to a liberal, democratic subjectivity (rational-critical reflection, autonomous agency, empowerment through civil as well as religious education, commitment to civic pluralism, and so on).[6] This conception of contemporary religious subjectivity is not supported everywhere in Indonesia's vast, 250-million-strong population, but it does find wide support in national policy, in public discourse, and in popular cultural representations.

Our method in this chapter is to trace the effects of this normative consensus on grave visiting. We do so by referring to a study of Mount Kawi pilgrimage practices made by a contributor to public discourse whose reasoning is strongly shaped by the consensus. Dr. H. Roibin is an academic at one of Indonesia's state-run Islamic universities. These institutions are an important part of Indonesia's national education infrastructure. Unlike the civil, nonreligious education system located within the Ministry of Research, Technology and Higher Education, the State Islamic University system is the responsibility of the Ministry of Religion. Established in 1962 with the purpose of suitably training Islamic scholars for the needs of the developing republic, the State Islamic University system has prioritized national unity above the particularity of specific Islamic constituencies in Indonesia. In other words, throughout its history, the State Islamic University system has given Islamic legitimacy to a plural Indonesia. Its academics perform research on Indonesia's Islamic communities using approaches and paradigms from Western social sciences as well as from Islamic sources. These academics have been influential in directing Indonesian society toward an inclusive, flexible mode of Islamic interpretation that has suited the developmental agendas of successive Indonesian governments.[7]

Roibin made an ethnographic study of the Mount Kawi gravesite for his doctoral research. In its evaluative analysis of the diverse observances taking place at the site, Roibin's account reveals the broadly supported idealization of the modern citizen/Muslim that we consider to constitute a normative center in Indonesian Islam and the perspective on grave visiting produced by that idealization. In what follows, we move between our observations of Mount Kawi grave-visiting practice and Roibin's ethnographic account. In the final part of the chapter, we identify materiality and narrative multivocality as the core properties that enable the site to appeal to an interreligious pilgrimage demographic.

Some initial stage-setting is required for those not familiar with Indonesian Islam. Indonesia is home to approximately 230 million Muslims, making up about 88 percent of its population. The first signs of an Islamic community being present in the territory of the current state date from the early thirteenth century, but the religion's diffusion cannot be understood as a single homogeneous process.[8] There were many points of initial contact, and Islam adapted to the wide ethnic, spiritual, and linguistic diversity of the archipelago's peoples. Contemporary Indonesian Muslims display a wide range of Islamic practices, beliefs, and outlooks. Almost all of them are Sunni Muslims, and in questions of law, Indonesia's ʿulama generally consult the Shafiʿi legal school.

Ziyara in Indonesia

Indonesian discourse around grave visiting can be understood on two planes. The first is the contestation concerning its validity as Islamic observance. This controversy replicates similar debates occurring in other Muslim communities (see Spadola's chapter in this volume). Reformist movements made the propriety and Islamic value of grave visiting points of contention. The global Islamic reform movement of the late nineteenth century manifested in early twentieth-century Indonesia in a groundswell of nationalist-oriented reformism at a time when Indonesia was still a Dutch colony. The main Indonesian vehicle of this reform was the mass organization Muhammadiyah, formed in 1912 by traders in the central Javanese city of Yogyakarta. Modernist critics focused on the efficacy paradigms through which Indonesians understood grave visiting as an Islamic observance. These critics argued that grave pilgrims were mistaken in their attribution of potency to deceased individuals, which showed a deficient understanding of the concept of *tawhid*. Furthermore, it was asserted that grave visitors held mistaken convictions about materiality and acts of supplication. Muslims erred if they thought that a specific place, such as a tomb, was a more efficacious site than others for supplicating. Modernists also expressed discomfort with the orientation of grave supplication toward obtaining worldly benefits. Islam had more important value than providing tools for Muslims to petition the Almighty for worldly wealth. Another objection focused on the way that gravesites combined Islamic elements with resources from other cultural and spiritual traditions. In many cases, gravesites were places that had been regarded as having spiritual potency before the arrival of Islam, and still today Muslim pilgrimage styles and practices are in dialogue with older routines of ancestor veneration.[9]

The Indonesian reform movement gained momentum because it was in harmony with twentieth-century concerns about political independence and sociopolitical progress, but it did not carry the day. Powerful Islamic elites were threatened by the momentum of the reform movement. Grave visiting was one of the key concerns of these elites. Many Netherlands Indies Muslims were concerned by the Wahhabi destruction of places in the Hijaz that were sacred pilgrimage places for Muslims in the Indies and elsewhere, and they organized themselves in response. The actors who led this response were the Islamic teachers (Javanese: *kyai*) in charge of Indonesia's Islamic schools (Indonesian/Javanese: *pesantren*). In 1926, they formed an organization to rival the modernists, the Rising of the Scholars (Nahdlatul 'Ulama, or NU). Their arguments against the modernists sought to defend a number of Islamic concepts with which the modernists had taken issue. Grave visiting was one such concept. NU elites, confronted by Islamic arguments that denied validity to grave visiting, were quick to summon authoritative Qur'anic verses and hadith that indicated that the practice was a valuable and correct Islamic observance.[10] These assertions provided countertexts to modernist positions and were significant discursive resources for Islamic communities, especially large rural ones for whom continuation of Indonesian Islamic practices such as grave visiting was a priority.

In the initial decades of the twentieth century, bitter disputes took place between the reformist and traditionalist movements. Over time, however, a respectful accommodation between these movements became a structural feature of Indonesian Islamic society, enabling Muslims affiliated with either of the two tendencies to feel that their aspirations are respected in the modern republic; as such, neither reformists nor traditionalists can lay claim to an exclusive monopoly on the national Islamic sensibility. This has been important for the public visibility of grave visiting. Despite the circulation of modernist critiques of grave visiting, some gravesites have developed as centers of massive pilgrimage activity. The graves of the nine saints (Javanese: *wali songo*)—commemorated as pioneers of Islam in Java—consistently draw large crowds, as they have done for centuries.[11] Graves of deceased religious leaders and national heroes are also favored sites. More recently, as Indonesian society has liberalized in the post-Suharto period, regional governments have supported grave visiting as a significant source of tourist income. Tour buses career around contemporary Java, ferrying groups to pilgrimage sites dotted around the island, and such tours even travel to sites in the neighboring islands of Madura and Bali.

Political aspirants and officeholders create positive impressions when they make well-publicized visits to graves.[12]

The second plane for understanding Indonesian dispositions toward grave visiting consists of the slippery conceptual terrain surrounding the notion of "modernization." When the republic's political and cultural elites make pronouncements about goals and aspirations in areas such as economics, education, and religion, they set up borders by distinguishing certain forms with the label of "modern" and consigning others to the past through labels such as "primitive," "anachronistic," and "traditional." The 1945 statement of national ideology by the first president, Sukarno, had such an effect. This national ideology, named the Five Principles (*Pancasila*), made "belief in one God" one of the five ideological principles of the republic. This was supported by modernizing elites of the mid-twentieth century—both Christian and Muslim—who were united in the opinion that monotheism had superseded animism and place-based spiritualities. (This was a view that Hindus and Buddhists chose not to dispute publicly.) The new republic, these reformers argued, would leave behind the days of superstition and magic.

This enshrinement of monotheism as a national value has had a profound effect on Indonesia's religious sphere since independence. Indonesians accept monotheism in its progressive forms as a core element of national modernity, and this shapes the public discourse around religion.[13] There is an aspect of compulsion in this, for Indonesian law has formally recognized only monotheisms—and religious forms that resemble them—as religions. As a result, Indonesians are compelled to identify themselves as followers of one of the world religions (atheism is an unacceptable category). Furthermore, the legalized recognition of the five official forms of monotheism has resulted in a number of exclusions, some of which are critical to our study of Mount Kawi. The state religious ideology excludes indigenous spiritualities, including the indigenous Javanese spirituality, by categorizing them as "customs" (*adat*) or "belief systems" (*kepercayaan*).[14] Although decades of Islamization have weakened Javanese spirituality as a publicly visible religious and spiritual affiliation, millions of Javanese still practice an Islam shaped by deeply respected Javanese spiritual conceptions (we refer to these Muslims as "Java-Muslims" in this chapter).[15] Chinese religions were also assigned to the status of "non-religion," a stance that reflected the official hostility to manifestations of Chinese culture and belief that prevailed in Indonesia between the 1960s and the early 2000s.[16] Chinese religious forms were also subjected to severe restrictions until the lifting of the government ban on

Chinese temples in 2000.[17] It is difficult to estimate the number of followers of Chinese religions. A recent estimate put the figure at "three to five million."[18] The exclusion of these spiritual systems is not just a symbolic issue, for affiliation with a "custom" or a "belief system" has in the past led to difficulties in legal/administrative matters such as marriage registration.

The monotheistic ethic signals an area of ongoing tension within Indonesian public life. In the post-authoritarian liberalization following the Suharto regime's fall in 1998, followers of indigenous religions have been emboldened to seek official recognition of their belief systems as religions. At the same time, some Islamic actors are determined to maintain monotheism as a national value. The tension is important to our consideration of Mount Kawi, for the site's visitors include many pilgrims self-identifying as followers of Chinese or Javanese religions.

The Site

Mount Kawi is located in a forested hilly region about sixty kilometers from the regional city of Malang, in East Java. The province of East Java is populous and strongly Islamic. At the time of this writing, about 97 percent of its population of 37,476,757 was Muslim. A visitor parks her car in the carpark at the foot of the hill, walks through an elaborate entranceway, and proceeds to climb a wide, well-preserved set of concrete stairs. Before reaching this point, a local person will have offered his services as a guide. The site's rich pilgrimage infrastructure unfolds to the eye as the visitor ascends the stairs. On the left and right appear small hotels and bed and breakfast accommodations, as well as restaurants. The pilgrim passes a *klenteng*, or place of worship for Chinese Indonesians. Then there is a facility for *wayang* (puppet theater), where visitors can make supplication by funding the performance of a puppetry performance. After that appears a kitchen, with a sign at the front reading "Registration for vows and ritual meals." A large menu board specifies the various ritual feasts (Indonesian/Javanese: *selamatan*) that can be ordered by pilgrims as offerings, ranging from relatively small, inexpensive offerings to feasts involving the slaughter of oxen. Drawing closer to the top, the visitor encounters the Baiturrohman Mosque. This stands beside a line of small stalls from which the pilgrim can buy flower offerings for the tomb lying ahead. On the right, just before the tomb enclosure, is the *ciam si* (Chinese: *Qianshi*, the divinatory poems used in some types of Chinese fortune-telling), a place where Chinese methods of divination are practiced. Opposite that is a temple dedicated to Kwan Im, (Chinese: *Guanyin*), the Chinese Bodhisattva of Mercy and one of the most important goddesses in Chinese popular religion.

The approach ends at an enclosure called the Resting Place (Javanese: *Pasarean*) of Iman Soedjono and Eyang Djoego. Within this enclosure is a "wishing-tree" (Javanese: *pohon dewandaru*), under which pilgrims wait, considering the falling of a leaf or a piece of fruit to be an omen of good fortune.[19] The guides tell visitors that the tree grew from the staff of Eyang Djoego. But the main focal point is the small building in which Iman Soedjono and Eyang Djoego lie. Only two people have the right to open the door to this building, and they do so at 3:30 P.M. every day. These men are guardians of the tomb (Javanese: *Kuncen*), a position they have inherited genealogically. They belong to families that have for generations performed such duties at the site. They will assist pilgrims in making offerings and prayers to the two occupants of the tomb. People visiting the tomb at other times are encouraged to make their prayers at the door and leave a floral offering, which the guardian takes before Iman Soedjono and Eyang Djoego when he arrives at 3:30 P.M.

Like all pilgrimage sites, this one is distinguished by narratives. The origin narratives of Mount Kawi reveal conflicting versions of the identities and origins of Eyang Djoego, who died at Mount Kawi in 1879, and of Iman Soedjono, who died after Djoego (the sources conflict about his death date). One version foregrounds the two heroes as descendants of the noble Javanese lineages of the Hamengkubuwana (Soedjono) and Pakubuwana (Djoego) dynasties.[20] According to this narrative, Eyang Djoego was born into the exalted lineage but chose to become a hermit; it is said that he left the palace to reside in the village of Jugo, about seventy kilometers from Mount Kawi. In this version, the two figures are advisers and followers of the rebel hero Pangeran Dipanagara, who was the son of Hamengkubuwana III and led the Javanese in the Java War (1825–30), before being exiled from Java in 1830. This narrative, which was related to us in this basic form by our Javanese guide at the tomb, locates the two figures in the lustrous lineages of Javanese sultanates and identifies them as nationalist heroes fighting the Dutch under Dipanagara in the Java War.

There is also a Chinese version. Oral tradition holds that after the Taiping rebellion, a disciple of Hong Xiuquan (the founder of the Taiping movement) fled to Java and adopted an ascetic life there; he became renowned as a teacher and healer among the Javanese and Chinese and eventually moved to Mount Kawi.[21]

These two versions point to the risk of disputes over "ownership" of Eyang Djoego, and not surprisingly, some accounts avoid this risk by navigating between the two. Im Yang Tju (Yinyangzi) published such an account in Chinese in 1953 and a version of the same text in Malay shortly afterward (previous scholarship holds that the Chinese version is a translation of the Malay text, but it appears that the reverse is the case).[22] Eyang Djoego was a hermit who walked out of the forest near the village of Djoego and cured the village's cattle of a disease. Late in his life, a man arrived in Djoego claiming to be his adopted son. He said that Eyang Djoego had adopted him when Djoego was in China, a claim affirmed by Djoego himself. This man became Iman Soedjono. Im Yang Tju is emphatic that Djoego's origins are unknown; he simply came to the village of Jugo as a hermit. But Im Yang Tju's account cleverly leaves open the possibility that he was in fact Chinese. Iman Soedjono's origins are also uncertain in this version, but once again there are a number of possibilities: he might have been Chinese, but he might also have been the son of the Javanese hero Pangeran Dipanagara.

All narratives agree that Eyang Djoego built up a reputation as a holy man and healer first in the village of Djoego and after 1876 in the village of Wonosari, which is the site of the tomb on Mount Kawi. After his death, his tomb gained a reputation as a potent place where good outcomes could be secured, and people began the custom of visiting the village bearing offerings. Without a doubt, Chinese financial support has been critical to the flourishing of the site. A major supporter in recent times was Liem Sioe Liong (Lin Shaoliang in Chinese), who was born in Fujian, China, in 1916 (d. Singapore, 2012). This man owned the Salim Group, a business conglomerate that enabled him to hold the title of richest man in Indonesia during most of the regime of his patron, President Suharto. Liem would consult the site's diviners before making difficult decisions or commencing large business undertakings. His donations supported general maintenance, road improvements, the building of dormitories, and the construction of the statue of Kwan Im.[23]

This summary of the site's spiritual and physical infrastructure and the narratives connected with them reveals a defining characteristic of this particular site: it is a resource that creates meaning for followers of a number of spiritual and religious traditions. First, the mosque and tomb highlight the site's value as a pilgrimage site for Muslims. Second, the *wayang* and ritual meal services point to the site's popularity with pilgrims for whom Javanese spirituality is an important reference. Third, the *ciam si*, Kwan Im shrine, and *klenteng* show the popularity of the site among followers of

Chinese religion. Fourth, the wishing tree provides the most prominent symbol of the site's value for people wishing to generate good outcomes without turning to any specific religious system. The narratives, and especially the Im Yang Tju version, do the same thing: they confirm the image of Mount Kawi as a site shared by followers approaching it through diverse spiritual and religious frames. The site's legitimizing narratives display a multivocality that resonates with that diversity.

A National Perspective

Dr. Roibin's PhD thesis is a valuable document for understanding the meanings given to grave visiting in Indonesian Islamic discourse.[24] Roibin is a Javanese academic who now leads the sharia faculty of the State Islamic University (UIN) in the regional center of Malang, less than an hour's drive from Mount Kawi. As previously noted, the State Islamic University system has throughout its history given Islamic legitimacy to a religiously plural Indonesia, a position that harmonizes with the developmental agendas of successive Indonesian governments. This makes Roibin's perspective valuable, for he reads Mount Kawi visitation practices through the lens of widely supported idealizations of Indonesian Muslim subjectivity. He writes from an academic and bureaucratic location heavily invested in the development of Indonesia as a progressive, liberal-democratic state.

Roibin is a Javanese Muslim sympathetic to the diversity of Islam in East Java, and his work succeeds in providing a comprehensive and sympathetic overview of the pilgrimage site. As such, his thesis is valuable as an ethnographic study of pilgrimage to Mount Kawi. But there is also value for the present discussion in the ways in which Roibin organizes the pilgrimage activities and the pilgrims themselves into a hierarchy of categories. The hierarchy reflects the borders between approved and objectionable forms of Islam that are authoritative in mainstream Indonesian Islamic discourse. In other words, the text reveals the ambivalences and tensions in contemporary Indonesian views on pilgrimage.

Roibin delineates three categories of pilgrims.[25] These categories are not innovations, as they are constructed out of concepts that hold currency in the academic literature on Islam in Java.[26] His first category is the *putihan*, or "white" Muslims. This term refers to a pious orthodox Islamic subjectivity, which in contemporary times harmonizes with idealizations of citizen subjectivity. The second category is *abangan* or *Muslim Kejawen*—Muslims whose understandings are shaped by Javanese spiritual conceptions. As previously noted, we translate this as "Java-Muslims." The third are supplicants whose pilgrimage practice is dedicated to achieving real-world outcomes in business; Roibin refers to these pilgrims as *bisnisan* (literally "doing business").

Roibin distinguishes the groups on a number of planes of difference. First, they differ in their preferences for specific parts of the Mount Kawi infrastructure. All groups patronize the tomb, participating in rituals that put Eyang Djoego and Iman Soedjono at the center of expectations of efficacy. All groups visit the wishing tree, albeit with different expectations and understandings. But the business pilgrims rarely patronize the mosque, while only a portion of the Java-Muslim pilgrims attend events in the mosque. Muslims from these categories prefer to avoid the symbolic implications of the mosque, which imply doctrinal constraints on the pilgrimage practices they enjoy. For the white Muslims, however, the mosque is the focal ritual site alongside the tomb.

Roibin maps these diverging preferences onto contrasting religio-spiritual understandings. For the white Muslims, Eyang Djoego and Iman Soedjono are mediating figures (Arabic: *wasilah*). Their efficacy paradigm is as follows: the pilgrim supplicates to Allah on behalf of Eyang Djoego and Iman Soedjono in the hope that these figures, who are within Allah's favor, will, in turn, intercede for them with Allah.[27] Furthermore, Eyang Djoego and Iman Soedjono are figures who are exemplary for their dedication to Islam and for their perceived involvement in the national struggle. Reflection on this dedication is a beneficial act, and if a white Muslim engages in a ritual feast, then this is an expression of thanks to Allah (Indonesian from Arabic: *syukuran*) for the efforts of the two men and is not to be understood as an offering for them.

The Java-Muslims, in Roibin's typology, understand Eyang Djoego and Iman Soedjono as *arwah leluhur* (Javanese: spirits of deceased ancestors), with the power to intervene in worldly affairs if proper offerings are made. Their grave rituals, of which the holding of a ritual feast is the most obvious, are oriented not to seeking Allah's favor through intercession but to making offerings to the spirits of the two deceased figures, whose contribution to the national struggle only increases their potency.

The business pilgrims' efficacy conception is, according to Roibin, dedicated to wealth seeking (Javanese/Indonesian: *pesugihan*). The grave and other infrastructure at Mount Kawi are places for making deals with unseen beings in the hope of success in business or of obtaining a windfall. The method is known among the Javanese as the *tumbal* or *imbalan* system, in which a pledge of sacrifice (animal, object, or even human spirit) is made to an unseen being in return for a favorable outcome. There is a strict rationality in their magical understandings of the site: unseen beings, if properly transacted with, can bring financial benefits. In performing the ritual, they consult with Chinese pilgrims, whom Roibin understands to share and have expertise in the methods and technology of this rational-magical approach.[28] The business practices are the most controversial of those cited by Roibin; the villagers living at the site were insistent that no *pesugihan* practices take place there, reflecting widely felt anxiety about their legitimacy.

The three groups also differ in their engagement with the material properties of the site. For white Muslims, the conception of divine oneness (*tawhid*) does not depend on the materiality of the site. The tomb is a suitable site for supplication to Allah because it is the resting place of the mediating figures Eyang Djoego and Iman Soedjono, not because it has any specific potency per se. Furthermore, the white Muslims value the natural surroundings as a place for reflection and humility among the beauty of Allah's creation. The other groups, by contrast, do not abstract spiritual potency as a portable thing. Rather, the spiritual properties of the site lie in its physical reality. Java-Muslims see the tomb as a source of power because it is the resting place of the spirits of ancestors, and these give the site potency as a place for supplications and offerings. For the business pilgrims, the physical sites are critical because they provide the opportunity for making transactions with unseen spirits. Java-Muslims and business pilgrims consider fulfillment of material conditions (offering feasts, catching a falling leaf, bathing in the site's pools) as conditions for successful supplication.

Roibin connects his observations about Mount Kawi pilgrimage practice with conceptions of national citizen subjectivity, leading him to identify deficient Indonesian subjectivities in all other groups besides white Muslims. In a telling passage, Roibin explores the contrasts between white and Java-Muslims by comparing their religious knowledge. The Java-Muslim is "limited in his understanding of religion," while the white Muslim "has a religious understanding that in a normative-theological sense is at a moderate or above moderate level."[29] The Java-Muslim is at a religious level that is "classic" (Indonesian: *klasik*) in the sense that it draws on long-standing Javanese models but also "primitive." The white Muslim's religious observance is also classic but is "modern" as well.[30] Roibin does not give any explanation of the modern–primitive dichotomy, assuming that his readers would recognize the practices of Java-Muslim and business pilgrims—especially the transactions for material gain—as signs of outdated religious subjectivities.

Education is another key variable through which Roibin makes connections to idealizations of national modernity. Although he did not collect any data on the education levels of pilgrims in his research, Roibin identifies education levels as a causative factor that determine pilgrims' positions on the hierarchy. According to Roibin, those with little formal education find the tomb's power in the spirits of deceased ancestors. The white Muslims, benefiting from their formal education, are enabled to see the almighty power of the Creator as the only source of potency.[31] Seen within the context of authoritative Indonesian opinion and religious discourse, Roibin's observations can be considered correct. They affirm the connection between monotheism and modernity, mentioned earlier, that is at the core of Indonesian self-imagination. When his analysis differentiates diverse ways of doing pilgrimage at Mount Kawi, Roibin reveals ambivalences about pilgrimage practice that correspond to broadly held conceptions of contemporary Muslim citizenship.

Although our analysis represents Roibin's perspective as one that reflects a national consensus, we need to qualify this. In Indonesia, the "center" is a pluralistic location where actors agree to disagree. Roibin's analysis reflects nationally supported norms about contemporary citizen subjectivity, but many members of Islamic elites would nevertheless disagree with his analysis. Roibin is familiar with and respectful of a theology that grants Islamic legitimacy to grave visiting. As previously mentioned, this theology is defended by the mass organization Nahdlatul 'Ulama, which has its heartland in East Java. Indeed, Roibin self-identifies as a supporter of NU. However, as also previously noted, the ideology of Indonesia's modernist Muslim organization, Muhammadiyah, denies legitimacy to grave visiting and to the practices associated with it. Muhammadiyah academics might support the sociological aspect of Roibin's thesis, but it is likely that they would find it too lax in its evaluation of grave pilgrimage as an Islamic observance. Roibin's white Muslims would not be "white" enough for the Muhammadiyah perspective.

Particularity and Materiality

Roibin's pilgrim informants were positive about the leveling effects of tomb ritual. They approved of the way differences between white Muslims, Java-Muslims, and even Chinese pilgrims seemed to melt away at the site. Roibin observed pilgrims from diverse religious backgrounds enjoying participation in the combination of Javanese mantras and Islamic supplications that are performed at the site of the tomb: "Perhaps because people's specific intentions [Indonesian from Arabic: *hajat*] dominate [their actions at the tomb], people feel required to shed the theological clothing of their own background. Or perhaps it is because of the welcoming nature of the teachings [in the mantras/supplications]."[32] The contrast here is with the normative religious trends apparent in the republic generally, which have encouraged people to develop unequivocal identities affiliated with one of the major religion options practiced within the republic.

We should not overestimate the extent of the interreligious activity. People visit the site in the company of their fellow believers and adhere to exclusive calendars that identify different dates as auspicious ones.[33] Although Tashadi and colleagues noted that pilgrims of all religious backgrounds enjoyed using the divination room (*ciam si*), Roibin noticed first-time Muslim visitors avoiding it, and it is likely that many Muslims would avoid the site altogether because of the facilities it provides for Chinese pilgrims.[34] The mosque is also a marker of difference. Non-Muslim Chinese pilgrims have little reason to enter the mosque, and as previously noted, some Java-Muslims might be discouraged by their association of the mosque with an Indonesian Islamic identity that differs from their own.

But these distinctions are brought by the pilgrims. In Millie's visit to the site, he did not notice any attempts or measures to direct followers of specific religions in predetermined directions, and the site arguably benefits from the relatively weak surveillance of borders that are heavily patrolled elsewhere in Indonesia. The site's guides did not inquire of him about his religious inclinations but encouraged him to make supplications at the tomb "in accordance with one's own convictions" (Indonesian: *sesuai dengan keyakinan masing-masing*). The prevailing ethic at Mount Kawi, in contrast to the formalization of boundaries implicit in Roibin's normative approach to religious identity, suggests that religious affiliations are private things that a visitor is not required to display.

If Mount Kawi does not clearly affirm the visitor's denominational identity, then what is it about the site that draws so many visitors? This is an important question because Mount Kawi is only one of a number of Indonesian gravesites that attract followers of diverse denominations. We suggest two factors, both of which are intrinsic to place-based spiritualities. The two factors are a strong emphasis on materiality in pilgrimage practice and the fact that the site is interpreted through multiple discourses that distinguish it without confining it in denominational terms; the site's legitimizing discourses (histories, anecdotes, and so on) are multivocal and fluid.

As previously noted, the materiality of objects and places is minimalized in Roibin's idealization of "white Islam". This is in harmony with an authoritative strain of Islamic thought that insists that religious practices must have low levels of engagement with their material and physical settings. On this point, modernist Muslims agreed with the founders of the Indonesian Republic. John Bowen pointed out that in the early twentieth-century Netherlands Indies, a nationalistic sense of supralocal bonds developed hand in hand with a universalistic Islamic view that valued uniformity in belief and practice irrespective of location.[35] Clifford Geertz identified a rationalizing turn in postindependence Indonesian religion: "The world was, in Weber's famous phrase, disenchanted: the locus of sacredness was removed from the rooftrees, graveyards and road crossings of everyday life and put, in some sense into another realm, where dwelt Yahweh, Logos, Tao or Brahman."[36] The generalization and formal integration of a religion of abstract concepts superseded object and place-oriented religion.

In contrast, the pilgrim to Mount Kawi approaches with relish the rich offerings of material resources that the site provides, such as its tomb, the wishing tree, the *ciam si's* divination gadgetry, the bathing spring, ritual meals, *wayang* performances, and so on. These resources enable pilgrims to make supplications that require their own bodily acts and sensory perception. The site is satisfying because its potency is accessed by the body of the pilgrim rather than through the mediation of a specialist. The visitor enjoys a physical sense of immediacy. Importantly, the material resources of the site are not mere copies of the same resources found elsewhere. If the pilgrim were to inquire into the properties that make these material props special, he or she would receive an answer in terms of the specific histories of Mount Kawi and those entombed there. These are the real thing, not reproductions of models located elsewhere.

But pilgrims' inquiries are not answered with uniform responses. As previously noted, the site is legitimized by a plurality of histories, meanings, and interpretations. The site has a particularity that is multivocal and slippery, with the result that pilgrims of diverse religious backgrounds understand the site as authentic *in terms of their own particular persuasion*. Popular gravesites in Indonesia abound in narrative materials, which concern not only the figures buried there but also the individual features of the site. In many narratives, material features of the site become significant because they feature in the narrative of the figure lying at rest there.[37] At Mount Kawi, different versions coexist. Were Eyang Djoego and Iman Soedjono exemplary Muslims who made heroic efforts in the struggle against colonialism?

Definitely. Were they experts in Javanese mysticism and healing techniques? The histories suggest this was the case. Could Eyang Djoego be considered the same person as Thay Lo Su (Chinese: Da Laoshi), and Iman Soedjono as Djie Lo Su (Chinese: Er Laoshi), as is suggested by Im Yang Tju?[38] Your answer will be in accordance with your individual conviction, say the hosts at the site. It is not their role to restrain the expansion of the site's narrative resources, which only increase Mount Kawi's distinction.

While the normative inclinations in Roibin's analysis point to processes of stabilizing, constraining, and homogenizing, the histories and origin stories of places like Mount Kawi multiply. The process is not random, for Roibin astutely points out that each interpretation brought to bear on the site is grounded in some understanding of the diverse religious forms invoked at the site. The Java-Muslim visitors might be lacking in their Islamic knowledge, but as Roibin points out, their understandings are grounded in classic Javanese philosophy, in widely practiced ascetic rites, in the repetition of stories about holy men, and in sayings and expressions that are part of everyday communication in Javanese life.[39] Sino-Indonesian traditions provide comparable resources for Chinese visitors. In effect, Roibin represents Mount Kawi as a place that followers of diverse religions/spiritualities read as a site for a unique and genuine experience of those religions/spiritualities.

Millie was given a striking demonstration of how the materiality and discursive particularity of the site brings dynamism to pilgrimage practice. The guides he encountered in the enclosure at the peak of the site sought to engage him and his Indonesian colleague with ever more sophisticated techniques and insights into the site as they journeyed through it. For example, a man he met inside the enclosure guided him in buying flowers and placing them with a cash offering at the door of the tomb structure in expectation of the arrival later in the day of the tomb's guardian. This man then instructed Millie and his colleague, rather aggressively, to circumambulate the tomb. In a quiet place at the back of the tomb, out of sight of the other visitors, the guide produced a small fruit, which he claimed had fallen from the wishing tree. He reminded Millie that this tree had grown from the staff of Eyang Djoego. He folded the fruit cleverly within a kind of envelope, verbalizing supplications to and blessings for Eyang Djoego and Iman Soedjono as he did so. He then made Millie and his colleague an offer. For a significant sum, he would ensure that the envelope was placed in the tomb by the tomb keeper when he arrived later that day. This, he claimed, was a powerful way to seek the favor of the tomb's occupants and was a proven means of obtaining benefit in worldly matters.[40]

The important point from this example is the way that the guide represented the site's potential through creative combinations of its materiality and history. These techniques had undoubtedly brought him success with other pilgrims. He cleverly sought to confirm and extend the pilgrims' convictions about the site's value as a place for supplication by expanding its material resources. His effort gave us a glimpse of the powers of attraction that draw so many visitors to Mount Kawi and similar locations. As we have observed, in the Republic of Indonesia of today, materiality is given limited approval in Islamic practice. The spiritual observances most welcome in normative public discourse occur in more or less the same forms without regard for place or material conditions. Mount Kawi works in the opposite direction. It offers the pilgrim intensely material forms of supplication that are directly legitimized by the occupants of the site and their histories and that are specific to that site. In a homogenizing national environment that to some degree confines Islamic meanings to those preferred by the white Muslims, Mount Kawi's narrative resources have actually multiplied, corresponding with the distinctive expectations of a diverse range of pilgrims.

Conclusion

What does this chapter add to this collection's coverage of Islamic pilgrimage? It brings the postcolonial state and its normative religious discourses into the picture. Indonesia is an ex-colonial state structured along constitutional-democratic lines in which modernizing elites feel responsible for enacting a pedagogical mission heavily shaped by a concept of the citizen as a rational, enlightened subject. This provides a compelling model for Indonesian citizenship that has been attractive to Indonesians of all religious affiliations and that authorizes a cultural normalization to which religious practices are required to submit.[41]

Although not all Indonesians would appreciate his sensitive positioning in relation to *ziyara*, Roibin's dissertation can be regarded as a normative statement of principles of a national Islamic culture that is as close to the Indonesian center as one might find. The assumptions and evaluations it presents about Islamic practice would have natural authority for many forward-looking Indonesian Muslims. Against that background, the materiality of what goes on at Mount Kawi are sticking points. In Roibin's analysis, some of its popular material practices point to citizen Muslims with inadequate education, little Islamic knowledge, incorrect ideas about the efficacy of divine power in the world, and incorrect methods for accessing that power.

It is not true that there is a general conflict between Islam and material religion per se. After all, the Hajj pilgrim pays great attention to practices connected to the material and historical properties of the Sacred Mosque of Mecca and the other locations involved in the pilgrimage. But the Hajj is underpinned by a wholly different authorizing discourse when considered against the practices discussed here. As Pinto's account reveals, the acts and utterances of the Hajj express membership of the global Muslim nation. In Indonesia also, the Hajj is constitutive of contemporary global Islamic identity. This is not so for Mount Kawi. Roibin objectifies its practices in the spirit and manner implied by the term "folk Islam": many Mount Kawi pilgrims observe practices that seem naturally to belong to the past and to the particularism of that locality rather than to the contemporary and the global.

We wish to conclude by restating another marker of the distance between authoritative notions about contemporary Muslim subjectivity in Indonesia and Roibin's representation of Mount Kawi: the weak demarcation of religious borders at the site. Mount Kawi is a religious site at which borders between denominations do not have the value that they are generally given in contemporary Indonesia. This is remarkable. Global developments since the Second World War have frequently seen the hardening of discrete religious identities.[42] Muslims in contemporary Indonesia (and also in Malaysia, Thailand, and Brunei) are now, more than ever, encouraged to consider their Islam as a core aspect of their personal identity. The same strengthening and differentiation of identities is experienced by many Christians and Hindus. By contrast, Mount Kawi visitors do not object to participating in spiritual practices at a site that is shared with members of other faiths. In addition, the site's management perpetuates Mount Kawi's legitimizing discourses in a way that ensures that they remain fluid and accommodate the expectations of the diverse demographic to which they appeal. We argue that there is a relationship between this relatively low concern for maintaining borders and the richness of the range of material engagements that the site offers. Both of these dimensions exist at the same distance from the normalizing discourses of contemporary Indonesian ideals about Muslim subjectivity.

Notes

1. The research on which this chapter is based was funded by the Australian Research Council's Discovery Grant program (DP1094913). The authors express grati-

tude to Prof. Dr. H. Roibin of the Maulana Malik Ibrahim State Islamic University, Malang, Indonesia. All errors are the responsibility of the authors.

2. Examples other than Mount Kawi include the grave of Sunan Gunung Jati in Cirebon, West Java, which attracts Muslim pilgrims as well as followers of Chinese spirituality, and a number of gravesites in Bali and Lombok, which attract pilgrims from Muslim, Balinese/Hindu, and Chinese communities. A. G. Muhaimin, *The Islamic Traditions of Cirebon: Ibadat and Adat among Javanese Muslims* (Jakarta: Centre for Research and Development of Socio-Religious Affairs, 2004); David Harnish, *Bridges to the Ancestors: Music, Myth and Cultural Politics at an Indonesian Festival* (Honolulu: University of Hawai'i Press, 2006); Martin Slama, "From Wali Songo to Wali Pitu: The Travelling of Islamic Saint Veneration to Bali," in *Between Harmony and Discrimination: Negotiating Religious Identities in Majority-Minority Relationships within Bali and Lombok*, ed. Brigitta Hauser-Schäublin and David D. Harnish (Leiden: Koninklijke Brill NV, 2014), 112–41. The forms of supplication popularly used in pilgrimage also facilitate invocations across denominational boundaries. J. Millie, "Supplicating, Naming, Offering; *Tawassul* in West Java," *Journal of Southeast Asian Studies* 39, no. 1 (2008): 107–22. Claudine Salmon provides an overview of Mount Kawi as a Chinese site. Claudine Salmon and Denys Lombard, *Les Chinois de Jakarta. Temples et vie collective* (Ann Arbor: Editions de la Maison des sciences de l'homme, 1993). In his study of Javanese and Catholic pilgrimage practices in south central Java, Laksana has noted pilgrims' hybrid identities and the encounters across religious traditions that they enable. Albertus Bagus Laksana, *Muslim and Catholic Pilgrimage Practices: Explorations through Java* (Surrey, Ashgate, 2014).

3. Matthew Engelke's study of Zimbabwe's Friday charismatics is a valuable study of religious ideas of materiality. Matthew Engelke, *A Problem of Presence: Beyond Scripture in an African Church* (Berkeley: University of California Press, 2007).

4. Paulo G. Pinto, chapter 3 in this volume.

5. Conflicts over the Islamic value of Islamic traditions practiced by Indonesian populations were more common in the early twentieth century. The diversity of modernist opposition to Javanese Islamic rituals, for example, is captured in the accounts of Clifford Geertz, *The Religion of Java* (Chicago: University of Chicago Press, 1960); Robert Hefner, *Hindu Javanese; Tengger Tradition and Islam* (Princeton, NJ: Princeton University Press, 1985), 241–47; Robert Hefner, "Islamizing Java? Religion and Politics in Rural East Java," *Journal of Asian Studies* 46 (1987): 533–54; A. Beatty, *Varieties of Javanese Religion: An Anthropological Account* (Cambridge: Cambridge University Press, 1999), 115–57; Howard M. Federspiel, *Islam and Ideology in the Emerging Indonesian State: The Persatuan Islam (PERSIS), 1923 to 1957* (Leiden: Brill, 2001); Abdul Munir Mulkhan, *Islam sejati; Kiai Ahmad Dahlan dan petani Muhammadiyah* (Jakarta: Serambi, 2003).

6. J. M. Atkinson, "Religions in Dialogue: The Construction of an Indonesian Minority Religion," *American Ethnologist* 10 (1983): 684–96; J. R. Bowen, *Muslims through Discourse: Religion and Ritual in Gayo Society* (Princeton, NJ: Princeton University Press, 1993).

7. Fuad Jabali and Jamhari, eds., *IAIN dan modernisasi Islam di Indonesia* (Jakarta: Logos Wacana Ilmu, 2002), 137–95. In doings so, it has attracted criticism from

Indonesian Muslim actors desiring that Islam should be a more influential and expansive presence in Indonesian life. A widely circulating critique of the State Islamic University System is Jaiz (Hartono Ahmad Jaiz, *Ada pemurtadan di IAIN* (Jakarta Timur: Al-Kautsar, 2005).

8. Ricklefs provides a useful summary of the issues around the arrival of Islam in Indonesia. M. C. Ricklefs, *A History of Modern Indonesia since c. 1200*, 3rd ed. (Basingstoke: Palgrave, 2001).

9. See, for example, Minako Sakai, "Modernising Sacred Sites in South Sumatra: Islamisation of Gumai Ancestral Places," in *The Potent Dead: Ancestors, Saints and Heroes in Contemporary Indonesia*, ed. Henri Chambert-Loir and Anthony Reid (Honolulu: Allen and Unwin, 2002), 103–16.

10. An exemplary defense of grave visiting, expressed in hadith and Qur'anic citations, is included in the biography of the Prophet written by one of the founding figures of NU, Hasyim Asy'ari (1875–1947). Hasyim Asy'ari, *Sang Kiai: Fatwa KH. M. Hasyim Asy'ari Seputar Islam dan Masyarakat* (Yogyakarta: Qirtas, 2005).

11. Useful overviews of Indonesian grave visiting include James J. Fox, "Ziarah Visits to the Tombs of the Wali, the Founders of Islam on Java," in *Islam in the Indonesian Social Context*, ed. M. C. Ricklefs (Clayton: Centre of Southeast Asian Studies, 1991), 19–38; J. Jamhari, "The Meaning Interpreted: The Concept of *Barakah* in *Ziarah*," *Studia Islamika* 8, no. 1 (2001): 87–128; George Quinn, "Throwing Money at the Holy Door: Commercial Aspects of Popular Pilgrimage in Java," in *Expressing Islam: Religious Life and Politics in Indonesia*, ed. Greg Fealy and Sally White (Singapore: Institute of Southeast Asian Studies, 2007), 63–79; Henri Chambert-Loir and Anthony Reid, introduction to *The Potent Dead*; Laksana, *Muslim and Catholic Pilgrimage Practices*.

12. Chambert-Loir and Reid, introduction to *The Potent Dead*.

13. Atkinson, "Religions in Dialogue"; R. S. Kipp and S. Rodgers, "Introduction: Indonesian Religions and Their Transformations," in *Indonesian Religions in Transition*, ed. R. Smith Kipp and S. Rodgers (Tucson: University of Arizona Press, 1987), 14–25; Hefner, "Islamizing Java?"

14. Niels Mulder, *Mysticism and Everyday Life in Contemporary Java* (Singapore: Singapore University Press, 1978).

15. Robert Hefner, "Where Have All the *abangan* Gone? Religionization and the Decline of Non-standard Islam in Contemporary Indonesia," in *The Politics of Religion in Indonesia: Syncretism, Orthodoxy, and Religious Contention in Java and Bali*, ed. Michel Picard and Rémy Madinier (London/New York: Routledge, 2011).

16. Lombard and Salmon provide a nuanced discussion of the relationship between Islam and Chinese culture in Indonesia from early times until the 1980s. Denys Lombard and Claudine Salmon, "Islam and Chineseness," *Indonesia* 57 (1994).

17. Koji Tsuda, "The Legal and Cultural Status of Chinese Temples in Contemporary Java," *Asian Ethnicity* 13, no. 4 (2012): 389–98.

18. "Umat menuntut, pemerintah menurut," *Gatra*, March 5, 2014, 32–33.

19. De Jonge describes the different uses made of the leaves by Javanese and Chinese pilgrims. Huub de Jonge, "Pilgrimages and Local Islam on Java," *Studia Islamika* 5, no. 2 (1998): 18.

20. This narrative is traced to documents held by the descendants of Iman Soedjono, described in Soeryowidagdo, a source we have not been able to locate. It is repeated approvingly by both Tashadi (and colleagues) and Roibin (Tashadi, Gatut Murniatmo, and Sumantarsih, *Budaya spiritual dalam situs keramat di Gunung Kawi Jawa Timur*, ed. Wiwik Pratiwi (Djakarta: Departemen Pendidikan dan Kebudayaan, Direktorat Jenderal Kebudayaan, Direktorat Sejarah dan Nilai Tradisional, Proyek Pengkajian dan Pembinaan Nilai-Nilai Budaya Pusat, 1995); Roibin, *Mitos pesugihan dalam tradisi keberagamaan masyarakat Muslim Kejawen (Studi konstruksi sosial mitos pesugihan para peziarah Muslim kejawen di Gunung Kawi, Malang, Jawa Timur)* (PhD thesis, submitted to Program Pascasarjana IAIN Sunan Ampel, Suryabaya, 2008)).

21. Claudine Salmon, "Cults Peculiar to the Chinese of Java," in *Chinese Beliefs and Practices in Southeast Asia: Studies on the Chinese Religion in Malaysia, Singapore, and Indonesia*, ed. T. Cheu (Petaling Jaya: Pelanduk Publications, 1993), 297–305.

22. Yinyangzi is a pseudonym meaning "Master of Yin and Yang." The author's real name was Tan Hong Boen (Chinese: Chen Fengwen).

23. Richard Borsuk and Nancy Chng, *Liem Sioe Liong dan Salim Group: Pilar bisnis Soeharto* (Jakarta: Kompas, 2016), 14–15.

24. Roibin, *Mitos pesughan dalam tradisi keberagamaan masyarakat Muslim Kejawen*.

25. In the early pages of his thesis, Roibin identifies a group in addition to the three he later analyzes later. This group is the Chinese business people, who have played a role in the history and development of the site. This group is not analyzed in the paper, as Roibin did no ethnographic work directly with Chinese pilgrims. Roibin, *Mitos pesughan dalam tradisi keberagamaan masyarakat Muslim Kejawen*, 102–4).

26. Roibin's categories reference Geertz's celebrated trichotomy. Geertz, *Religion of Java*. Ricklefs took the term *Putihan* from the Dutchman Poensen (1836–1919), using it as a corrective to what he sees as Geertz's inaccurate use of *santri* (scholar). M. C. Ricklefs, *Polarising Javanese Society: Islamic and Other Visions (c. 1830–1930)* (Singapore: NUS Press, 2007): 97–104.

27. Regarding this paradigm, see J. Millie, "Creating Islamic Places: Tombs and Sanctity in West Java," *ISIM Review* 17 (2006): 12–13.

28. Roibin, *Mitos pesughan dalam tradisi keberagamaan masyarakat Muslim Kejawen*, 252–53.

29. Roibin, 307.

30. Roibin, 306.

31. Roibin, 350–51.

32. Roibin, 263.

33. De Jonge, "Pilgrimages and Local Islam on Java," 18.

34. Roibin, *Mitos pesugihan dalam tradisi keberagamaan masyarakat Muslim Kejawen*, 266. De Jonge makes a valuable comparison between the Mount Kawi site and the burial place of Sunan Ampel, one of the nine saints of Java, which is located in the nearby city of Surabaya. Both sites evolved out of similar social, economic, and religious developments on Java and, for that reason, are intelligible as sites that draw on similar traditions and histories. Mount Kawi is known as an interreligious site that draws people wishing to supplicate for material gain, whereas the grave of Sunan Ampel in Surabaya is visited by orthodox Muslims for whom pilgrimage is an opportunity

not just for supplication but also for worshipping Allah in ways popular in Javanese tradition. It is more restrained in the range of material possibilities it offers than Mount Kawi. De Jonge, "Pilgrimages and Local Islam on Java," 22–23.

35. Bowen, *Muslims through Discourse*.

36. Cliford Geertz, *The Interpretation of Cultures* (New York: Basic Books, 1973), 174.

37. Millie, "Creating Islamic Places."

38. Im Yang Tju, *Riwajat Ejang Djugo Panembahan Gunung Kawi* (Surabaja: Toko Astagina. 1955), 53.

39. Roibin, *Mitos pesughan dalam tradisi keberagamaan masyarakat Muslim Kejawen*, 292.

40. This performance seemed to Millie to be extremely insincere, so he did not accept the offer. The Indonesian friend who accompanied Millie, a Muhammadiyah scholar who had never before attended a grave pilgrimage site, was disgusted by the display, which confirmed his deepest prejudices about pilgrimage practice. At the same time, he told Millie that if Millie had not been there, he would have certainly paid the money to the guide. The guide had cornered Millie and friend in a quiet spot and had been so insistent in his presentation that if Millie had been there on his own, he would have found it impossible not to hand over the requested sum. It was explained sheepishly by our colleagues from Malang that these guides were actually gangsters who occupied the enclosure at certain times in order to make money from visitors. This was not surprising. In our experience, the economic potential of Indonesian pilgrimage sites is sometimes exploited by actors whose conduct is not much restrained by religious and spiritual propriety.

41. Our understanding of postcolonial modernity draws chiefly on the classic work of Chatterjee. Partha Chatterjee, *The Nation and Its Fragments: Colonial and Postcolonial Histories* (Princeton, NJ: Princeton University Press, 1993).

42. The global trend toward the systematization of religious identities is described in Peter Beyer, *Religions in Global Society* (Abingdon Oxon: Routledge, 2006). Indonesian case studies include those of Ramstedt for Bali and Mulder for Java. Martin Ramstedt, ed., *Hinduism in Modern Indonesia: A Minority Religion between Local, National, and Global Interests* (New York: RoutledgeCurzon, 2004); Mulder, *Mysticism and Everyday Life in Contemporary Java*.

PART III | Communication, (New) Media, and Space

CHAPTER NINE

Jamkaran

Embodiment and Messianic Experience in the Making of Digital Pilgrimage

BABAK RAHIMI

Located six kilometers south of the shrine city of Qum, Iran, the Masjid-e Moqaddas-i Jamkaran is a major Shi'I pilgrimage site near a village known as Jamkaran.[1] The shrine mosque has been a leading *ziyaratgah* (place of visitation) for devotees of the "Hidden Imam"—Muhammad al-Mahdi (b. 869 C.E.), Twelfth Imam of Twelver Shi'i (also known as Imami Shi'ism)— whose return before the Day of Judgment, it is believed, will bring an end to injustice on earth. Since his Major Occultation in 941 C.E., seventy years after his birth according to the lunar calendar, the concept of Minor Occultation has played a central role in the history of Shi'i communities.[2] Associated with Mahdi's return is not only divine vengeance for the unjust treatment of the Prophet's household (*Ahl-i Bayt*), in particular the martyrdom of the Prophet's grandson, Husayn, in 680 C.E., but also an eschatological posture in a final day of reckoning, bringing justice to all at the end of time.

Historically speaking, Shi'i messianic traditions have been subject to changes in spiritual authority and popular understanding of sacred experience, along with material spirituality revolving around shrines. By material spirituality, I refer to devotional practices that are built around material ambience, wherein devotees seek a spiritual mode of life. Such material spirituality includes text and paper media, such as prayer books, designed for devotional practices. Shi'i identity, as Najam Haider argues, has been closely connected to the growth of pilgrimage literature for shrine-specific devotional rites and the proliferation of mosques and shrines since the eighth century.[3] The prominent Shi'i scholar Shaykh al-Tusi (995–1067 C.E.) devoted separate sections of his *Tahdhib al-Ahkam* (Ordinance of Judgments) to *ziyara*, sites associated with the Mahdi. The al-'Askariyya Shrine in Samarra would become as popular as shrines in Karbala and Najaf.

With the institutionalization of clerical authority as state apparatus under the Safavids in the sixteenth century and the triumph of the rationalist school of thought (known by scholars as "new-*Usulism*") in the late eighteenth century, popular expressions of Mahdism have provided an interpretive paradigm for religious experiences.[4] Under sometimes contentious clerical authority, Mahdism has fostered for Shiʻi communities the shared belief of redemption in historic time. At the heart of many rituals is the attempt to enact, communicate, and dramatize through symbolic, individual, and collective performative acts the expectation of a redeemable time under the leadership of a mystical messianic figure.

In this chapter, I examine pilgrimage rituals of messianic expectations associated with the Jamkaran mosque and focus on the use of digital technology in the ways distinct religious experiences are performed. In broad terms, I emphasize that pilgrimage in the digital domain is not subordinate to a more authentic form of physical sacred journey but a unique experience in connection with a technologically enhanced set of emotive interactions with a perceived sacred site and its embodied and communicative practices. A key concept that I propose is that although digital technology creates a distinct and different kind of experience, it nonetheless has many of the intimate and physical features of so-called traditional pilgrimage performances. Here I am following Victor and Edith Turner's famous claim that pilgrimage is "some form of deliberate travel to a far place intimately associated with the deepest, most cherished axiomatic values of the traveler."[5] However, I also identify the relationship between "travel" and "values," axiomatic or otherwise, in terms of reconstructing a new sense of modernity in terms of messianic spirituality enhanced through media technologies. At the core of this study are the claims of a symbiotic relationship between religious mediation and technology and of a relationship that ultimately contributes to the construction of ritual subjectivities.

I first examine the history and ritual culture of the Jamkaran mosque, paying particular attention to the role of emotions and embodiment, together with the materiality of religious experience in making messianic expectations manifest at the Jamkaran pilgrimage site. I identify digital forms of Jamkaran pilgrimage in terms of three sets of practices: (1) social media pilgrimage, (2) digitized pilgrimage, and (3) digital embodiment. In each feature, I examine how digital media enhances ways of practicing pilgrimage with varied modes of messianic hope. The common theme that emerges here is not just how technology is used to reinforce more traditional notions of shrine visitation but the shaping of a felt community of Shiʻi devotees who experience Jamkaran as a site of messianic regeneration. What digital technologies provide is a different experience in the realization of such a community.

Jamkaran: A Messianic Dwelling

In essence, Jamkaran represents a place of messianic dwelling where the Mahdi hardly resides but frequently visits, making himself and his promise for a better future felt by his devotees. Like any other sanctuary of apparition, the Jamkaran mosque, its physical presence, carries a sensation of spiritual healing and tales of miracles for Shi'i devotees. As a site of pilgrimage on the outskirts of Qum, the foundation of the mosque is attributed to a miraculous encounter with the sacred persona, the Hidden Imam. The mystical origins of the mosque date back to February 22, 984 C.E. (17 Ramadan 373 A.H.), when Shaykh Hasan Jamkarani, a farmer and a Shi'i devotee, experienced a Mahdistic apparition.[6]

The story is as follows: Shaykh Hasan Jamkarani is abruptly awakened after midnight and informed that Sahib-i zaman (the Lord of Age) has requested his audience. Surprised by the news, he is brought to a nearby place, where a young man, the Hidden Imam, is seated on a throne next to the Prophet Khidr, who is known in Islamic tradition as a spiritual guide to Moses. The Hidden Imam requests that Jamkarani meet with the landowner and get him to give up his land, which is holy. After giving back the profits from farming the land and gathering funds from other local landowners, he was to begin building a mosque on the land. As a miraculous sign, a goat was offered for sacrifice to sanctify the site, followed by instructions to perform prayers, liturgical rites, and salutations for the imams, the Prophet Muhammad, and his daughter Fatima.[7]

Narrative discourses of appropriation are replete with devotional accounts. In the ritual performances, the desire for a renewed relationship between the spiritual and the mundane is expressed and hence forms a new subjectivity. The origin story of Jamkaran is also full of devotional rites associated with the site of appropriation. According to one tradition, the Hidden Imam instructed Jamkarani to tell the faithful to do four *rak'a* prayers, with two of them counting as if done in the Ka'ba.[8] Along with prayers, other spiritual beliefs associated with the mosque include the healing powers of the sacrificed goat, which was found among a flock of sheep and provided a *shafa* (miracle) for the person who consumed its meat. According to tradition, objects such as chains and nails from the mosque were brought back to Qum, where at a certain sayyid's house they had healing powers for the sick and afflicted.[9] Objects such as chains and nails became vestiges, as they were perceived to be traces of spiritual blessing in earthly forms.

Since the tenth century, pilgrims to Jamkaran have focused on miraculous events, spiritual blessings, and intercessions by the Hidden Imam for worldly afflictions that appear insoluble. In fieldwork conducted in 2002, I met a young cleric who had come to Jamkaran in the hope of finding a remedy for pain that had caused him considerable suffering.[10] On a Tuesday night, when devotees of the Hidden Imam gathered for *faraj* (release) prayers at the mosque, the young cleric discovered that Sahib-i zaman had interceded on his behalf for God's help. His weekly return to the mosque served as a way to pay tribute to the imam, whose presence he felt whenever he visited the mosque. The apparition of a sacred persona is difficult to explain, but what is made present to the devotees seeking mostly earthly blessings is the *hes* (feeling) of a personal spiritual manifestation, which is revealed as a miraculous event associated with the mosque. The *hes* is more enunciated with the understanding that the mosque is a site of visitation not because of a grave or tomb but because of the promise of Mahdi's return. Accordingly, this makes the case of Jamkaran unique in the *ziyara* ritual landscape.

The role of intercession, as an act of arbitration on behalf of someone performing prayers, plays an integral role in various miracle stories associated with Jamkaran. Based on testimonies of pilgrims, women and men, old and young, perform prayers, seeking intercession from the Hidden Imam for personal or familial problems. In one account, a young man with inadequate funds to pay off the loan on his house visited the mosque for the usual Tuesday prayers. On his return home the following day, after asking the imam for help, he met a friend, a sayyid, who deposited the money in his bank account.[11] Several other reports also narrate experiences of apparitions, including personal conversations with the Mahdi.[12] In the mountains near the mosque, an elderly man saw the Hidden Imam, who informed him of a long and healthy life ahead. An infertile woman became pregnant weeks after the Tuesday prayers at the mosque. An elderly cancer patient was cured because of the Imam's blessing, and his doctor ridiculed him by saying "Imam zaman dar chah ast" (The Lord of the Age [the promised Mahdi] is in the well).[13]

Here, the well plays an important role, as many pilgrims believe the well serves as a link between the Jamkaran shrine and the spiritual world. The link of the well, I should note, is similar to that of a tomb, which serves as a portal connecting this world with the beyond. While performances associated with the well can be described as techniques of devotion, they can also represent visitation practices that resemble *ziyara* of entombed figures with the spiritual value of intercession. In the case of Jamkaran, it is as though the living but hidden body of Mahdi has visited, though hardly resided in, the well, and a devotee who visits with good intentions can experience miracles because of the site's capacity for intercession. Jamkaran's *ziyara*, after all, is a different kind of visitation rite, for it is a physical place where the Mahdi once visited and yet it is entangled in the anticipation of a future encounter with the Hidden Imam, whose return is expected to change the world. This encounter can be realized at the well, where devotion is performed, and the *hes* of an arriving Mahdi can be experienced during the visit. It is no wonder that the mosque is also commonly known as a *ziyaratgah*, or a place of visitation. Along with references to the name *ziyaratgah*, some pilgrims describe their devotional encounters in terms of the physical traces left behind by the imam in what can be described as *ghadamgah*, or spiritual dwelling.[14] Depending on the pilgrim's perspective, then, Jamkaran could be uniquely identified as mosque, *ghadamgah*, and *ziyaratgah*, hence underlying the multilayered spatial practice of ambiguous pilgrimage oriented toward the inevitable rupture of messianic time. The well, in this view, becomes the material manifestation of the messianic sacred. Spirituality can only be realized when materiality is performed.

As a devotional tradition, pilgrims write their requests on a form provided by the mosque and drop it into the well. Doing so provides a sense perception of a material object (the paper) as an animate object of desire, a longing for a way to overcome earthly suffering for something beyond. The letter is not merely a tool of communication with the Mahdi but an experience associated in terms of an encounter with the spiritual realm, where earthly and otherworldly desires intermingle in devotional acts of prayers and requests. Dropping the letter into the well is therefore a performance of spirituality through which a person attains access to an alternative world where desire can be affirmed if one's intention is pure. Several pilgrims speak of the letter and the well as crossing an invisible boundary between the earthly realm and the Hidden Imam's domain, where all desires and wishes can come true if one has a *qalbi-i pak* (clean heart).

Especially in light of the letter ritual, there seems something meditative about Jamkaran. In fact, throughout the nineteenth and twentieth centuries, Jamkaran was a small village that provided a place of meditation for pilgrims who came to visit the Qum shrine. As a collective site of pilgrimage in its own right, Jamkaran emphasizes a personalized space of spirituality, where direct encounters with the divine in its messianic manifestation are ventured through individuated ritualized performances, such as prayers and letters. What identifies Jamkaran as a shrine is the Mahdiastic abode, a messianic dwelling place where, through spiritual encounters, redemptive time is felt and otherworldly transformations are realized in a this-world context.

With the establishment of the Islamic Republic in 1979, Jamkaran gradually gained religious importance with the backing of several high-ranking clerics. As 'Abbas Amanat explains, the messianic fervor of the 1960s and 1970s played a major role in the Islamist revolutionary movement, which led to the 1979 revolution and the institutionalization of new religious sites for political legitimacy of the ruling clerics.[15] By the mid-1990s, Jamkaran had become a major messianic shrine in transnational Shi'ism, so popular that the mosque expanded in size due to increasing clerical support from Qum, state funds, and the rising number of pilgrims from Iran and abroad.[16] In 2000, Ayatollah 'Ali Khamenei, who regularly visits the shrine, appointed Jamkaran's first official trustee.[17] By the late 2000s, Jamkaran had become a major shrine, known to many Shi'is in the world.

Social Media Networking Pilgrimage

As a religious institution and a popular shrine with over fifteen million visitors from fifty-two countries each year, Jamkaran makes up a large mosque-shrine complex.[18] For example, one department deals with the affairs of international pilgrims, particularly those from neighboring Arab countries. It also has a research center and a publishing house, and the mosque has been actively appropriating digital media since the late 1990s. The emergence of Jamkaran as a leading Shi'i center for digital production coincided with the seminary at Qum adopting new technologies for disseminating religious texts, speeches, poems, songs, and other devotional materials. By the 2000s, Jamkaran and Qum expanded Shi'i Islam's internet presence, which became more widespread in the form of blogs and worldwide social media.

The use of the internet in particular has been increasingly embedded in Jamkaran as a transnational institutional complex. With local area networking technologies such as Wi-Fi throughout the mosque complex, pilgrims and visitors can share their experiences.[19] The internet has also become a popular means for communicating with those outside Iran. Wi-Fi technology also enables the mosque to accommodate an increasing number of visitors with a networking feature that is being developed by various Islamic institutions around the world.[20] Network domains, though not distinct to information technologies, can transcend physical space limitations by constructing an alternative space for distant connectivity, linkages that may or may not resemble everyday social ties. As a wired religious space, Jamkaran is representative of an increasingly transnational mediated community.

Perhaps the most evident networking feature is requiring pilgrims to register online before making an *i'tikaf*, or visitation stay in a mosque to perform a religious ceremony, which usually takes place during major religious festivals.[21] Pilgrims need to participate in a digital network that then allows them to make the physical pilgrimage. Likewise, with the rising popularity of mobile technology and social media sites, Jamkaran continues to experiment with new ways of providing interactive spiritual experiences online.[22] This is similar to the internetization of other practices associated with Muslim pilgrimage traditions, as in the case of seeking Hajj guidance online as a way to disseminate and consume information, particularly questions related to the field of Islamic jurisprudence.[23]

Jamkaran's digitization efforts during the 1990s coincided with the development of information technologies in post-revolutionary Iran, which involved several changes in the way Shi'i pilgrimage was performed. The most significant was what can be described as "spreadable media," with social media outlets emerging as a many-to-many participatory source of disseminating news and information related to Mahdistic themes and Jamkaran.[24] Jamkaran's use of networked information on the internet has marked a radical break from the traditional notion of pilgrimage as essentially a corporeal experience of sacred travel. Although virtual pilgrimage has in a way been practiced for centuries in the form of orating, reading, and writing about spiritual journeys, the internet experience of pilgrimage is a recent development with distinct characteristics. With growing technological use in everyday contexts, the implications of internet use are numerous and growing, but one of the most important remains the dissemination of news and information. The target audience is, by and large, transnational Shi'is.

Jamkaran's social media outlets are diverse. The majority involve the dissemination of news, prayers, events, lectures, and, most importantly, audiovisual materials for a sense of shared identity associated with the shrine. Through email, websites, and social media (particularly the popular instant-messaging service Telegram), news and events related to Jamkaran are posted for various religious activities. Friday lectures, workshops on the Hidden Imam, news bulletins, and hashtags are used for a growing online community of Jamkaran devotees. On Instagram, personalized photos and comments are liked and reposted on Telegram and other mobile apps on both individual and group channels, where audios, photos, and videos are shared.

Devotional rituals and prayers for the Prophet or imams are posted on various social media sites, shared by Shi'is across the world.

An equally important feature of the Jamkaran online community is the emphasis on offline events, such as weddings at the shrine or photo contests. Boundaries between offline and online become blurry as participants encounter a new form of sociability, which Allucquere R. Stone has described as "passage points for collections of common beliefs and practices that unite people who were physically separate."[25] The passage point can also be identified as the compression of time and space, wherein new social encounters are constructed in social media in which Shi'i devotees form networks of connections across different sociocultural contexts in their shared visitation of Jamkaran as the site of destiny on a par with Mecca or Medina. The establishment of a research center devoted to Mahdi studies speaks of attempts to connect the devotional aspects of Jamkaran with jurisprudence research activities, but doing so through the internet and the use of websites (see http://mfsrc.isca.ac.ir/Portal/Home).

The relationship between social media and pilgrimage is less about spreading information about events or news and more about finding oneself in a perceived sacred place where pilgrimage is performed through traversing diverse networks. A Friday lecture posted on Telegram reaches users who have not met in person, but what is collectively experienced is the shared practice of attending the lecture, spreading audio and videos across wide networks on multiple social media sites, and at times converging on mainstream media. Such media convergence can be described as participatory, but it is also about sharing an experience, which in the case of Jamkaran pilgrimage is not felt at the physical site but relived through social media in the very act of sharing the felt sacred in networked ways.

Digitized Pilgrimage

"Live" visitation of Jamkaran is a unique pilgrimage experience in its digital form, boasting one of the best live streaming services of Shi'i sites. In fact, Jamkaran administrators claim that the mosque was the first to initiate live streaming.[26] On the website http://www.jamkaran.ir/live/, live feeds from the mosque are shown, while similar sites include links to other major Islamic sites, including Masjid al-Haram in Mecca.[27] What the element of live broadcast introduces to virtual pilgrimage is the sense of copresence at the shrine, where participants can experience the sacred while being linked with other pilgrims at the site or present online. Software that allows "virtual travel to Jamkaran," along with professional photos of the mosque for pilgrims to purchase from the cultural center of the mosque, is another case in point.[28] This multilingual software provides scenes and images of Jamkaran with the purpose of performing pilgrimage from a distance. The cultivation of a shared experience of pilgrimage in the form of live streaming or photographic ensembles highlights a mediated sense of community of Mahdi devotees who reconstruct rituals of shrine visitation through digital technologies of copresence. Moving images of Jamkaran are not merely representations for viewership but a distinct kind of visitation centered on the emotive dimension of immersive traveling from a distance.

In an important way, digitized pilgrimage is less about networking and more about traversing into a sacred site through digital means. There is a distinct ambience of social experience in live streaming. The experience of being there, at the shrine, entails a unique awareness of visitation based on interaction in a shared virtual setting. Meanwhile, the technology enhances the experience of travel as an imagined experience and is not a marker of separation between the viewer and the object of pilgrimage. Turner's idea of "deliberate travel to a far place" in terms of being "intimately associated with the deepest, most cherished axiomatic values" underscores the imaginative ability to place oneself in the live experience of digital visitation of Jamkaran. Consider the following account by a pilgrim: "I feel I am there when I see the video. It is not that I am there, but it feels like I am there. But it is just a different *ziyara*, especially if I enter the website with a clean intention for Imam." This statement made by a middle-aged man from Tehran is important because first, it signals the integral role of emotions in "deliberate travel to a far place." Travel from where the live stream is experienced takes place in the form of an emotive passage, a transportation that though nonphysical is essentially performed in the medium of digital materiality. Emotions are embedded in the digital interaction between the pilgrim and the site of visitation. Though emotions can be displayed according to cultural expressions, emotions of digitized pilgrimage take on a virtualized reality in the mediated domain of live streaming.

Second, the notion of "clean intention" evokes an important state of mind, a perceived spiritual purity actualized in a situation that a pilgrim encounters and ultimately immerses him- or herself from a distant space and time. Purity of intended action refers to a disciplinary practice in which purity, detached from worldly desire, is emphasized, with the aim of performing pilgrimage. It is not the act of travel but the intention of doing pilgrimage, digitized or otherwise, that underlies the act of visitation of Jamkaran, and a particular pilgrim is able to perform this distinct rituality through live streaming. Intention also renders the salience of consciousness, in this case a spiritual perception, which can be present regardless of situated contexts and which can be collapsed and transcended in relation to the objective of (spiritual) desire—namely, the shrine.

The implicit dynamic of a pilgrimage experience collapses everyday time and space and reconfigures one's ordinary sense of being—that is, it reconstructs a stable reality in the process of travel, arrival, visitation, and departure from the sacred site. With digitized pilgrimage, the collapse of time and space occurs in the contextual collapse of a social body in the reappropriation of self and reality in an alternative surrounding, though one still perceived as authentic, hence intermingling the material with the digital in ways that make pilgrimage undergo a transformation of substance rather than kind. As Tom Boellstorff has shown, virtual world experience always entails a distinct form of embodiment but is contextually dependent on a socially interactive "virtual world" as a distinct space.[29] The relationship between virtual and body is as complex as the physical body situated in social reality, since perception always carries a multiplicity of experiences. Digitized pilgrimage does not imitate the "real" pilgrimage experience but expands on it through emotive actions that render pilgrimage ritual possible in the first place.

Digital Embodiment

Digitized pilgrimage carries the assumption of a form of ritualized practice that undergoes a distinct embodied experience of digitization. But does the "digitized" merely involve an intimate reconnection in distance with a sacred site through digital technology? In this final section, I examine how the digital can serve as an embodied event at the actual pilgrimage site, rather than just a means to visit a sacred site. Digital embodiment is about how the body in terms of perceptions, senses, feelings, and experiences incorporates digitality into the practice of pilgrimage at the physical site. By "incorporation" I refer to a form of embodiment in that experience becomes immersed in digital technological practices, activities in which subjective encounters with the world become mediated through social technologies such as mobile phones, social media, or blogging. Digital incorporation is a mediated experience of being physically present at the pilgrimage site, with digitally enhanced forms of communication interactively involved with the sacred space on individual and collective levels.

Behind the mosque, the famous Jamkaran water well brings together pilgrims for the letter-dropping ritual. Some write notes or letters and pin them on designated spaces on the wall near the well. The well of Jamkaran is where Mahdi can listen to his devotees, as he occasionally visits the place and will one day return before the end of time. Regardless of variation of beliefs about the well, letters written by devotees can serve as a way to connect with the *aqa*, the Lord of Age. Pilgrims' letters are personal, private, and rarely shared with others. When asked about their content, several persons I interviewed described, without going into detail, prayers for healing, regaining lost love, or increasing income via a new marriage. In my fieldwork, I have mostly observed male pilgrims, who generally engage in the letter-writing ritual in a quiet and solitary manner. But this is also true for women. Clad in black chadors, female pilgrims engage in similar performances, although as a male, I had to observe them at a distance.

Here, the meditative theme is pervasive. In one case, a man described his sister dropping a letter with a prayer for passing the entrance exam to the university—a prayer for personal improvement, though it was shared with relatives and even a stranger (me). The meditative ambience around the well, with separate sections for men and women, speaks of an introspective spatial practice that resembles what Turner famously described as a "liminal space"—an in-between, transitional realm of everyday transfiguration, which sharply contrasts with the structured and institutionalized domain of daily life.[30] What technology enhances in ritual performance is the dynamics of liminal space.

Since 2008, I have increasingly become aware of the use of blogging to narrate pilgrimage experience at a specific time, primarily during a major religious event. With the rising popularity of social media, Facebook narratives posted after a pilgrimage have less to do with networking than with being a reflective performance articulating a pilgrim's experience as a spiritual transformation. Such narratives put the physical presence of the shrine center stage in the narrative Facebook scheme. When examining numerous examples of technological use in the pilgrimage experience, one is often struck by the way technology becomes, in the words of Marshall McLuhan, extensions of corporeal reality, an augmentation of senses and consciousness with a heightened awareness.[31] A Facebook site, a cell phone camera, a Telegram posting of communal prayers, an Instagram photo of a wedding at the mosque, can all serve as extensions of the emotive experience of pilgrimage, rather than its mere substitute or representation. The extension of experience can perhaps be described as a simulacrum—that is, not a mere reproduction of an original experience but a distinct experience that undermines, to use Gilles Deleuze's words, "a privileged position."[32]

In light of the preceding discussion on experience and technological use, I want to take up an important feature of embodiment. I use the concept "digital embodiment," since most discussions on digital pilgrimage have focused on how technology operates as something to and from the "physical" or "actual" domain of the pilgrimage site. What I suggest here, however, is how digital technologies foster distinct practices of embodiment that reconfigure corporeal practices such as pilgrimage in a radically different way. How can we best describe such a radical difference?

During my June 2016 field trip, I observed a young man in his early twenties quietly engaging in the letter-dropping ritual. Like other male visitors who visited the well, the young man was focused and mostly detached from his surroundings. He seemed to be in his own world. Concentration displays an inward movement, marked by flexibility and fragility of circumstances, which the young man was fully aware of yet embraced as a way to do his prayer—that is, with tears. What transformed were the body and the senses into a digital creation and a medium for resituating oneself in an encounter with the pilgrimage site.

This transformation, in particular, became more pronounced when, after dropping the letter, the young man took out his cell phone and began to record the event of letter dropping (see figure 9.1). He stared into the dark well through his cell phone camera, as though the device could give him a special ability to see beyond into the darkness of the well. Minutes passed, and he still looked into the well through his cell phone. He appeared to occasionally take photos, but much of the activity was recording the depth of the well, tracing the fall of the letter into the darkness. I decided not to approach the man, as I wanted the experience to speak for itself. And what the experience demonstrated is that embodiment cannot be detached from the technology, which is used to perform the ritual. The cell phone, in a sense, became an extension of the young man's perception, enhancing his felt and visual experience with the technology, which is deliberately inserted into a situation perceived in spiritual value. Travel here is one of digital enhancement of the body rather than virtual transportation, as in the case of digitized pilgrimage. The sensory is projected into a material substance, technology, which in itself carries a magical force of trans-human quality. What happened here is that the cell phone did what the naked eye was incapable of performing: seeing beyond the present time and expanding the pilgrim in his experience to encounter the Mahdi. In this capacity, what precisely

FIGURE 9.1 A young pilgrim after dropping his letter down the well, Jamkaran, June 25, 2016 (photograph by author).

identifies embodiment is conceived out of digital sensory, an emotive process that renders technology essential to the experience of pilgrimage.

In the case of digital embodiment of letter dropping, memory plays a crucial role. There is an intimate relationship between material and technology in the ways memory is shaped. Pilgrims write wishes, desires, dreams, and prayers on printed papers, on reproduced objects made personalized through various practices, technological or otherwise, that make religious experience possible in the first place. What the well becomes is the physical-spiritual containment of pilgrims' aspirations, a keeper of desires, where affective capacity to link the human world with the supernatural is affirmed in the materiality of the printed paper, pen, and ink. Desire in the performance of well letters also becomes a practice of carving out a history of a future yet to come, a future of messianic hope involving uncanny knowledge of a forthcoming promise. The experience of hope nevertheless includes encounters with a future time that unfolds a new tomorrow, where sensory linkages with earthly concerns through materialized memory, ironically, serve as a medium to transcend the human everyday. In the case of the young man at the well, the experience of memory and the cell phone camera absorb more than just scenes from the well. While a photo or a video is captured as a memorial to the moment of dropping the letter into the well, memory of the experience becomes what Walter Benjamin described as the recognizable now, a living experience "in which things adopt their true—surrealistic—face."[33] The "surrealistic" truth here is a trace of a future, a personalized tomorrow with the promise of the Mahdi and his power of intercession reenacted in the performance of recording the letter dropping. Time here collapses in physical space, and technology as embodiment attains agency in this transformative experience.

Conclusion

In this chapter, I have attempted to show the relationship between digital technology and pilgrimage as a set of individual and social experiences. The relationship between pilgrimage and digital technology is the ability to transform experience in ways that cause new forms of pilgrimage to emerge. The modern Muslim pilgrimage experience is undergoing changes with digital technologies, in particular the rising popularity of app culture tied to mobile technology. What emerges in consequence to appropriation of digital practices is not merely a change in pilgrimage performances but a change in the ways of seeing and being Muslim in a perceived globalized world, where technology is viewed as an enhancement of being (or becoming) modern without contradicting spiritual traditions sought to be synthesized with notions of progress. Moreover, digital technology affirms social solidarity with the production of new networks of ritual communities, networks that construct new conceptions and practices of self and reality in complex and multiple, shifting experiences of time and space.

In the case of Jamkaran, digital pilgrimage has and continues to provide new ways of staging a collective shared experience of pilgrimage. Social solidarity of technological imaginative form is heightened with Jamkaran, not just as a mosque but also as an administrative-communication institution, producing online web streaming of mosque events broadcast to the world. Transnational perceptions significantly matter when such scenes are viewed by Shiʿis across the world. More than alternative reality, it is the experiential impact in terms of subjective and networking practices that render technology a significantly new feature in pilgrimage rites. And in this process, Jamkaran has been a leading shrine complex in the realization of a distinct form of digital pilgrimage.

Notes

1. Derived from *Jam-kard* (Built by Jam), the name Jamkaran also means "the margin of Jam." See Amir-Moezzi, "Jamkaran et Mahan: Deux pèlerinages insolites en Iran," in *Lieux d'Islam: Cultes et cultures de l'Afrique à Java* (Paris: Editions Autrement, 1996), 109–35; Jean Calmard, "Jamkarān," in *Encyclopaedia Iranica*, last updated June 28, 2011, http://iranicaonline.org/articles/jamkaran.

2. For a study of the history and theology of Shi'i Islamic Mahdism, see Abdulaziz Abdulhussein Sachedina, *Islamic Messianism: The Idea of the Mahdī in Twelver Shī'ism* (Albany: State University of New York Press, 1981); Seyyed Hossein Nasr, Hamid Dabashi, and Seyyed Vali Reza Nasr, eds., *Expectation of the Millennium: Shi'ism in History* (Albany: State University of New York Press, 1989).

3. Najam Haider, *The Origins of the Shī'a: Identity, Ritual, and Sacred Space in Eighth-Century Kūfa* (Cambridge: Cambridge University Press, 2011), 231–48.

4. For a study of Akhbari-Usuli (scripturalist-rationalist) conflict and the debate over the nature of Shi'i Islam in the eighteenth century, see Zackery M. Heern, *The Emergence of Modern Shi'ism: Islamic Reform in Iraq and Iran* (London: One World, 2015).

5. Victor Turner and Edith Turner, *Image and Pilgrimage in Christian Culture* (Oxford: Blackwell, 1978), 241.

6. Calmard, "Jamkarān."

7. Calmard, "Jamkarān"; Amir-Azimi, *Masjidi Muqaddasi Jamkarān Tajallīgāhi Imām Zamān* (Jamkaran: Intishārāti Masjidi Muqaddasi Jamkarān, 2000), 27–31. While some Shi'i scholars have questioned the authenticity of this narrative, there have been leading grand ayatollahs, such as Abdul-Karim Ha'eri Yazdi, Mar'ashi Najafi, and Ruhallah Khomeini, who have revered the mosque as a site of the Imam Mahdi. For the supreme leader, Ayatollah 'Ali Khamenei, Jamkaran is a "sacred place" and of "lightness," and a major "base" for Shi'i Muslims. "Imam Khamenei: Bi Masjidii Jamkarān raftan, sāzandi ast," July 4, 2015, http://welayatnet.com/fa/news/68422.

8. Amir-Azami, *Masjidi Muqaddasi Jamkarān Tajallīgāhi Imām Zamān*, 29.

9. Amir-Azami, 30–31.

10. Since 2002, I have made a total of six field trips to Jamkaran, with the last trip in June 2016, conducting interviews and making ethnographic observations.

11. Amir-Azami, *Masjidi Muqaddasi Jamkarān Tajallīgāhi Imām Zamān*, 136–37.

12. Sayyid Hassan Abtahi, *Mulāqāt bā Imām Zamān* (Tehran: Nidāyi Muslih, 2001/2002), 62–65.

13. Mir-Azami, *Masjidi Muqaddasi Jamkarān Tajallīgāhi Imām Zamān*, 137–38.

14. For the relationship between *ziyaratgah* and *ghadamgah* in reference to the sacred history of Mahdi appearances at various earthly locations, see Ahmad 'Ali Majid Hali, *Tārīkhi Maqām Sāhibi al-Asri wa al-Zamān 'Alayhi al-Salam fī al-Hilla* (Qum: Markaz al-Dirasāt al-Takhassusiyi fī al-Īmām al-Mahdī, 2005/2006).

15. Abbas Amanat, *Apocalyptic Islam and Iranian Shi'ism* (London: I. B. Tauris, 2009).

16. Calmard, "Jamkarān"; Amanat, 249.

17. Amanat, 230.

18. On Tuesdays and Fridays, nearly 250,000 pilgrims visit Jamkaran. ‎-52- ‎از-زائرانی‎-‎ ‎جمکران-مسجد-در-جهان-کشور‎, May 22, 2016, http://tasnimnews.com/fa/news/1395/03/02/1081316/.

19. The mosque provides Wi-Fi uploading during major festivals, which can be activated through personal cell phones using numerical codes. See "Masjidi Jamkarān tahti pūshishi internet 'Wi-Fi' qarār girift," May 18, 2016, http://mehrnews.com/news/3662021/.

20. Gary Bunt, "Defining Islamic Interconnectivity," in *Muslim Networks: From Hajj to Hip Hop*, ed. Miriam Cook and Bruce B. Lawrence (Chapel Hill: University of North Carolina Press, 2005), 235–51.

21. Internet registration is not limited to Jamkaran but extends to other religious shrine sites in Iran.

22. Jamkaran also provides free SIM cards for cell phone use. "Interneti rāygān dar masjidi jamkarān tawassuti hamrāhi awwal," May 21, 2016, https://rond.ir/News/695/.

23. Gary Bunt, "Decoding the Hajj in Cyberspce," in *The Hajj: Pilgrimage in Islam*, ed. Eric Tagliacozzo and Shawkat M. Toorawa (Cambridge: Cambridge University Press, 2016), 231–41.

24. Henry Jenkins, *Spreadable Media: Creating Value and Meaning in a Networked Culture* (New York: New York University Press, 2013).

25. Allucquere R. Stone, "Will the Real Body Please Stand Up? Boundary Stories about Virtual Cultures," in *Cyberspace: First Steps*, ed. Michael Benedikt (Cambridge, MA: MIT Press, 1991), 81.

26. According to Qudsonline, Jamkaran began live streaming the shrine in 2000/2001. "Pakhshi zindiyi marāsimi masjidi muqaddasi jamkarān dar internet," September 26, 2012, http://qudsonline.ir/news/73374/‎پخش-زنده-مراسم-مراسم-مسجد-مقدس-جمکران‎-‎ ‎در-اینترنت‎.

27. See also www.shiayan.ir, where a "live" section includes links to various religious sites in Iraq, Iran, and Saudi Arabia. https://www.shiayan.ir/‎پخش-زنده-و‎- ‎مستقیم-مسجدالحرام-مکه-مکرمه‎/.

28. "Safar-i majazi be jamkaran ba narm afzar-i safar-i bihisht," Fars News, March 19, 2013, http://farsnews.com/newstext.php?nn=13911228000170.

29. Tom Boellstorff, "Virtuality: Lacing the Virtual Body: Avator, Chora, Cypherg," in *Companion to the Anthropology of the Body and Embodiment*, ed. F. E. Mascia-Lees (Oxford: Wiley-Blackwell, 2011), 504–20.

30. Victor Turner, *The Forest of Symbols: Aspects of Ndembu Ritual* (Ithaca, NY: Cornell University Press, 1967), 93–111.

31. Marshall McLuhan, *Understanding Media: The Extensions of Man* (New York: Routledge, 1964).

32. Gilles Deleuze, *Difference and Repetition*, trans. Paul Patton (New York: Columbia University Press, 69.

33. Walter Benjamin, *The Arcades Project* (Cambridge, MA: Belknap Press, 1999), 486.

CHAPTER TEN

On Mediation and Magnetism: Or, Why Destroy Saint Shrines?

EMILIO SPADOLA

As the studies in this volume attest, tombs and shrines of exemplary Muslims or saints (*awliya'*, or *wali*) have long been compelling centers of devotional pilgrimage (*ziyara*) and thus critical sites for the production and reproduction of Muslim authorities and communal norms. In implicit acknowledgment of their "spiritual magnetism," episodic reformist movements have criticized such "non-Hajj pilgrimage" sites—and saint veneration more generally—as idolatrous threats to Islam's fundamental monotheism.[1] This chapter analyzes recent Muslim reformist movement challenges to shrine pilgrimage practices by examining the recent spread of highly publicized destruction of popular saints' shrines. What, if anything, is historically specific to this current tactic?[2] And what can shrine destruction tell us about contemporary Muslim piety and pilgrimage more broadly?

The Call of the Shrine

Shrine desecration and destruction are recognized political gestures. In medieval Islam's complex of "shrine-centered sovereignty," the destruction of old shrines or the building of new ones vividly demonstrated new claims to power.[3] A strictly *antishrine* reformism emerged with the late medieval scholar Ibn Abd al-Wahhab, whose followers in Iraq and Arabia went so far as to demolish shrines of the Prophet's family.[4] A century later, colonial-era Salafi modernists dismantled numerous popular Sufi shrines in North and West Africa and called fellow Muslims to reject local pilgrimage practices as doctrinally unsound and incompatible with new political logics of Muslim public life and piety.[5]

Since the turn of the millennium, acts of shrine destruction have taken a spectacular turn, addressed at times as much to non-Muslim as to Muslim audiences. For many Euro-American observers and regional allies, the Afghan Taliban's televised demolition of the Bamiyan Buddha statues in 2001 epitomized the group's failure to meet global standards of political civility. In similarly publicized and condemned acts, Islamic State militants destroyed

223

Muslim shrines as well as pre-Islamic architecture and museum relics in Iraq and Syria.[6] In the meantime, militant reformists and Sunni militias challenged national regimes by targeting Sufi and Shi'i shrines and worshippers in Mali, Tunisia, Libya, Egypt, Somalia, and Pakistan.

While these recent acts of shrine destruction claim adherence to the Qur'an and the Sunna of the Prophet, they call not for a fantastical return to scriptural origins but declaim these scriptures' contemporary relevance. Conflicts over non-Hajj pilgrimages and saints' shrines, as over public piety more broadly, confirm Talal Asad's description of Islam's "discursive traditions" as being built on, rather than free of, interpretive differences and debates. In framing shrine destruction as acts of doctrinal fidelity and public piety, reformists seek recognition of their call, aiming, in Asad's terms, to *"win someone over"* to particular interpretations of "apt practice" (original emphasis).[7] Indeed, insofar as contemporary shrine destructions claim coherence *as calls*, analysis must attend not only to social conditions and political norms surrounding a particular shrine or reformist movement but also to the technological media spheres that transcend them—to the online video sites and global television networks by which these acts of destruction circulate, and to the mass publics they address.

Bringing our focus, as reformists do, to the mass publicity of shrine destruction confirms that the chosen media of Islamic discourse are indeed the message. Particular media do not merely archive and transmit authoritative claims to "apt practice" but rather shape the terms and contexts of that discourse—and thus define what counts *as* apt: Islam's discursive tradition is not simply a contest of interpretation but a contest of mediation. In this light, modern reformists' framing of shrine destruction as calls to public reform helps us grasp the analogous communicative power of shrines within the multiple Muslim traditions of saint veneration and pilgrimage. Specifically, it prompts analysis of saints' shrines as channels of spiritual command—as the media platforms of a saintly call. Put simply, as militants aim to reform or eliminate saintly authority and the reverential acts of pilgrimage and publics they summon, it is shrines' literal *appeal*—the call of the shrine—that they must destroy.

In this chapter, I revisit anthropological studies of pilgrimage, including Muslim traditions of visits (*ziyara*) to saints' shrines, to draw out themes of mediation—that is, to discern in non-Hajj pilgrimages the spiritual "call of the shrine." I then examine reformist calls, including online videos of attacks on saints' shrines and online fatwas approving of the destruction of shrines. The key aim is less to identify Islamic doctrinal interpretive differences than to discern contestations over the distinct media they deploy—from saints' shrines to YouTube—and the normative Muslim publics and pieties they solicit. In the final analysis, this focus on the call of shrines and reformists' counter-calls highlights basic tensions of dissemination and coherence internal to contemporary Muslim politics: between Islam's multiplicity of mediations and distinctly modern calls for a unified, and ideally uniform, Muslim *umma* and discursive tradition.[8]

"Spiritual Magnetism" and Shrines as Media

Addressing the social and spiritual attraction of pilgrimage centers across religious traditions, James J. Preston develops two notions of their communicative power: namely "spiritual magnetism" and "tracing."[9] Regarding the first, Preston writes that as communities of believers invest specific material sites with spiritual significance, these destinations seem to mysteriously *compel* visitors. Spiritual magnetism, he argues, "is not an intrinsic 'holy' quality of mysterious origins that radiates objectively from a place of pilgrimage"; rather, it "derives from human concepts and values, via historical, geographical, social, and other forces that coalesce in a sacred center."[10] Shrines compel or call to visitors due to "traceable forces that seem mysterious to participants but have measurable referents in empirical reality": if devotees associate the site with miraculous healing and with past manifestations of supernatural power, if the locale and the land is considered holy, and if reaching the site is made difficult by distance or rules of approach, then the site will maintain its magnetic aura.[11] Preston's concept of "tracing," adopted from nuclear physics, concerns these "measurable referents" of a shrine's magnetism. "Spiritual magnetism" may not "radiate objectively" from shrines, but it nonetheless takes form in *objects*: "the invisible world of atomic structure [i.e., a 'mysterious' magnetism] becomes tangible through traces left in other media."[12] It is toward such traces, and not some ineffable or compelling power of the sacred, Preston concludes, that scholars must direct their inquiries.

Preston's reading of "magnetism" and "tracing" thus rejects pilgrims' beliefs in the metaphysical power of the sacred for the observable "media" that embody it, an argument that would seem to sympathize with pilgrims' desire for tactile encounters and material relics, including photographs and other technical reproductions of the journey. Yet Preston suggests that a site's spiritual magnetism or call is not merely reproduced by, but fundamentally *depends* on, some minimal medium or archival trace—the recollections and stories of prior miracles at the site, or even the emergence and maintenance of a pathway to the shrine. ("Trace," as Preston notes, not only refers to "sign" but also bears the archaic definition of "path or trail.")[13] Put otherwise, for Preston, these media traces do not simply copy or reproduce a sacred presence summoning the faithful to pilgrimage; rather, they constitute the shrine's very *"source* of spiritual magnetism" (my emphasis).[14]

In his emphasis on the material (human) origins of the shrine's call, Preston's argument hews quite close to militant reformist criticisms of pilgrimage as idolatrous. From both perspectives, it is not the sacred which creates pilgrims, but the converse; the community of devotees invests the shrine with sacred value, and the shrine in turn mediates that collective force. Put in Durkheimian terms, it is the pilgrims' society that calls itself via the shrine as totemic medium.[15] Yet while anthropologists and historians of Islam consider "non-Hajj pilgrimage" to be part of a larger Muslim tradition,[16] reformists consider it to be a deviation from the tradition. What in reformists' view warrants a shrine's destruction is its call (and command) to worship a power other than God. And because that call emanates not merely from individual pilgrims but from the norms of their social collective, the destruction of the shrine must constitute a counter-call addressed to that same collective.

Studies of Muslim pilgrimage provide numerous examples of shrines' embodiment of a command. Indeed, while Bhardwaj's taxonomy of Muslim pilgrimage (or "religious circulation") attempts to distinguish the "obligatory" Hajj from the "voluntary" *ziyara*, he nevertheless notes that acts of shrine visitation are often "virtually contractual" and made in "fulfillment of a vow."[17] In these traditions—common across the Muslim world, including at sites of shrine destruction—the act of pilgrimage is not at all voluntary; rather, the sovereign forces embedded in the shrine impose the duty to visit. Such contractual conditions include illnesses and afflictions of pilgrims or their loved ones—illnesses that, imposed by honored saints, may only be alleviated by them.[18] In some Egyptian and Moroccan practices, for example, a Sufi saint (or tutelary spirit) initiates the contract in a dream or a waking vision. As Amira Mittermaier observes, "It is considered a special blessing to be called upon by a saint."[19] But the blessing is unequivocally a command: "The blessing of being visited by a saint comes with an obligation. The visit has to be reciprocated as soon as possible, usually by the dreamer herself but sometimes also by someone close to her. The urgency that evokes the counter visit to the shrine is most clearly expressed when visitors at shrines state that they have received an order (*ga li al-amr*)."[20]

Similarly, in some Moroccan Sufi traditions, pilgrims' shrine visits are preceded by the saint's prior visitation and summons in dreams, and the dreamer's failure to respond risks further afflictions. In southern regions, this appearance is explicitly described in colloquial Arabic as *"ntiq"* — that is, the saint's pronouncement or summons, or "the call of the saint."[21] In northern Morocco, as in Egypt, terms describing the saint's visitation in dreams are likewise understood to be a call or command; thus, as Muhammad Maarouf describes it, someone who "has a dream in which the saint appears to him in person and summons him to his shrine . . . immediately fulfills the vision" to make the pilgrimage.[22]

That dreams and visions are interior and otherworldly makes their force no less collective: "Spiritual magnetism" compels pilgrims only insofar as its traces (whether material or oneiric) are recognized by others as signs of an otherworldly command. Khadija Naamouni summarizes the point: "The call is a subjective sign of [*jinn*] possession seeming in some way imposed by the logic of popular beliefs that hold that only a judgment rendered by the saint [against the *jinn*] can resolve the patient's troubles. The *ntiq* is considered *by other people* to be an incontrovertible sign by which the patient may invest all hopes in the recourse to the saint [i.e., by making a pilgrimage to the saint]" (my emphasis).[23]

DURKHEIMIAN THEORY might seem quite foreign to Muslim reformists' concerns, but it is in fact entirely relevant. In destroying a shrine, reformists surely mean to enjoin individual Muslims to pious practice; in disseminating the act of destruction as a collective call, however, they acknowledge the collective source of the shrine's value. Destroying the shrine aims to destroy the primary medium, and thus the power, of a collective's call to pilgrimage. Of course, were reformists merely concerned to harness the loyalty of the community as it is, another shrine would do. Yet rather than simply build another shrine to a competing saint, reformists disseminate their counter-call in other media. At issue here is not simply competing claims to political loyalty, nor even interpretive differences within the discursive tradition, but the media that shape discourse, and the forms of individual piety and communal publics these media solicit.

Differing Calls, Competing Mediations

The spate of recent attacks on pilgrimage shrines in the Middle East, North and West Africa, and Central Asia claim the historically recognized aim of enforcing *tawhid*, the doctrine of God's unicity, by which shrine visitations embody *shirk*, or polytheism, the unforgivable sin of ascribing partners to God. Yet as central a role as this doctrine plays, more notable are efforts to publicize the act of destruction, or indeed to stage the act itself as a media spectacle for further technical reproduction and consumption. The new millennium marks a crucial turning point, with the Afghan Taliban's efforts to publicize its demolitions of the Buddha statues in Bamiyan—a move only seemingly at odds with the group's temporary ban on television.[24] The September 11 attacks of the same year, aimed at the World Trade Center and the U.S. Pentagon, may mark the most globally mediated shrine destructions yet.[25] These attacks did not aim merely to destroy the World Trade Center as a putatively sacred object but, as W. J. T. Mitchell observes, to "stage its destruction as a media spectacle."[26]

The question is, staging it for whom? The majority of shrine destructions today take place in spaces of political contestation, lethal social disintegration, and outright civil war. Yet as with colonial-era reforms, these spaces of contestation are difficult if not impossible to limit: Just as the Taliban demonstrated (local) state sovereignty, they anticipated a global audience—the necessary locus of any nation-state's political recognition. Indeed, every attack on a shrine, no matter how ostensibly local the shrine's community of devotees, is made potentially global by virtue of its televisual or online reproducibility. Sunni militant attacks on Iraq's al-'Askariyya shrine in 2006 and 2007; the post–Arab Spring destruction of Sufi shrines in Tunisia, Libya, Egypt, and Syria; the Shabab movement's (*harakat al-shabab al-mujahidin*) attacks in Somalia; Ansar al-Dine's (*ansar al-din*) attacks on Sufi shrines, mosques, and Arabic manuscript repositories in Timbuktu; the Islamic State's demolition of Assyrian relics in Nimrud, Mosul, and Palmyra—all of these garnered global attention.[27] More precisely, by choosing to document and disseminate acts of shrine destruction on global networks, these groups explicitly performed local sovereignty for a global audience.[28]

One effect of this dissemination is to situate the modes of piety and sociability the shrine solicits within a global space of comparison and critique. A Kata'ib News Channel video identified with al-Shabab in the Islamic State of Jubba (southern Somalia) titled "Destruction of Idolatrous Shrines in the Village of *Balad al-Karim*" explicitly addresses a transnational Arab Muslim audience. Although narrated in a distinct dialect of Arabic (and therefore limited in its comprehensibility among native Arabic speakers), the Kata'ib channel's reportage includes subtitles in *fusha*, or Standard Arabic, the lingua franca of the Arab world. In analogous ways, the producers appeal to putatively universal, rather than narrowly local and thus illegitimate, Islamic norms of saint veneration.

The video begins with a Shabab member providing viewers with an ethnographic tour of the shrine, with its tombs of a saint, Shaykh Nur Husayn, and his sons. The guide, pointing out the tombs and sheets of cloth inscribed with the saints' legends, explains their local uses and meanings: "This rope tied around the tomb is used by pilgrims [*zuwwar*] who come for healing or to have children. Behind this curtain there's an opening to the tomb where the pilgrim reaches for a handful of earth for healing purposes. He rubs it on his face or on his relatives, his children, or painful spots or ailing limbs."

After the tour, the video cuts to the immediate exterior of the shrine, where militants cast relics of the saints onto a bonfire while the villagers look on. The camera lingers on the flames and then cuts abruptly back to the inner sanctum of the shrine, now subject to the reformists' happy destruction. As with the image of fire, the video's power rests not so much on discursive persuasion as on shock and awe. The camera pans across a group of men with sledgehammers who work together to break open one of the tombs. There is no narrative, only the visceral hammering of the shrine and joyous shouts of *Allahu Akbar!* The men appear physically imposing, formidable. In contrast, the shrine, with its splintering boards and shattering tiles, appears suddenly flimsy—hardly the abode of authority.[29]

Now the video shifts once more to Shabab addressing a large circle of villagers. An Arabic caption reads, "Discourse and lecture to the locals following the shrine destruction"; loudspeakers broadcast Qur'anic verse. The lecture is brief. A reformist reminds the villagers: "After today, this place will count among the Houses of God, where He alone is worshipped." The video closes with a Shabab reformist's clear and practiced recitation of the *adhan* (the call to prayer).

A second video features Shaykh Hassan al-Husayni, a prominent reformist preacher and satellite media figure, in an occasional series documenting his travels in the Muslim world. Posted on al-Husayni's YouTube channel and titled "Destroying an Idolatrous Building [*bina' shirki*] in Tunis," it features the burly and bearded shaykh walking through a pleasant urban neighborhood of Gabès (Qabis) and stopping in front of rubble. A yellow backhoe digs at the pile. Al-Husayni explains: "[Here] people came to praise deities other than God, and to sacrifice to deities other than God. They came day and night and would stay three days, dedicating their sacrifices to 'Saint so-and-so' [*sidi fulan*]." "Thank God!" he continues. "This [destruction] is one of the results of the awakening of the Tunisian youth [during the revolution]!"

The video cuts to a local man, perhaps in his thirties, who repeats the description of idolatry and adds that, in place of the shrine, a Qur'anic education and outreach center will be founded: "Here, where Qur'anic recitation was *prohibited*—we'll have a *Dar al-Qur'an!*" Al-Husayni interviews a second local man who repeats, more vehemently, "We *don't want idolatry* in Tunis! We want *tawhid* in Tunis!"[30]

The video closes with a stirring anthem over silent footage of al-Husayni lecturing a group of young boys gathered in the street in front of the rubble. He gestures to the empty spot where once idolatry ruled, then faces his local audience. The video's placement of the anthem over the shaykh's speech mutes the content of his address, but as with the previous video, physical acts enforce the message: wiping his hands clean, al-Husayni models total refusal of the shrine's call for the local boys who might otherwise constitute its future pilgrims.

The videos differ in terms of locale, but they share themes. These include discursive content, namely critiques of *shirk* (polytheism), that contrast the illicit call of the shrine to their own legitimate call to Islam. The first video, beginning with an educational tour, focuses on what draws pilgrims to the shrine. The reformist guide, explaining the social significance of putatively sacred objects, explains that the pilgrims come for *al-tabarruk*—that is, to seek transmissions of the saint's blessing (*baraka*) embedded in the tomb and its soil. It is a matter of the blessing's communication from God to pilgrim through the essential medium of the saint's shrine. In the reformist's view, pilgrims think they communicate with God not by responding to the adhan and the video but by responding to the shrine's call and rubbing dirt on children and ailing limbs.

The question of licit or illicit calls is not only a matter of discourse. The online video and the saint shrine and sacred soil mediate different things and differ as media.[31] A major difference is their presence in space and time; that is, their susceptibility to reproduction and circulation. We may assume that for pilgrims the particularity of this saint and this soil is crucial. It cannot be merely any soil, any tomb. Rather, this saint and this soil bear what Walter Benjamin characterized as the "aura" or "cult value" of a singular object; these traces call in their absolute particularity.[32] The value of the saint's body and baraka is also singular: it may be reproduced or, rather, extended through his sons and the soil, and indeed, through the indexical medium of the photograph, but for pilgrims these extensions do not usurp but rather enhance the saint's power. The shrine, like that of the saint's body and tomb, is the irreplaceably particular medium of blessing. As such, it summons devotees to its unique site rather than to any other. In stark contrast, the reformists' video of its destruction is not merely reproducible in multiple copies but, rather like any commodity, *made* to be reproduced and exchanged. As Benjamin observes, the value of this commoditized medium rests precisely on its capacity for multiple simultaneous "exhibitions," that is, on the fetishistic force of copies *with no original*.

In terms of Islam, the stakes of these media differences concern the nature of social collectivity as much as subjective piety and discursive debate. Of course, the very fact that modern reformist movements are typically figured *as* calls signals their collective aims. But reformists' recourse to one medium or set of media over others speaks to the production and reproduction of particular forms of collectivity and sociability—in short, to mediation. In Benjamin's terms, the auratic force of the shrine would produce or mediate hierarchies grounded in spiritual proximity or distance from its unique placement in time and space. The devotional collective would assume spiritual hierarchy rather than equality, exclusive access to sacred power rather than its general dissemination. In stark contrast, technologically mediated calls to reform would assume egalitarian, or at least horizontal, access to the sacred. Collectivities grounded in this ostensibly egalitarian ideal can neither presume nor guarantee democratized authority or a bourgeois public sphere. But in an age of technologically reproducible (i.e., mass-mediated) address, Muslim reformists can imagine multiplicity in the service of unity—Muslim cohesion and discursive coherence resulting from a uniform call.[33]

Inasmuch as the Shabab movement's call demonstrates the power of a medium, it does so at the expense of the saint, whose sacred baraka now seems, like his shrine, disposable. The call of a provincial hierarchy to itself via the shrine pales before the reformists' universalizing call and its potentially global public. The reformists' "discourse and lecture" is inaudible for precisely this reason. What matters is not so much doctrinal argumentation as the force of its transmission on a global platform.

Shaykh Husayni's video from Tunisia likewise implies that the destruction of a local shrine and replacement by a new outreach center is necessary but insufficient without its televisual and online dissemination. A caption accompanying the video emphasizes that the shrine is not a merely provincial medium but an extension of the Tunisian state: "The people of Gabès, Tunisia, carried out the destruction of a building constructed by the former Tunisian regime, used for spreading [*nashr*] superstitions and ignorance." As a result of such publicity, the caption clarifies, "common folk [*'awam al-nas*] came to sacrifice to deities other than God the Most High and indulge in [illicit] worship for three days." The danger of the shrine rested not only with its bygone presence but also with the state power it mediated and the corrupt public it sowed.[34]

A key point should also be reiterated: If militants destroy the shrines, it is not to *deny* their power to attract pilgrims but to acknowledge and warn against it. For the reformists, this power is grounded in the people's beliefs and practices of pilgrimage and thus with the subjects and social collective these forged. By staging scenes of education with local reformists acknowledge the shrine as a medium of social reproduction; the call of the shrine is the call of a misguided community to itself. The destruction of the medium is the message.

A Fatwa on Sufi Shrines: Rejecting Idolatry, Rejecting "Heritage"

The videos I have discussed here share colonial-era reformists' efforts to forge not only pious Muslim subjects but also potentially uniform and coherent social collectives, or, more specifically, mass publics, connected by virtue of the call itself.[35] The Islamic State of Jubba video closes with reformists' direct plea to the online viewer to "not forget us in your prayers"; in the YouTube comments section, the post reiterates the request. That YouTube viewers are being recruited to fight the call of the shrine points to the global dimensions of modern Muslim pilgrimage sites, including those supposedly peripheral or merely local shrines. Such shrines acquire global value because their calls resonate through global circuits of communication and power. Along the way, however, the call of the shrine acquires different values, including that of a putatively universal heritage.[36]

Global outrage provoked by reformists' almost gleeful shrine destructions only confirms the breadth of these shrine's calls—and this, too, is the point. Such reformists are aware of their global value as "cultural heritage," which may in turn reinforce their local value as spiritual centers. Indeed, this heritage discourse enhances the call of the shrine as the command not only of an individual state, but of a global sociopolitical order. A fatwa provided by the legal committee of a militant reformist group, Minbar al-Tawhid wa-l-Jihad [The Unicity and Jihad Pulpit], addresses the legality of Sufi shrine destruction in Tunisia following the 2010–11 revolution with explicit reference to "heritage." A petitioner identified as Abu Ahmad from Qayrawan, a notable center of Sufi history in Tunisia, writes:

Very often these days so-called saint's shrines [*maqamat al-'awliya' al-salihin*] are burnt. God knows who's behind these acts, but the media, as usual, blame Salafis for most of it. Some in the general public support the media's opinion, while others see it as a political game played by the left-wing unbelievers to cripple the country's development in order to take power by spreading fear of Islamists [*al-islamiyyin*]. . . . What are the rules regarding the burning of these shrines? What are the rules regarding the view that [shrines] are part of our heritage, customs and traditions?[37]

Although the nature of "heritage, customs and traditions" is unspecified, the petitioner is familiar with Tunisian national politics in which shrines mediate conflicting political claims. The petitioner is likewise familiar with two distinct discourses in which the conflict is grounded: the one, for which the fatwa is sought, based in Islamic law; and the other, based on a public discourse of saints' shrines as "heritage." In a complex set of suspicions, some propose that "left-wing unbelievers," being cognizant of the (secular) call of "heritage," sow fear by blaming Salafis, whose lack of respect for these shrines only reinforces their departure from global "civilized" norms. The competition over calls is indexed by the petitioner's references to "the media" as indirectly bolstering the value of shrines.

The committee begins with reference to the commands of the law: "If those dedicated to *tawhid* [God's unicity] occupy a position of power, their first obligation is to destroy the idolatrous shrines, that is, the pilgrimage sites [*mazarat*] where followers [*ashabuha*] worship deities other than God." Still, the committee is aware of reformists' political limits: "At present, however, that power is not ours; therefore [reformists] must focus their efforts on spreading God's call, and warning people of the dangers of idolatry, and publicizing and teaching the [true] creed [*al-'aqida*]." Of course, under better circumstances, shrine demolition would form part of this call. However, under current circumstances, the committee continues, "The quest [of those in favor of *tawhid*] to destroy tombs will be used as an excuse [by the powerful] to prohibit and obstruct the call to *tawhid*."

For the militants, shrines and idolatry are positioned as explicit objects of and obstacles to God's call. If they do not explicitly say that shrines "call" those to *shirk*, they nonetheless treat idolaters' form of worship as "obedience" (*'ibada*) to another deity, against which God's call must be spread. And they acknowledge the complex ways in which the state and a related mass technological apparatus ("the media") may reinforce the shrine as a medium of a mass public. The solutions to idolatry are thus to destroy the medium of this idolatrous call (the shrine) or, if that is not possible, to spread another call with enough force and clarity to appeal to and convert that public.

The committee responds to the petitioner's question regarding "our heritage, customs and traditions" by discrediting the discourse of heritage: "If someone knows what takes place [in shrines] to be idolatry, and nonetheless defends it and accepts it, then that person is [also] an idolater. To *accept* idolatry *is* idolatry." Here, the shrine as medium is the message of a mass public: its material presence promotes idolatry, even among those who do not respond to it directly. The mere existence of the shrine bespeaks their failure to negate its call.

Conclusion

If making pilgrimage to shrines—or, to put it otherwise, *heeding the call of the shrine*—has historically reproduced the power invested in the shrine, then in the age of mass media and mass publics, the force of that call is enhanced by state sponsorship and recognition and by the circulation of photographic relics and other media. Such mediations build on older "traces" of shrines' "spiritual magnetism," but now even ostensibly local saints' shrines have found novel global relevance, including as embodiments of "universal heritage."[38]

The countervailing episodic destruction of shrines is no less concerned with acknowledging the call of the shrine. Reformists' mass mediatizing of shrine destruction as calls to Islam proves as much. But as the figure of the call itself indicates, the politics of shrines and Muslim pilgrimage more generally is not limited to doctrinal difference and the discursive tradition's internal divisions. Rather, the shrine destructions, and their documentation and dissemination, signal a contest over media and the forms of piety and collective they summon.

When Talal Asad argued for the recognition of difference within Islam's discursive tradition, he noted the recent historical emergence of uniformity as an ideal: only modern Muslims immersed in mass media and mass politics *imagined* Islam to be a unitary and uniform tradition.[39] Of course, the mass mediation of Islamic discourse has in practice produced no such uniformity. Continuing traditions of non-Hajj pilgrimage—indeed, the enhanced political focus on local shrines—suggests as much. Nevertheless, modern reformist movements, immersed by choice or not in mass media and mass publics, have often explicitly criticized the older norms of hierarchical and embodied authority that shrine visitations reproduce. Rather than privileging the hierarchical and exclusive power embodied in the unique and particular saint and shrine, reformist movements framed as acts of communication—as calls—have tended to emphasize the universalizing logic of exchangeability and "exhibition value" embedded in technologically reproducible media.

Yet acts of shrine destruction, as technologically reproducible calls to Islam, also confirm what they destroy—namely a lengthy history of multipolarity and multiplicity of practice, piety, and authority within the Muslim world. Perhaps at no prior historical moment have Muslims so forcefully experienced this tension between forces of dissemination and desires for unity, between proliferating calls to pilgrimage and fantasies of a single call from a single shrine that might guarantee discursive coherence and Muslim community.

Notes

1. James J. Preston, "Spiritual Magnetism: An Organizing Principle for the Study of Pilgrimage," in *Sacred Journeys: The Anthropology of Pilgrimage*, ed. E. Alan Morinis (Westport, CT: Greenwood Press, 1992); Surinder M. Bhardwaj, "Non-Hajj Pilgrimage in Islam: A Neglected Dimension of Religious Circulation," *Journal of Cultural Geography* 17, no. 2 (1998): 69–87.

2. In the Qur'an (21:50–68), the prophet Abraham denounces and then destroys his people's "false gods," revealing their fragility as mere human creations. The Qur'an and Sunna, however, have also been adduced in support of building and visiting shrines (see, for example, Qur'an 18:21). For *fatawa* defending shrines written in the wake of recent acts of destruction, see the Islamic Text Institute, "Building Domes and Shrines over the Deceased: Fatwa by the Mufti of Egypt, Ali Jumua," accessed October 7, 2018, https://islamictext.wordpress.com/building-domes-and-shrines-over-the-deceased-fata-by-the-mufti-of-egypt-ali-jumua/; Faraz Rabbani, "The Loss of Meaning: The Destruction of Muslim Holy Sites," SeekersHub, August 28, 2012, http://seekershub.org/blog/2012/08/the-loss-of-meaning-the-destruction-of-muslim-holy-sites/. I thank Aaron Spevack for these references.

3. Describing the Timurid prince Babur's destruction of an Afghan Sufi shrine, Azfar Moin writes, "His conduct resembled less that of a Muslim seeking salvation and more that of a king enacting his sovereignty." A. Azfar Moin, "Sovereign Violence: Temple Destruction in India and Shrine Desecration in Iran and Central Asia," *Comparative Studies in Society and History* 57, no. 2 (2015): 494.

4. Natana J. DeLong-Bas, *Wahhabi Islam: From Revival and Reform to Global Jihad* (New York: Oxford University Press, 2004), 24–26.

5. Brian James Peterson, *Islamization from Below: The Making of Muslim Communities in Rural French Sudan, 1880–1960* (New Haven, CT: Yale University Press, 2011); Emilio

Spadola, *The Calls of Islam: Sufis, Islamists, and Mass Mediation in Urban Morocco* (Bloomington: Indiana University Press, 2014), chapter 2.

6. Elliott Colla, "ISIL vs the Graven Idols of History," *Informed Comment*, March 7, 2015, http://www.juancole.com/2015/03/graven-idols-history.html. For a periodically updated list of demolitions beginning with post-invasion Iraq, see the public outreach project, the Muslim 500, established by the Amman-based Royal Islamic Strategic Studies Centre, an independent international research center. Editorial Board, "Issues of the Day: Destruction of Holy Sites," accessed October 7, 2018, http://themuslim500.com/2014-pages/issues-of-the-day. See also Christoph Machat, Michael Petzet, and John Ziesemer, eds., *Heritage at Risk: World Report 2011–2013 on Monuments and Sites in Danger* (Berlin: hendrik Bäßler verlag, 2014), http://www.icomos.org/images/DOCUMENTS/Publications/HR2011-13final.pdf.

7. Talal Asad, *The Idea of an Anthropology of Islam* (Washington, DC: Georgetown University Center for Contemporary Arab Studies, Occasional Papers Series, 1986), 16.

8. Asad, 16.

9. Preston, "Spiritual Magnetism," 33.

10. Preston, 33.

11. Preston, 33–34.

12. Preston, 40.

13. Preston, 41.

14. Preston, 41. For works on pilgrimage related to media, one may start with Stewart M. Hoover's characterization of television viewing as "armchair pilgrimage." Stewart M. Hoover, "Television, Myth, and Ritual: The Role of Substantive Meaning and Spatiality," in *Media, Myths, and Narratives: Television and the Press*, ed. J. Carey (Beverly Hills, CA: Sage, 1988), 171. Hoover's argument does not, however, speak to media traces as *inciting* pilgrimage—that is, as calls to pilgrimage. For this, see the outstanding works by Maria José de Abreu and Jennifer Sime on Catholic traditions in Portugal and Spain. Maria José de Abreu, "Erring Like a Bullet" (unpublished manuscript, n.d.); Jennifer N. Sime, "The Aura of Pilgrimage: Traveling toward Santiago de Compostela in Modern Spain" (PhD diss., Columbia University, 2009); Jennifer N. Sime, "The Mass-Mediatized Call to Pilgrimage in Santiago de Compostela, Spain: Voice, Photography, and the Deathly Origins of Europe" (presentation, American Anthropological Association Annual Meetings, San Francisco, CA, November 2012). Sime's work on the modern history and culture of the Santiago de Compostela pilgrimage in northern Spain demonstrates that the mass mediation of sacred traces of the Catholic shrine has regenerated popular desires to undertake the pilgrimage and, more specifically, to experience the authentic *presence* of the sacred. Abreu addresses the sanctuary of Fátima in Portugal and specifically the "call" of a relic contained within, a bullet recovered from an assassination attempt on Pope John Paul II. For Abreu, the appeal of the relic is a desire for presence but more specifically a *future* presence; the bullet does not so much offer a compelling secret apotropaic power as it does invoke the threat of an evil event to come.

15. Emile Durkheim, *The Elementary Forms of Religious Life*, trans. Karen E. Fields (New York: Free Press, 1995).

16. Bhardwaj, "Non-Hajj Pilgrimage in Islam."

17. Bhardwaj, 71–72.

18. Amira Mittermaier, *Dreams That Matter: Egyptian Landscapes of the Imagination* (Berkeley: University of California Press, 2011); Mohammed Maarouf, *Jinn Eviction as a Discourse of Power: A Multidisciplinary Approach to Moroccan Magical Beliefs and Practices* (Leiden: Brill, 2007); Khadija Naamouni, *Le Culte de Bouya Omar* (Casablanca: Editions EDDIF, 1995).

19. Mittermaier, *Dreams That Matter*, 157.

20. Mittermaier, 157.

21. Maarouf, *Jinn Eviction as a Discourse of Power*, 239; Naamouni, *Le Culte de Bouya Omar*, 112.

22. Maarouf, 239. The language of the "call" of the shrine (and of the interred saint) extends to Shi'i traditions. See Pinto's description of Shi'i pilgrims' repeated cries of "Labayk ya Husayn!" (At your call, Oh Husayn!).

23. Naamouni, *Le Culte de Bouya Omar*, 112.

24. Having set to destroy the Buddhas in early March 2001, the Taliban granted Al Jazeera television exclusive coverage of the destruction on March 19, 2001. Mohammed el-Nawawy and Adel Iskandar, *Al Jazeera: How the Free Arab News Network Scooped the World and Changed the Middle East* (Cambridge, MA: Westview Press, 2002), 149. Later, on March 26, the Taliban specifically flew journalists to Bamiyan to report on the destruction. Pierre Centlivres, "The Death of the Buddhas of Bamiyan," Middle East Institute, April 18, 2012, http://www.mideasti.org/content/death-buddhas-bamiyan. As Centlivres writes, "The victory over the Buddhas could only be won if there were witnesses." More specifically, the destructions required mass media coverage to communicate effectively with Western and Muslim nations, the intended audience of the acts.

25. Regarding Al-Qaeda's destruction of the World Trade Center towers, W. J. T. Mitchell points to the choice of targets based on their mediating power as globally recognized images of U.S. wealth and power. W. J. T. Mitchell, *What Do Pictures Want? The Lives and Loves of Images* (Chicago: University of Chicago Press, 2005), 13–14. A similar aim is apparent in the U.S. military's much publicized toppling of Saddam Hussein's statue in 2003. Colla, "ISIL vs the Graven Idols of History."

26. Mitchell, *What Do Pictures Want?*, 14.

27. ICOMOS, "Planned Destruction of Sufi Architectural Heritage in Tunisia," press release, March 11, 2013, https://www.icomos.org/en/178-english-categories/news/590-planned-destruction-of-sufi-architectural-heritage-in-tunisia. See also Benjamin Soares, "Islam in Mali since the 2012 Coup," Hot Spots, *Cultural Anthropology*, June 10, 2013, https://culanth.org/fieldsights/321-islam-in-mali-since-the-2012-coup.

28. Muslim and Western investment in shrines and relics, along with militants' dissemination of their demolition, actively elevates shrines and pilgrimage to global political objects. And indeed shrine destructions have prompted global objections. An ongoing public appeal against the shrine demolitions issued by an Amman-based independent international Islamic research center speaking for "the world's most influential Muslims" captures the starkly divided views of militants and the mainstream: "The past few years [have] seen a troubling trend of systematic grave desecration and destruction of holy places carried out by various Wahhabi groups in Libya, Mali,

and Egypt. With the fall of ruling powers resulting from the Arab Spring many Wahhabis have decided to utilize power vacuums that opened up in Libya and subsequently Mali to ravage these lands by destroying all signs of their holy sites, which according to their puritanical view are heretical, pagan-like, grave worshipping, despite the fact that the vast majority of Sunni scholars throughout history have held them to be valid and even praiseworthy to maintain. Spurred on by extremist preachers, the destruction of centuries old heritage continues to spread to other countries despite it being condemned by all other Muslims as sacrilege" (Editorial Board 2014). Similar denunciations of shrine destruction in North Africa by the UN-affiliated International Council on Monuments and Sites (ICOMOS) refer broadly to the "Sufi heritage" embodied in the material sites. Regarding attacks in Tunisia in 2013, ICOMOS writes: "Having always been esteemed and regarded with affection, Sufi architectural heritage in Tunisia is now threatened by planned acts of destruction which began shortly after the revolution of 17 December 2010-14 January 2011. Destruction has focused on the *zaouias*—mausoleums housing the tombs of patron saints—which serve as important places of pilgrimage for communities. The Sufi heritage occupies a special place in the daily lives of Tunisian communities. . . . Any damage to this heritage will harm the identity of a community and inflict irreparable loss to local spiritual and social values." ICOMOS, "Planned Destruction of Sufi Architectural Heritage in Tunisia." While ICOMOS emphasizes the shrines as sites of pilgrimage, both statements identify the shrine's value with its recognition by a social collective.

29. On the production of Muslim publics through the visceral force of transmission, see Patricia Spyer's study of the visual "aesthetic of accident" in clandestine videos calling to Muslims to jihad in 2000s Maluku. For Spyer, this aesthetic, involving rapid and repeated cuts of wounded bodies and destroyed mosques, refuses narrative order or closure. In contrast, the shrine destruction videos highlight not so much Muslim victimization as militants' own destructive power. Nevertheless, the videos are similar insofar as they juxtapose destructive force with a recuperating or reassuring authority. In the videos Spyer highlights, militants are reminded of the laws of jihad; similarly, the shrine destruction videos include scenes of the militants summoning and guiding the local community to God's call. Patricia Spyer, "Reel Accidents: Screening the *Ummah* under Siege in Wartime Maluku," *Current Anthropology* 58, no. S15 (February 2017): S27–S40. See also Hirschkind, *Ethical Soundscape*.

30. "Destroying an Idolatrous Building in Tunis: [Reportage by] Hassan al-Husayni" [*hadm binā' shirkiī fī tūnis—hassan al-hussayni*], February 26, 2012, https://www.youtube.com/watch?v=dbn8tUX79.

31. This contest of media may also be read as a hermeneutic difference regarding language and signs—that is, as a difference of "semiotic ideology." Webb Keane, *Christian Moderns: Freedom and Fetish in the Mission Encounter* (Berkeley: University of California Press, 2007). Scholars of Islamic reform and revival often read "semiotic ideologies" as differentiating secular and Protestant norms of immaterial belief and disembodied publicness from distinct Islamic traditions of embodied ethics. See Patrick Eisenlohr, "Technologies of the Spirit: Devotional Islam, Sound Reproduction and the Dialectics of Mediation and Immediacy in Mauritius," *Anthropological Theory* 9, no. 3 (2009): 273–96; Hirschkind, *Ethical Soundscape*; Saba Mahmood, *Poli-*

tics of Piety: The Islamic Revival and the Feminist Subject (Princeton, NJ: Princeton University Press, 2005); Saba Mahmood, "Religious Reason and Secular Affect: An Incommensurable Divide?," in "The Fate of Disciplines," ed. James Chandler and Arnold I. Davidson, special issue, *Critical Inquiry* 35, no. 4 (Summer 2009): 836–62.

32. Walter Benjamin, "The Work of Art in the Age of Its Technological Reproducibility (Second Version)," *The Work of Art in the Age of Its Technological Reproducibility, and Other Writings on Media*, ed. Michael W. Jennings, Brigid Doherty, and Thomas Y. Levin (Cambridge, MA: Harvard Belknap Press, 2008).

33. On mass media and the unprecedented modernist ideal of discursive uniformity, see Asad, *Idea of an Anthropology of Islam*. For emphasis on democratization and the Habermasian public sphere, see Dale F. Eickelman and Jon W. Anderson, eds., *New Media in the Muslim World: The Emerging Public Sphere*, 2nd ed. (Bloomington: University of Indiana Press, 2003). For Habermasian readings of technological reproducibility and a democratized public sphere, also see Eickelman and Anderson, *New Media*, and Dale F. Eickelman, "Mass Higher Education and the Religious Imagination in Contemporary Arab Societies," *American Ethnologist* 19, no. 4 (1992): 643–55.

34. As Kasmani, Bianchi, Szanto, and Millie and Mayo (this volume) observe in Pakistan, China, Syria, and Indonesia, contemporary statecraft includes recognizing and thus enhancing the calls of particular shrines (including the Kaʿba at the center of the Muslim Hajj) to claim some part of their symbolic capital as well as tourist revenue.

35. Francis Cody, "Publics and Politics," *Annual Review of Anthropology* 40 (2011): 37–58; Michael Warner, *Publics and Counterpublics* (Cambridge: MIT Press, 2002).

36. See, for example, the ICOMOS statement cited above. To name such objects as universal itself signals a shift in the value of shrines. In a recent commentary on the Islamic State's demolition of archaeological objects in the Iraqi cities of Nimrud and Mosul, Elliott Colla examines the West's discourse of heritage as a putatively secular interest in sacred objects and sites. It is, he writes, a particularly modern form of veneration of such objects not as sacred or holy but as nonetheless "sacrosanct." Rather than veneration, such objects are to be "appreciated," and one's capacity to "appreciate" (without explicitly venerating) signals one's civilized taste compared to those who would lack such refinement. For Colla, most critics denounce the Islamic State's destruction of sacrosanct objects as absolutist, without acknowledging "appreciation" as our own "absolutist claim, since [we] also insist that anyone who disagrees with this proposition is, in effect, uneducated, uncultured and probably a barbarian." The West invests the shrines with "universal" value but fails to admit to the parochialism of its own investment. Colla, "ISIL vs the Graven Idols of History."

37. Minbar al-Tawhid wa-l-Jihad, "What Is the Ruling concerning the Burning of Saints' Shrines in Tunisia? [*mā hukm harq maqāmāt al-sālihīn fī tūnis?*], accessed October 7, 2018, http://www.ilmway.com/site/maqdis/FAQ/MS_3326.html.

38. Preston, "Spiritual Magnetism."

39. Asad, *Idea of an Anthropology of Islam*, 16.

CHAPTER ELEVEN

Pilgrimage to a Ritual
The Fluid Sacred Geography of the Bohras' Muharram

REZA MASOUDI NEJAD

> Since the Sayyidna speech is considered sacred for every Bohra, there is a great rush to be at his majlis. The attendees received their invitations after registering by e-mail. Nearly two lakh [200,000] Bohras from across the world are in town and around 32,000 get to sit in the massive mosque at a time.
>
> —M. WAJIHUDDIN, *Times of India*, November 14, 2010

A pilgrimage is a journey to a holy place, a journey throughout which individuals receive an ultimate spiritual experience. Many pilgrimages end in a congress at a sacred place, creating a socio-religious solidarity among those who share the sacred geography where a spiritual moment is collectively experienced. "Pilgrimage" is commonly defined, conceived, and illustrated based on previously demarcated holy places. A stereotypical definition of pilgrimage might resemble this: "A journey to a shrine or place of religious importance."[1] Common examples are places and cities such as the old temple wall in Jerusalem, Mecca, or Buddha's footprint. However, this chapter illustrates a pilgrimage and congress that is defined not by arrival at a holy place but by sacred sermons. The pilgrimage of the Dawoodi Bohras is to wherever their spiritual leader chooses to deliver his Muharram sermons.[2] The geography of the Muharram sermons is rather different when compared to that of other important sermons, such as the Pope's at St. Peter's Square, since it is not continually held at the same place.

The spiritual significance of the Muharram sermons inspires the over 200,000 members of the Dawoodi Bohra community,[3] which are dispersed from India to East Africa, the Far East, Europe, and more recently North America and Australia. 'Abbas Master, who is a highly influential member of the community, explained, "Every year before Muharram, the highness Sayyidna Muhammad Burhanuddin announces where he is going to deliver his Muharram sermons, then the Bohras will travel from all over the world to that place."[4] Over the years, the Sayyidna (1915–2014) held his

FIGURE 11.1 Dr. Sayyidna Mohammed Burhanuddin (1915–2014), the spiritual leader of the Dawoodi Bohra, after one of his Muharram sermons, December 2010, Mumbai (photograph by author).

sermons in various cities, including Mumbai (the Bohras' capital city), Cairo, Colombo, Nairobi, and Dar-e-Salaam. Not only does this pilgrimage not have a perpetual place, but it is differentiated from typical diasporic community pilgrimages that are commonly oriented toward a *homeland*.

In this chapter, I articulate the unique geography of the Bohras' Muharram ritual, a geography that has been crucial to the maintenance of an ethnoreligious solidarity among the Gujarati trading community. The Bohras follow the Masta'ali branch of Isma'ili Shi'i Islam. The discussions in this chapter will reveal the creative approach of this orthodox community in producing a "fluid sacred geography" that is well suited to this diasporic community. Toward this premise, the chapter begins with introductions on (1) the observance of the *'ashura* tragedy during Muharram in Mumbai and (2) the Bohra community. The discussion follows by narrating my participatory experience in the ritual in 2010 in Mumbai, through which I will explain different aspects of the fluid geography of the Bohras' Muharram ritual.

'Ashura Observance, Then and Now

'Ashura day, the tenth day of Muharram, is observed by Shi'i Muslims as the day of the martyrdom of Husayn ibn 'Ali, a grandson of the prophet, and his few companions in the tragic battle of Karbala in the seventh century. The 'ashura tragedy was significant in the process of establishing the division of Muslims into Shi'i and Sunni sects. Michael Fischer argues that the tragedy "provides a way of clearly demarcating Shi'i understanding from the Sunni understanding of Islam and Islamic history."[5] The narration of 'ashura as "the Shi'i myth" has profoundly influenced creed and rituals. From Shi'i Muslims' point of view, the tragic battle of Karbala is more than a historic battle and has since transcended into "meta-history."[6] The battle of Karbala is regarded as "a cosmic event around which the entire history of the world, prior as well as subsequent to it, revolves."[7]

Shi'i Muslims have developed diverse rituals to commemorate 'ashura; these rituals originated in the Arab environment in Iraq and were developed under the Buyid dynasty (ca. tenth–eleventh century) in Iran and Iraq and by the Fatimid dynasty in Egypt. In particular, the Iranian Safavid dynasty substantially contributed to developing and enriching the rituals. The commemoration also spread throughout the Indian subcontinent.[8] Indian diasporic communities contributed to expanding the geography of the ritual during the colonial era to as far as East Africa and the Trinidad islands.[9] Although the Muharram ritual delineates the Shi'i–Sunni division in the Middle East, the ritual metamorphosed into a non-Shi'i festival in India, where not only Sunni but also Hindu communities were involved in the 'ashura observance.

It is often argued that the intercommunity remembrance of 'ashura has historically been a mechanism for creating communal harmony in India. For example, Hasnain has mentioned that some of the Hindu rulers of Gwalior and Jalpur were patrons of Muharram rituals for the purposes of encouraging harmony between their Muslim and Hindu subjects.[10] However, I would like to resituate this as the result of the cultural process of localizing a ritual. The Shi'i myth of 'ashura, which is a complex metahistorical narration, has been well received and absorbed in the Indian subcontinent, where religious culture is predominantly constituted by myths.[11] The cultural process of localizing a ritual almost always involves reinventing and metamorphosing the ritual. Therefore, the 'ashura observance in India has been strikingly different in comparison to its Middle Eastern origins.

The 'ashura observance was the largest and the most important festival of Bombay[12] in the nineteenth century. Sunni communities not only dominated

Muharram commemoration and processions but also claimed authority over the rituals.[13] As I have extensively discussed elsewhere, the Shi'i communities of Bombay were mainly the Iranians (often called Moghuls), the Khojas, and the Bohras.[14] Interestingly, these communities were marginalized by Sunni communities during Muharram commemoration. The Konkonis, a Sunni community, used the mechanism of the legal system to suppress the Iranians' Horse Procession, a kind of street passion play, by getting it banned from public streets. The Khojas, who follow Aga Khan, were not allowed to carry their *tabuts*, the symbolic coffins of Karbala martyrdoms, beyond their private grounds.[15] Moreover, the Bohra community was often targeted by Sunnis whenever tensions were raised during Muharram.[16]

In the nineteenth century, Bombay emerged as "the cosmopolis of the Indian Ocean,"[17] bringing linguistically, ethnically, and religiously diverse Muslim groups together to an unprecedented degree. Among Shi'i Muslims in Bombay, the religious diversity was multiplied by the ethnic diversity, with the Shi'i community including such groups as the Khujas, the Bohras, the Iranians, the Hindustanis, and the Baluchis. The full picture of this diversity can be perceived only by taking into account the fact that the Khujas divided into the Ithna-Asharis and the Nizari Isma'ilis (followers of Aga Khan) and that the Bohras were Isma'ili but followed the school of Musta'ali Isma'ili. There are few, if any, cities in the world where we can discover as many sects of Shi'i as in Mumbai. These Shi'i communities did not collapse themselves into an indistinguishable and uniform religious community, since they have always insisted on their own distinct identity. In this complex social setting, the Muharram ritual constituted intense interaction and tension among diverse ethnic and religious groups encountering one another in Bombay. While the ritual was a crucial social medium for redefining identities, this situation intensified the need for reinvention of the ritual. Therefore, the Muharram ritual was constantly changing, making Muharram rituals in Mumbai unlike those practiced anywhere else. While it used to be an intercommunity festival, the commemoration is predominantly a Shi'i ritual today.[18]

The Bohras and Their Muharram Observance

The Bohras are a Gujarati community who follow the Musta'ali Isma'ili school of Shi'i Islam. Shi'i and Sunni sects divided due to a dispute over the successor to the Prophet and the legitimate leadership of the Muslim community. Tabatabai explains that the Shi'i doctrine of *imama* differentiates Shi'i and Sunni sects. Shi'i argues that a spiritual religious leader, known as an imam, should lead the Muslim community, and not a caliph, which has a political connotation.[19] However, the disputes over identifying the imam have subdivided the Shi'i Muslims into the sects of Ithna-Ashari, Isma'ili, Zaidi, and Alavi.[20] For example, the Isma'ili branched over a disagreement on identifying the seventh imam. Furthermore, the Isma'ili sect, like other schools, has been divided into subsects throughout history. The Nizari Isma'ilis currently follow the forty-seventh living imam of Nizari Isma'ili, better known as Aga Khan IV.[21] However, the Bohras are led by their spiritual leader, known as Da'ei al-Mutlaq (absolute missionary), who serves as the representative of the Hidden Imam, who supposedly lives on in seclusion. This historical process entwined the religious and ethnic identities of the Bohras, making it difficult to determine if the subdivisions had either strictly theological or ethnic-social logics.

The Bohras, like many other ethnoreligious groups, moved to Bombay during the nineteenth century and made this great city not only their new home but also their cultural capital. As previously mentioned, the Bohras encountered many other Shi'i communities in Bombay. Therefore, distinguishing ethnoreligious identity for the Bohras, as well as other communities, was an inevitable social practice in the cosmopolitan context of Bombay. The Bohras practice and maintain their solidarity—especially during Muharram, when their identity is redefined.[22] One of the ways that the Isma'ili Bohras chose to differentiate themselves from other Shi'i is by using the traditional Egyptian lunar calendar instead of the common Arabic lunar calendar. Use of the traditional Egyptian lunar calendar signifies how the background of Isma'ilism is associated with the Fatimid dynasty established in Egypt in the tenth century. The dynasty played a significant role in establishing the Shi'i Isma'ili school and made a splendid contribution to the development of Shi'i culture, theology, and philosophy.[23] By the Egyptian lunar calendar, the Bohras identify the beginning of the lunar month differently when compared to other Shi'i communities. In 2010, when I did my second fieldwork in Mumbai, the Bohras' Muharram began a day earlier; therefore, the Bohras and Ithna-Ashari communities observe 'ashura, the tenth of Muharram, on different days. This meant that I was able to experience the devotion and emotion of 'ashura twice, as I participated in both the Bohras' and the Ithna-Asharis' rituals of 'ashura; very convenient for fieldwork, indeed.

Dongri, in the south of Mumbai, is the cultural heart of Shi'i communities and is transformed into a ritual arena within the first few days of Muharram. The cityscape is drastically changed with flags, banners, and *sabils*. *Sabil*

FIGURE 11.2 A Bohras' *sabil* in Bohra Muhalla, Mumbai, December 2009 (photograph by author).

means "donation" in Arabic; in Mumbai, however, it refers to booths that are temporarily set up in the streets, where water, sherbet, tea, and food are served as *niyaz* (donation). The first thing that anyone would notice on a short walk around Dongri during Muharram is the transition from the Ithna-Asharis' territory into the Bohras'. The Ithna-Asharis' *sabils* are mainly covered with black textiles. However, the Bohras' *sabils* are very colorful and covered with flowers (see figure 11.2). This spectacle points to the Hindu background of the Bohras;[24] it can also be perceived as a symbolic way of glorifying the status of the Karbala martyrdoms.

All Shi'i communities commonly observe the *'ashura* tragedy,[25] which creates a degree of intimacy among all Shi'i groups in Mumbai. Nonetheless, since solidarity within each community is stimulated during Muharram, the intercommunity relationship is weakened. Peter van der Veer argues that religious rituals create boundaries by defining a *self* and bonding the members of a community together; simultaneously, the created boundaries separate them from others.[26] This idea particularly applies to the case of the Bohras; the Muharram commemoration is the most important annual event for them to define, reinforce, and practice social solidarity, as well as distinguish themselves from others. The Bohras do not organize a procession; they commemorate the *'ashura* tragedy solely through service sessions (*majlises*) that are exclusively for members of the community. Although such exclusiveness may not be officially announced, it is evidently practiced.

I did participatory observation during Muharram in 2009 and 2010 in Mumbai. During my first fieldwork, I quickly realized that it is rather difficult to attend a Bohra *majlis*. As the community is hierarchically constituted, for an outsider to attend a *majlis*, he or she would need to be invited and accompanied by an influential member of the community. In 2009, I was not able to attend a *majlis*; however, after a lot of networking, I eventually had enough privilege to be invited by Mr. 'Abbas Master to a *majlis* in 2010. 'Abbas Master was the CEO of the Saifee Burhani Upliftment Trust (SBUT), a company responsible for the major initiative for uplifting the Bendhi Bazaar area, also known as Bohra Muhalla, in Mumbai. After a long wait, 'Abbas Master called me late one night to confirm that I was invited to the *majlis* on the very next day. Then he added that I might have the privilege of meeting the highness Sayyidna Mohammed Burhanuddin, the spiritual leader of the Bohras, who would address "the service session on *'ashura* day". I replied, "But *'ashura* is not tomorrow, it is the day after tomorrow." When I expressed confusion, he explained: "According to the Egyptian lunar calendar, *'ashura* is tomorrow." That telephone conversation marked the moment I realized that the Bohras use a different lunar calendar.

'Abbas Master asked me to meet him at his office in Bendhi Bazaar early in the morning, as a great rush was expected before the *majlises*. Arriving in Bendhi Bazaar, I observed that the entire area was changed and gated for the event. In order to control the large number of attendees, who had registered via email, all roads around Saifee Masjid and Rowzat al-Tahirah, the heart of the Bohra Muhalla, were gated and assigned a number. People entered the gates by showing a registration card and their spot in the *majlis*. In the company of 'Abbas Master, I passed through the gates and sat at Rowzat al-Tahirah. Shortly after, not only Saifee Masjid and Rowzat al-Tahirah but all the surrounding streets were packed. In fact, the official number of 32,000, reported by the *Times of India*, accounted only for those Bohras who sat inside Saifee Masjid and Rowzat al-Tahirah, not the ones who stood in the streets (see figure 11.3). A bridge temporarily connected the two buildings, and the crowd could see their spiritual leader, who would cross the bridge after his sermon to visit his father's shrine at Rowzat al-Tahirah. There was literally no "outsider" in the whole crowd, inside or outside the two places. I was, indeed, the only outsider attendee at the service session. The event

FIGURE 11.3 The Bohras packed the Bendi Bazaar area during the Muharram service session, December 2010, Mumbai (photograph by author).

was very exclusive; this was visually evident, as Bohra men wear white dresses and *topi*, and the women wear colorful dresses, called *rida*.

A Sacred Sermon and Spiritual Acoustic Experience

As an outsider, I was very careful not to violate any norms. At the same time, I was very attentive to observing, absorbing, and capturing the atmosphere of this very emotional ritual. I asked my host if I could take pictures, and thankfully the answer was positive; this gave me the opportunity to freely move around and capture the very emotional scenes. I also had a voice recorder by which I recorded the soundscape of rituals I participated in during Muharram, including the emotional chanting of the Bohras at that very session. After a long wait, eventually Sayyidna Muhammed Burhanuddin arrived and began his sermon. 'Abbas Master told me that the sermon is delivered not in the everyday Gujarati language but in Dawati Zaban, also known as Lisaan al-Dawati. Shortly after he began, I took out my voice recorder to record the sermon. Quickly but gently 'Abbas Master whispered in my ear, "I think you are not allowed to record the sermon."

Dawati Zaban literarily means "the language of invitation" or "the language of sermon or preaching." Dawati Zaban refers to the language that Isma'ili missionaries, known as Da'ies, used to promote the Isma'ili school of Islam in India. The language has its roots in the Gujarati language but heavily amalgamates Arabic, Urdu, and Farsi. Asghar 'Ali Engineer explained that this priesthood language has a very high content of Arabic words; "therefore many Bohras, who are not acquainted with Arabic, can hardly follow sermons."[27] But as Lambertz has extensively discussed, the spiritual experience during religious sessions is not merely based on the semantic dimension of preaching or prayer. He argues that listening to prayers or sermons in a language semantically empty for audiences is a purely iconic acoustic experience.[28] In fact, all "celestial languages" — or "otherworldly languages," as Peek would call them — are powerful linguistic tools for producing spiritual acoustic experiences.[29] This is like the recitation of Qur'anic verses or Arabic prayers by non-Arabic-speaking Muslims, Christian orthodox prayers by non-Greek-speaking Christians, Sanskrit *shlokas* for Brahmanic instruction of the Vedas, and Pali texts for Buddhists.[30] Tambiah challenges the idea that using divine languages is irrational because they may be unintelligible to their users.[31] He argues that language is not just supposed to be listened to; rather, because it is foremost a sonic phenomenon, the sounds of language have to be heard within their own cultural phenomenology.

The significance of the sonic spiritual experience of a sermon can be compared to the sacred aesthetic calligraphies of Qur'anic verses on the facades of mosques. In fact, these calligraphic masterpieces are not supposed to be read, as the calligraphic styles used often transfigure the text into a motif, which creates a sacred visual experience for visitors within its own cultural landscape.

The ritual performance is orchestrated through a set of ritual repertoire, including auditory recital. Peek explains that "the ritual period of a sacred presence must be signaled sonically, just as physical space is marked off visually."[32] Shortly after we arrived, Bohra Muhalla was packed; then a series of rites were performed, including the singing of dirges. These performances gradually built up an emotional atmosphere toward the most important moment, the Sayyidna's sermon. When the spiritual leader of Bohras was about to deliver his sermon, the whole arena went into an extreme emotional moment of chanting "*Mola, mola, mola.*"[33] The mighty sound of the passionate chanting by the huge crowd suddenly ceased when the very calm and gentle voice of their hundred-year-old spiritual leader began speaking. This sharp acoustic threshold created an ultimate spiritual experience, even for me as an outsider. After this aural inauguration, the sermon went on for more than two hours. The gentle, low, and soft voice of the Sayyidna over such a long sermon created a surreal space that even a recording could not have reproduced the spirituality of the moment. Tambiah argues that "celestial languages" should be listened to and heard;[34] I would add that such an acoustic sacred space is based not only on otherworldly languages but also on the spiritual voice of a human. This particularly revealed to me that at least my own experience was profoundly based on the sacred acoustic space and not on the physical space of the ritual venue. With such an experience, I grasped why the Bohras' Muharram congress/pilgrimage is organized around their spiritual leader's sermon and not a fixed holy place.

After the service session, we went to 'Abbas Master's office, where I interviewed him. He explained that in recent years, the highness's sermons had been about two hours long, but when he was younger, he would preach for three to four hours. The subject of sermon for the day is not only about the tragedy of *'ashura* but also about the Bohras' way of life and how they can be in harmony with their host societies. He explained that due to the significance of Muharram sermons, the representative committee of different Bohra communities around the world meet with the highness every year a few months before Muharram, proposing cities for him to host his Muharram *majlises*. Apart from Mumbai, there are Bohra communities in Pakistan,

FIGURE 11.4 An emotional time for the Bohras at Rowzat al-Tahirah, when their spiritual leader visits his fathers' shrine after giving his Muharram sermon (photograph by author).

Yemen, Tanzania, Madagascar, Zanzibar, Kenya, and, in more recent years, North America. A few weeks before Muharram, Sayyidna Muhammed Burhanuddin announces where he is going to deliver his sermon; then the Bohras will travel from all over the world to that place. The Sayyidna addressed the *majlises* in Dongri in 2010, the Safiee Mashid of Marol in the north of Mumbai in 2009, and in Tanzania in 2008. In the past, the Sayyidna had addressed the *majlises* in "Cairo, Dubai, Houston, Colombo, Nairobi, and Dar-e-Salaam."[35]

Diaspora and Pilgrimage

The rise and development of Bombay during the nineteenth century made it the capital city of many ethnoreligious communities, including the Bohras. The city was an urban magnet and attracted people from the entire subcontinent, the Indian Ocean region, and beyond. In the nineteenth century, Bombay emerged as "the cosmopolis of the Indian Ocean" and was the colonial counterpart to New York City and Chicago in the nineteenth century, with its own urban processes and city fascination.[36] More importantly, this cosmopolitan city was a hub from where Indians dispersed into almost every corner of the British Empire, the largest empire in history. I would argue, therefore, that Bombay (now Mumbai) remains a unique city when compared to New York City, since this young city became the cultural heart for many Indian diasporic communities for whom Bombay symbolizes the "homeland." For example, the Bohras are a Gujarati trading community that have dispersed across the Indian Ocean and beyond; however, it is Bombay that functions as the administrative capital and cultural heart of the community. This is the case for many other communities as well, such as the Zoroastrian Parses and the Hindu Sindhis.[37]

Brah explains that *diaspora* means "dispersing from"; "hence the word embodies a notion of a center, a locus, a 'home' from where the dispersion occurs."[38] As Vertovec has explained, the term *diaspora* is commonly associated with dispersed peoples who share a common religious or cultural heritage;[39] hence, a "cultural homeland" is not only the origin of a community but also a sacred land where the most important religious places are located. The homeland is not only a symbolic place that shapes the world cognitive map of a diasporic community; it is an actual center around which the translocal network of a diasporic community is configured. A translocal network is based on a center, or homeland, and peripheries, or host lands—a network that is practiced through financial, cultural, and religious activities.[40] In such translocal systems, pilgrimages actively shape a sacred geography in which "homeland" is the place where the most holy places are located.

Every translocal network is configured based on the center and peripheries; therefore, it naturally creates superiority for the center. Although this is the geographical nature of all pilgrimages, the pilgrimages practiced by diasporic communities particularly create superiority for the homeland. However, the policy of hosting the Sayyidna's Muharram sermons in different places creates a polarized sacred geography; this can be called a *fluid sacred geography*, since the center of the Muharram congress is not defined based on a perpetual sacred place. Rather, this sacred geography is defined by the Muharram sermons, thereby implying the significance of the spiritual leader of a hierarchical community instead of a holy place. However, this is not aimed solely at representing a hierarchical social system and offers much more complex spatial practice. Here I discuss two implications of this fluid geography.

The first implication: The Bohras are dispersed all over the world, and many of them live in the geographical periphery of the community. This positions these diasporic communities on the social periphery of the main community; in other words, spatial periphery causes social segregation. However, the fluid geography of Muharram sermons creates *temporal centers* during the ritual time, forming a *liminal translocal geography* in which the center and periphery of the community are temporarily redefined. In other words, the fluid geography is based on the liminal sacred spaces of the Muharram sermons.

Victor Turner theorized the notion of liminal status during ritual; he formulated how the social structure of a community is temporarily altered during ritual. The significance of the liminal status was initially considered by Turner in *The Drums of Affliction* and then further developed in *The Ritual Process*.[41] He reformulated the idea of Ven Gennep's "the rites of passage"[42] as a process of moving a society from a specific structure into an antistructure and then returning them to a structure. As Turner explains, liminal status is a transitional time in which individuals or social groups have a social position and status that they do not have normally. In this liminal status, the social interactions are constituted based not on normal social structure but on antistructure—or *communitas*, as he has also called it. Turner argues that the antistructural social order during ritual should not be conceived as chaos and disorder but as a transitional social order, a status that is rather acute for a sustainable social organization. Here I am not only employing the idea of *liminality* to articulate the "fluid geography" of Bohras' Muharram; I am also arguing that this sacred geography that temporally alters the center and peripheries is a critical part of a mechanism that maintains the solidarity of the Bohras' diasporic community.

The second implication of the Bohras' fluid geography is in negotiating their authority over different territories around the world, wherever they have settled. This is manifested in two ways: (1) negotiating rights to a city and for exclusive access to a large urban area during the ritual time, and (2) legitimizing their permanent physical interventions—that is, building and urban development projects—in different cities around the world. In practice, mobilizing a large number of Bohras (often reported to be as many as 200,000 people) to the location of a Muharram sermon involves major sociopolitical negotiations. This includes a wide range of arrangements, from easing visa procedures for Bohras, to police and traffic arrangement, to security management for large urban areas that will be gated during the Muharram ritual. All these arrangements need a well-institutionalized and influential organization that is active in different countries. Currently, these arrangements are coordinated by the International Ashura Mubaraka Com-

FIGURE 11.5 Dongri area, looking toward Bohra Muhalla (to the east), April 2010, Mumbai (photograph by author).

mittee. The application of the Muharram rituals for justifying more permanent urban changes is even more interesting. The major urban development in Bendhi Bazaar in the old part of Mumbai well illuminates this point.

The Saifee Burhani Upliftment Trust was established to manage redevelopment of the Bendhi Bazaar area, also known as Bohra Muhalla (Bohra's residency). This ambitious project, which would transform this old and busy area of the city, is a socially complex exercise. Although it is known as Bohra Muhalla, it is an ethno-religiously mixed area. Apart from negotiations with the municipality, the project is continually engaged in convincing shopkeepers and residents of the area who will be temporarily displaced until the completion of each phase of the project. In the context of India, this is an incredibly difficult and exhausting process. In 2010, when the project was in its early stages, I was interested in seeing to what extent choosing the Bendhi Bazaar for the Muharram sermon was part of the negotiation. The best person to ask about this curiosity was 'Abbas Master (CEO of SBUT). However, I did not want to exploit the interview with a direct question on this subject, especially knowing that Bohras are not often willing to share

Pilgrimage to a Ritual 253

community policy and affairs with an outsider. Nonetheless, I could not resist asking the question at the end of the interview: "Was hosting the Sayyidna's sermon here at Bendhi Bazaar aimed at legitimizing your right to carry out such a major urban development project?" "Obviously yes!" he simply and sharply replied.

Conclusion

The Bohras' Muharram ritual has a complex geography that serves a wide range of purposes, including creating an ultimate sacred experience, maintaining the social structure of a diasporic community, and negotiating with those that the Bohras encounter. Although this orthodox community is attached to its ethnoreligious values, it does not mean that they are uncreative. They do welcome all new technologies, such as using electronic services to register the members of the community for the Muharram ritual. In fact, the Bohras not only use information technology to manage the administration of a traditional social organization but also, as Blank comprehensively shows, embrace all aspects of modern culture without directly conflicting with their core traditional beliefs.[43] However, in this chapter, I am more interested in articulating the Bohras' creative approach to inventing a complex fluid sacred geography. The discussions here show that the ritual of Muharram sermons that defines the Bohras' fluid geography is not merely a religious or a social practice but is a more complex practice that blurs the border between sacred and profane practices. On one hand, the community's annual congress is structured around the Sayyenda's Muharram sermon, the moment of an ultimate collective spiritual experience. On the other hand, the ritual is plainly arranged to promote an urban development project. However, the point is that SBUT is run like any other urban development company; nonetheless, 'Abbas Master, CEO of SBUT, sees this practice as a religious duty to serve his community. In fact, while a modern mind-set would divide sacred and profane, traditional and contemporary, the Bohras entwine these paradoxical notions, since such a border does not exist in their epistemology. It seems that this is the source of their creativity.

Notes

This chapter was written when I was an Alexander von Humboldt Fellow at the Centre of Modern Oriental Studies (ZMO, Berlin). However, it is the result of my research project at the Max Planck Institute for Religious and Ethnic Diversities (MPI-MMG,

Göttingen). My fieldworks during 2009–2010 were carried out under the financial support of the MPI-MMG.

1. W. R. F. Browning, *A Dictionary of the Bible*, 2nd ed. (Oxford: Oxford University Press, 2009). See also S. G. F. Brandon, ed., *A Dictionary of Comparative Religion* (London: Weidenfeld & Nicolson, 1970); Keith Crim, *Abingdon Dictionary of Living Religions* (Nashville, TN: Abingdon Press, 1981); J. B. Sykes, *The Concise Oxford Dictionary of Current English* (Oxford: Clarendon Press, 1982); John Bowker, *The Concise Oxford Dictionary of World Religions* (Oxford: Oxford University Press, 2000); André Vauchez, *Encyclopedia of the Middle Ages* (Cambridge: James Clarke, 2002); *World Encyclopedia* (Seattle, WA: Philip's, 2004); Damien Keown, ed., *A Dictionary of Buddhism* (Oxford: Oxford University Press, 2004); David Leeming, ed., *The Oxford Companion to World Mythology* (Oxford: Oxford University Press, 2005); E. A. Livingstone, *The Concise Oxford Dictionary of the Christian Church*, rev. ed. (Oxford: Oxford University Press, 2006); Peter N. Stearns, *Oxford Encyclopedia of the Modern World* (Oxford: Oxford University Press, 2008); Allen Beaver, ed., *A Dictionary of Travel and Tourism* (Oxford: Oxford University Press, 2012).

2. Dr. Sayyidna Mohammed Burhanuddin was the spiritual leader of Dawoodi Bohra and died in January 2014. He was the 52nd Da'i al-Mutlaq of the Dawoodi Bohras, who follow Musta'ali Isma'ili Shi'i Islam.

3. As this chapter is only about the Dawoodi Bohras, hereafter they will be addressed as "the Bohras." The Sulaymanis, the Aliyas, and the Hebtiahs are other divisions of this Gujarati community that branched off in dispute over recognizing the spiritual leader of the community, known as *Da'i*.

4. 'Abbas Master, interview by author, December 2010, Mumbai.

5. Michael M. J. Fischer, *Iran: From Religious Dispute to Revolution* (Cambridge, MA: Harvard University Press, 1980), 21.

6. Peter J. Chelkowski, "Diverse Religous Practices," in *Shi'ism: Doctrines, Thought, and Spirituality*, ed. Seyyed Hossein Nasr, Hamid Dabashi, and Seyyed Vali Reza Nasr (Albany: State University of New York Press, 1988), 263.

7. M. Ayoub, *Redemptive Suffering in Islam: A Study of the Devotional Aspects of `Āshūrā in Twelver Shī`ism* (The Hague: Mouton, 1978), 141.

8. See Yitzhak Nakash, "An Attempt to Trace the Origin of the Rituals of 'Āshūrā'," *Die Welt Des Islams (N.S.)* 33, no. 2 (1993): 161–81; J. Calmard, "The Consolidation of Safavid Shi'ism: Folklore and Popular Religion," in *Safavid Persia: The History and Politics of an Islamic Society*, ed. Charles Melville (London: I. B. Tauris, 1996). See also A. J. Hussain, "The Mourning of History and the History of Mourning: The Evolution of Ritual Commemoration of the Battle of Karbala," *Comparative Studies of South Asia, Africa and the Middle East* 25, no. 1 (2005): 78–88; C. E. Bosworth, C. Hillenbrand, and L. P. Elwell-Sutton, eds., *Qajar Iran: Political, Social and Cultural Change, 1800–1925* (Edinburgh: Edinburgh University Press, 1983); Mahmud Ayoub, "Diverse Religious Practices," in Nasr, Dabashi, and Nasr, *Shi'ism*, 258–259.

9. Frank J. Korom, *Hosay Trinidad: Muharram Performances in an Indo-Caribbean Diaspora* (Philadelphia: University of Pennsylvania Press, 2003).

10. Nadeem Hasnain, *Shias and Shia Islam in India: A Study in Society and* Culture (New Delhi: Harnam, 1988), 48.

11. Scott and Simpson-Housley explain that the historicity of the "religions of the Book" (Judaism, Christianity, and Islam) is the crucial factor in differentiating them from Asian religions (Hinduism, Buddhism, Taoism, and Shinto), which are predominantly constituted by the mythical myriad of arbitrary divinities. See Jamie S. Scott and Paul Simpson-Housley, eds., *Sacred Places and Profane Spaces: Essays in the Geographies of Judaism, Christianity, and Islam* (New York: Greenwood Press, 1991), xi.

12. Bombay was officially renamed Mumbai in the 1990s; I use "Bombay" if the discussion refers to the city before the 1990s.

13. Jim Masselos, "Change and Custom in the Format of Bombay Moharram during Nineteenth and Twentieth Centuries," *South Asia: Journal of South Asian Studies* 50, 5, no. 2 (1982): 47–67; Jim Masselos, *The City in Action: Bombay Struggles for Power* (New Delhi: Oxford University Press, 2007); Prashant Kidambi, *The Making of an Indian Metropolis: Colonial Governance and Public Culture in Bombay, 1890–1920* (Aldershot, UK: Ashgate, 2007).

14. See Reza Masoudi Nejad, "Practising Fractal Shi'i Identities through Muharram Rituals in Mumbai," *Diversities* 14, no. 2 (2012): 103–17; Reza Masoudi Nejad, "The Muharram Procession of Mumbai: From Seafront to Cemetery," in *Handbook of Religion and the Asian City*, ed. Peter van der Veer (Oakland: University of California Press, 2015).

15. *The Times of India*, "The Mohurram in Bombay," April 14, 1871, 3.

16. See, for example, Masoudi Nejad, "Muharram Procession of Mumbai," 94, 98.

17. Nile Green, *Bombay Islam: The Religious Economy of the West Indian Ocean, 1840–1915* (Cambridge: Cambridge University Press, 2011), 3.

18. For comprehensive historical reviews, see Masoudi Nejad, "Muharram Procession of Mumbai"; Masselos, "Change and Custom in the Format of Bombay Moharram during Nineteenth and Twentieth Centuries."

19. Muhammad Husayn Tabatabaei, "Shiism and Sunnism," in Nasr, Dabashi, and Nasr, *Shi'ism*, 85.

20. See Heinz Halm, *Shiism* (Edinburgh: Edinburgh University Press, 1991); Moojan Momen, *An Introduction to Shi'i Islam: The History and Doctrines of Twelver Shi'ism* (New Haven, CT: Yale University Press, 1985).

21. Full name: Prince Shah Karim Al Hussaini Aga Khan.

22. Jonah Blank, *Mullahs on the Mainframe: Islam and Modernity among the Daudi Bohras* (Chicago: University of Chicago Press, 2001).

23. See Farhad Daftary, *The Ismāʿīlīs: Their History and Doctrines* (Cambridge: Cambridge University Press, 1990), 144.

24. Engineer argues that the Bohras were locally converted. Therefore, they continue to follow many Hindu traditions and festivals, including Diwali. Asghar ʿAli Engineer, *The Bohras* (Ghaziabad: Vikas, 1980), 161.

25. There is an exception, as the Shi'i Isma'ili Nizaris no longer commemorate ʿashura day. This is the consequence of the reform of creed and ritual that Aga Khan III introduced in the 1910s. For more information, see Masoudi Nejad, "Practising Fractal Shi'i Identities through Muharram Rituals in Mumbai," 108; Farhad Daftary, *The Ismāʿılıs: Their History and Doctrines*, 2nd ed. (New York: Cambridge University Press, 2007), 492.

26. Peter van der Veer, *Religious Nationalism: Hindus and Muslims in India* (Berkeley: University of California Press, 1994), 11.

27. Engineer, *The Bohras*, 151.

28. Peter Lambertz, "Divisive Matters: Aesthetic Difference and Authority in a Congolese Spiritual Movement 'from Japan'" (PhD diss., University of Utrecht and the University of Leipzig, 2015), 232–46.

29. Wyatt MacGaffey, *Modern Kongo Prophets: Religion in a Plural Society* (Bloomington: Indiana University Press, 1983), 69; Philip M. Peek, "The Sounds of Silence: Cross-World Communication and the Auditory Arts in African Societies," *American Ethnologist* 21, no. 3 (1994): 474–94.

30. Lambertz, "Divisive Matters," 233, 244.

31. Stanley Jeyaraja Tambiah, "The Magical Power of Words," *MAN* 3, no. 2 (1968): 175–208.

32. Peek, "Sounds of Silence," 481.

33. *Mola* literally means the "lord" or "master."

34. Tambiah, "Magical Power of Words."

35. "Bohra Community Holding Muharram Discourses in Suburban Mumbai," *TwoCircles.net*, December 22, 2009.

36. Green, *Bombay Islam*, 3.

37. The Hindu Sindhis' homeland is Sind in Pakistan, and they are dispersed in well over a hundred countries. "Today, the primordial homeland (Sind) survives as little more than a nostalgic memory; instead, Bombay functions as a node that connects and organizes translocality—it is the 'cultural heart' of the cosmopolitan Sindhis." Mark-Anthony Falzon, "Bombay, Our Cultural Heart: Rethinking the Relation between Homeland and Diaspora," *Ethnic and Racial Studies* 26, no. 4 (2003): 662.

38. Avtar Brah, *Cartographies of Diaspora: Contesting Identities* (London: Routledge, 1996), 181.

39. Steven Vertovec, "Religion and Diaspora," in *New Approaches to the Study of Religion: Textual, Comparative, Sociological, and Cognitive Approaches*, ed. Peter Antes, Armin W. Geertz, and Randi Ruth Warne (Berlin: Walter de Gruyter, 2004), 275.

40. See Ulrike Freitag, Achim Von Oppen, and Elisabeth Boesen, *Translocality: The Study of Globalising Processes from a Southern Perspective* (Leiden: Brill, 2009).

41. Victor Turner, *The Drums of Affliction: A Study of Religious Processes among the Ndembu of Zambia* (Oxford: Clarendon Press and International African Institute, 1968); Victor Turner, *The Ritual Process: Structure and Anti-Structure* (London: Routledge & Kegan Paul, 1969).

42. Arnold Van Gennep, *The Rites of Passage* (London: Routledge & Kegan Paul, 1960).

43. Blank, *Mullahs on the Mainframe*.

Glossary

Ar. = Arabic

Pr. = Persian

Tr. = Turkish

Ur. = Urdu

'Abaya (Ar.) a simple, loose overgarment, essentially a robe-like dress.

'Ada (Ar.) pl. of *'adat*; customs, habits, and traditions observed by Muslims.

Adhan (Ar.) the Islamic call to daily prayer.

Ahl-i Bayt (Ar.) the household of the Prophet Muhammad.

Agha (Pr. & Tr.) sir, lord, master.

Arba'in (Ar.) literary meaning: "the fortieth"; forty days after *'ashura*, the day on which Imam Husayn was killed in the battle of Karbala, 680 C.E.

'Ashura (Ar.) the tenth day of Muharram in the Islamic calendar, on which Imam Husayn was killed in the battle of Karbala, 680 C.E.

Awliya (Ar.) plural form of *wali*.

Baba (Ar.) father, also an honorific title for a Sufi saint.

Baraka (Ar.) spiritual force that can radiate through God's creation to ordinary humans in their presence.

Bid'a (Ar.) act of innovation in religious matters.

Daira (Ar.) Sufi lodge among Wolofs (people living in Senegal and Gambia).

Dargah (Pr. Ur.) tomb, shrine.

Da'wa (Ar.) proselytizing or preaching of Islam.

Dhamal (Ar.) a ritual dance in South Asia.

Didar (Pr.) literary meaning: "meeting"; in Shi'ism, encounter with an Imam with spiritual implications.

'Eid (Ar.) Islamic feast.

Faraj (Ar.) literary meaning: "release"; reappearance of Mahdi at the End of Time.

Fatiha (Ar.) the first Sura of the Quran.

Galabiyya (Ar.) traditional Arab Middle Eastern menswear.

Ghadamgah (Pr.) literary meaning: "site of footsteps"; a domain of visitation by a saint.

Hajat (Ar.) people's special intentions and need.

Hajj (Ar.) pilgrimage of Muslims to Mecca.

Hajja (Ar.) a title given to a female Muslim person who has performed the Hajj to Mecca.

Hajji (Ar.) a title given to a male Muslim person who has performed the Hajj to Mecca.

Halal (Ar.) permissible to use or engage in, according to Islamic law.

Husayniyya (Ar.) an assembly hall where Shiʻi Muslims perform commemorative ceremonies.

Ibada (Ar.) literary meaning: "service"; also worship.

Ihram (Ar.) state of consecration for Hajj. Includes dress and/or prayer.

Imam (Ar.) literary meaning: "leader"; generally one of the Twelve divine leaders of Shiʻi Muslims who lived in the first centuries of Islam.

Imama (Ar.) leadership; in Twelver Shiʻism, the Twelve Imams who are religious and political successors to the Prophet of Islam.

Imamzadah (Ar.) literary meaning: "an offspring of an Imam," a descent of the Prophet.

Istalam (Ar.) Touching and kissing the "blacked stone" (part of *Kaʻba's* wall) while doing Hajj.

Iʻtikaf (Ar.) pious seclusion in the *masjid* in order to worship for a certain time.

Jinn (Ar.) an invisible being with lower status than the angels.

Kaʻba (Ar.) a cubic building at the center of Islam's most important mosque (Al-Masjid Al-Haram) in the city of Mecca, Saudi Arabia.

Karbalayi (Ar.) *ziyara* pilgrim who has performed visitation to Karbala, Iraq.

Khuja (Pr.) a common name given to people from South Asia who convert to Islam.

Kirama (Ar.) literary meaning: "generosity"; in Sunni Islam, magical and spiritual miracles performed by saints.

Kiramat (Ar.) plural of *Kirama*.

Kiswa (Ar.) the cloth that covers the Kaʻba in Mecca.

Mahram (Ar.) a relative of the opposite gender, usually described as being "within the forbidden limits."

Majlis (Ar.) literary meaning: "place of siting"; usually referred to a gathering or a council session.

Maqam (Ar.) literary meaning: "place"; a sanctified space associated with a saint.

Mawlid (Ar.) observation of the birthday of Prophet Muhammad.

Mazarat (Ar.) plural of *mazar*, literally "the place that is visited"; graves.

Muharram (Ar.) the first month of the Islamic calendar.

Mujtahid (Ar.) literary meaning: "diligent"; a high-level religious scholar.

Murid (Ar.) disciple, especially in Sufi orders.

Musalla (Ar.) literary meaning: "the place of worship"; special hall for religious ceremonies.

Mutibarrik (Ar.) blessed.

Nadhr (Ar.) pious vow to perform a good deed or forsake a bad deed.

Namaz (Pr.) daily prayers of Muslims.

Nasab-nama (Pr.) book of genealogy.

Na'␣t (Ar.) praise, eulogy.

Niyaz (Pr.) donation, gift.

Niyya (Ar.) intention.

Nowruz (Pr.) Persian New Year.

Pir (Pr.) patron, especially in Sufi orders.

Rak'␣a (Ar.) each unit of Islamic daily prayer.

Rida (Ar.) robe.

Rihla (Ar.) travelogue, travel diary.

Sabil (Ar., Ur.) literary meaning: "path" or "way"; public booth.

Sadaqa (Ar.) charity and voluntary alms.

Salafiyya (Ar.) a revivalist movement within Sunni Islam which emerged in North Africa and with roots in the Wahhabi movement in eighteenth-century Arabian Peninsula.

Salah (Ar.) Muslim daily prayers.

Sayyid (Ar.) descendant of the Prophet Muhammad.

Shafa' (Ar.) miraculous healing.

Shahada (Ar.) testimony to Islamic faith.

Shahid (Ar.) martyr.

Shaykh (Ar.) literary meaning: "old man"; Muslim saint and pious man.

Shirk (Ar.) idolatry and polytheism.

Sowqat (Ar.) souvenir of travel.

Sukut (Ar.) pious silence and seclusion.

Sura (Ar.) each of the 114 chapters of the Qur'an.

Tabarruk (Ar.) ritual practice for seeking bless from God, prophets and saints.

Tabut (Ar.) coffin.

Tahannuth (Ar.) pious seclusion.

Taqiyya (Ar.) short and rounded skullcap worn for religious purposes.

Tariqa (Ar.) literary meaning: "path" or "way"; Sufi order.

Tasbih (Ar.) Islamic rosary and prayer beads.

Tawaf (Ar.) ritual circulation around Kaʿba during Hajj and ʿUmrah.

Tawhid (Ar.) unity of God.

Tekke (Tr.) Sufi lodge in Turkish.

Thavab (Ar.) otherworldly reward according to Islamic theology.

Thawb (Ar.) robe, ankle-length Arab garment.

Topi (Ur.) Cap.

Turba (Ar.) literary meaning: "soil"; in Shiʿism, the soil around the body of Imam Husayn.

ʿUlama (Ar.) scholar of Islamic jurisprudence.

Umma (Ar.) community of Muslims wherever they live.

ʿUmra (Ar.) the pilgrimage to Mecca lesser than Hajj.

ʿUrs (Ar.) the death anniversary of a Sufi saint in South Asia.

Wali (Ar.) saint and pious Muslim, especially in Sufi circles.

Walima (Ar.) ritual meal for returning from Hajj and weddings.

Waqf (Ar.) religious endowment.

Wasila (Ar.) mediating feature that may help others get closer toward God.

Wuquf (Ar.) ceremonial standing at the plain of ʿArafat and Mashʿar, east of Mecca city.

Za'ir (Ar.) pilgrim.

Zamzam (Ar.) a well located near Kaʿba, with blessed source of water which, Muslims believe, sprang during the time of the prophet Abraham.

Zarih (Ar.) grave of a Muslim saint or the box put on his or her grave.

Zawiya (Ar.) Sufi lodge, a term commonly used in North Africa.

Ziyara (Ar.) pilgrimage, generally made in reference to non-Hajj pilgrimage.

Ziyaratgah (Pr.) place of visitation where a saint, an Imam or a prophet were buried.

Zuwwar (Ar.) plural of *zair*, pilgrim.

Contributor Biographies

SOPHIA ROSE ARJANA was appointed visiting assistant professor of Islamic Studies in 2011. Her teaching areas include courses on comparative religion and Islam. Her primary areas of research are monstrous Western representations of Muslim men, liberation theology, postcolonial discourse, Shiʻa and Sufi pilgrimage, and the holy sites associated with these traditions. Arjana has published work on several subjects in the study of Islam, including pilgrimage, Islamophobia, and Orientalism. Two of these contributions include an article in Shiʻa studies, a journal published by the Centre for Islamic Shiʻa Studies in London, and an article in *ARTS: The Journal of the Society of Arts in Religion and Theological Studies*. She has also published a book chapter on the trope of "Turning Turk" in Orientalist discourse, which looks at the role of race in Western discourse about Islam. In addition, she has two encyclopedia articles in print on Islamic subjects, and a third that is forthcoming. In 2015, Dr. Arjana saw the publication of her first book, *Muslims in the Western Imagination* (Oxford University Press); book chapters on Jewish and Islamic liberation theology and female and queer imams in North America; and a critique of Islamism and post-Islamism in relation to the theology of Ali Shari'ati.

ROSE ASLAN is an assistant professor of religion at California Lutheran University. She teaches courses on global religions, the Abrahamic traditions in comparative focus, and Islam. Her research focuses on the construction of sacred space, ritual, and pilgrimage in a variety of medieval and contemporary Muslim contexts, and also studies different aspects of sacred spaces around the world from different traditions. She received her PhD in religious studies from the University of North Carolina and her MA in Arabic studies from the American University in Cairo.

ROBERT R. BIANCHI is a political scientist and international lawyer who has lived and worked in China and the Islamic world for nearly two decades. He earned his PhD and law degree at the University of Chicago, where he also served on the faculty of the political science department and the law school. He is a former Peace Corps volunteer, a three-time Fulbright-Hays grantee, and a recipient of the Albert Hourani Book Prize.

PEYMAN ESHAGHI is a doctoral student in anthropology and sociology of religion at the University of Chicago. Prior to his graduate studies, he studied in Germany, Turkey, and Iran. His main areas of research are Muslim pilgrimage and the cult of saints, religion and politics, and Shiʻi Islam. Among his publications are "Quietness beyond Political Power: Politics of Taking Sanctuary (Bast Neshini) in the Shiʻite Shrines of Iran" (*Iranian Studies*, 2016) and "To Capture a Cherished Past: Pilgrimage

Photography at Imam Riza's Shrine, Iran" (*Middle East Journal of Culture and Communication*, 2015).

OMAR KASMANI is a postdoctoral research fellow in Social and Cultural Anthropology at the Collaborative Research Center Affective Societies at Freie Universität, Berlin. With an overarching interest in ideas of place and public intimacy, his research is situated at the crossroads of affect, queer futurities, and the politics of Sufi religious life-worlds. He has previously conducted long-term fieldwork in a pilgrimage town in Pakistan. He teaches on gender, queer theory, and religion in South Asia, and has coedited the volume *Muslim Matter* (Revolver, 2016).

AZIM MALIKOV currently works as a senior researcher in the Faculty of Arts of Palacký University, Olomouc, in the Czech Republic (the EU-funded project on Sinophone Borderlands: Interaction at the Edges). He was a senior research fellow affiliated with the Department of Anthropology and Ethnology of the Institute of History, Academy of Sciences of the Republic of Uzbekistan, Tashkent. Between 2010 and 2013, he was a postdoctoral fellow at the Max Planck Institute for Social Anthropology (Halle/Saale, Germany).

LEWIS MAYO teaches Chinese language and culture at the Asia Institute, University of Melbourne. He has published mainly on Chinese intellectual traditions. A sample publication is "Birds and the Hand of Power: A Political Geography of Avian Life in the Gansu Corridor, Ninth to Tenth Centuries" (2002, *East Asian History* 24).

JULIAN MILLIE is senior lecturer in the anthropology program of the School of Political and Social Inquiry at Monash University. His research interests include religious communication and Islamic forms of social life in Indonesia. A recent publication of his is *Splashed by the Saint: Ritual Reading and Islamic Sanctity in West Java* (2009, KITLV Press).

REZA MASOUDI NEJAD is a native southwestern Iranian who lives in London. As an urbanist, his work focuses on the geography of crowds and protests, urban violence, and extensive studies of religious rituals in public spaces in Iran and India. He has been a Research Fellow at the Max Planck Institute for the Study of Religious and Ethnic Diversity in Göttingen (Germany) and an Alexander von Humboldt Fellow at the Centre for Modern Oriental Studies (ZMO) in Berlin. Reza is currently a Research Associate at SOAS, University of London. He received his PhD from the Bartlett Faculty of the Built Environment, UCL (2009).

PAULO G. PINTO earned his PhD in anthropology from Boston University. He is professor of anthropology at the Universidade Federal Fluminense, Brazil, where he is also director of the Center for Middle East Studies. He did ethnographic fieldwork in Syria in various periods from 1999 to 2010. In 2012–13, he did ethnographic fieldwork of the ziyāra al-arba'iyyn in Najaf and Karbala, Iraq. He has also done fieldwork with the Muslim communities in Brazil (2003–17), Paraguay (2005, 2006, 2011, 2015), and

Argentina (2018). He is the author of articles and books on Sufism and other forms of Islam in contemporary Syria, as well as on Arab ethnicity and Muslim communities in Brazil. His recent publications include *Ethnographies of Islam: Ritual Performances and Everyday Practices* (Edinburgh: Edinburgh University Press, 2013), which he coedited with Baudoin Dupret, Thomas Pierret, and Kathryn Spelman-Poots; and *Crescent over Another Horizon: Islam in Latin America, the Caribbean and Latino USA* (Austin: University of Texas Press, 2015), which he coedited with John Karam and Maria del Mar Logroño Narbona.

BABAK RAHIMI is associate professor of Communication, Culture, and Religion and the director of the Program for the Study of Religion at the University of California, San Diego. His monograph, *Theater-State and Formation of the Early Modern Public Sphere in Iran: Studies on Safavid Muharram Rituals, 1590-1641 C.E.* (Brill 2011), traces the origins of the Iranian public sphere in the early seventeenth-century Safavid period, with a focus on the relationship between state building, urban space, and ritual culture. Rahimi is also the coeditor (with David Faris) of *Social Media in Iran* (SUNY Press 2015) and the coeditor (with Armando Salvatore and Roberto Tottoli) of *The Wiley Blackwell History of Islam*. Rahimi's research interests concern the relationship between culture, religion, and technology. The historical and social contexts that inspire his research range from early modern Islamicate societies to contemporary Iran.

EMILIO SPADOLA is associate professor of Anthropology and Middle East and Islamic Studies at Colgate University, Visiting Associate Professor of Anthropology at Tufts University, and president of the Middle East Section of the American Anthropological Association (2016-18). His work examines the intersections of religion, media, security, and modernity in Morocco and the Muslim world. His book, *The Calls of Islam: Sufis, Islamists, and Mass Mediation in Urban Morocco* (Indiana, 2014) was awarded Honorable Mention for both the 2014 Clifford Geertz Book Prize, by the Society for the Anthropology of Religion, and the 2015 L. Carl Brown Book Prize, by the American Institute of Maghrib Studies. He is a 2018-19 grantee of Notre Dame's Global Religions Research Initiative, studying Moroccan Sufism, security, and diplomacy.

EDITH SZANTO is an assistant professor at the American University of Iraq, Sulaimani, where she teaches classes on religion and history. Dr. Szanto received her PhD in religious studies from the University of Toronto in 2012. She is the author of "Challenging Transnational Shi'i Authority in Ba'th Syria," published by the *British Journal of Middle East Studies* in 2018, as well as "Sayyida Zaynab in the State of Exception: Shi'i Sainthood as 'Qualified Life' in Contemporary Syria," published by the *International Journal of Middle East Studies* in 2012. Her current project examines contemporary Islam in Iraqi Kurdistan.

BRANNON WHEELER teaches history of religions, Islamic studies, and Middle East history at the United States Naval Academy in Annapolis. He has published nine books, including *Mecca and Eden: Ritual, Relics, and Territory in Islam* (Chicago, 2006). He has held visiting positions throughout the Middle East and Europe, most recently as a fellow at the King Faisal Center for Research and Islamic Studies in Riyadh. His current research is on pre-Islamic camel sacrifice and the role of ritualized violence at the origins of Islam.

Index

Note: Page numbers in italics indicate illustrations; those with a *t* indicate tables.

ʿAbdudjalil-bab, 153
ʿAbdullah, king of Jordan, 13
ʿAbdullah, Zain, 113
Ablay-khan (d. 1781), 162, 163
Abreu, Maria José de, 236n14
Afghanistan, 11, 223, 228, 237n24
African American Muslims, 18, 23, 113–15, 120
Aga Khan, 243
Aga Khan III, 256n25
Aga Khan IV, 244, 256n21
Ahbar, Kaʿb al-, 57
Ahl-i Bayt, 207, 259
Ahmed, Qanta, 33–35
al-ʿAskariyya shrine, 207, 228
Albera, Dionigi, 4, 8
al-Busiri (d. ca. 1296), 146n16
Al-i Ahmad, Jalal, 24
Algar, Hamid, 13
Algeria, 12, 94–96, 102
Alilat (deity), 49
Al Jazeera (news network), 237n24
Alpamys mystics, 153
Al-Tusi, Shaykh (d. 1067), 207
Amal Movement (Lebanon), 174
Amanat, ʿAbbas, 212
American Muslims, 112–28; of Brazil, 89–107
Amin, Sayyid Muhsin al- (d. 1952), 173
Ampel, Sunan (saint), 203n34
ancestor veneration, 152, 158, 160, 186, 193, 195
Anderson, Benedict, 108n6
animism, Indonesian, 188. *See also* shamanism
Ansar al-Dine, 228

Arab Spring (2010), 228, 238n28
arbaʿin pilgrimage, 99–100, 103–4, 106, 107n1, 179
Argentina, 107n3, 108n11
Arjana, Sophia Rose, 8, 27, 112–28
arwah. *See* ancestor veneration
Arystan-bab (saint), 167n18
Asad, Hafez al-, 174
Asad, Talal, 224, 234
ʿashura, 110n33, 173, 179, 242–46, 249, 256n25
Aslan, Reza, 113
Aslan, Rose, 27, 112–28
Asyʾari, Hasyim, 202n10
Ata Zholy (Way of Forefathers), 157–58
Awrangabad, 141, 147n27
Aysha-bibi (saint), 168n18
Azraqi, Muhammad b. ʿAbdallah al-, 55

Bab al-Saghir cemetery, 180
Babak, Sasan b., 52
Babur (Timurid prince), 235n3
Baiturrohman Mosque (Java), 189
Bakhtin, Mikhail, 173
Bamba, Ahmadou, 102
Bamiyan Buddha statues (Afghanistan), 223, 228, 237n24
Bangladesh, 12
baraka (saint's blessing), 9, 96, 160, 230–31; of pilgrims' souvenirs, 100, 104; as religious reward, 179
Baydabek-ata (saint), 167n18
Begim, Rabiya Sultan (d. 1485), 162
Benjamin, Walter, 220, 231
Bianchi, Robert R., 18, 25–26, 68–87
Bibi Mariyam (saint), 168n18

269

Birk, Sandow, 113
Biruni, Muhammad b. Ahmad al-, 52
Bodei, Remo, 30
Boellstorff, Tom, 216
Bohras, 240–54; Dawoodi, 37, 240, 255n3; diaspora of, 250–53; homeland of, 251, 257n37; Muharram ritual of, 240–50, 241, 245, 247, 250
Boissevain, Katia, 5, 14
Boivin, Michel, 146n12, 148n34
Bokhari brothers, 147n23
Bombay, 242–43, 247n37
Bowen, John, 197
Brandon, George Frederick, 149
Brazilian Muslims, 26–27, 89–107, 183; population of, 108n10; sociocultural context of, 90–95, 105
Buddhism, 188, 223, 228, 248, 256n11
Burhanuddin, Sayyidna Mohammed, 240, 241, 246–51, 255n2

Campo, Juan E., 23
Center for the Spreading of Islam in Latin America (CDIAL), 92, 98, 109n14
Centlivres, Pierre, 237n24
charitable societies, 90–91, 97
Chinese Indonesians, 189–92, 194–96, 198, 203n25
Chinese Islamic Association, 68
Chinese Muslims, 25–26, 68–87, 72
Christianity, 7, 18, 256n11; Brazilian Muslim converts from, 110n35; hospitality in, 181n2; in Indonesia, 188, 200; pilgrimage in, 4, 7–8, 53; sacrifice in, 50
ciam si (Chinese divinatory poems), 189, 191, 196
Cibal Halal, 91
Civil Rights Act (1964), 23
Cohen, Erik, 18
Coleman, James S., 116
Colla, Elliott, 239n36
communitas, 32, 113, 172, 177–81, 252; Turner on, 19–20, 180

Coptic churches, 7
Couroucli, Maria, 8

Daulatzai, Sohail, 113
Dar Al Ber Society, 109n13
dargah, 10, 259
Daʿwa Party, 173
Dawati Zaban, 248
de Jong, Huub, 203n34
Deleuze, Gilles, 217
Delval, Raymond, 108n10
dervishes, 137, 145n2, 158. *See also* fakirs
Dharr, Abu, 55
"digital embodiment," 36, 208, 216, 218–19
digital technology, for pilgrimage, 34–36, 207–9, 212–21
Dikan-ata (saint), 167n18
Dilger, Hansjörg, 146n9
Dilthey, Wilhelm, 34
Diwali, 256n24
Djie Lo Su (Er Laoshi), 198
Djoego, Eyang, 190–98
Domalak Ana (saint), 168n18
Domalak-ata (saint), 167n18
dreams, 51, 219, 226–27; healing, 146n16; of pilgrimage, 3, 9–11, 29, 32, 133–44; "spiritual magnetism" and, 227
Druze, 90–91
Dubai Charity Association, 109n13
Durkheim, Emile, 227
Dushares (deity), 56

Eade, John, 20
Echchaibi, Nabil, 114
Egypt, 53, 108n11, 118, 134, 173; Brazilian Muslims and, 91, 94, 97; Coptic church in, 7; Herodotus on, 49; lunar calendar of, 244, 246; shrine destruction in, 224, 228, 238n28
Eickelman, Dale F., 17, 30, 89, 108n6
Eliade, Mircea, 19
Engelke, Matthew, 201n3
Engineer, Asghar Ali, 248, 256n24
Enuma Elish, 59, 60

Erdoğan, Recep Tayyip, 171n73
Eshaghi, Peyman, 1–37
Esim, Kazakh khan, 161
Eurasian Economic Belt, 71, 86

fakirs, 32, 137–39, 146n14. *See also* dervishes
faraj (release) prayers, 210
fatiha prayers, 14
Fatima (wife of ʿAli), 125, 152, 173
Fátima shrine (Portugal), 236n14
Federation of Muslim Associations of Brazil (FAMBRAS), 91–93, 98–99, 109nn13–14, 110n29
Fischer, Michael, 242
Flood, Finnbarr B., 146n16
"folk Islam," 156, 200. *See also* "normative Islams"
Foucault, Michel, 134, 145n8
Frembgen, Jürgen W., 147n24
fusha (Standard Arabic), 228

Gansu Hajjis, 69, 71, 73–78, 75–80t, 80, 81
Gaukhar-ana (saint), 167n18, 168n18
Geertz, Clifford, 107, 197, 203n26
"gender police" (Saudi Arabia), 121
gender roles, 12, 112; fluid, 139, 145n1; on Hajj, 74–84, 75–80t, 81, 83, 98–99, 119–23
ghadamgah (spiritual dwelling), 211, 221n14
gifting practices, 32, 172–81; Mauss on, 173; Moufahim on, 172–73, 176; Pinto on, 100, 172; types of, 176
globalization, 86, 89, 107n4
Golani Syrians, 173, 175
Gomez, Michael, 114
Gormez, Mehmet, 171n73
Grabar, Oleg, 11
grave visiting, 3, 13, 30, 53–54, 152; hadith on, 157, 187; in Indonesia, 33, 183–200; interreligious appeal of, 183, 192–96, 201n2; Qurʾan on, 184
Green, Nile, 30, 141, 143, 147n27, 184
Grewal, Zareena, 113

Guanyin (Bodhisattva of Mercy), 190
Gujaratis, 243, 248, 255n3

Habermas, Jürgen, 239n33
Haider, Najam, 207
Hajj, 13, 18, 24, 97, 116–19; costs of, 117–18; gender issues and, 74–84, 75–80t, 81, 83, 98–99, 119–23; *ihram* garment for, 20, 23, 29, 119, 126, 127; narratives of, 120–27; Organization of Islamic Cooperation and, 81; public health concerns with, 18; quotas for, 68, 81; Qurʾan on, 38n2; religious observances during, 97; *rihlas* of, 41n18; selection criteria for, 68–69; sponsoring of, 91, 96–98, 109n13, 118; "substitution," 115; symbolic capital of, 16, 90; ʿUmra and, 95–96, 103; visas for, 99, 119; *ziyara* versus, 4–14, 200, 226. *See also* pilgrimage
Halabi, Nur al-Din al- (d. 1635), 55
Hamawi, Yaqut b. ʿAbdallah al- (d. 1229), 53
Hammoudi, Abdellah, 28–29
Hanafiya, Muhammad, 153–55
Harani, Abu ʿArubah al-, 52
Hasnain, Nadeem, 242
Hénaff, Marcel, 11
Henan, China, 84–85
Herodotus, 49
"Hidden Imam." *See* Mahdi, Muhammad al-
hijab (headscarf), 122, 127
Hijaz, 10, 23, 44n53, 54, 187
hijra, 145n1, 147n17
Hinduism, 8, 200, 256n11; Bohras and, 256n24; in Indonesia, 188; Shiva and, 142, 147n21, 148n34
Hobsbawm, Eric J., 14
Hoover, Stewart M., 236n14
hospitality, 32, 172–73, 179–81
Huber, Valeska, 18
Hudaybiyyah, Treaty of (628 C.E.), 38n1
Hui Chinese Muslims, 26, 69–70, 73–74, 78, 82, 82–85, 83

Index 271

Hurayrah, Abu, 52
Husayn, Nur (saint), 229
Husayn ibn ʿAli (Prophet's grandson, d. 680 C.E.), 9, 207, 242; grave of, 17, 17, 104; martyrdom of, 8, 173
Husayni, Hassan al-, 229–31
husayniyya (assembly hall), 91, 260
Hussain, Ashiq, 141

Ibn ʿAbd al-Barr (d. 1071), 57
Ibn Abd al-Wahhab, 6, 223
Ibn Abi al-Khayr al-ʿUmrani, 56–57
Ibn al-Hawrani (d. 1596), 58
Ibn al-Kalbi, 52
Ibn Hanbal, Ahmad b. (d. 855), 56
Ibn Hisham, 55
Ibn Ishaq, 51–52
Ibn Mikhsan, Ukasha, 165
Ibn Saʿd, Ahmad, 52
Ibn Taymiyyah (d. 1328), 6
Ibn ʿUmar, 52
ihram garment, 20, 23, 29, 119, 126, 127, 260
Im Yang Tju (Yinyangzi), 191, 192, 198
imama doctrine, 243–44, 260
imamzadah, 12, 260
India, 13, 54; ʿAshura observance in, 242–43; Muharram observance in, 240–50, 241, 245, 247, 250; Tablighi Jamaat in, 94, 109n19
Indonesia, 33, 74, 115, 122–23, 183–200
International Ashura Mubaraka Committee, 252–53
Iran, 103; China and, 68; Qum in, 95, 103, 212; Revolution of 1979 in, 8, 13, 91, 212; Sahib al-Zaman Mosque in, 207–21; Syria and, 174, 175
Iraq, 242; archaeological destruction in, 239n36; Najaf in, 6, 17, 95, 99–100, 103–4. *See also* Karbala
Isbelle brothers, 97
Isfahani, Abu al-Faraj al- (d. 967), 54
Ishak-bab (saint), 153, 167n18
Ishmael, 49, 53, 55, 57

Islamic State (ISIS), 9; Assyrian relics destroyed by, 223–24, 228; Iraqi archaeological destruction by, 239n36; Salafism of, 7
Ismaʾil, 1, 32n2
Ismaʾili Nizaris, 241, 243, 256n25
Ismailiyah, Egypt, 49
iʿtikaf (visitation stay), 213

Jabal al-Nur (Mountain of Light), 125
Jahan, Noor, 141
Jamkaran shrine mosque, 35–36, 207–21; expansion of, 212; website of, 214; well at, 210–11, 217–20, 219; yearly visitors at, 212
Jamkarani, Hasan, 209
Jannat al-Baqi cemetery (Medina), 125
Jati, Sunan Gunung, 201n2
Java War (1825–1830), 190
Jerusalem, 53, 56–61, 240
Jhok Sharif, 146n12
jinns, 143, 227
John Paul II (pope), 236n14
Jordan, 13
Judaism, 8, 50, 256n11; shrines of, 7

Kaʿba, 10, 25, 37, 127; history of, 1, 51–52, 54–56; "relativisation" of, 13; souvenirs of, 99–100, 183, 260; Ukasha-ata shrine and, 164
Kalbi, Hisham b. al-, 56
karamat (proofs of saintliness), 184
Karamustafa, Ahmet, 145n2
Karashah Ana, 168n18
Karbala, Iraq, 95; battle of, 173, 242; martyrs of, 8, 243; as pilgrimage site, 6, 17, 103–5, 104
Kasmani, Omar, 32, 133–44, 184
Kataʾib News Channel, 228
Kawi, Mount (Java), 32, 183–85, 188–200
Kazakhstan, 32, 69, 83, 149–66
Kedar tribes, 49
Khamenei, ʿAli, 177, 178, 212, 221n7
Khattab, ʿUmar b. al-, 52
Khojas, 243

272 Index

Khomeini, Ruhallah, 221n7
Khuja descent groups, 150, 152–57, 160, 162, 167n9, 243, 260. *See also* Yassevi, Khuja Ahmad
Khurasan Ata, 154
Kirama tradition, 9
klenteng (Chinese Indonesian shrine), 189, 191
Knight, Michael Muhammad, 124–26
Konkonis, 243
Koshkar-ata (saint), 168n18
Kurds, 178
Kwan Im shrine, 191

Laksana, Albertus Bagus, 201n2
Lambertz, Peter, 248
Lanzhou Muslims, 71–72, 72, 75–80t, 77, 80, 81
Lapidus, Ira Marvin, 152
Latif, Khalid, 118
Lebanon, 90–91, 93, 95, 97, 174; Hezbollah movement in, 177, 178
Libya, 96; shrine destruction in, 224, 228, 237n28
Liem Sioe Liong (Lin Shaoliang), 191
Linxia Muslims, 71, 72, 74–75, 75–80t, 77, 80, 81
literacy, among Chinese Muslims, 26, 76t, 77, 79t

MacWilliams, Mark, 35
"magnetism, spiritual," 225–27, 234
Mahdi, Muhammad al- (b. 869 C.E.), 12, 36, 207–20, 221b7, 244
Mahrij, Ahmad, 107n3
majlis, 246
Makki, Taqi al-Din Ahmad b. ʿAli al- (d.1429), 53
malang (mentor), 137–39, 146n14
Malaysia, 8–9, 68
Malcolm X, 18, 23, 113, 120
Mali, 224, 228, 237n28
Malikov, Azim, 32, 149–66
Marwandi, ʿUthman, 145n2
Masjid al-Haram (Mecca), 214

Masjid-e Moqadas-i Jamkaran. *See* Jamkaran shrine mosque
Masoudi Nejad, Reza, 37, 240–54
Massignon, Louis, 173, 179; on hospitality, 181n2
Master, ʿAbbas, 240, 246–49, 253, 254
Masʿudi, Abu al-Hasan ʿAli al-, 52
materiality, religious beliefs about, 183, 195–200; business success and, 191, 193–94; pilgrimage and, 11, 30, 100
Mauss, Marcel, 173
Mayo, Lewis, 32, 33, 183–200
mazarat (visitation), 9, 149, 160–62; types of, 152–53, 168n21; Ukasha-ata, 165
McLuhan, Marshall, 217
Mecca, 60–62; Grand Mosque of, 120, 125; graves in, 55–56, 61; as pilgrimage site, 6, 53, 93; souvenir shop in, 122
Medina, 11, 112, 120; Jannat al-Baqi cemetery in, 125; as pilgrimage site, 6, 93, 100
Mehdi, Anisa, 112
messianic experience, 207–21
Metcalf, Barbara D., 31
Millie, Julian, 32, 33, 183–200
Mitchell, W. J. T., 228
Mittermaier, Amira, 10, 134, 226, 243
Mogahed, Mohamed Magid Yasmin, 118
Moin, Azfar, 235n3
Morocco, 12, 17, 114; Sufism of, 13, 14, 226–27; Wolfe on, 126
Moufahim, Mona, 172–73, 176
Mountain of Light (Jabal al-Nur), 125
Muhammadiyah (organization), 184, 186, 195
Muharram ritual, 9, 240–50, 241, 245, 247, 250
mukams (female saint shrines), 12
Mumbai, 242–43, 247n37
Muminov, Ashirbek, 152
Muqatil b. Sulayman (d. 767), 55
Muslim Renaissance, in Central Asia, 155

Index   273

Mutlaq, Da'ei al-, 244
Muttalib, 'Abd al-, 52

Naamouni, Khadija, 227
Nahdlatul 'Ulama (organization), 184, 187, 195
Najaf, Iraq, 6, 17, 95, 99–100, 103–5
Najafi, Mar'ashi, 221n7
Naqshbandiyya Haqqaniyya, 93
Naqshband, Bakhauddin (saint), 153
Nasser, Gamal Abdel, 108n11
Nayman, Tolegetay Sadir, 157
Nazarbayev, Nursultan, 156, 164, 171n73
neoliberalism, 86, 89, 107n4
new-Usulism, 208
Nigeria, 116
Ningxia Muslims, 69, 71, 73, 78
"normative Islams," 184–86, 192–93, 200

Obeyesekere, Gananath, 111n37
"One Belt, One Road" project (China), 71, 86
Organization of Islamic Cooperation, 81

Pakistan, 32; China and, 68, 86; pilgrimage in, 133–44; shrine destruction in, 224
Palestinians, 90, 93, 95; at Sayyida Zaynab, 173, 175
Parramore, Thomas, 114
Peek, Philip M., 248–49
pesugihan (wealth seeking), 193, 194
piety, economies of, 172, 176–81
pilgrimage, 56–58, 223, 234–35; *arba'in*, 99–100, 103–4, 106, 107n1, 179; "armchair," 236n14; categories of, 192, 203nn25–26; Christian, 4, 7–8, 53; definitions of, 4, 208, 215, 240; digital technology for, 34–36, 207–9, 212–21; dreams of, 3, 9–11, 29, 32, 133–44; German words for, 179; history of, 38n1, 50–61; to Jerusalem, 57; Kazakh, 149–66; meanings of, 1–3, 19; networks of, 13; politics of, 112–28; rituals and, 158–59; as self-negotiation, 15–16; souvenirs from, 99–100, 122, 183; transnational religious imagination and, 89–107; Turners on, 113, 208, 215. *See also* Hajj; saints' shrines
Pinto, Paulo G., 26–27, 30, 89–107, 172, 183, 200
Piscatori, James, 89, 108n6
Preston, James J., 225–26
Provansal, Danielle, 12
Puar, Jasbir K., 115

Qadhi, Yasir, 118
Qalandar, Lal Shahbaz (saint), 133, 145n2
Qasidah burdah sharif (Egyptian Sufi poem), 146n16
Qinghai Muslims, 69, 71, 73, 78
Qum, Iran, 95; as pilgrimage site, 103; seminary at, 212
Qur'an, 60, 113; on grave visiting, 184, 187; on Hajj, 38n2; on saints' shrines, 235n2
Qureishi, Amira, 112
Qyzylorda, 149, 155, 157

Rahimi, Babak, 1–37, 207–21
rainmaking ritual (*tasattyk*), 161
rak'a prayers, 209
Rashid, Samory, 114
Razi, Fakhr al-Din al-, 60
Restall, Matthew, 114
Ricklefs, M. C., 203n26
Rodrigues, Renan de Araujo, 109n15
Roibin, H., 185, 192–96, 198, 200, 203nn25–26
Royal Islamic Strategic Studies Centre (Jordan), 236n6
Rumi, Nasir al-Din Muhammad al-, 57

sabils (donations), 244, 244–45
sacrifice, 50–61, 61; animal, 25, 50, 51, 53, 54, 58–59
Sadr, Muqtada, 178

Sadr, Musa al-, 174
Safi, Omid, 113
Saifee Burhani Upliftment Trust (SBUT), 246, 253
saints' shrines, 151–52, 223–35; destruction of, 10, 120, 187, 223–25; dreams of, 133–44; fatwa on, 232–34; interreligious appeal of, 7–8, 183, 192–96, 201n2; Kazakh, 155–61; as media, 225–27; public administration of, 139–43; Qur'an on, 235n2; spiritual attraction of, 225–27; symbolic capital of, 239n34. *See also* pilgrimage
Salafiyya movement, 7, 36, 109n18, 261; in Brazil, 93–94, 102; shrine destruction by, 223. *See also* Wahhabis
Sallnow, Michael, 20
Sarhan, Saud al-, 3
Sasan, Babak b., 52
Saudi Arabia, 23–24; Brazilian Muslims and, 89, 99, 112–28; Hajj quotas of, 68, 81; religious police of, 121, 125; shrine destruction in, 10, 187. *See also* Mecca; Medina
Sayyid 'Uthman Marwandi shrine, 145n2
Sayyida Ruqayya shrine, 180
Sayyida Zaynab shrine, 32, 172–81, 184
Schwab, Wendell, 159–60
Sehwan, Pakistan, 133–44, 145n2, 147n21
Senegal, 13, 14, 93–96, 102–3, 109n15
September 11 attacks (2001), 228, 237n25
al-Shabab movement, 228–31
Shadhili, Abu al-Hasan ash- (d. 1258), 7
Shadhiliyya 'Alawiyya, 102
Shadhiliyya Yashrutiyya, 93
Shahrastani, Muhammad b. 'Abd al-Karim al- (d. 1153), 54
Shakhan-ata (saint), 167n18
shamanism, 156, 159, 161, 167n18, 188
Shanghai Cooperation Organization, 86
Shannahan, Dervla, 179
Shariati, 'Ali, 174

Shaykh, Hayder, 8
Shirazi, Sadiq, 178
Shiva (Hindu deity), 142, 147n21, 148n34
Shrine of the Cloak (Qandahar), 11
Siddiqi, Muzammil, 118
Silk Roads, 71, 86
Sime, Jennifer, 236n14
Sistani, 'Ali, 182n16
social capital, 12, 16–17, 26, 116. *See also* symbolic capital
social media, 99, 129n25; digital pilgrimage and, 34–36, 212–21
Soedjono, Iman, 190–98, 203n20
Somalia, 224, 228
Spadola, Emilio, 36–37, 183, 223–35
Spiritual Administration of Muslims of Kazakhstan (SAMK), 156
"spiritual magnetism," 225–27, 234
Spyer, Patricia, 238n29
Stone, Allucquere R., 214
Straitwell, Jane, 121–24, 126–27
Strothmann, Linus, 142
Subki, Taqi al-Din al- (d.1355), 57
Sudan, 123
Sufism, 114; in Brazil, 93, 95, 96, 102; Kazakh, 150–54; Moroccan, 13, 14, 226–27; Pakistani, 144; saints of, 10, 167n18; Uighur, 12
Suharto, 189, 191
Sukarno, 188
Sultan-Begim, Rabiya, 161
Supreme Council of Theologians and Islamic Affairs of Brazil, 92
symbolic capital, 16, 90, 239n34. *See also* social capital
Syria, 90, 93, 172–81; John the Baptist's tomb in, 58; shrine destruction in, 228
Szanto, Edith, 32, 172–81, 184

Tabari, Jarir al- (d. 923), 50–51, 60
Tablighi Jamaat, 94, 109n19
tabuts (symbolic coffins), 243
Tagliacozzo, Eric, 13, 18

Taiping Rebellion (1850–1864), 190
Tajani, Sidi Ahmad el, 14
Tajikistan, 150
Taliban, 223, 228, 237n24
Taribaev, Qydyrali, 158
tariqa (Sufi order), 93, 95–96, 102, 109n16
tawaf (prayer custom), 163
tawhid (unity of God), 186, 228, 233, 256n11; Indonesian Muslims and, 188–89, 194
taz'iya, 8
ta'ziya-khana, 42n25
Tell al-Maskhuta shrine (Egypt), 49
Thay Lo Su (Da Laoshi), 198
Tibetan Muslims, 69, 78
Timur, Amir, 161, 162
Touba, Senegal, 102–3
tourism, religious, 150, 174–76
trans* communities, 139, 145n1, 147n17
Tubba' king, 50–52
Tunisia, 224, 228, 229, 231–33, 238n28
Turkey, 68, 86, 94–96
Turkish Religious Foundation (TDV), 164
Turkistan, 150–52, 162, 164
Turner, Victor, 19–20, 252; on *communitas*, 19–20, 113, 180; on liminal space, 217; on pilgrimage, 113, 208, 215
Twelver Shi'i Islam, 17, 36, 172, 174

Uighurs, 12
Ukasha-ata (saint), 153, 164–65, 167n18
umma (Muslim community), 2, 97, 102
'Umra, 2, 26–27, 124, 128, 262; funding of, 91; Hajj and, 95–96, 103; visa for, 99, 119
United Arab Emirates, 109n13
United States Muslims, 112–28
Usulism, 208
Uyghur Muslims, 69–70, 81–84, *83*
Uzbekistan, 150–53, 162

van der Veer, Peter, 245
Van Gennep, Arnold, 252

visas, Hajj, 99, 119
votive offerings, 49–50

Wadud, Amina, 120–21, 123, 126
Wahhabis, 6–8, 10–11, 41n19, 104, 124; in Indonesia, 187; Kazakhstan and, 157; sack of Karbala by, 10–11; shrine destruction by, 237n28. *See also* Salafiyya movement
Wajihuddin, M., 240
waqf (religious endowments), 139–42
wayang (puppet theater), 189, 191
Weber, Max, 197
Weinhart, Martin, 147n24
Wheeler, Brannon, 25, 49–61, 180
Wilson, G. Willow, 113
"wishing tree" (*pohon dewandaru*), 190, 192
Wolfe, Michael, 125–27
World Assembly of Muslim Youth (WAMY), 92, 98, 109n14

Xinjiang, China, 70–71, 73–74, 77, 81–84, *82*, *83*

Yada^{x}il Bayyin, king of Hadramawt, 58
Ya'qubi, Ahmad b. Abi Ya'qub al- (d. 905), 52
Yassevi, Khuja Ahmad (saint), 153–54, 161–64, 166, 167n18, 171n73
Yasuda, Shin, 174, 180
Yazdi, Abdul-Karim Ha'eri, 221n7
Yemen, 55
Yeoh Seng-Guan, 8–9
Yinyangzi (Im Yang Tju), 191, 192, 198
Yunnan Muslims, 69, 72, 73, 84

Zamzam, well of, 1, 52, 55–56, 96, 127, 263
zaouias (saints' mausoleums), 238n28
Zarcone, Thierry, 13–14
zawiya (Sufi lodge), 93, 102
Zayed Charitable Foundation, 109n13
Zaynab, Sayyida, 173. *See also* Sayyida Zaynab shrine

Zholy, Ata, 158
Zimbabwe, 201n3
ziyara (pilgrimage), 3, 105, 159, 163, 263; *al-arbaʿin*, 99–100, 103–4, 106, 107n1; Boivin on, 146n12; definitions of, 7–8, 179; "digital," 214–21; dreams of, 133, 136–37, 143; as grave visiting, 3, 30, 157, 183–200; during Hajj, 14; Hajj versus, 4–14, 200, 226; in Indonesia, 33, 183–200; Jamkaran as, 207–21; Kasmani on, 32; symbolic importance of, 9–10
ziyaratgah (place of visitation), 9, 207, 211, 221n14
Zubayr, ʿAbdullah b. al-, 55

Islamic Civilization and Muslim Networks

BABAK RAHIMI AND PEYMAN ESHAGHI, *Muslim Pilgrimage in the Modern World* (2019).

SIMON WOLFGANG FUCHS, *In a Pure Muslim Land: Shiʿism between Pakistan and the Middle East* (2019).

GARY R. BUNT, *Hashtag Islam: How Cyber Islamic Environments Are Transforming Religious Authority* (2018).

AHMAD DALLAL, *Islam without Europe: Traditions of Reform in Eighteenth-Century Islamic Thought* (2018).

IRFAN AHMAD, *Religion as Critique: Islamic Critical Thinking from Mecca to the Marketplace* (2017).

SCOTT KUGLE, *When Sun Meets Moon: Gender, Eros, and Ecstasy in Urdu Poetry* (2016).

KISHWAR RIZVI, *The Transnational Mosque: Architecture, Historical Memory, and the Contemporary Middle East* (2015).

EBRAHIM MOOSA, *What Is a Madrasa?* (2015).

BRUCE LAWRENCE, *Who Is Allah?* (2015).

EDWARD E. CURTIS IV, *The Call of Bilal: Islam in the African Diaspora* (2014).

SAHAR AMER, *What Is Veiling?* (2014).

RUDOLPH T. WARE III, *The Walking Qurʾan: Islamic Education, Embodied Knowledge, and History in West Africa* (2014).

SAʿDIYYA SHAIKH, *Sufi Narratives of Intimacy: Ibn ʿArabī, Gender, and Sexuality* (2012).

KAREN G. RUFFLE, *Gender, Sainthood, and Everyday Practice in South Asian Shiʿism* (2011).

JONAH STEINBERG, *Ismaʿili Modern: Globalization and Identity in a Muslim Community* (2011).

IFTIKHAR DADI, *Modernism and the Art of Muslim South Asia* (2010).

GARY R. BUNT, *iMuslims: Rewiring the House of Islam* (2009).

FATEMEH KESHAVARZ, *Jasmine and Stars: Reading More Than "Lolita" in Tehran* (2007).

SCOTT KUGLE, *Sufis and Saints' Bodies: Mysticism, Corporeality, and Sacred Power in Islam* (2007).

ROXANI ELENI MARGARITI, *Aden and the Indian Ocean Trade: 150 Years in the Life of a Medieval Arabian Port* (2007).

SUFIA M. UDDIN, *Constructing Bangladesh: Religion, Ethnicity, and Language in an Islamic Nation* (2006).

OMID SAFI, *The Politics of Knowledge in Premodern Islam: Negotiating Ideology and Religious Inquiry* (2006).

EBRAHIM MOOSA, *Ghazālī and the Poetics of Imagination* (2005).

MIRIAM COOKE AND BRUCE B. Lawrence, eds., *Muslim Networks from Hajj to Hip Hop* (2005).

CARL W. ERNST, *Following Muhammad: Rethinking Islam in the Contemporary World* (2003).

www.ingramcontent.com/pod-product-compliance
Lightning Source LLC
Chambersburg PA
CBHW030528230426
43665CB00010B/809